Writing the Politics of Difference

Selected Studies in Phenomenology and Existential Philosophy 14

Writing the Politics of Difference

Edited by
Hugh J. Silverman

STATE UNIVERSITY OF NEW YORK PRESS

Production by Ruth East
Marketing by Fran Keneston

Published by
State University of New York Press, Albany

For information, address State University of New York
Press, State University Plaza, Albany, N.Y. 12246

Library of Congress Cataloging-in-Publication Data

Silverman, Hugh J.
    Writing the politics of difference/Hugh J. Silverman.
        p.   cm. — (Selected studies in phenomenology and existential
    philosophy ; 14)
    Includes bibliographical references.
    ISBN 0-7914-0497-8 (alk. paper).—ISBN 0-7914-0498-6 (pbk. :
alk. paper)
    1. Difference (Philosophy) 2. Philosophy, Modern— 19th century.
3. Philosophy, Modern—20th century. 4. Philosophy, European.
5. Existentialism. 6. Phenomenology. I. Title. II. Series.
B809.9.S54   1991
190—dc20   90-32126
                                                                    CIP

10 9 8 7 6 5 4 3 2 1

Contents

III. Toward a Sartrean Ethics

IV. Dialectic of Desire and Identity

**PART TWO: Writing Differences in
Continental Philosophy**

V. Dialogue and Difference

Introduction

Hugh J. Silverman

Continental philosophy is in its adolescence. Its future(s) will doubtless be rich and rewarding; its past is inscribed within a variety of traditions that still remain to be reread; its present is one of many differences. This volume addresses various phases of continental philosophy —both in the context of its multiple traditions and in relation to the politics of difference that mark the understanding of its present and future(s). Divided into two parts, *Writing the Politics of Difference* focuses on the traditions of difference in continental philosophy, most notably in connection with the texts of Hegel, Marx, Kierkegaard, Sartre, and de Beauvoir; and it stresses the reality of differences (social, political, sexual, and philosophical) as well as the various theoretical operations that identify features of difference in contemporary continental thought.

The politics of difference is not new. And yet the term has come to operate particularly in the context of both feminism and deconstruction. Correspondingly, the profound philosophical differences that, in recent years, have marked professional debates concerning the official program of the American Philosophical Association and the effects of its representation have come under the aegis of pluralism. Furthermore, the political differences that characterize theoretical work on the nature, role, and status of democracy (in relation to totalitarianism) broaden the inquiry (especially in relation to current Eastern European realities). The critical differences that prevail in questions of interpretation relate to the understanding of how the texts of a tradition can be understood and what is to be done about the alternatives that inevitably arise both theoretically and practically. In short, how do differences operate together in a context of viable communication. This book is about these sorts of differences and the possible futures that they carry with them.

The occasion for these essays was the twenty-fifth anniversary conference of the Society for Phenomenology and Existential Philosophy held at the University of Toronto in Ontario, Canada. This momentous event was also a time of thresholds. In the 1980s, the society established itself as the dominant professional framework for continental philosophy and its practice in North America. It had definitively moved beyond the narrower self-definition of a limited group concerned exclusively with transcendental and existential phenomenology. At the banquet celebrating the twenty-fifth anniversary (with symposium speeches by some of its founders such as James Edie, George Schrader, David Carr, Don Ihde, and Edward Casey) the more than one hundred persons present were reminded of the early debates at Northwestern University concerning the name of the society—whether it should highlight existentialism and phenomenology, existential philosophy, or some other version of these terms. Curiously, in the first of my six years as executive director of the Society, one of the aforementioned founders recommended at an executive committee meeting that the name be changed to Society for Continental Philosophy. Although it was decided to retain the palyonym, the ensuing six years marked a profound difference in the society's self-understanding.

By the time of the anniversary conference in 1986, it was generally understood that the purpose of SPEP annual meetings was to address current issues in continental philosophy (in its broadest formulation). Sessions could be devoted not only to readings of Husserl, Heidegger, Sartre, de Beauvoir, Merleau-Ponty, Gurwitsch, and Schütz or to phenomenologies of art, society, psychology, science, and technology, but also to current debates in critical and dialectical phenomenology, semiotics and post-structuralism, hermeneutics and deconstruction, feminism and postmodernism. Common figures to be discussed, presented, and debated now included Gadamer, Ricoeur, Lacan, Derrida, Foucault, Deleuze, Lyotard, Adorno, Habermas, Vattimo, Lefort, Kristeva, and Irigaray. Even the "figure" itself came to constitute a locus of philosophical elaboration, disagreement, and creative de- and re-construction. The frame was also opened for renewed examination and reading of Kant, Hegel, Marx, Kierkegaard, and Nietzsche. Furthermore, a number of important names in the North American context had already begun to emerge as foci for philosophical scrutiny. This shift in attention from a continental philosophy based solely in Europe to one highly animated on the other side of the Atlantic as well was concomitant with the introduction of SPEP conference "current research sessions" addressing recent publications by North American philosophers. In such a context, the work of Edward Casey, Alphonso Lingis, Reiner Schurmann, James Edie, John Sallis, Calvin Schrag, Bruce Wilshire, Fred Dallmayr, Charles Scott, John Caputo, William Richardson, J. N. Mohanty, Joan

Stambaugh, Joseph Kockelmans, David Michael Levin, John McCumber, and even Hugh Silverman (to name just a few) have come to be an integral part of the ongoing discourse.

In the 1980s, continental philosophy became as much a North American philosophy as an European derivative. Continental philosophy was no longer a regional, geographical name but rather a designation for an international philosophical style, a way of philosophizing that moved beyond the earlier antagonisms between phenomenology and analytic philosophy, that brought American philosophy into dialogue with and beyond its roots in pragmatism, naturalism, and process philosophy. The twenty-fifth anniversary of SPEP marked these changes in atmosphere, tenor, and assumed commitment of a revitalized society with its invigorated set of philosophical practices.

But if all of these differences are to be understood as part of the context, then one might assume that there is no basis for any disagreement? As in any group, there is never simple acceptance of the status quo nor should there be. What became a matter for debate was the degree and extent to which a particular component of the society's new set of commitments should be represented. And although the broad range of orientations could be called *continental philosophy,* any number of particular positions and even alternative philosophical views made themselves known within the context. Feminism—growing steadily into one of the dominant concerns of SPEP and particularly in connection with French Feminism—demanded and needed more space. The election of Arleen Dallery along with Charles Scott as codirectors in 1986 was symbolic of this important new thrust. Postmodernism came to be an important element in the response to traditional semiotics, phenomenology, and even post-structuralism. Dialectical phenomenology demanding a reinscription of traditional transcendental thinking fought for its identity. Deconstruction, already a major force in a literary context found its proper space in continental philosophy. And the human sciences—whose practices had come to be affected by phenomenology in particular—grew to the extent that a whole new society was created. Tensions arose as these differing orientations came to vie for a central place in the sun.

The task of those of us expected to respond to the growing needs and changing interests of the society was to provide both balance and new representation of the full range of these concerns. Where this response was adequate, the result was appreciation. Where members felt that their context was underrepresented, there was discontent. In the last half-decade or so, SPEP more than doubled in size. This increase reflects not only the growth in interest in continental philosophy but also its greater diversity. More and more, younger philosophers and fellow-travelers entered the field. No longer were all sessions plenary, and by the time of the an-

niversary conference, there were in some instances as many as five concurrent sessions. And even this was not enough . . .

   This book is situated precisely at a moment of juncture — the place
where the pyjamas outgrow the child — necessitating either expansion or
replacement. It has been suggested that SPEP had gone into hibernation
in the late 1970s. In the 1980s it came alive with so much energy and enthusiasm that an increasing number of those attending were thirty-five or
younger. Correspondingly, graduate programs with a strong emphasis in
continental thought at universities such as Stony Brook, Penn State, Boston College, Loyola of Chicago, Purdue, Emory, Vanderbilt, and even
Northwestern again gained special prominence in the field. Although the
proliferation of these programs came to meet an increasing need, they
could still accept only a small number of the many qualified and aspiring
applicants. SPEP became the meeting place for both younger and more
established philosophers and interested scholars from a wide range of in-
terdisciplinary interest groups. The society's annual conferences in October established themselves solidly as one of the dominant contexts for
exchange, debate, and growth in continental philosophy.

   In the light of this new growth and expanded program, William
Eastman, director of SUNY Press, graciously agreed to celebrate the occasion of the twenty-fifth anniversary of the Society with a book devoted
to this one year. The essays here moulded to form an independent, coherent framework mark the traditions and politics of difference in continental philosophy. One will find alternative readings of Hegel, Marx, Kierkegaard, Sartre, and de Beauvoir as well as moments of difference in the
context of contemporary (philosophical, sexual, and political) debate.
The book concludes with some reflections on the futures of continental
philosophy — through readings of Heidegger, postmodernism, and deconstruction from American, British, and Italian perspectives.

   The inscription of Hegel in continental thought can be regarded as
central. And yet the multitude of readings of Hegel is nothing short of dis-
persive. What Kierkegaard or Marx make of Hegel is very different from
what Heidegger, Adorno, or Derrida find in the corpus. And these differences highlight the readings of Gary Shapiro, John McCumber, and Martin Donougho, who study carefully the subversion of Hegel's system in
the philosophies of Heidegger and Adorno — two different (and in many
ways) opposing German philosophies. The shift to Kierkegaard, with his
own vociferous rejection of the System, nevertheless still operates within
the Hegelian framework. The essays by John Michelsen, Merold Westphal, and C. Stephen Evans establish Kierkegaard's link with philosophies of acting, choice, and religion. The discussion of Sartre's ethics by
Linda Bell, Thomas Anderson, Robert Stone, and Elizabeth Bowman is
a natural outgrowth of the Hegelian and Kiergaardian traditions. Here,

the highlighting of posthumous material that still is not translated into English introduces new perspectives in continental philosophy's contribution to ethical theory. And further discussions by Patricia Mills, Christie McDonald, and Jo-Ann Pilardi concerning questions of identity and desire by returning to Hegel and Freud (out of Adorno and Marcuse), Proust (out of Barthes and Deleuze), and de Beauvoir (out of Sartre and Merleau-Ponty) are logical conclusions to the question of the practice of difference in the traditions of continental philosophy.

The second part of the book focuses more specifically on the writing of difference in contemporary thought. Bernhard Waldenfels, Martin Dillon, and Wayne Froman are all concerned in one form or another with the implications of Merleau-Ponty's philosophy for a theory of language and dialogue. They indicate alternative directions arising from Merleau-Ponty's phenomenology. Waldenfels moves toward a theory of dialogue and discourse (in relation to both Gadamer and Foucault), Martin Dillon offers a controversial critique of what he calls "post-hermeneutic skepticism" and "semiological reductionism" in favor of the broader experiential account paramount in Merleau-Ponty's ontology. And by contrast Wayne Froman juxtaposes the Derridean theory of "writing" with Merleau-Ponty's interrogation of speech.

Following the discussion of language and speech is a section concerned quite directly with questions of sexual difference. Here the stress is on gender differences and the groundwork for a politics of difference. Susan Bordo in a Foucauldian vein examines "the body as a text of femininity" with its contradictory effects. Reading Irigaray, Kristeva, Felman, and Wittig, Eleanor Kuykendall asks whether women's bodies constitute or are constituted by language and explores its epistemological and ethical implications. Terry Winant shows that, in relation to gender differences, relativism about rationality need not entail epistemological relativism. She picks up on two dominant concerns of this volume by arguing for various forms of methodological and political relativism.

Claude Lefort, Dick Howard, and Claude Piché bring out aspects of a democratic theory concerned with "the *sense* of social action" and an account of "the political" as founded in the philosophy of Merleau-Ponty, as linked with that of Hannah Arendt, and as ultimately providing a basis for what might become a Habermasian theory of the social role of art. Out of this discussion of democracy, it follows that another politics should complete the book; namely, a philosophical politics in which the question of the future is raised: in Heideggerian (Joan Stambaugh), postmodern (Gianni Vattimo), and deconstructive (David Wood) modes.

Unlike previous books in the SPEP series, a bibliography has been included here to guide the reader and to provide a referential frame for following the itinerary though the tradition from Hegel to de Beauvoir and into the complex of debate concerning the philosophy of language, gender politics, democratic theory, and the question of the future. Hence issues surrounding the role of philosophical systems, ethical choice, relations with others, the gendered body, language, socialization, and the status of philosophy today constitute the fabric of the present volume.

Writing the Politics of Difference was to be called "The Future of Continental Philosophy," which was the guiding theme for the anniversary conference. It would have made an excellent antecedent to the new SUNY Press Contemporary Studies in Philosophy and Literature book entitled *After the Future* and edited by Gary Shapiro (who also has an essay here). However, in the light of the contributions themselves, it seemed more appropriate to stress the writing of differences as a political practice, particularly as it has come to characterize discussions in the Society itself and in the broader context framed by its nearly thirteen hundred members. What brings together a theory of difference, feminism, the issue of democracy, and the question of the future of continental philosophy will be evident from the links that constitute this particular inscription of the politics of difference.

Acknowledgments

Writing the Politics of Difference concludes the set of five volumes[1] resulting from conferences in which I have had a directorial role in the Society for Phenomenology and Existential Philosophy between 1980 and 1986. During these two three-year terms, I have been pleased to work with effective, dedicated, and committed executive committee members, including David Carr, Joseph Kockelmans, Bernard Dauenhauer, Harold Alderman, Arleen Dallery, Thomas Flynn, and Graeme Nicholson. Their grace and good will has contributed to the growth and well-being of one of the largest philosophical societies in the English-speaking world. But, above all, the SPEP members who have attended the annual meetings regularly, participated in its programs, and worked actively toward the development of continental philosophy in North America have made these volumes possible.

For the twenty-fifth anniversary conference at the University of Toronto both Graeme Nicholson and Henry Pietersma devoted much of their time during the 1986 year to the development of superb local arrangements and a delightful three days of meetings at several Victoria University sites on the University of Toronto campus. To them special gratitude is owed. And to the Social Sciences and Humanities Research Council of Canada our sincere acknowledgment for its generous support of the conference. This was the first time that SPEP has held a number of its sessions in French as well as in English. And two of the essays in this volume are translated from the French.

1. These include *Hermeneutics and Deconstruction*, edited by Hugh J. Silverman and Don Ihde (Albany: SUNY Press, 1985); *Descriptions*, edited by Don Ihde and Hugh J. Silverman (Albany: SUNY Press, 1985); *Critical and Dialectical Phenomenology*, edited by Donn Welton and Hugh J. Silverman (Albany: SUNY Press, 1987); *Postmodernism and Continental Philosophy*, edited by Hugh J. Silverman and Donn Welton (Albany: SUNY Press, 1988); and the present volume, *Writing the Politics of Difference*, edited by Hugh J. Silverman (Albany: SUNY Press, 1991).

For their many labors in helping to prepare the manuscript for publication, I should like to express my thanks to Jean Keller and especially to Nina Belmonte (who prepared the Index and offered her editorial skills throughout); also to James Hatley for his expertise in developing the bibliography. They were each supported in part through the SUNY/Stony Brook Summer Work-Study Program. And to Harriet Sheridan my warm gratitude for her valuable assistance in this and related editorial activities that are so essential to the vitality of the Philosophy Department at Stony Brook.

Part One

Rereading the Traditions of Difference in Continental Philosophy

I Hegel and the Subversion of the System

1

Subversion of System/Systems of Subversion

Gary Shapiro

Dear Reader: I wonder if you may not sometimes have felt inclined to doubt a little the correctness of the familiar philosophic maxim that the external is the internal, and the internal the external.

—Victor Eremita, Preface to Either/Or

What might it mean to think outside or beyond the Hegelian system of philosophy? Already in Hegel's own time this was a question that came to occupy those who labored under the weight of his speculative and comprehensive system of thought. The easiest and most immediately appealing strategy was to seize upon some category that seemed to be relatively neglected within the system, something that seemed to have been too easily *aufgehoben* into the totality. Kierkegaard is sometimes represented as centering his challenges to the Hegelian system around the valorization of the unhappy consciousness; that is, the consciousness aware of the immensity of the gap between itself and the infinite for which it longs.[1] There is a danger in choosing just one category from the entire Hegelian array, however, or in wanting to reverse the privileged status that the system accords to one of a pair of values (in Kierkegaard's case the reversal of the values given to the happy and unhappy consciousness). The danger is one that, as Derrida formulates it, is an ingredient in any practice that "put[s] the old names to work, or even just leave[s] them in circulation"; it is "the risk of settling down or of regressing into the system that has been, or is in the process of being deconstructed. To deny

1

this risk would be to confirm it.''[2] So Kierkegaard, who rejects the system so vehemently, can be and has been read as elaborating a dialectics of existence that is simply the Hegelian system inverted or reversed. The reasons are not difficult to see. To the extent that the old terms bear their old meanings and affiliations with the other terms of the system, simply denying those meanings and affiliations is to invite a return of the repressed. Marx himself introduced the figure of inversion or reversal for the operations he intended to perform on Hegel, although he was much more respectful of the system than Kierkegaard, and most plausible reconstructions of Marxist thought still tend to be Hegelian. Sartre, in *Being and Nothingness,* aimed at a certain transformation of the *Logic* by radicalizing nothingness. Twenty years later, in *The Critique of Dialectical Reason,* he had come to embrace a much more explicitly Hegelian position, as abstract Being had been transformed into the practico-inert and the drama of human freedom was no longer played out in the *Phenomenology's* early chapter on ''Independence and Dependence of Self-Consciousness'' but had advanced all the way to ''Absolute Freedom and Terror.'' These subversions of the Hegelian system are not entirely unsuccessful; but they do raise the question of whether and to what extent a subversion more profound than inversion or reversal is possible. We might note that all of these subversions of the system could equally well be described as systems of subversion. In this respect we could point out that Hegel's philosophy is itself a system of subversion: one that sees the negative everywhere, that applies criticism universally (beyond the limits assigned to it in the Kantian critique), and that deploys a set of categories that will throw into high relief the actual and potential contradictions of whatever exists. More specifically, Hegel aims at a subversion of the systems of Fichte and Schelling. One sense of the equation of the actual and the rational is surely that the actual shares in the movements, contradictions, and tensions of reason and that its limits are accordingly subject to reasonable articulation and critique. To the extent that a subversion of the Hegelian system operates in the spirit of this (left) Hegelian system of subversion we detect a certain modification and diversification of the Hegelian enterprise as well as its reconfirmation.

Perhaps Heidegger's questioning of Hegel does appropriately seek to establish a distance between itself and these various systems of subversion. As Heidegger pointed out in his ''Letter on Humanism'' the reversal of a metaphysical formula simply reconfirms metaphysics.[3] Although provoked by Sartre's formula ''existence precedes essence,'' it could be amplified to include his variation on being and nothingness from the *Logic,* or lord and bondsman from the *Phenomenology.* Heidegger's own questioning of Hegel proceeds not by isolating an aspect of the Hegelian system but by interrogating the spirit of the system itself. It is not enough, Heidegger notes, in the rich pages he devotes to systematicity in his book on Schelling, to set oneself against all systems.[4] We must ask what is presupposed, and most fundamentally presupposed, by the project of systematicity itself. Like the other systems of German idealism, Hegel's seeks to demonstrate the identity in difference of subject and object, to manifest an Absolute that knows itself. In "The End of Philosophy and the Task of Thinking," Heidegger attempts to show that what remains unthought in this call to "the thing itself " (*die Sache selbst*) is the metaphysics of presence and its limits. It is assumed by the system that its task is to present the way in which the thing itself becomes present: "Hegel's speculative dialectic is the movement in which the matter as such comes to itself, comes to its own presence."[5] The system, along with Husserl's phenomenological "principle of principles," is the most advanced realization of the metaphysics of presence. Heidegger aims at subverting the metaphysics of presence by means of a *historical reduction* or bracketing, in which the entire sequence of thought from Plato to Hegel, Nietzsche, and Husserl is put into parentheses. Outside those parentheses lies a different kind of thinking, a play of absence and presence, lighting and concealment, in which truth is not the *telos* of a system but an inevitably partial dis-closure that always wavers or trembles between presence and absence.

To what extent does Heidegger's subversion of system then still remain indebted to Hegel? To what extent is he practicing a system of subversion that leans upon Hegelian modes of thought? The context within which such questions are to be explored is perhaps suggested by Heidegger's way of telling a story and by his use of the first person plural. The story of the metaphysics of presence, from Plato through the *Gestell* of the technological world (the Plato to NATO story) comes to seem more and more Hegelian as we acquire a certain distance from its initial shock and as more of the details are filled in. Certainly it has all the earmarks of the *grand recit* or metanarrative; the ghost of *Geist* seems to haunt it still.[6] And Derrida's question to Heidegger — "Who we?" — is not coincidentally the question that Kierkegaard and Marx asked of Hegel. In the same essay Derrida suggests that Hegel, too, could say with Heidegger and Foucault that the end of philosophy is the end of man because man has no role or activity beyond the completion of the system. In this sense Derrida can also state more explicitly than Heidegger will allow himself, albeit with the qualification that it is said "within the metaphysics of presence" (where Heidegger would not like to speak), that: "we believe, quite simply and literally, in absolute knowledge as the *closure* if not the end of history. And we believe *that such a closure has taken place*."[7]

When Derrida says that, he also anticipates speaking with another voice, or writing otherwise, that is, a voice that can give up the claim to a logocentric legitimation and a writing that is no longer constrained by the boundaries of the book. This "voice" and "place" can be anticipated only in the form of "monstrosity." The key to the Derridean project of subversion will be to speak and write in both ways at the same time. What is called a *double reading* and a *double writing*, then, is one that refuses the forced alternative between subversion from within and subversion from without. And this is because the inside/outside binary itself is precisely one from which the Hegelian system derives much of its nourishment; it is a prime motor of its machinery. Every theme, category, or topic that might be valorized from within — nothingness, labor, and the unhappy consciousness, for example — will prove to have limits that point to the need for totality. At the same time going outside — to Feuerbachian sensuous immediacy or to the Heideggerean history of Being — will turn into an illusory exercise in so far as these apparently absolute "others" will turn out to have been already comprehended in the system and in fact will push us toward increasingly comprehensive and totalistic readings of the system itself. For the internal/external binary, simply interpreted, is but an egregious form of that abstraction of the understanding that can also be formulated as the contrast between the finite and the (bad) infinite. To choose one or the other is to invite Hegel to explain once more the systematic distinction between the finite and the (good) infinite, that is the whole or totality.

When Derrida describes the work of *differance* as operating "at a point of almost absolute proximity to Hegel," he is refusing the strategies of extremist subversion that would look for weapons only within or without the system.[8] The point of absolute proximity itself can be understood in (at least) two ways (and not surprisingly, for both Hegel and Derrida are suspicious of any reductionist approach to limits that would yield an absolutely determinate point—the "almost" indicates the movement here). One focus of the ellipse that deforms or displaces the circle of the system will be a vigilant attention to the constant use of the inside/outside binary itself. The other focus will be the interrogation of the workings of the Hegelian text. In a certain sense these two foci correspond to Hegel's own distinction, articulated in the Preface to the *Phenomenology* and elsewhere, between the rational core of the system and its external literary expression. Due to Hegel's systematic and literal insistence on such a distinction we find here a kind of fissure or gap that, like the other wounds of the spirit, cannot be healed without leaving a scar. How great is the distance between these two foci? The point of Derrida's textual labor is to establish that distance or, in other words, to investigate the various forms it takes when the system is interrogated with different strategies. The opening of deconstruction, and its territory or field, are made possible because there is indeed a spacing or difference here that the system simultaneously calls for and rejects. Hegel sees the same problem in the systems that he explicitly criticizes. In his essay on *The Difference Between Fichte's and Schelling's System of Philosophy* he notes that at the "center" of Fichte's system, speculation and reflection do not quite coincide; "the two standpoints," he writes, "that of speculation and that of reflection are absolutely necessary and without union at the center of the system."[9] Hegel suggests a way of systematically raising a question about any claim to systematicity: Do the two poles or dimensions that the system attempts to identify really come to coincide in the system? Hegel poses this question to previous philosophy, where it then operates as a system of subversion in regard to the systematic as such. But the question may also be asked of Hegel's system itself. Consider the way Hegel announces the identity of the internal and the external sides of the system at the beginning of the *Phenomenology*:

> The true shape in which truth exists can only be the scientific system of such truth. To help bring philosophy closer to the form of science, to the goal where it can lay aside the title "*love* of knowing," and be *actual* knowing — that is what I have set myself to do. The inner necessity that knowing should be science lies in its nature, and only the systematic exposition of philosophy itself provides it. But the *external* necessity, so far as it is grasped in a general way, setting aside accidental matters of person and motivation, is the same as the inner, or in other words it lies in the shape in which time sets forth the sequential existence of its moments. (*Phenomenology*, p. 3)[10]

The Preface itself is external, Hegel says, to the genuine movement of science, but to the extent that it orients us to that movement it is internal to it. This orientation to distinguish and identify the internal and external necessities impels knowing to become science or system or to attain its "true shape" (*wahre Gestalt*). Yet if the Preface is not part of the "true shape," does it distort that shape and impair the perfection of the circle? At the same time it is suggested that science may not yet have attained this "true shape," for as Hegel announces (in the first person), this is the project he has set for himself. The internal necessity is timeless, the external necessity is temporal and historical, and these are said to be the *same*. Hegel finds it necessary to distinguish between the "external necessity grasped in a general way" and "accidental matters of person and motivation." This sounds like good scientific procedure. The circle, the "true shape," will be produced from either the internal or the external center, and because these are the same center, the two circles coincide. If we press this geometrical figure or analogy too far, we will find ourselves involved in the interminable problems that arise from attempts to map the *Logic* and the *Phenomenology* onto each other. Hegel might well point out that the mathematical figure of the circle is itself only an external image of the "true shape" of a scientific system. Because the Preface is self-excluded from the system, there should be no problem in placing any particular aspect of it under erasure. However, similar figures crop up throughout the Hegelian text, subverting its own claims to accomplishing an inside/outside distinction of prefaces and books or figures and thoughts.

The point to be noticed about this binary of the inside and the outside is that Hegel himself judges systematic thinking in terms of its ability to deploy and reconcile this opposition. In the *Phenomenology*, whose own status as inside or outside the system must remain puzzling, he does this in two places that must at first seem quite removed from one another. The question of system is first brought together with the inside/outside binary in the Preface (an outside of the outside?) and in a range of other observations on the relation of philosophical science to various mathematical, historical, or literary forms with which it might be confused. The second occurs in the analysis of the *Beobachtung der Natur* ("Observation of Nature"). The coincidence is marked by the fact that the word *System* and its derivatives occur much more frequently in these two sections of the *Phenomenology* than anywhere else in the text. Yet it might be objected that the mere appearance of the word is hardly a sign that the same issues are at stake; for a *System* of philosophy, it could be argued, is a very different thing from a biological organism considered as a system or from the systems (as Kielmayer and Schelling called them) of sensibility, irritability, and reproduction that help to constitute an organism. It may also seen that Hegel's discussion of observational reason and the biologically organic is the most outdated section of the *Phenomenology*, tied as it is to the methods and findings of the empirical and speculative natural sciences of 1806, whereas the Preface still speaks to us about the question of how one ought to "do" philosophy. The contrast cannot be drawn so easily, however. As Hegel pointed out, the text of the *Phenomenology* is a complex network of references, interlocking back and forth.

One model of *System* that Hegel wants to subvert is the abstract Schellingian *Naturphilosophie*, which comes in for critique in both sections of the text. In both contexts system is something more than an ordered or comprehensive form of knowledge. System is a crucial concept in the analysis of observational reason because what is in question there is *life*, understood as a certain unity of the inside and the outside; specifically life is conceived on the model of an exterior as an *expression* of the interior. These very aspects of systematicity — life, expression, and a certain relation of interior and exterior — are also decisive in the thought of the Preface.

In the section *Beobachtung der Natur,* Hegel's analysis of systematic thinking is placed, it seems, between what could be called *structuralist* or *post-structuralist* alternatives. Systematic thinking is preceded by a stage at which reason notices only the *signs* by which organisms are differentiated. These *Merkmale* (signs, marks, indications), however, are not purely arbitrary. They are *"differentiae"* (as Miller translates *Merkmale*) that not only "enable cognition to distinguish one thing from another" but they are also that by which the organisms *"break loose* from the general continuity of being as such, *separate* themselves from others and are explicitly *for themselves"* (*Phenomenology,* p. 149). The differences are marked by such things as claws, teeth, and sexual division, which actually *make* a difference. It is not simply a question of constructing taxonomic schemes of classification into which these features of life might be inserted; it is part of the experience of reason to see system, in the first instance, as a system of difference. "Our artificial system," Hegel notes, "is supposed to accord with nature's own system" (*Phenomenology,* p. 149). Yet what is discovered is not system in the form of totality, but rather system as sheer differentiation, what Hegel had called *"absolut differente Beziehung"* in the *Jena Logic.*[11] This collapse of our expectation of systematic unity is one that is reiterated in the *Phenomenology,* very often recurring in this figure of nature differentiating itself endlessly, "nature red in tooth and claw"; for example, the expectation of an intellectual system that is aroused by the social institutions and practices of the intellectual is discovered to have as its *truth* an "intellectual jungle" (*das geistige Tierreich*).[12] To escape from this relentless system of differences, consciousness moves on to the search for laws and relations. The search is important, and the reasons for its failure are significant, but let us first look at the results of this failure, upon the eventual collapse of the quest for lawful systematicity in the world of life. We will be left in a condition in which we have a certain freedom with regard to the assignment of meaning; it will be a state that might variously be called *pre-systematic* or *post-systematic.* Such an "unspiritual freedom of 'meaning' (*Meinen*) will offer on all sides the beginnings of laws, traces (*Spuren*) of necessity, allusions to order and system, witty and plausible connections" (*Phenomenology,* p. 179). These comments can be read as pertaining to more than biology; they are also an account of what remains after the deconstruction of a classical philosophical text or system like the Hegelian one. We must return to the question whether Hegel himself gives us grounds for such a reading.

After experiencing the disorder of a world of signs or *differentiae,* observational reason turns not only toward laws and relations as such but to that which appears to be its own law: the organism considered as self-preserving and autotelic. In such an investigation, we are told, reason seeks its own *Begriff,* which has been displaced onto the organism. Here the *Begriff* is to be thought of as coinciding with actuality, but because of the displacement, the *Begriff* "is taken roughly to mean the *inner,* and actuality the *outer;* and their relation produces the law that *the outer is the expression of the inner*" (*Phenomenology,* pp. 159–160). Given this law it becomes important to see what *shape* is attained by both the inner and the outer. In the Preface the *shape* of the system of science is one of Hegel's major concerns; in this text external shape has an apparently more univocal sense than it does in the case of *the* system. But in so far as the "shape" of the system is something external, perhaps in so far as the system can be said to have a shape at all, are not the spatial and visual aspects of *Gestalt* implicated in what Hegel has to say about the order and structure of the system? I will not lead you through the torturous paths of Hegel's discussion of the systems of sensibility, irritability, and reproduction. But it is clear that his general verdict on the search for systematic unity that those concepts were intended to enable, that is, the demonstration of a systematic expression of the inner by the outer, is a failure because it leads to trivial and tautologous pseudo-laws. It becomes an "empty play of formulating laws" that "can be practiced everywhere and with everything and rests in general on a lack of acquaintance with the logical nature of these antitheses" (*Phenomenology,* p. 164). By such criteria everything whatsoever becomes a system and it becomes impossible to rank and differentiate systems with regard to their degree of comprehensiveness and totality.

The *denouement* of reason's experience of the principle that the outer is the expression of the inner is reached with the discovery that each of these terms itself has an inner and an outer dimension. The inner has an inner and an outer; the outer has both an outer and an inner (*Phenomenology,* pp. 171–172). The outer is both the "inner outer" of a purely mathematical description and the "outer outer" of (literal) shape. The inner is both the "inner inner" of the *Begriff* as the "unrest of abstractions" and the "outer inner" of its more specific form of teleology. Rather than a third term, *expression,* which would provide a *systematic* interrelationship of inner and outer we seem to have arrived at something like the typical structuralist double binary matrix that can be used for generating an indefinite series of differences. And so we arrive at the post-systematic state, or the ruins of system, at which we glanced earlier. Thus Hegel subverts one variety of organic system based on the coincidence of the inside and the outside.

There is some mutual resonance, I suggest, between these concerns with "true shape," "inner and outer," "system," and "life," and those that Hegel addresses with the same language when he comes to discuss the ground, status, and texture of a philosophical system. The difference, it seems, is that in the Hegelian system the *Begriff* is always both subject and object; it is not displaced into the world of life in the mundane sense. Rather it is the systematic comprehension of the ways in which such displacement operates and points the way beyond, so that the displacements are simultaneously the movements along the "highway of despair" and the road to wisdom. However, Hegel himself explicitly distinguishes a level of the merely accidental within the external dimension of systematic necessity that he describes as details of language and "accidental matters of person and motivation." Here, too, there is both an inner and an outer *of the outer*. We could establish even a further dichotomy of the inner and the outer of the inner; namely, between the most general sense of the system's purpose and its articulation in the form of a certain categorial apparatus and order. In Hegel's critique of the sytems of *Naturphilosophie* it is the mathematical character of the inner outer that "is just that completely quiescent, lifeless, and indifferent determinateness in which all movement and relation is extinguished" (*Phenomenology*, p. 172). Now the outer side of the necessity of science becoming a system is *time*, which is also susceptible to mathematical ordering, and the outer side of the system as a work or accomplishment is a written text that is articulated mathematically in chapters, subchapters, and sequential pages. Is this not the same matrix for generating differences and undecidable meanings as what Hegel found in the systems of biology? Perhaps we will be dealing with the machinery of the text whenever we are concerned with the system of truth. The *Gestalt* as spacing appears where we had expected only the conceptual form of the system. This occurrence seems to be what Derrida has in mind (or in the machinery that operates his text) when he interrogates the status of the Hegelian preface, not just the Preface to the *Phenomenology* but the preface as a structural possibility that renders uncanny the system's claims to systematicity. In his essay "Outwork" (*Hors livre*), he observes, for example:

> Hegel's preface elaborates a critique of prefatory formality as it critiques mathematicism and formalism in general. It is one and the same critique. As a discourse external to the concept and to the thing itself, as a machine devoid of meaning or life, as an *anatomical* structure, the preface always has some affinity with the procedure of mathematics.[13]

Subversion of system, then, can proceed by reading the system against itself. The price to be paid (or perhaps the reward) is that one never quite escapes from the system but reads it differently. The more that Hegel succeeds at the construction of system, the more he fails; for in succeeding he elaborates a systematic way of assessing claims to systematicity that can then be turned upon the system he is presenting. Above all, Hegel insists, "the true shape of truth is scientific," and science is to be contrasted with an intuitive immediacy that would escape analysis by claiming "immediate knowledge of the Absolute, religion, or being" (*Phenomenology*, p. 4). But scientific truth, like the scientific systems that emerge in *Naturphilosophie* must allow of an *articulated* distinction into inside and outside that will yet be recuperated at the higher level of expression.

Hegel himself has already read system differently in exposing the difficulties that ensue upon the construction of such expressive unities. He details its dissolution into "beginnings of laws, traces of necessity, allusions to order and system, witty and plausible connections." That is to say:

1. "Beginnings" not in the sense of *archai,* first principles, but anticipations or gropings toward lawfulness.

2. "Traces" (*Spuren*) of a necessity that, according to the logic of the trace has never been present.

3. "Allusions" (or hints) in the direction of order, where it is not possible to decide once and for all whether an order is cited or demonstrated, used or mentioned.

4. Witty connections because, like Rameau's nephew in another section of the *Phenomenology,* wit makes linguistic connections that are deeper than the empty laws of the understanding in announcing the "*absolute Verkehrung*" or subversion of the simple and discrete.

In Hegel's narrative of the systematic impulse in the "Observation of Nature," we have something like an allegory of how the human sciences deal with texts, including the Hegelian text. A typology of interpretive stances is sketched, beginning with the pre-systematic, proto-structuralist effort to understand the subject-matter by sheerly differentiating marks, with opposed and opposing sets of features; then there is the inquiry that postulates an expressive and systematic identity of inside and outside. When that effort collapses because structural oppositions appear within the inside and outside themselves, we are left with a different kind of order, an economy of phonemes, mythemes, or in the crucial case, philosophemes, which exhibit some interrelationships even if they do not constitute a classical, totalistic system. Hegel himself provides such allegories of the subversion of system that are themselves systematic operations of subversion.

Derrida calls Hegel "the last philosopher of the book and the first thinker of writing."[14] As the philosopher of the book, he is the encyclopedagogue, presenting his system as a fully rounded volume with no outside. As the thinker of writing, Hegel constantly deforms and subverts that volume by adding prefaces, introducing tropes that are irreducible to the *Begriff* (itself a trope for grasping or comprehending), and by writing of writing in a way that makes visible his own writing and prevents it from becoming part of a seamless sphere. In "Outwork" Derrida gives a rigorous reading of the relation between system and preface along these lines, which I will not continue to repeat here. The Hegel of the system, Adorno says, would have us read only "between the lines," but how can we avoid reading the lines as well and noting their words, margins, and spacings?[15] As a piece of writing, the Hegelian text then produces a *moirē* effect of presence/absence and turns upon itself to perform topological variations on its "true shape." If the inside "is" the outside, this may be so only in the degenerate, mathematical sense in which this is the case for the Moebius strip. There the nonidentity is as patent as the identity; what we have is not an expressive unity but (because this construction can be indefinitely divided to generate more like itself), a permanent possibility of subversion.

2

Essence and Subversion in Hegel and Heidegger

John McCumber

INTRODUCTION

If continental philosophy were one thing, it could have a unitary future, but the different threads that make it up are not woven into a single tapestry. Indeed, they are not static "threads" at all, but independent and changing discourses: pathways on which philosophers are already underway. One such pathway to the future, I think, leads through what I will call the Hegel-Heidegger "topos:" through the conceptual web that relates to Hegel's and Heidegger's thought, through the interplays in which those bodies of thought engage and that engage them.

This topos is something unthought in the thinking of Heidegger. On December 2, 1971, Heidegger wrote the following to Hans-Georg Gadamer: "I myself do not yet know with sufficient clarity how my 'position' with respect to Hegel is to be characterized — 'opposite position' would be too little; any characterization in terms of 'position' is itself connected with the mystery of the 'beginning' ... Time and time again I have objected to the talk of a 'collapse' of the Hegelian system. What has collapsed, i.e. degenerated, is what followed — Nietzsche included.[1]

This quote suggests two things. One is that the Hegel-Heidegger topos was important to Heidegger — so important that his own position within it remained a matter of concern to him until almost the end of his life. His bewilderment over that position suggests further that, in spite of the efforts not only of Heidegger himself but of thinkers as powerful as Gadamer and Sartre (to name only two) the topos remains obscure — so obscure that any attempt to map it must begin with the possibility that

13

even essential questions with regard to it, to say nothing of answers, are lacking.[2]

How can we obtain an "essential question?" How would we ask one? What, indeed, is one?

Essence is, among other things, a category of Hegel's *Logic* and there connotes, in the first instance, the other of Being. If Being is indeterminate immediacy, then Essence as the other of *Being* will be determinate mediacy. If Essence is the other *of* Being, the original immediacy that it mediates must be nothing other than Being itself. Hence, Essence is a determinate mediacy that mediates (that can be reached from) indeterminate immediacy. Considered in Hegelian terms, an "essential question" follows in this way.

The "reach" from Being to Essence is itself, in the Logic, immediate; mediation of the relation will come only in the Logic of the Notion. This immediacy means, among other things, that when we reach Essence, Being has been thrown away, has vanished or resolved into its Hegelian correlate—Nothing. To ask an essential question about a thing is then to ask after something hidden behind an indeterminate variety of nullities that can be safely thrown away. Such a question thus begins with what I will call a "peremptory dismissal" of some givens as mere appearances.

If what we must leave behind to reach it is a mere nullity, then Essence is all reality: it is the true nature that lies behind the immediacy of Appearance. But (to continue the dialectic), Appearance as immediate nullity is a mere set of contingencies and thus can have no "real nature"; or, we might equally say, anything can be its "real nature." Appearance thus turns out to be a set of anomalies to any formulation of Essence itself and will eventually show any such formulation to have been false. So all "essences" are temporary. An essential question can never be finally answered; any real nature it may ask for can never be definitively formulated.[3] Because a Hegelian essential question unmasks appearances as nullities without arriving at any final formulation of the reality of which they are appearances, I call such a question "subversive."

For Heidegger, the "essence" of a thing is ultimately to be understood verbally; it is precisely not a common feature behind a number of givens (e.g., appearances), but the way a thing "holds sway, administers itself, develops and decays."[4] In this, Heidegger remains true to one traditional account of essence, that of it as the "internal possibility" of a thing.[5] But that internal possibility, as unique to the entity it enables, is not something that can be put into words: it is a mystery or (seen from the traditional perspective) a dis-sence, an *Unwesen*.[6]

Insofar as the aim of thinking is to "serve, attend to, watch over" something in its essence, thought for Heidegger must incorporate a moment of calling attention to mystery, of questioning.[7] Such questioning is, in keeping with Heidegger's general view of thinking as a "way," a step-by-step process.[8] As a series of questions, thinking is governed by a lack, a need. The need is not for a definitive answer to the questions but for continual transformations in thinking, new formulations, approaches, and retreats. The necessity in question here is a needful twisting, in Heidegger's term a *Not-wende*.[9] Such twisting is a continual subversion and resubversion.

Our question about essential questions, interpreted via the thought of Hegel and Heidegger, reveals ground common to the two philosophies, at least as regards the nature of essential questions. I will articulate that common ground by saying that my original statement that "essential questions are lacking for the Hegel-Heidegger topos" implies that

1. The relations and interplays that constitute the topos are hidden behind various appearances that must, if we are to reach it, be peremptorily dismissed (though, of course, they will be held in reserve for other questions and topics, indeed for other investigations of this same essence that may undo this one).

2. Dismissal must be in the service, not of an ultimate answer, but of a new approach.

3. This new approach must allow the topos to unfold and prevail in previously unthought ways.

One obvious fact about the relation of Hegel and Heidegger is that, although Heidegger writes about Hegel, Hegel nowhere discusses Heidegger. This chronological circumstance is, indeed, essential to their relation. Heidegger would not be able to question metaphysics in the way that he does had Hegel not previously brought it to completion. Nor could Hegel have completed metaphysics without opening it up to the later questioning of Heidegger. The two bodies of thought thus refer to each other internally; that is, neither would be what it is without the other. But the reference is asymmetrical: the Hegel-Heidegger topos is articulated, first and foremost, in the writings of Heidegger on Hegel.

Because of this internal-but-asymmetrical reference, an essential question for the Hegel-Heidegger topos will be one that questions not only the relation of the two thinkers, but the essence of each. We cannot seek to open up the topos with a question that presupposes that we understand what either thinker is about. We cannot put Hegel and Heidegger into relation without a willingness to challenge our own preconceptions concerning their philosophies.

Fortunately, the asymmetry I mentioned gives us a place to begin. For if we have no essences to presuppose, we can—and must—look first for an appearance, a candidate for peremptory dismissal. The first "appearance" we have for the Hegel-Heidegger topos, as we have noted, is its articulation in the writings of Heidegger. Our first move, then, will be to find a dismissable appearance — something Heidegger says about Hegel that is clearly wrong—and dismiss it. The appearance in question will turn out, I am afraid, to be deeply rooted — in a sort of preconception Heidegger has about Hegel's thought and ultimately in a certain view of the basic structure of the Hegel-Heidegger topos itself. These preconceptions, too, will be formulated and dismissed. What remains after these three dismissals will be a provisional circumscription of the Hegel-Heidegger topos, and of the essence of Hegel within that topos, which we can question—essentially—from a Heideggerean point of view. Then we will do something similar with Heidegger.

QUESTIONING HEGEL

Heidegger's treatment of Hegel contains an anomaly. On the one hand, early and late, Heidegger treats Hegel as the culmination of the modern philosophy of subjectivity.[10] One of Hegel's standard and basic claims, however, is that the standpoint of subjectivity, or of consciousness certain of itself, is overcome in the *Phenomenology of Spirit* and that his later system is beyond it. Hegel's later, systematic writings, it would seem, are the crucial ones against which Heidegger must test his assignment of Hegel to modern philosophy. But Heidegger rarely turns to them; when he does so it is, as Jacques Taminiaux has noted, to identify them as the point where Hegel became "blind" to the ontological difference.[11]

Another approach possible for Heidegger—one taken, for example, by Kojève — would be simply to discard the system, as well as the final chapter of the *Phenomenology* that reaches it, as some sort of mistake.[12] Heidegger argues instead, in the opening pages of his *Hegels Phänomenologie des Geistes,* that the *Phenomenology* and the system, far from being separable, are so interwoven that their joint nature can be understood from the *Phenomenology* alone.[13] This attempt to digest the system by devouring the *Phenomenology* leads Heidegger to some very strong claims. In particular, though he recognizes that Hegel's concept of system went through several versions, he insists that it was thought through simultaneously with the *Phenomenology.* By the time Hegel went to Berlin its basic nature was clear and unchangeable, "das System stand fest": "Except for the *Philosophy of Right* (1821) and a few reviews, Hegel in his Berlin period published nothing of fundamental significance for his philosophy. His activity as a lecturer [only] develops the system, which had already received its decisive and final form in 1817, in the Heidelberg Encyclopedia."[14]

This claim, for all its vigor, is falsified by comparing virtually any two editions or versions of texts from different phases of Hegel's Berlin period. The system never got any "entscheidende und endgültige Gestalt" but was to Hegel's death in a state of radical revision and flux, not merely with regard to particular contents but in its basic nature and strategy.[15] If the formulation of an essential question begins from a peremptory dismissal, then, a good candidate for such dismissal would be Heidegger's argument here. But that requires us also to dispense with the *Phenomenology* itself, for Heidegger's basic point is that the system is to be understood out of that work. Our essential question must, then, ask after the essence of Hegel independent of the *Phenomenology*.

Though Heidegger's lecture-course on the *Phenomenology* breaks off with no statement of what the book can ultimately teach us about the system, his project of understanding system and *Phenomenology* together turns out to rely upon a particular preconception of the system. This preconception contains for our purposes three ingredients:

1. The system is "absolute knowing" in that, rather than being bound to the contents known (as is "finite knowing"), it binds them to it; that is, it determines their nature.

2. The binding of known contents is the presentation of absolute knowing itself.

3. This presentative binding is the self-construction of absolute knowing.[16]

The view that the system is "absolute knowing" is indisputable within the context of the *Phenomenology*—for "das absolute Wissen" is the title of its final chapter. It thus forms the bridge between the end of the *Phenomenology* and the beginning of the system—a bridge that, as we have seen, still preoccupied Heidegger in 1971. Projecting absolute knowing onto the system means that what the system constructs—the totality of its known content—is what Heidegger calls its matter, its *Sache*. Using *matter* in this sense in "Die Onto-theologische Verfassung der Metaphysik," Heidegger claims that "for Hegel, the matter of thought is Being in respect of its quality of being thought in absolute thinking, and as this. . . . [It is] thought as absolute concept." The "matter" of Hegel's system is just that which is articulated *within* the system itself and as such, Heidegger notes, is to be contrasted with the matter of his own thinking; that is, Being with regard to its *difference* from beings.[17] I will argue that this view of Hegel's system is not false, but incomplete.

The claim that the system successfully conforms to the threefold preconception given earlier is the success claim of absolute knowing and in fact is the system's truth claim: for truth, in its broadest philosophical sense, is the goal of cognitive activity, and to claim success in knowing is to claim truth.[18] Thus, in positing "absolute knowing" as the essence of Hegel's thought, Heidegger is suggesting that truth—its nature as beginning, originating, or calling forth thought—is what structures the Hegel-Heidegger topos. It appears that our search for an essential question must ask after the truth claim of Hegel's system. Let us follow this out a bit, sketching how the Hegel-Heidegger topos appears from the point of view of truth.

Hegel and Heidegger stand on common ground in that both, as we well know, reject the correspondence theory of truth. Hegel replaces the correspondence theory with what could be called an *identity-theory*. Things are "true," he says, insofar as they correspond to their articulable "Notion"; that is, insofar as they can be *said* to be what they are.[19] In contrast to the correspondence theory's definition, the "truth" of a thing is its own articulable identity, and this identity is presented in the system itself. Hence, from the point of view of truth, Heidegger's three points stand verified: the system, as the self-constructive presentation of the Notion, determines the natures of what is to be known in the world.

Heidegger's concept of truth as disclosure cannot be understood in such terms. For disclosure comes about not through the demonstration of a seamless unity between a thing and its Notion, but via a series of what Graeme Nicholson has called "dislocations" in the experience of the thing. Through these dislocations the Being of the being stands forth; to experience a being as "disclosed" is to experience it in terms of a fundamental rupture or nonidentity that Heidegger, in contrast to Hegel (as we have seen), calls "difference." So I suggest we can call Heidegger's a *nonidentity* view of truth.[20]

Given the fundamental role theories of truth traditionally play in philosophy, it is not surprising that Hegel's and Heidegger's disagreement on the nature of truth leads to further opposition, which I will not rehearse here.[21] In general, it seems that the two bodies of thought diverge right at the beginning. So both thinkers cannot be acceptable, it appears; and our problem is to decide which, if either, is right about the nature of truth. If that is the case, there is no common topos of interplay for Hegel and Heidegger; rather, we find only the once-for-all parting of their ways, and any decision for one or the other can only be arbitrary. No wonder, then, Heidegger remained confused to the end about his own position with respect to Hegel or that he thought his divergence from Hegel was too great even to be called an "opposite position." But is this really the case?

The properly *philosophical* sense of *truth,* Hegel tells us, is entirely different from the notion of correspondence: *eine ganz andere Bedeutung.* Truth in this particular sense does not supplant the traditional notion of it as correspondence. For example, the *Encyclopedia* tells us that philosophy requires the results of empirical science, especially physics; in Hegel's view the correspondence theory *holds* for empirical science. The *Phenomenology* is Hegel's argument that the *similarity* of thought and thing postulated in the correspondence conception of truth turns dialectically into his own concept of *identity* if it is pushed far enough. But there are, he thinks, reasons for not always pushing it that far.[22]

In *Being and Time* and "On the Essence of Truth," Heidegger argues that the notion of truth as correspondence presupposes his own concept of truth as disclosure, both *seinsgeschichtlich* (in the primal Greek experience of truth) and logically. He also recognizes, however (e.g. in "Zur Sache des Denkens") that presupposition is not identity: "the question of 'Αληθεια, of unconcealment as such, is not the question of truth."[23]

Both Hegel and Heidegger, then, accept the correspondence view of truth as valid within its own sphere: their rejection of it is *local*.[24] If their "local" definitions of truth can both coexist with the correspondence theory, might they not also be able to coexist with each other? May we not view their concepts of truth, not as in themselves conflicting general theories of something homogenous called *truth,* but in the first instance as stipulations, perhaps complementary, of what they themselves, as thinkers, are after?

At its most grandiose, this question suggests a bipartite research program that would show that truth as correspondence, on the one hand, presupposes a Heideggerean acount of truth as disclosure and, on the other, transforms dialectically into a Hegelian account of truth as identity. But the correspondence theory of truth itself is in no great shape, as much recent analytical philosophy can teach us.[25] Dismissing it from our discussion would require us to consider Hegel's and Heidegger's views not as mediated by the correspondence theory, but as directly related to each other. This would give us the question: Can Hegel's thought be "true" in Heidegger's sense?

We are now approaching our essential question; but in its present form, the question can be misleading. If the goals of Hegel's and Heidegger's forms of inquiry are so different from truth viewed as correspondence, sharing with it only the virtually meaningless genus "success in cognitive activity" (or perhaps "stipulated goal of thinking"), maybe we should peremptorily dismiss talk of "truth" altogether, leaving the concept to the correspondence theory. Let us do so, and abandon all inquiry into the "truth" of Hegel's system. This brings to the fore two other features of Hegel's system, which he did maintain from first to last, through all changes in content and strategy: its *necessity* and its *completeness*.[26] As complete, Hegel's system aims to comprehend—to know absolutely

—the totality of "forms of finite thought" stored, the *Logic* tells us, in language.[27] As necessary, it claims to put these into a self-constructed and fully determinate logical order. Because of Hegel's claim to completeness, his system will be of the greatest possible conceptual magnitude; because of his necessity-claim, its order will be perfect. These two demands, I suggest, amount to radicalizations of Aristotle's concept of the καλόυ. For the καλόυ, Aristotle tells us, "'εν μεγεθει και ταξει 'εστιυ," is in order and size or is order over size.[28] The standard translation of καλόυ is, not "truth," but "beauty."

To be sure, beauty and truth are not unrelated for Hegel: "beauty is only a specific way of expressing and representing the true," viz. as encountered immediately in a sensuous object.[29] My claim is not that we can definitively leave behind all questions of truth, but that for the present we will do better to understand what Hegel means by "truth" in terms of what he means by "beauty" rather than the other way around. The system, we may say, exhibits on an intellectual level the same sort of "order over size" that an artwork exhibits in sensuous immediacy. It claims something akin to a sort of intellectual beauty, and this—not its construction of its subject-matter—may well be its essence, in the Heideggerean sense sketched earlier. We may do well, then, to look at Hegel's system together with Heidegger's "The Origin of the Work of Art." This, at last, gives us our essential question: Can Hegel's system be said to function similarly to the way Heidegger claims that works of art operate? Beginning with dismissals of the *Phenomenology* and of all talk of truth, this question asks after the nature of Hegel's system, the way it administers itself and prevails over us. And, though not a question Heidegger himself asks, it is asked from a Heideggerean perspective. Answering it will show Hegel's thought functioning with respect to Heidegger's thought, in their common topos. It seems, then, that we have found our essential question. What is left to do?

ANSWERING THE QUESTION

"The Origin of the Work of Art" explores two "essential tendencies" (*Wesenszüge*) of the work of art: the "setting up" of a world and the "setting-forth" of earth. The work of art "sets up" a world by bringing into presence, by "fitting together," and even by existing *as,* the basic determinants—pathways and deities—in the lives of a historical people: in it, "things come to appear as what they really are." The work both stands on and is made from the earth. It has a ground that itself cannot be opened up in this way but immediately closes itself off and in this escape is set forth precisely *as* that which can never be made present. Moreover, these two tendencies—opening up a world and setting forth the earth—are not separate from one another: it is because the work of art can make some things present that it highlights what it cannot make present. Earth and world are thus not mutually indifferent, but in conflict, *Streit,* πολεμος.[30]

Hegel's system aims to state accurately and articulately the Notion, which is just the rational structure of actually existing entities. In this, it does not go directly *to* such entities but to the "forms of finite thought" that, in *their* own way, articulate them, for example, as physics articulates the nature of such entities as time, space, and light. These forms of finite thought, by articulating the natures of entities we actually encounter in the world, give us clues or "hints" on how to deal with those entities.[31] Without denying obvious differences, we may suggest that Hegel's forms of finite thought function as basic determinants of human existence, similar to Heidegger's "pathways and deities."

The system, then (somehow) "fits" these "together" by incorporating them into its own coherent order. Moreover, the system is a conceptually purified articulation of the rational natures of those things—of their identities, as we saw. We may say that the finite forms of thought are given a *purified linguistic presence* in the system: the system "exists as" those moments.[32] Fitting together and existing as the essential content of its time, the system seeks to accomplish, in a logically transparent way, one "essential tendency" of Heidegger's work of art. It seeks to open up a world.

The claim to logical transparence, clearly un-Heideggerean, has two sides. First, Hegel claims that the system is itself immanently developed in a necessary way. Second, he also seems to claim that it has a transparent relation to the historical processes that have produced the world it seeks to comprehend. It is the second claim that confronts us most directly with the "Origin of the Work of Art."

For the question of whether the system stands in a transparent relation to the concrete, extrasystematic world turns out to be the question of the other essential tendency of artwork for Heidegger. If the relation between system and historical reality is not transparent, there must be something in the reality that the system cannot articulate. Is it, then, also something that the system can set back into its originary muteness in such a way as to highlight its nature? I think such is indeed the case for Hegel. To see this we must turn briefly to Hegel's view of the relation of art—especially poetry—to philosophy.

The essential content of poetry and philosophy is for Hegel one and the same: poetry presents "the entire world of ideas developed with a wealth of imagination." Indeed, poetry is *wider* than philosophy, for it presents not only "essential" content, but a wealth of accidental empirical detail; in Hegel's language, poetry does not "present" thoughts but "contains" them. In a sense, then, philosophy has a content more restricted than that of art: it takes the "essential" aspects of what art presents and gives them necessary order or logical form.[33]

What if there is something the artist cannot portray but that is an important part of at least some human lives? Because the artist cannot portray it, it must also remain philosophically unarticulated; it will not find its way into the "world" the system claims to open up. What if the system can provide ways to articulate it, so to speak, negatively, *as* something that cannot be brought into the system? Then we could say that Hegel's system has revealed that thing in its philosophical undisclosability; that is, set it forth as incomprehensible — as Heidegger's work of art reveals Heidegger's earth. Moreover, because the keystone of Hegel's aesthetics is his concept of "reconciliation" — a concept that, like beauty, is not merely aesthetic but taken up in his philosophy[34] — it will be a reality that is not only incomprehensible by Spirit and Reason, but to which they cannot be reconciled. *Streit,* of a sort, is then guaranteed.

Such disclosure of the undisclosable is possible only if the system is essentially, like a work of art, καλόν. It cannot even be asked about if we remain directed on the system as absolute knowing; that is, upon its truth claim. For as philosophically incomprehensible, the "unportrayable" we are seeking is untrue, without identity — what the system *refuses* to claim. If there proves to be such an unportrayable, Heidegger's preconception of Hegel's system, although valid as far as it goes, must ultimately be incomplete. Rather, the system must be understood, not solely in terms of what it articulates and presents in the course of its self-construction, but also in terms of things it does not present.

Does Hegel think there is any such thing? Yes, and his most important example of it in the *Aesthetics* is perhaps a surprising one: the oppression of Jews in Eastern Europe.[35] This, Hegel says, cannot be depicted artistically: it must be *fought* or, if fighting is useless, *endured.* The choice of which is up to the Jew, as a "reasonable man" (*vernünftiger Mensch*): the philosopher cannot make that decision for him.

The oppression of Jews in 1823–1829, while Hegel was lecturing on aesthetics, was far from the unique horror of the Holocaust, unthinkable today and undreamt of then. What Hegel talks about here is the denial of civil rights and social opportunities to some people because of their birth. Such oppression, sadly, is widely distributed in the contemporary world. It is felt in the daily grind of blacks in South Africa and South Chicago; of Italians, between the wars, in the South of France; of the Indians and French of Northern Canada; of women, everywhere.

As undepictable, such oppression is not "beautiful" or "true." It has no place in art and clearly has none in the system: the oppression of Jews is mentioned, in the *Philosophy of Right,* in a footnote.[36] It is absent from the *Encyclopedia,* the *Philosophy of History,* and as far as I know from the *Philosophy of Religion.* But the system does have a categorial locus for this absence.

Evil, writes Hegel in the *Science of Logic,* is a concrete form of what is there called the "exclusion of the One."[37] This occurs when we have a plurality of units, Ones, that are qualitatively identical and can therefore maintain their separate existence only by a rigid repulsion, in which each One posits its other as merely other. Because, in its true nature, it is the same as that other, this repulsion is a denial of the One's own true nature: a dynamic denial that, as a denial of true nature, is a "loss of inner meaning." This loss is presented in "Being-for-self," the generic heading under which "the One" appears in the Logic.[38]

In more concrete forms, this "loss of inner meaning" would not result in an empty repulsion or exclusion but in an affirmation of merely meaningless finitude—of nonessential, indeed silly, content that, as such, cannot be comprehended philosophically. That Hegel was aware of this sort of affirmation and of the inability of his future system to comprehend it was announced in the Introduction to the *Phenomenology:* "this vanity, which understands how to frustrate every truth and to return from truth to itself, and which revels in this understanding; which always knows how to dissolve all thoughts and, instead of any content, to find only [its own] jejune ego; is a satisfaction *which must be left to itself;* for it flees the universal and seeks only Being-for-self.[39]

Shlomo Avineri has documented Hegel's probable role in opening up the student league at Heidelberg to Jewish students during Hegel's stay here.[40] Avineri notes that the main ally, among the professoriat, of the anit-Semitic students was Jakob Fries. If we examine passages where Hegel discusses Fries, we find a rhetorical portrait of the "excluding One" in human form. In the *Philosophy of Right,* Fries is the "generalissimo of the hosts of superficiality" who "bases philosophical science . . . on immediate sense-perception and the play of fancy"; after several similar sentences, Hegel concludes by (mis)quoting Goethe at Fries: "*so hast dem Teufel dich ergeben/und musst zugrunde gehen.*"[41]

Fries's philosophy, a "brew of plundered ideas," is said in the *Philosophy of Mind* to be "the opposite of truth," with which no "reasonable man" (*sinniger Mensch* — Hegel is apparently thinking of intelligent students momentarily seduced by Fries) will stay for long.[42] Fries cannot even get along with others of his ilk. Unable to make positive discoveries, they write polemics against each other, a fact that forces Hegel into French: "*ils se sont battus les flancs pour être de grands hommes.*"[43] Fries's thought is "subjectivity of arbitrary will, ignorance; . . . comfortable . . . lazy reason." In it, "everything was rested upon particular subjectivity; each was haughty and contemptuous of others."[44]

Striking, in addition to the violence of Hegel's rhetoric, is his refusal to engage Fries on a philosophical level. Fries was important, if only as the main academic rationalizer of Jewish oppression; he was a personal opponent of Hegel's at Heidelberg and a political one elsewhere. Hegel knew he was important: Rosenkranz reports that Hegel tried to close down the *Allgemeine Literaturzeitung* after it defended Fries against him.[45] Not only does Hegel attempt no rational dialogue directly with Fries, he makes no effort even to demonstrate Fries's errors in any detail to others, let alone try and comprehend the Friesian "brew" in his system. Fries's philosophy, we may say, is not a "form of finite thought" but a deformation of narrow thoughtlessness. It will defeat any attempt to comprehend philosophically its mishmash of ideas, for the simple reason that such comprehension would have to descend to its level. In any case (as the past tense in the final quote indicates) the philosophy will self-destruct, as does the excluding One: "Since their negating effects nothing . . . they do not return to themselves, do not maintain themselves, and are not."[46]

If Hegel's philosophy cannot deal philosophically with a man who, after all, is a well-known philosopher, there is no point in expecting him to deal with other, presumably even less articulate manifestations of anti-Semitism. But it does not follow that the system is indifferent to Jewish oppression (as it is indifferent, for example, to the "impotence of nature" or to the oppressive "prose of the modern world" also discussed in the *Aesthetics*).[47] For the "reasonable man," the oppressed Jew himself, has a decision to make concerning whether to fight or to endure, and the system, although it cannot make that decision for him, can give him some important information.

For one thing,[48] the system teaches, *as the complete truth about human beings,* the infinite nobility of the human Spirit. There is thus no question of the oppression being in any way justified: "maybe I really am inferior" can be a tempting thought for the oppressed, but the system forecloses it. The system also teaches that the modern state derives its legitimacy from that same concept of the infinite nobility of humanity.[49] It can make clear to the "reasonable man" that his oppression is not necessitated by historical givens, but that those givens are in fact his allies against it. It is a result, not of nature or history, but of the mere irrationality of others.

Without treating oppression systematically — indeed, *by* not so doing — the system thus reveals its true nature and hands it back to those who suffer from it as what it truly is — not merely painful, but incomprehensible and irreconciliable with reason and Spirit. In this sense, I suggest, Hegel's system, like a Heideggerean work of art, does "set forth" an earth: the leaden, unvoiced realities of human oppression.

Though the Hegelian system does not grow out of or contain oppression the way the Heideggerean temple grows from and contains earth, the two must remain for Hegel in conflictual interplay. As long as human oppression surges up from the nowhere-in-particular of others' irrational vanity and takes new forms in so doing, different aspects of the system will be highlighted: a contemporary woman or South African black would read the system differently than would a Jew of the early nineteenth century. System and oppression, neither grounding the other, encounter each other in an everchanging strife of equiprimordials.

All this seems most un-Hegelian. To grasp any of it we must listen for the *silences* of his thought: those contents of the contemporary world that it cannot discuss because to discuss them would be to justify them. That Hegel intended his students to listen for such silences is perhaps suggested by the fact that his philosophical grandchildren included such thinkers as Feuerbach, Marx, Arnold Ruge, August Czieskowski—and Moses Hess. Heidegger, though, is the one who articulates, as a central trait of language, the idea that "one who keeps silent in discussion can 'make something understood' more authentically . . . than someone whom words never fail."[50] Heidegger can articulate this idea because he is open to "dislocation" in speech, to the interstices in talk through which truth can shine or out of which earth can surge forward.

To find silences in Hegel is to place him in the Hegel-Heidegger topos. In so doing we subvert the reactionary Hegel, who thinks he can "bind" the entire current state of the world to absolute knowing and thus provide rational warrant for it all. Placing Hegel's thought in the Hegel-Heidegger topos, allowing its essence to be questioned from a Heideggerean perspective (though not the stated perspective of Heidegger himself), reveals that Hegel's thought prevails through its silences, and that its prevalence is subversive.

QUESTIONING HEIDEGGER

Can we ask a similarly essential question of Heidegger as well—one that questions his thought from a Hegelian perspective? In this attempt we will follow roughly the same procedure as for Hegel but will remain on the terrain already marked out: the terrain that dismisses talk of "truth" as such and holds itself to the "aesthetic" dimension in both thinkers. Using a later author, we will locate something in Heidegger that can be dismissed. We shall then suggest that failure in this dismissal results in a certain preconception of Heidegger's thought, which must be dismissed as well, along with the question in terms of which that preconception would structure the Hegel-Heidegger topos. We shall then ask a related question that will reveal the Hegelian subversion of Heidegger.

Because our point of contact between the two bodies of thought is now "The Origin of the Work of Art," we will turn to a comment Gadamer makes on it. The key to the essay, as we shall see, is its account of the Two-fold of earth and world. And as Gadamer notes, this account is a radical break with all philosophy up to that point, including *Being and Time*: "That 'earth' was used as a philosophical concept was something almost perplexingly new. To be sure, Heidegger's analysis [in *Being and Time*] of the concept of world . . . signified a new twist to [that concept] for the philosophical tradition as well. . . . Yet it did have its theological and moral-philosophical predecessors. However, that "earth" now became the theme of philosophy—this elevation of a poetically charged world to the position of a central conceptual metaphor — signified a true breakthrough."[51]

If "The Origin of the Work of Art" is in its invocation of earth so fundamentally new, we can for our purposes dismiss what preceded it—especially *Being and Time*, where world alone is the ultimate horizon of meaning.[52] The Two-fold of earth and world, then, is the essence of Heidegger in the Hegel-Heidegger topos. It must be understood without regard to *Being and Time*.

If we are to designate the Two-fold of earth and world as the essence of Heidegger, it must also be shown to hold sway in, prevail over, his later thought. This can hardly be done here as I did it for Hegel, with a few quick quotes about necessity and completeness from 1801 to 1831. It might be relatively easy to do, however, if we could take Heidegger's later thought to be concentrated in his accounts of the "Fourfold" of earth, sky, mortals, and immortals.[53] For it seems that the world, already depicted in "The Origin of the Work of Art" as a place of light and air, later becomes the sky, from which the immortals beckon. The mortals are those who inhabit the earth, located under the sky that is the home of the immortals.[54] Earth and world, the latter reinterpreted as sky, prevail in the later Fourfold as the regions which circumscribe the dwellings of mortals and immortals.

Indeed, our essential question for Hegel already engaged the Fourfold. In showing how the system worked we were required to mention, in addition to earth and world, two further types of thing. One was the infinite essence of man, which was articulated in and clarified by the system itself, but which beckoned from out of it toward extrasystematic reality: something on the order, then, of a Heideggerean immortal. Finally, there were the entities *to* whom the infinite essence of man beckoned: Fries, the seduced student, and the oppressed Jew. One is a man *der faulen Ver-*

nunft, one a *sinniger Mensch,* and the third a *vernünftiger Mensch;* but all three are *Menschen,* mortals. My claim is then that the Two-fold prevails in the later Fourfold, and that this is implied not only by Heidegger's texts but by our essential question for Hegel. It seems that we can digest the Fourfold while devouring the Two-fold, just as Heidegger tried to digest the system while devouring the *Phenomenology.* This points to future dismissals of the present effort, the possibility of which I would not deny: as we are seeing, essence and dismissal, or more generally essence and subversion, are intrinsically related.

Let us now formulate for Heidegger the mirror image of the question we formulated for Hegel. It will ask whether Heidegger's account of the Two-fold can function like a Hegelian work of art. Works of art function for Hegel, as we have seen, in ways very similar to the way his system functions, so what we are asking turns out to be whether Heidegger's thought can be καλόν in the sense of Hegel's system—whether it can be necessary and complete.

This question, however, remains bound to its own preconception of Heidegger's thought; namely, that Heidegger even aims at providing a complete and necessary account of something (as Hegel's system, considered as absolute knowledge, was supposed to be a complete and necessary account of everything). The role of earth in "The Origin of the Work of Art" is ignored in the formulation of this question. For the undisclosable intrusions of earth into world mean that the work of art—and thinking itself—is irretrievably fragmented, conditioned by mystery. Neglecting the role of earth, this preconception of Heidegger remains determined by the horizon of *Being and Time,* as Heidegger's preconception of Hegel was determined by the *Phenomenology.*[55] If Heidegger's account of the temple and the Two-fold does not even aspire to the status of Hegel's system, then there is no point in investigating whether it attains that status, and we have the opportunity for another peremptory dismissal. We can dismiss this whole question in favor of another that asks, not whether it is possible for Heidegger's thought to be καλόν in Hegel's sense, but more generally what it would be like for it to do so.

This question, in fact, is more in keeping with the essence of Hegel as we have opened that up. Heidegger's preconception of Hegel's system saw it as, in a loosely Kantian sense, "constitutive" of its matter or *Sache;* for its matter is just what it articulates in the course of its self-construction. The Heideggerean subversion of that essence has shown the system to confront a reality radically other than it, to which it can relate in what might, with equal looseness, be styled "regulatory." The infinite essence of man, like Kantian freedom a rationally constructed idea, provides a standard by which to judge given realities, for example Fries and the anti-Semites, and find them radically defective.[56] We will then hold

Hegel's system over against Heidegger's thought as beckoning to it in a regulative way, telling it what (from Hegel's standpoint) it should be; and we will ask what kinds of modifications in Heidegger's thought would constitute an affirmative response to such beckoning. This will enable us to put into question the essence of Heidegger, as adumbrated earlier.

To think like Hegel, Heidegger would have to view the Greek temple as a moment of a larger whole; an expression of, let us say, the Absolute in nature. What is the Absolute here? Surely we are not going to revert to considerations of truth as correspondence and hypostasize it as some sort of theological or metaphysical reality about which propositions could be asserted (such as, in Hegel's case, that it exists, and in Heidegger's that it does not). For the "Absolute," in the sense of "absolute knowing" for example, constructs itself in the system and therefore *is* the system itself in its development, necessary and complete.

As Joan Stambaugh notes, Hegel's thought begins with the concept of dialectic and then seeks to understand time in terms of that — as an "externalized" version of the rational structure of thesis-antithesis-synthesis, if we may use those terms.[57] This means that Hegel will view something that, like the Two-fold of earth and world, is itself *in* time as exhibiting rational development *over* time — as material for a narrative: where, by *narrative,* I mean something like the concept of μυθos in Aristotle's *Poetics* — a temporal development exhibiting a logical structure; that is, one in which post hoc ergo propter hoc is not a fallacy.[58] In Hegelian terms, this rational development, as καλόν, must also be complete: none of its stages can be omitted.

How, then, would Hegel plot the Two-fold? He could not simply have earth, world, and temple as equiprimordial in their interplay but would have to begin from one of them, which presumably would be earth. Then, via minimal (or, as Hegel calls them, determinate) negations, he would advance to the world and then on to the temple itself, which would synthesize the two. This in fact is roughly how Hegel views art in general: as an expression (synthesis) of Spirit (world) in nature (on earth). But his μυθos is not yet καλos because it is not yet complete. For he must also view the temple, not merely as a synthesis of the two realms of earth and world, but as negating each.

This negation turns out to be the same for both earth and world. The religious work of art, according to the *Phenomenology,* negates the previous status of deities in that it constructs them, rather than merely finding them in natural phenomena: the artist is a "spiritual worker."[59] The temple's negation of nature is likewise the process of its construction, to which the *Aesthetics'* account of the Greek temple is keyed.[60] To amend Heidegger's account in the direction of Hegel would then require attention to the process by which the temple was constructed. The temple would have to be shown as coming forth, in part, from the earth.

The temple in fact, of course, is built by human beings and, in particular, by slaves. This point is nowhere hinted at in Heidegger's account, any more than Heidegger the man was willing to recognize the realities of Jewish oppression in his own day. Instead, the work of art is viewed as coming to be through a purely "creative" process.[61] Correspondingly, in the "Origin of the Work of Art," earth is considered as a "heimatlicher Grund," a "homey ground" on which the Greek temple stands and not as a realm of possible oppression that the temple could somehow articulate.[62] Such considerations, to be sure, are lacking as well in Hegel's *Aesthetics*, but he, unlike Heidegger, makes up the deficiency elsewhere, identifying slavery as both the ground and nemesis of Greek civilization.[63] Slavery is for Hegel, like all human oppression, the reduction of Spirit (in the form of another human being) to nature (seeing the other person as intrinsically determined by mere birth).[64]

Heidegger's account of human oppression, as realized in what he called the "Gestell," locates it outside the Fourfold, and indeed as resulting from the forgetting of the Fourfold.[65] He never asserts, or even implies, that earth can contain, as well as elements of a "homey ground," mortals who have been pushed back into earth, who are deprived of their very mortality because they are deprived of the chance to live their lives. But, I think this view is also not incompatible with anything Heidegger acutally says. Articulating it subverts the reactionary Heidegger — the Heidegger who thinks he can avoid talking about political matters by invoking such "deeper" concepts as Being, Appropriation, and the Fourfold. The regulative use of Hegel's system, accomplishing that subversion and articulation, can perhaps allow Heidegger's thought, unable to escape politics on any level, to prevail over us in new ways.

My point is not that Hegel is right and Heidegger wrong: no account of how a temple was built, or for which purposes, could ever articulate its role in the strife between world and earth. The two bodies of thought rather hold sway over one another, in that they can be used as checks on each other. Heideggerean thought gives us an ear for what is not articulated in Hegel's system. Hegelian thought gives us a check on the silences of Heidegger, some of which can and should be filled in. Each body of thought, in holding sway over the other, subverts it, and through this mutual subversion the two bodies of thought prevail together. The terms *essence* and *subversion*, as I have articulated them here, both name the same. That same is the Hegel-Heidegger topos.

3

Hegel and the Subversion of System: Der Fall Adorno

Martin Donougho

Freud liked to quote Sophocles to the effect that even the ruins of the world would slay the most intrepid of men. The same is true of Hegel's system. It is noteworthy how much recent continental philosophy has been carried out in the shadows cast by that system. In turn its interpretation has constantly to be revised in the light of contemporary developments. What I offer here, out of self-defense perhaps, are a few remarks —on life among the ruins—intended only as signposts for further exploration.

A natural place to begin is with Adorno's often-quoted aphorism in *Minima Moralia* (still used as epigraph to the much later *Aspekte der Hegelschen Philosophie* [1957]): "The whole is the untrue"—which plays on Hegel's own "*Das Wahre ist das Ganze*" ("The true is the whole") from the Preface to the *Phenomenology*.[1] To this aphorism may be added another, from Friedrich Schlegel: "It is equally fatal to the spirit to have a system and to have none: the only way out is to combine both."[2] Such a combination is exactly what Hegel attempted. He tried, that is, to establish a philosophical system unified by a model of subjectivity or self-reflection derived essentially from Fichte, while avoiding the reduction of the whole to pure self-relation; that is, the mere projection of the ego's self-positing. From the difficulty of the task comes a certain ambiguity, and not merely for us, in retrospect; Hegel was himself aware of the stakes. His thought employs a dialectic of reflection that aims finally to close upon itself in an encyclopaedic system—the true, comprehensive whole—that nevertheless claims to be more than a subjective, formalist postulate, a mere short-circuit.

Adorno's relations to Hegel display a similar ambivalence. Adorno's vocabulary, for example, is Hegelian even in its denunciations of Hegel (admittedly his style is very different: paratactic, fragmentary, full of *Stichworte*, cues for the entry of our own thinking). More substantively, Adorno emphasizes that Hegel carries through Fichte's program — to show how the a priori is also the a posteriori—and so opposes both stubborn empiricism and static apriorism (*"Aspekte,"* p. 252). He notes, too, that unlike Fichte, Hegel does not presuppose subjectivity as axiomatic: "His system is less a scientific construction than a conglomerate of original observations" (*"Aspekte,"* p. 253)—a dynamic totality of propositions rather than derived theorems. Yet he concludes that in the final reckoning Hegel *imposes* an identity upon the world he observes, and reason thereby becomes instrumental, repressive, masterful.

Adorno wants to go further however. For if—to return to the initial aphorism—the whole is the un-true, it is so dialectically: there is truth in the un-truth. Hegel is convicted of hypostatizing the concept of the subject and so mystifying it. Hence, we should learn not so much to spell Hegel (which some have urged) as to *dis*pel the mystification his system works on our ways of thinking. We demystify by seeing through its allure to the hidden meaning: a social labor that throughout conditions its production. Thus Hegel's placement of nonidentity under the aspect of identity may be interpreted as mimicking the systemic aspect of capitalist society, which likewise subsumes the individual subject into the illusory but dominant whole. Adorno goes further still: the truth that Hegel's system discloses is that of the whole; that is, an unrealized utopia. Like the work of art, it shows through its *Schein* to an exemplary falsity and thence to its truth, its utopian gesture, its sense of a possible reconciliation — but not yet (Bloch) and not for us (Benjamin).

These intricate doublings help us explicate the opaque opening sentence of *Negative Dialectics*: "Philosophy, which once seemed obsolete, continues to survive because the moment of its actualization was let slip."[3] It was *Hegelian* philosophy that seemed (to Marx) obsolete; and it was due to Marxism's lost opportunity, Adorno thinks, that the dialectic retains its power, though in negative mode. Ironically, then, the critique of instrumental or identity reasoning is to be conducted *by* reason, if now a reason that is dialectical, negative, and nontotalizing. Adorno would dispel the illusion of absolute subjectivity, while nevertheless holding fast to subjectivity itself. Hence, the goal of *Negative Dialectics*: to "use the power [*Kraft*] of the subject in order to break through the deceit [*Trug*] of constitutive subjectivity" (ND, p. xx/11). Or to express the paradox another way, built into philosophy "is the effort to transcend the concept by means of the concept" (ND, p. 15/27). Reason, so to say, is the cure for which (in its instrumental guise) it was meant to be the disease.

The brief remarks that follow ask how, with respect to Hegelian *Vernunft,* the cure might be effected — perhaps by Hegel himself. They will address, in the first place, Adorno's model for reading Hegel, then three crucial texts — the *Logic,* the *Phenomenology,* and the *Aesthetics* — with suggestions for their further rereading.

THE ADORNO READER

"Skoteinos, oder Wie zu lesen sei" is a 1963 essay that brilliantly teaches us how to approach Hegel, that master of enlightening obscurity, of "darkness visible."[4] Let me review some of its points.

1. Adorno remarks, rightly enough, that Hegel's mode of address is oral; his "works" are not some mythic final word but derive mostly from lectures, the notes for which are rudely "printed without permission." Even the few properly dialectical works (the *Phenomenology,* above all the *Logic*) retain the gesture of oral presentation and give-and-take that teaching imparts. Adorno instances the beginning of the *Greater Logic:* "*Sein, reines Sein* — ohne alle weitere Bestimmung."[5] Such an expression strives to say what cannot be said in a discursive sentence or sequence, yet must be *said* all the same. Hegel negates all presentation; his books vanish as we read them. "Just as one today speaks of anti-matter, so the Hegelian texts are anti-texts" ("Skoteinos," p. 351), Adorno writes. We listen to the words as if to musical cues for our attempted performance of the thought. Adorno compares the statement, reversal, doubling back, and restatement so characteristic of this procedure first to the description of the dialectic at the end of the "Subjective Logic," then again to the peculiarities of Hegel's stumbling lecturing style (as reported by Hotho), and lastly (and most surprisingly), to Beethoven's sonata-form (theme or motif, development, recapitulation, coda, etc.). We listen, in sum, as if to the music of Hegel's thinking.

2. Adorno locates the main reason for Hegel's obscurity in the dialectical need to say everything at once. No sentence is adequate to its content but must always implicate every other sentence. Reading Hegel is reading both beyond and between the lines. He is trying to express what cannot be expressed, trying to articulate the nonidentical, to bring the speechless to expression. If he continually fails in the attempt, the failure is necessary, and con-

stitutes the motor of philosophical rectification and restatement. His language may indeed lie convicted of equivocation, but only because Hegel uses language to criticize and correct language. The thought is always in process. Adorno even compares the experience of reading Hegel to that of watching films: we do not attend to the moments save insofar as we look at stills of the action. At the same time, attention to such moments—in a kind of slow motion thinking—is precisely what the dialectic demands of its reader. Adorno would make of the *Greater Logic* a veritable "micrologic." Or, to use one of his key figures, the individual moments should be read as forming "constellations," the parts of which illuminate one another and may thus be read as "determinate signs and legible script" (*"Skoteinos,"* p. 342).[6]

3. Nevertheless, in Adorno's view, Hegel falls back on schematic representation rather than trust his experience, tends to offer common sense assurances of overall coherence: a conceptual legerdemain that would separate a completed thought from an expression (or presentation) to which the thought is then indifferent. We should see through it, Adorno suggests, and read Hegel otherwise—with imagination, against the grain if need be—as if he were trying out a series of experiments that in themselves have no guarantee of success.[7]

4. As a result of this strategy, Hegel's comforting assertion of an overall identity of thought serves instead to bring out all the more strongly the negative that is thereby suppressed—the whole system cries out, with pathos, "Nonidentity" (*"Skoteinos,"* p. 375).

Such a reading is in part subversive of Hegel's positive message of reconciliation within an absolute subjectivity or Idea. In part it suggests that, if we take its dialectic of reflection seriously, the system explodes itself from within. The following three sections look at how such inner contestation might be found in specific texts.

THE PHENOMENOLOGY

Adorno holds that Hegel's philosophy is the continual effort to express experience in terms of concepts. The *Phenomenology* certainly attempts that by Hegel's own admission and representation in the Introduction; and by the end the claim is made not only to have succeeded in the quest, but also to have proven it—in absolute knowing, which Derrida calls *Sa,* or the eternal feminine that draws Hegel on. Adorno shares Derrida's skepticism about the legitimacy of this claim to absolute knowing, and, like Derrida, he looks for discordant signs in the text itself.

Horkheimer and Adorno's *Dialectic of Enlightenment* takes a leaf or two from Hegel's book, in arguing that enlightened reason risks short-circuiting itself. In their view, modernity is marked by the subject's subordination of nature to its own instrumental reason. As such it celebrates the rise to power of the individual, bourgeois self; but equally and more insidiously it is marked by the fall of the individual subject, by his or her effacement before the nameless power of the whole social system. Hegel, too, gives clear voice to both movements, the fabrication of the self, as well as its vulnerability to the world it has made. The *Phenomenology* tells an enthralling story of subjectivity's quest for self, for knowledge of itself. But it also tells a more subversive tale, a not-so-tall story, of how the individual constitutes itself — and at the same time is constituted — within the realm of *Bildung,* culture, language, or what one might almost call, in Lacanian terms, the Symbolic (*bildlich*) Order.[8]

Self-constituting comes about in three stages. The first stage is the forging of the self as legal *person,* stemming from the disintegration of the ancient Greek ideal of ethos or character and the transformation of *persona* into the individual self, subject (in both senses) of the Roman-Christian imperium. The second stage is the revolutionary citizen, at once particular and universal, but unstably so (because unified by the disinterested yet arbitrary force of justice). The third is the self of *conscience (Gewissen),* a development of the Kantian subject as inhabitant of a moral and political kingdom of ends. None of these is exactly a role-model for true subjectivity; or rather, a mere role model is exactly what each amounts to. Ultimately the moral self becomes the "beautiful soul," which Hegel describes as self-sufficient "introverted being" (*Insichsein*), inwardly certain of itself, exclusive, and proud, but able to exist only in constant flight from the world. (The "beautiful soul" has a precursor in the purely linguistic self of Rameau's nephew — a virtuoso of expression without substance, who pulls out all the stops of *ressentiment* long before Nietzsche had diagnosed that characteristically modern disease.)

In this impasse Hegel looks beyond the self-reflection of Romantic subjectivism and toward a radical openness to otherness and contingency, namely, in religious experience and cultic community.[9] His move has its parallel in Adorno, as we may see from some remarks by Albrecht Wellmer: "The critique of identity-logical reason appears to issue in the alternative, cynicism or theology; unless of course one wants to become the advocate of a joyous regression or disintegration of self without concern for the consequences."[10] Now, Adorno wanted at all costs to avoid such an irrationalist regression (associated with someone like Ludwig

Klages), just as he would never resort to cynicism. For the "theological" option, Wellmer has in mind Adorno's reliance on a utopian perspective to hold open the possibility of critique. The *Phenomenology,* too, proceeds via religion, and does so in a salvational mode. Yet Hegel at this point (the transition from "Spirit" to "Religion") chooses to resolve any utopian hope into a strict dialectic of form and content. Whereas religious representation frames a content set over against the self, philosophical knowing (theme of the chapter after that on religion) identifies content with form, so that its object becomes its own self, or rather, its own act of knowing itself. This absolute, philosophical identity marks the return of none other than the "beautiful soul":

> The beautiful soul . . . is its own knowing of itself in its pure transparent unity — the self-consciousness which knows this pure knowledge of *pure introverted-being* [*Insichsein*] as spirit. It is not only an intuition of the divine but also the divine's intuition of itself [*Selbstanschauung*] . . . The self has attained the life of absolute spirit . . . what in religion was *content,* or a form for the presenting of an *other,* . . . is here the *self*'s own *act.*[11]

The philosopher is the truly beautiful soul, therefore, because he acts and is actual, showing himself open to the whole panoply of finitude and determinacy, to nature and history alike. His is the self that is finally free, the absolute self.

The solution may not convince. Yet the important thing here is that Hegel's *problem* foreshadows Adorno's: how to preserve subjectivity and hence critical distance from a reified world, without at the same time resorting to the decentered, schizoid self celebrated by Deleuze and Guattari, described by Lacan, and effected by Althusser.

THE LOGIC

Hegel's *Science of Logic* is the most baffling of texts because (to put it in Adornian terms) it attends seriously to the baffles that language puts in the path of dialectic — a dialectic that nevertheless exists only *through* language. Enough has been said about the celebrated triad. I wish instead to glance at the career of Being *after* it has gone through Nothing and Becoming, to be thematized as *Dasein* or Determinate Being. Hegel tries to express the very lability of thought categories: how we can think them only as immediately (sc. mediately) passing over into their opposites, in a process of becoming that itself cannot be thought for the same reason, though it at least has a name. Even so, calling the new thought content "*Dasein*" does not help much, for we (readers) have immediately to think of the negativity that infects such determinate being in general. A thought determination must put the accent on being and identity (which at this stage appears as the relatively indefinite "self-sameness") rather than nonbeing and difference. (In the Jena Logic he thematizes the latter as *differente Beziehung,* about which Derrida offers some perceptive and even crucial remarks for his own thinking[12]). Is the emphasis in fact no more than a procedural convenience? Or is there an ontological lesson here? It is difficult to decide whether Hegel stubbornly holds to identity—having continually to make amends for it—or whether he is pointing to the difference or otherness that escapes capture by determining thought. After all, how *can* we express nonidentity (the task that Adorno sees as central to Hegel's thinking)? How can we figure the ground that grounds figure? (We might recall that Spinoza's *Omnis determinatio est negatio,* which Hegel quotes in this section, was applied specifically to the notion of *figura.*)

Hegel's fascinating quest seems on the face of it bound to fail, yet he sets off with a will. In an initial step, *Dasein* is determined as quality, then as the unity of reality and negation, and eventually as the "something" (*Etwas*), or that which can be thought only as bounded and limited by otherness. As such it is finitude, and Hegel next enquires into how determinate things can be determined as what they are by what they are not, by a limit (*Grenze*) that is both inside and outside. It is a kind of double game that makes itself out to be neutral and "indifferent," but that as a result can only be lost.

This is one of the densest parts of the Hegelian forest, and one of the most important. Yet there is no time to explore it here, and no guarantee of escape. Suffice it to make two comments. First, Hegel brings out the evil of sheer self-relation by labeling it *Insichsein*—precisely the "introverted-being" of pure reflection that demonstrated the downfall of the (Romantic) self in the *Phenomenology.* He also points to its positive side, just as in the *Phenomenology,* for it is the very principle of subjectivity. It prefigures the Concept and what Hegel terms the "concrete intensity of the subject."[13] Here in miniature we have played out the drama of Hegel's entire system: the attempt to take account of otherness while not reducing it to the "ego = ego" of an empty formalism. Second, the dialectic of determination that Hegel develops through the thematics of *Sollen*—the never ending "is-to-be"—parallels his metacritique of the Kantian critical system, which in his view lays itself open to determination *ab extra.* In neither instance is Hegel taking a systematic position. Instead he observes the thought-determination and attempts to mediate the relational terms (self-sameness and otherness), maintaining each through the agility of his (and our) thinking of them. It is a long process. At the end of the section we are left with a *new* determination — *Fürsichsein* — that promptly undergoes the same deconstructive treatment.

Now, the question is whether Hegel falls into an identity-philosophy in following this sort of procedure, always pulling out the positive moment just when it seemed to be engulfed in the negative — the resolution of the negation of the negation that shows only, as Adorno puts it, that the negative was not negative enough. Or is he really trying to think otherness as such — the other to other, in Hegel's phrase?[14] The latter sounds very much like the project of negative dialectics, for which positing (*Setzen*) is always provisional and reflection the only article of faith. The question submits of no easy answer (and certainly not in a brief essay). I would merely point to several studies along these lines, notably the dense and itself "experimental" attempt by Theunissen in his *Sein und Schein* to see how far Hegel masks difference behind identity, how far he enacts a dominating form of speculative reason.[15]

LECTURES ON THE PHILOSOPHY OF FINE ART

Aesthetic Theory—Adorno's opus posthumous and in effect his last testament — as any would-be reader knows, is extraordinarily difficult. Fragmentary, polemical, filled with gnomic utterances (especially on Hegel), sometimes micrological in approach and sometimes infuriatingly general, it is so indirect as almost to amount to a giant set of paralipomena (as indeed one of its sections is labeled). To complete the symmetry, it is also a parergon—the ergon in this case being Hegel's *Aesthetics,* to which Adorno constantly alludes. In particular, Adorno plays variations on the Hegelian theme of the essential pastness of art, adding only that the pastness has itself become thematic matter for art; presumably he has in mind modernism's tradition of the new, its tendency to flout the rules and attack the institution or industry of art that supports it. How is art possible, now that its cultic function has passed? He poses the question with the realization that it may no longer *be* possible at all. Adorno's worry is even larger, however. It echoes the worry in *Negative Dialectics* as to the very survival of philosophy. For as Hegel's absolute spirit came crashing down, according to Adorno, so did the spiritual (sc. subjective) basis of art, or more precisely, of the *work* of art; art risks becoming inhuman, objectivist, all on the surface with no allegorical content. "Originally patterned after art," he declares, "the metaphysics of spirit, once destroyed, must restore spirit to art."[16] Adorno wishes to retain the element of subjectivity in modern art, the element he sees as central to modernism and its protest against the culture industry—the element, we might add, that has recently come under attack from the tendency called *post-modernism* (whose motto seems to be "Anything human is alien").

Adorno wishes, in other words, to retain the *auratic* quality in the work of art, its work-ness, its symbolic (or allegorical) dimension, which announces hope even in desperate times. He does not wish the *work* to become *text* (to employ Roland Barthes's useful distinction).[17] For the work of art constitutes a mimesis of natural beauty; that is, of a meaning in sensuous nature, of its aura or archaic aspect. The trouble is that the aura has faded. Modernism can no longer take plot or centered character-agent as given for its own refashioning: the modernist work must create its own conventions, genres, meanings, and Adorno calls it "nominalist" for that reason. In this respect Hegel remained old-fashioned, according to Adorno, spellbound by the classical Ideal that saw meaning in nature and the work in its context of tradition. If he is still useful, it is only by being turned against himself. It follows that, just as Hegelian philosophy attains a kind of afterlife in negative dialectics, "Hegelian aesthetics can be brought to itself only through the experience of a radically nominalistic modern art" (AT, pp. 398, 377).

It seems to me, however, that the *Aesthetics* need not be turned inside out to apply it to modernism. It can be seen as responding to an increasingly "nominalist" tendency in the art of Hegel's own time, a tendency Hegel detects in the artist's formal and thematic freedom of treatment. Moreover, far from imposing a framework of classical beauty derived from the ancient Greek Ideal, Hegel shows himself more sympathetic to the sublime, the symbolic, the sheer falling together of nature and subjectivity. The time has come, as Paul de Man and Peter Szondi both saw, for a certain rehabilitation of the *un*-classical Hegel. Consider for instance a remarkable passage from the *Aesthetics,* where Hegel describes the romantic (sc. Christian) art-form–world-view; and because it seems to deal with peripheral matters, it is in fact, central to an understanding of Hegel's conception of art:

> Thus in the romantic we have two worlds: a spiritual realm, complete within itself, feeling [*Gemüt*], which is reconciled within itself and now bends back the otherwise linear repetition of birth, death and rebirth into a new cycle, to return into itself, into the genuine phoenix-life of the spirit; on the other side, the realm of the external as such, which released from the fixedly secure unification with spirit now becomes a purely empirical reality, by whose shape the soul is unencumbered . . . now the inner life is indifferent to the mode of shaping [*Gestaltungsweise*] of the immediate world, because immediacy is unworthy of the soul's inward bliss [*Seligkeit*]

. . . it is to express not merely the inner [*Innerliche*] but also inwardness [*Innigkeit*], which instead of fusing with the external appears as reconciled with itself only within itself. In this relation the inner, pushed thus to an extreme, is expression without externality [*äusserlichkeitslose Ausserung*], invisibly as it were perceiving only its own self: a sounding as such, without objectivity and shape, a hovering over the waters, a ringing over a world which in and on its heterogeneous appearances can assume and mirror only a reflexion of this inward-being [*Insichsein*] of the soul.

If we sum up in *one* word this relation of content and form in the romantic, then we can say that the basic note of the romantic is *musical,* and with determinate content of representation, *lyrical.*[18]

It hardly needs remarking that the romantic, creational model this passage embodies parodies the first genesis of Genesis. We might add, with Adorno in mind, that *aura* means breath, the atmosphere of divine meaning that breathes over nature and the work of art alike. And other associations are readily made. For example, creation would seem to be inherently musical (and all art, in Hegel's developmental view aspires to the condition of music). In Hegel's account of it, music sets in motion a primal *Stimmung* or mood infusing and charging the whole world (the German has such cosmic associations), conjuring up a primal attitude toward the world. Romantic music (in our sense of *romantic*) has a more specific meaning for Hegel: it realizes just one idea or inspiration (*Einfall*) and then elaborates upon it in a complex arabesque (Adorno uses the term *Einfall* for many of his explanations of the work of art). Furthermore, music could be thought of as the embodiment of the sublime, breathing over the waters, sounding over the sheer inanimateness of nature to give it meaning even though the surface is meaningless. The transitions between world-views are marked, for Hegel, by a return of the epigraphic, symbolic moment in which external and inner are separate and yet coincide. That is no less true of the transition from romantic art (in Hegel's sense) to whatever is to come. Here the epigraphic marker is so-called objective humor: the artist—for whom no art of the past is alien, its genres, techniques, and themes all being available material—ranges over the surfaces of the past in search of inspiration, an *Einfall* we might say, a momentary touching of subject and object. I have elsewhere compared this moment to the end of *Faust II* and the often-cited lines "*Alles vergängliche ist nur ein Gleichnis*" ("Everything transitory is but a figure").[19] The *Aesthetics'* historicizing mode of treatment mortifies its object into yielding its hidden (but superficial) allegorical meaning.

Perversely, Adorno makes Hegel sound old-fashioned. The philosopher stands accused of subordinating natural beauty to art (born again from the spirit, as Hegel says), of being against the sublime, of having an aesthetics of content, of displaying a crippling bias toward the classical norm. None of these charges stands up, at least if we probe the texts just a little. Hegel's aesthetics may be read as one of disintegration, whereby the very terms that make art possible—a classical separation of form(ing) and content—are gradually dissolved.[20] Hegel points, at the edges of his account, to the sublime limits of classical beauty. In Berlin he displays enormous and growing fascination with the symbolic, little with the Greeks' "cold pastoral." He shows, in effect, how the classical Ideal (of self-transparent action, demeanor, work, etc,) is subverted from within precisely by its mode of presentation (*Darstellungsweise*), most notably through tragic drama. The classical artist presents a phantasmagoria that on its surface belies the human origin—its "construction" in Adorno's terms—but on inspection or in practice shows through such a semblance or *Schein*. Just as Adorno thought, art requires the philosopher to interpret what it cannot say, even though in its historical practices it comes more and more to reflect on its own materials, activity, and status.

I have been trying to make Hegel sound like Adorno. After all that is not so difficult. Hegel invites reading "against the grain," with panache, just as Adorno himself recommends. If we do read him in this way, we find that his melancholy gaze very much resembles Adorno's, indeed much more than Adorno realizes. Doubtless my examples from the three chosen texts could be multiplied and extended. They suffice however to show that Hegel may be read as mimesis of Adorno.

4

Kierkegaard's Stages on Life's Way: How Many Are There?

John M. Michelsen

It is common knowledge that Kierkegaard distinguishes three "stages on life's way": the aesthetic, the ethical, and the religious. Although there is no simple correlation between these stages and the chronological development of an individual from childhood to old age, they can be said to be stages of maturation. The maturation of the *spirit* is involved, and progression through the stages can be said to involve increasing degrees of authenticity, culminating (ideally) in an existence where the individual is completely grounded in the ground of his being or — in more Christian terms — where he achieves eternal salvation. The aesthetic stage is characterized by a search for various forms of enjoyment, ranging from the purely sensuous to the most refined and cultivated artistic and intellectual. The ethical stage is characterized by moral guilt and the striving to realize the good; and the religious stage by suffering and salvation through an irrational faith in Christ. The relationship between these stages is dialectical in the sense that a contradiction within a lower stage necessitates the transformation to a higher one insofar as the self *demands* such a development. The three stages are therefore not simply three different life orientations or three different value systems; the fulfillment of the individual as an authentic self necessitates the progression through these stages.

There is however one major complication on this rather neat, albeit complex, structure. In Kierkegaard's own discussion of his writings in *The Point of View for My Work as an Author,* the central point discussed is the polarity between the aesthetic and the religious. The question that he raises is how one is to understand his writings of the previous five years, and in particular how one is to understand the pseudonymous writings. Do they have an essentially aesthetic purpose or an essentially religious one? It is fairly clear that the aesthetic and the religious are the two stages[1] competing for Kierkegaard's allegiance, and this has been sensed by many readers who have found in his discussion of these two stages a passion and a beauty that is lacking in his discussion of the ethical. Significantly, the ethical is all but absent from his discussion in *The Point of View*.

One may therefore ask the following question: how does one reconcile the formulation of the three stages with the emphasis on the aesthetic-religious polarity? It is not difficult to establish that the polarity must be given priority, a point I will discuss later. Let us first look at an interesting question that arises if one adopts the "two-stages" position: what becomes of the ethical stage? Because it obviously cannot be excised, one is left with the options of uniting it with one or the other of the two remaining stages, so that the polarity comes to be either the aesthetic-ethical vs. the religious or the aesthetic vs. the ethico-religious. Again, it is not difficult to establish that Kierkegaard would opt for the latter, for there are countless passages in his most central works where this point is made explicitly. Even in the work in which he deals with the question of the Good in almost entirely nontheological terms, *Purity of Heart,* he says that to will the Good is the same thing as to will to hold fast to God.[2]

What I wish to explore here is the significance of the fact that Kierkegaard treats the ethical and the religious as inseparable. I will also explore the possibility that the essence of his entire philosophy supports a radically different polarity — one that he would find very disturbing.

Before turning to his analyses of the ethical and the religious stages, it will be helpful to look at how he characterizes the general human condition in his marvellous description of modern society in *The Present Age,* a little work that has had such a profound influence on many of the greatest thinkers in the tradition of existentialism and phenomenology. "Our age," he says in the opening paragraph, "is essentially one of understanding and reflection, without passion, momentarily bursting into enthusiasm, and shrewdly relapsing into repose."[3] The discussion that follows is a lament for the loss of the individual, the submersion of the individual in the crowd, the lack of courage to act on one's own, and the tendency always to join with a group, to form a committee. What characterizes the age is the process of leveling, establishing the worst kind of equality by reducing everyone to the lowest common denominator and failing to recognize, admire, and respect the outstanding individual. This process of leveling produces people who are lacking in true moral character, people who are individually in contradiction with themselves and whose relationship to one another is characterized by envy and the love of money rather than a commitment to value. Throughout the discussion runs the distinction between, on the one hand, reflection, understanding, abstraction, and the quantitative, and, on the other hand, passion, action, the concrete individual, and the qualitative. One of the striking things about this description is that much of it could have been written by Karl Marx. It is very reminiscent of the analysis of the alienation of the individual from himself and other men found in the *Paris Manuscripts,* written only two years earlier.

However, when we turn to Kierkegaard's diagnosis of this condition and the cure he recommends, we of course find a parting of the ways with Marx. Loss of the individual occurs because "eternal responsibility, and the religious singling out of the individual before God, is ignored."[4] The lack of authentic religion being the cause, it is not difficult to imagine what will be recommended as the cure for the malady: "man's only salvation lies in the reality of religion for each individual."[5] The individual is faced with the choice between *either* being "lost in the dizziness of unending abstractions" *or* being "saved for ever in the reality of religion."[6]

In another passage where he again posits the alernatives of being lost or finding oneself religiously, he goes on to make the following remark: "Dialectically the position is this: the principle of association, by strengthening the individual, enervates him; it strengthens numerically, but ethically that is a weakening. It is only after the individual has acquired an ethical outlook, in face of the whole world, that there can be any suggestion of really joining together."[7]

This passage is interesting for several reasons. It makes it clear how naturally Kierkegaard slides from talking about the religious to talking about the ethical. It also makes it clear that there is nothing wrong with an association of individuals per se. The important thing is that for an association to have positive value it must be ethically based, and this suggests that the ethical as such is more fundamental than even such an association. I will return to this point later.

First let us ask, why does Kierkegaard think of the ethical and the religious as being so closely related? To answer this question, we have to look at works where he analyzes these stages in considerable depth and detail. I have chosen the *Postscript* for the religious, for this contains what is no doubt his most famous analysis of faith, and the *Equilibrium* essay in *Either/Or,* vol. 2, which contains an equally familiar statement of the ethical. In both works the subjective-objective distinction is central, and this in turn is parallel to the passion-reflection distinction in *The Present Age,* thus giving the clue to the whole puzzle.

Spelled out already in the Introduction to the *Postscript*[8] is the distinction between the objective and the subjective points of view: *objectively,* the problem of Christianity consists of an inquiry into the truth of

Christianity; *subjectively*, the problem concerns the relationship of the individual to Christianity. The book does not concern itself with the objective truth of Christianity, except to set that problem aside; rather, it concerns itself with the problem of how to become a Christian. It eventually becomes clear that the objective-subjective dichotomy, which is also said to be the distinction between the WHAT and the HOW, is not quite correctly characterized as a distinction between a concern with truth and a concern with something else. For Kierkegaard[9] there are two kinds of truth—objective truth and subjective truth—and the main purpose of the *Postscript* is to elaborate the idea that, as far as religious faith is concerned, truth is subjective or — more accurately — that subjectivity is truth and that the religious task of the individual is to become subjective.

In a nutshell, this view amounts to the following: the subjective question is a question of the mode of the subject's acceptance of that which he believes. Objectively, the Christian doctrine is no doubt either true or false but, subjectively, one is in the truth if one relates oneself to that doctrine in such a manner that one's relationship is in truth a God-relationship, regardless of whether the doctrine itself is objectively true or false. What must be the manner of one's acceptance for one to be in the truth? A primary condition is that there can be no *knowledge* of the (objective) truth of Christianity. *Certainty* would destroy the possibility of *belief*: "without risk there is no faith."[10] So there must at least be uncertainty, and subjective truth can be defined as "An objective uncertainty held fast in an appropriation-process of the most passionate inwardness."[11] But in the case of Christianity it is not merely a matter of uncertainty whether God exists, whether Christ was God incarnate, and whether man possesses an immortal soul; the central tenet of the Christian doctrine is known to be a paradox, an absurdity: "The absurd is — that the eternal truth has come into being in time, that God has come into being, has been born, has grown up, and so forth, has come into being precisely like any other individual human being, quite indistinguishable from other individuals."[12]

That the eternal has become temporal and historical is the paradox at the heart of Christianity. And to endure the crucifixion of the understanding and accept this with passionate inwardness is the highest expression of faith. Why should an individual become subjective and develop such a faith? Kierkegaard gives essentially two related answers. First, Christianity promises the individual eternal happiness on the condition that he accept Christ in faith. Second, and because of the nature of faith as understood by Kierkegaard, Christianity intensifies passion to its highest pitch, and this is itself something that consolidates the personality and gives one a certain self-assurance in spite of the suffering that of necessity attends faith.

One can easily see the parallel between *The Present Age* and the *Postscript*. The distinction between understanding and passion is identical to that between the objective and the subjective points of view. But whereas the former work talked only of the importance of individual religious faith, in the *Postscript* we find articulated the inherent opposition between faith and understanding, and this gives a stronger sense to the dimension of *commitment* as the essence of faith. This is closely related to the term *inwardness* that occurs throughout the *Postscript* as well as elsewhere, and about which I will have more to say presently.

Turning to the *Equilibrium* essay[13] in the second volume of *Either/ Or*, we find that this is in the form of a letter from the ethicist, Judge William, to his young aestheticist friend. It is a lengthy exhortation to him to abandon his current mode of existence and take the existential leap into the ethico-religious realm.

The main point that Kierkegaard[14] makes is that the ethical dimension of life properly speaking has to grow out of the aesthetical, or pre-ethical, dimension, and—more specifically—that the transition from the lower to the higher stage has to be motivated by an existential failure on the aesthetic plane. The aesthetic, moreover, must fail from its own point of view; it is not just from the ethical point of view that such a personality fails. When this failure is somehow recognized by the aestheticist himself, the transition becomes an existential imperative. The failure of the aesthetic is what Kierkegaard calls *despair*. And why can the aesthetic person be said to be in despair? Because he is guided by the principle that "one must enjoy life,"[15] that the significance and purpose in life lies in various froms of enjoyment, ranging from the purely sensuous to the most refined and cultivated artistic and intellectual. But such a life exists in the moment and lacks continuity. Above all, the aesthetic personality is characterized by having the condition of life external to the self. This means that success or failure in one's pursuit of enjoyment depends on conditions which are beyond one's control and contingent. To be thus dependent on conditions outside is to be in despair, and this condition — this "doubt of the personality"[16]—is independent of whether one is joyful or sorrowful. It is also independent of whether one knows that one is in despair. Yet the aesthetic individual must come to realize that he is in despair if he is to overcome it. Otherwise, his spirit will continue to be repressed and will not be granted the higher form of existence it craves.

What, then, is this person to do? Judge Williams's answer is that he must choose the ethical or, what amounts to the same thing, *choose himself,* for through this choice of oneself is the transition to the ethical effected. What is it then to choose oneself? What is involved is a transformation of the self or — better — a transfiguration: "[It is] the whole aesthetical self which is chosen ethically — He becomes himself, quite the same self he was before, down to the least significant peculiarity, and yet he becomes another, for the choice permeates everything and transforms it."[17]

What is involved in this transformation of the self can be understood when one sees that through this choice the ethical as such comes into being. The basic choice is not between good and evil; it is "the choice whereby one chooses good *and* evil/or excludes them."[18] The aesthetic, then, is the realm of neutrality or indifference that excludes good and evil. Thus it seems that the choice of which Kierkegaard is speaking is not precisely a choosing in the ordinary sense but a kind of *positing*. A self is posited and, insofar as the ethical person recognizes himself as being guilty, that guilt is not *discovered* through the choice himself; it is *posited* in that choice. The self is transformed because a totally new attitude is adopted toward oneself. This is a matter of adopting responsibility for oneself, of introducing a dimension of seriousness into one's life, and of becoming free in the sense of being sovereign over oneself. The condition of one's life has now come to be internal to the self. What is involved in this distinction between externality and internality becomes clearer if one looks at Kierkegaard's conception of *duty*.

Kierkegaard contrasts his view of duty with that contained in the common conception of morality, according to which duty consists of a multiplicity of demands placed upon one from without, making the life of duty "very uncomely and tiresome."[19] The attractiveness, indeed the beauty, of the moral life can be realized only when one comes to see that the ethical has a far deeper connection with personality, that it is in fact *internal* to the subject. If to be truly ethical is to choose oneself in the sense of adopting a certain attitude of seriousness and responsibility toward oneself, then one's duty is to become a certain sort of person, rather than to conform to certain laws or customs, or to be obedient to a set of commandments or prohibitions. What a particular person's duty is on a particular occasion does not follow simply from the empirical facts of the case. The duty will emerge from the particular facts and relations *given* that the individual has adopted the requisite attitude of seriousness and responsibility. If one does not recognize this, empiricism becomes the only road open to one, and morality will be totally relative and ultimately without source.

By willing the good, says Kierkegaard, one falls under "perfectly general categories."[20] From the aesthetic point of view, one may cherish one's individuality, that whereby one is *different* from all others. However, to adopt the ethical point of view is to consider oneself from the point of view of *identity* and — more important — *unity* with others. It is in fact the social dimension which is realized through the choice of oneself. The aesthetic individual is characterized as someone who has not found his place in the world.[21] The self that is realized through the ethical choice "is not merely a personal self but a social, a civic self."[22] And this point is crucial, for it contains what I take to be an essential truth in Kierkegaard's position.

Thus far, Kierkegaard's position might be summarized as follows:

1. Prior to the act of choosing himself the individual exists on the aesthetic plane and at best is related to morality as something external and imposed. As such, he is in despair.

2. Through the act of choosing himself, which is demanded by his repressed self, he enters the ethical plane properly speaking and thereby posits the absolute difference between good and evil. Through this act he achieves true freedom and unity of personality.

Now, we might well ask, what truth is there in all this? More specifically, what truth can attach to the view that moral value, or morality as such, is *created* through the act of choosing oneself? I have said that by choosing oneself Kierkegaard means something like taking responsibility for oneself, adopting an attitude of seriousness toward oneself. I would like to suggest further that what is involved are the elements of *commitment* and *honesty*. Judge William says of the aestheticist that he hides behind masks, and the transformation that is required is expressed in the question, "Do you not know that there comes a midnight hour when everyone has to throw off his mask?"[23] The ethical person by contrast aims to be transparent to himself.[24] To throw off one's mask and become transparent to oneself is clearly a matter of overcoming self-deception and becoming honest with oneself about oneself, and this development extends far beyond the process of coming to know oneself. It is a matter of arriving at the ethical and achieving authenticity, and it is something of great concern to later existentialists, especially Jean-Paul Sartre in his analysis of bad faith.

But, given the intersubjective nature of the human self, the relationship that one has to oneself is inseparable from one's relationship to others. The self that is realized in choosing oneself was said to be the social, the civic self. It is not surprising that when Judge William in the last third of his letter turns to a lengthy discussion of specific ethical duties, the ones he selects are the duties of work, marriage, and friendship, for these all involve the relationship between self and other. It can be seen from his discussion that what is involved is an element of commitment to the other, and this requires honesty not only with the other but also with oneself. This honesty is a matter of openness and, as far as the relationship with the other is concerned, it is a matter of love and trust: "But he who can-

not reveal himself cannot love, and he who cannot love is the most unhappy man of all.''[25]

If I am right in suggesting that the ethical in the fullest sense involves adopting an attitude of commitment, love, and trust toward the
other, how does this *create* value and why does failing to adopt this attitude leave empiricism as the only alternative, with the attendant relativism, scepticism, and despair? Put most simply, I would say that the question of whether other people are worthy of trust, love, and commitment
cannot be an empirical one. If one treats it as an empirical question, one
is most likely to conclude, unless one is naive, that cynicism is the only
"rational" position. The challenge of the ethical is, without falling into
naiveté, to perform something like a leap of moral faith and, through
one's own act of trust, to *create* trust. This is perhaps the central way in
which the choosing of the ethical can be said to be the act that generates
moral value and brings into existence the entire moral dimension. This
choice can be said to be absolute in the sense that it involves adopting an
attitude toward oneself and others that is totally different from the aesthetic, empirical, and rationalistic one. In light of later developments in
phenomenology one can see the thrust of Kierkegaard's philosophy as
being antiempiricist, antiobjectivist, antipositivist. What it affirms is the
subject as intersubjective, the subject as creative of meaning and value.

The parallel between the analysis of religious faith in the *Postscript*
and the analysis of what I have called moral faith in the *Equilibrium* can
now be seen. In both cases what is involved is a leap beyond the merely
empirical and the purely rational. More specifically, it is in both cases a
matter of commitment through love and trust. It is not surprising that he
several times in the *Postscript* and elsewhere draws an analogy between
religious faith and love. In both cases it is a matter of transcending the
objective point of view. In both cases it is a matter of passionate subjectivity, which is said to consolidate personality by transfiguring the contingent, the temporal, and the multifarious through an infusion of the eternal
and universal dimension. In both cases it is a matter of *inwardness*. This
word, which is so central to his discussion of the ethical and especially
the religious, deserves some comment. The Danish word, *Inderlighed*,
unlike the corresponding English word, is actually a very common word
in ordinary discourse—it is not a technical philosophical term at all. Acceptable translations of it are "heartfelt sincerity" or "intensity." The
term does not therefore suggest simply the inner, the purely personal, or
the subjective as ordinarily understood; it carries primarily the meaning
of passion and intensity. The step from this to what I have emphasized as
commitment, love, and trust is a slight one. When he therefore says that
religious faith is a matter of *Inderlighed*, the point that it is a matter of intense commitment rather than intellectual conviction is much more directly conveyed than through the English notion of *inwardness*.

If any further documentation of the parallel between the analyses of religious and moral faith should be required, it can easily be found, especially in *The Sickness unto Death,* to which I must of necessity refer in the briefest possible way. This powerful study in religious psychology, or — better — phenomenology of religious consciousness, centers around the distinction between sin and faith, not sin and virtue. The central point is that not to be in faith is to be in sin, and this in turn is to be in despair. We find, signficantly, that this term, which is the central one in the *Equilibrium* and captures the malady of the aesthetic person, is equally central in *The Sickness* and captures the malady of sin. In short, both the absence of moral faith and the absence of religious faith are characterized as despair, as doubt of the personality. According to the analysis of *The Sickness,* despair can be conquered by overcoming a certain disrelation in the structure of personality by relating oneself in the appropriate way to God: "by relating itself to its own self and by willing to be itself the self is grounded transparently in the Power which posited it."[26] This faith, this health unto life, is also said to be *freedom.*

On this interpretation of what is the essence of faith, one can easily see why Kierkegaard conceived of the ethical and the religious as being virtually identical and certainly inseparable, and why he saw this attitude as being essentially contrasted with the aesthetic one. But can one accept this position? If one does, then one is faced with the view that is expressed so forcefully in *The Present Age*: the only possible escape from the objectivistic and positivistic world-view so destructive of the individual and human value lies in the religious life of the individual Christian. Although this may be a comforting view for some, it cannot really be supported. What I wish to suggest in my concluding remarks is that the feature that constitutes the strength of Kierkegaard's position is precisely that which — paradoxically — makes his identification of the ethical with the religious untenable. This is not to reject Kierkegaard's philosophy entirely. On the contrary, I consider his various analyses of human existence to the among the most profound in the entire tradition of Western philosophy. His examination of the various dimensions of human consciousness constitutes a phenomenological analysis of astonishing depth not equaled by anyone since the origin of the phenomenological method proper by Husserl half a century later. More specifically, I believe that his analysis of the essence of Christian faith and the essence of morality, both of which have only been sketched in earlier, are fundamentally correct. On what grounds can I then reject his identification of the two?

Put most briefly, I would say that the flaw in his analysis lies in his tendency to emphasize the similarities between moral and religious faith while ignoring, or at least minimizing, the differences. Put in Husserlian terms, Kierkegaard is not sufficiently aware of the interdependence of the *noetic* and the *noematic* poles of experience. He does not sufficiently understand *intentionality*. What one would have to do, without necessarily departing from the thrust of Kierkegaard's analysis, would be to attend to the differences between the respective intentional objects of moral and religious faith and show how these objects determine the two modes of consciousness. It is not difficult to say what the object of Christian faith is: the divinity of Christ and other dogmas, such as that regarding eternal salvation. And it is quite clear that the believer, although he abandons the objective, historical, and speculative point of view, still presupposes the objective truth of Christiantity. Although he "rejects" these dogmas as being absurd, he still accepts them, for otherwise there would not be the basis for this passion of the highest intensity called *faith*. And that this is the intentional object of faith cannot but affect the nature of this consciousness itself. Kierkegaard of course demonstrates this at length himself.

When we turn to that which I have called *moral faith,* it becomes more difficult to specify the corresponding intentional object. It is quite clear however that it is nothing remotely like the object of religious faith. It might be said to be something like the perfectibility of man, or—more modestly—the conception of human community as something that is cemented by mutual respect, love, and trust. There is a wonderful passage in *Purity of Heart*[27] where he says that to will one thing, which is to will the Good in truth, is to reject all divisive selfishness and clannishness and to will universal humanity. Although Kierkegaard is absolutely right in suggesting that this sort of attitude is a kind of faith that transcends the purely empirical and objective, a kind of positing and creating of value, there is nothing irrational about it. No crucifixion of the understanding is required. Moral consciousness therefore must be radically different from religious consciousness, in spite of their parallel faith-structures. It would be incorrect to claim that Kierkegaard is in no way aware of this difference. For instance, he insists strongly on the difference between guilt-consciousness and sin-consciousness, and yet his phenomenology of the moral life is permeated with Christian values and categories. One might give a biographical explanation for his inability to conceive of true morality apart from the Christian faith, but—although this might be revealing—it would not be of much philosophical interest.

If we were to sustain an even more thoroughgoing analysis along the lines I have just suggested and hence be able to make a fundamental distinction between the ethical and the religious, would this bring us back to a "three-stages" position? No. One would still be working with the ultimate distinction between, on the one hand, the objectivist attitude, prejudice in favor of the world, and calculative thinking, and, on the other hand, passionate commitment in the face of uncertainty and the creation of value through the integration of personality. This would not only be consistent with the polarity of *The Present Age*, but also—and more important—it would retain the existential-dramatic urgency of the either/or to which Kierkegaard seemed to be irresistibly drawn. But what I have dealt with in this paper is the tension in his thinking between a dramatic either/or and a philosophy of three stages. If one is forced—as I have suggested one must be — to make a radical distinction between the ethical and the religious types of faith, how *can* one retain the either/or? I would like to conclude by suggesting a different way of looking at the "reduction" of the three stages to two, a way that rests on extracting from his philosophy what is phenomenologically sound and rejecting what might be said to rest upon personal religious conviction. This could be said to capture the spirit of Kierkegaard's philosophy better than the distinction between the aesthetic and the ethico-religious, although it is a way that might well have shocked him. I said toward the beginning of this essay that some of us have noticed in his discussion of the aesthetic and the religious stages a passion and a beauty lacking in his discussion of the ethical. I also pointed out that the ethical is all but absent from his autobiographical work. Why is there this difference in his treatment of the different stages? It is no doubt because he was most strongly attracted to the aesthetic and the religious stages. And why is that? It is because they deal with the solitary individual, either alone or alone before God, whereas the ethical stage is the realm of intersubjectivity, the realm of the social, the civic self. This is a dimension of human existence that appealed less to Kierkegaard, although he could recognize it and do it considerable justice in his philosophical analysis. Let us not forget that his entire authorship is said to be devoted to *hün Enkelte* — that solitary individual. The dichotomy we are left with then has as one of its terms the passionate but solitary and inward-turning individual, with or without religious faith, and as its other term the no less passionate but outward-turning individual who, without the aid of religious faith, realizes an authentic self by committing himself to universal humanity and solidarity with others. The dichotomy is between the aesthetic-religious and the ethical. And *that* is ultimately Kierkegaard's either/or!

5

Kierkegaard's Phenomenology of Faith as Suffering

Merold Westphal

In this essay I want to sketch what I understand to be Kierkegaard's phenomenology of faith as suffering and then discuss the ramifications of this reading for the interpretation of his writings and for philosophy in general. Although suffering is an important theme of the authorship prior to the *Concluding Unscientific Postscript,* my point of departure will be the latter's analysis of suffering as the essential expression of existential pathos.

The initial expression, it will be recalled, is resignation. It might seem only reasonable that we should be absolutely committed to absolute ends and only relatively committed to relative ends. But whenever a moment of spiritual awakening occurs, whenever we hear the call of our truest and deepest selves, we find ourselves already stuck fast in an immediacy that is defined as absolute commitment to relative ends. Resignation is the deliberate denial of this worldly worship of the finite. "Just as the dentist has loosened the soft tissues about a tooth and cut the nerve, so [in resignation] the roots of [our] life in the finite have been severed."[1] This does not mean a cloistered withdrawal from the stage on which the dramas of finitude are acted out. We remain on that stage, but in resignation the finite is "deprived . . . of its unchecked vitality" (CUP, p. 368).[2]

As soon as we understand what resignation involves, we understand that it is not a task for some of the people some of the time but for all of the people all of the time. The pain of resignation (which is inseparable from the joy of being related to the absolute) becomes suffering in the

55

recognition that the task is the task of a lifetime, neither accidental nor temporary but essential and permanent. Suffering is the perpetual dying from immediacy that knows itself to be such.

We miss the power of this account if we link it too tightly to the context in which it occurs, the presentation of Religiousness A. Kierkegaard's account of this first mode of the religious life is shaped by his polemic against aesthetic immediacy. But aesthetic immediacy is not the only immediacy and, just to the degree that there are other kinds, the suffering that is essential to the life of faith will consist in more than one kind of dying.

The beginning of Hegel's *Logic* can help us understand the concept of immediacy at work here. Being, the category with which the whole show begins, is presented as pure or indeterminate immediacy. This means we are dealing with Being "as it is immediately in its own self alone."[3] In its "indeterminate immediacy," pure Being "is identical only to itself. It is not different relatively to any other; it has no diversity within itself nor any with a reference outwards" (SL, p. 82).[4] This also means that Being "cannot be mediated by anything. . . . for all mediation implies advance made from a first on to a second, and proceeding from something different."[5] This immediacy is indeterminate because "we cannot determine unless there is both one and another; and in the beginning there is yet no other" (SL, p. 159).

This "there is yet no other" is as crucial to Kierkegaard's understanding of immediacy as it is to Hegel's. Though aesthetic immediacy is deeply connected in Kierkegaard's writings with both hedonism and average everydayness, neither of these plays a definitional role for immediacy as such. What does define immediacy is this notion of unrelatedness or self-sufficiency. Anything that relates only to itself and lacks all outward reference because for it there is as yet no other is immediate. The absolutizing of relative ends can be described as immediacy, not because that is where we find ourselves most of the time, however true that may be, but because what we find when we find ourselves there is the "unchecked vitality" of some finite moment of our life. Suffering is the process in which parts that have taken themselves for the whole are put in their place.

Because this suggests a dialectical journey something like that of Hegel's *Phenomenology,* Hegel can be helpful to us a second time. For Kierkegaard's phenomenology of faith as a practice essentially involving suffering[6] is indeed, if you like, a deconstructive dialectic in which more than one stage on life's way is exposed in its immediacy and challenged to abandon its unchecked vitality, acknowledging its other and thus its place of relative importance in a larger scheme of things.[7] I shall suggest four such immediacies from which faith represents the perpetual dying away and thus suffering. They are the Aesthetic, the Ethical, Religiousness A, *and* Religiousness B. Whereas these stages are familiar, what I have just suggested about them is not. But once we see the generic character of immediacy we would be in bad faith to try to restrict the meaning of religious suffering to the critique of aesthetic immediacy that is the prime target in the *Postscript*'s discussion of suffering. This would be especially true if we, like the "good and the just" who regularly evoke the scorn of Nietzsche's Zarathustra, do not find aesthetic immediacy to be our besetting sin. In any case, Kierkegaard himself does not so restrict his concept of suffering.

I can be brief about the first three moments, but not because dying to the immediacy of the Aesthetic, the Ethical, or the Religion of Immanence is a task briefly accomplished or, in any instance, once and for all. Each represents the task of a lifetime, a task that remains to be accomplished even when one has gone on ahead to the next task. Religious suffering will turn out to be multidimensional in its essential permanence. Still, the first three moments can be treated briefly because it comes as no surprise that Kierkegaard sees them as to be transcended (not abolished, but dethroned). But we are not entirely prepared to discover that he seeks to deconstruct Religiousness B just as thoroughly. Yet, to anticipate, that is the meaning of the attack upon Christendom that increasingly dominates his later writings. I hope to show that this attack is a critique of the immediacy of Religiousness B and, as such, simply a consistent extension of the phenomenology of faith as suffering whose first moment is the *Aufhebung* of the Aesthetic.

The description of the move from the Aesthetic to the Ethical in *Either/Or* is far richer than is necessary for our present purposes. The central theme of the *Postscript*'s contrast of ethico-religious subjectivity with aesthetic objectivity is what we need to notice. "When an aesthetic sufferer bemoans his fate and seeks solace in the ethical, the ethical really has solace for him, but first it makes him suffer more than he did before . . . when he sends for the ethical it first helps him from the fryingpan into the fire, so that he gets something to complain about in real earnest —and then only does it give him help" (CUP, p. 384). This painful move from the fryingpan into the fire is the abandonment of the "unchecked vitality" of a life lived exclusively in pre-ethical categories. Such categories lack the existential pathos of implying a thoroughgoing transformation of the individual's existence with reference to objective norms.

Although the dipolar category boring-interesting plays a central role in *Either/Or,* in the *Postscript* it is the category fortune-misfortune that primarily expresses aesthetic immediacy. Were he writing today, Kierkegaard would surely have included the categories wealth-sufficiency, high status–low status, high sex appeal–low sex appeal, and even high self-esteem–low self-esteem. For the Aesthetic, these are the criteria of success in life. The Ethical, whose concept of success essentially involves that of the good will, is the other that does not yet exist for aesthetic immediacy, that cannot get beyond such pre-ethical categories as those just mentioned in its understanding of the good life.[8]

One vivid expression of this involves the concrete otherness of other persons. "The 'neighbor' does not yet come into existence until in self-denial one has died to earthly happiness and joys and comforts [the interesting, good fortune, etc.]. Therefore the spontaneous, immediate person cannot be censured for not loving the neighbor, because the spontaneous, immediate person is too happy for 'the neighbor' to exist for him."[9] The sheer self-relatedness of my pursuit of self-satisfaction, in which other persons are but means to my ends, comes to an end when by virtue of the Ethical they become genuine others, ends in themselves, neighbors. The joy of having neighbors, other people in my world, is inseparable from the perpetual dying to the tendency to reduce them to things, mere conditions of my own happiness.

As already mentioned, it would be a mistake, even a mystification, to read the *Postscript* as if this were the only dying to immediacy essential to the life of faith. In its polemic against aesthetic immediacy (along with a speculative immediacy not addressed in *Either/Or*), the *Postscript* lumps the Ethical and the Religious together under the rubrics of subjectivity and inwardness. But Kierkegaard has not forgotten the differences between these two stages, and he reaffirms the need to transcend the Ethical as well as the Aesthetic if one is to reach the Religious. In short, dying from ethical immediacy is another mode of religious suffering.

The Ethical has accepted the other that the Aesthetic sought to evade, the requirement of self-transformation in a world of neighbors. But in its own immediacy it, too, has an other whose acknowledgment would drive it beyond itself. That other is moral failure. Kierkegaard writes, "An ethics that ignores sin is a completely futile discipline, but if it affirms sin, then it has *eo ipso* exceeded itself. ... As soon as sin emerges, ethics founders precisely on repentance; for repentance is the highest ethical expression, but precisely as such it is the deepest ethical self-contradiction" (FT, pp. 98–99, 98 n).[10]

The *Postscript* renews and illumines this claim. It suggests that the Ethical is a realm of action and victory, whereas the Religious is one of suffering (CUP, p. 261). Furthermore, "ethical interest is interest in one's own reality," whereas "the believer differs from the ethicist in being infinitely interested in the reality of another," namely, God as Savior (CUP, p. 288). Finally, we hear that "in the immediate consciousness there is rooted the wish to have the power to do everything" (CUP, p. 412). These passages interpret each other as well as the claim of *Fear and Trembling* that in sin and repentance the Ethical meets its other. Whereas aesthetic immediacy is the desire to preside (have the power) over my happiness, ethical immediacy, having accepted the significance of moral categories for interpreting my existence, wishes to preside over my goodness. Its triumphalist orientation focuses on its own actions and victories. There is a peculiarly religious suffering in the discovery that I cannot win my moral battles and must turn in confession and repentance to another, God, both for forgiveness and for help in the self-transformation required by the ethical standards I have accepted as valid. Kant's inability to accept the notion of forgiveness illustrates quite eloquently the nature of this suffering.

Johannes Climacus sums this up for us nicely. The Ethical adopts the moral meaning of good and bad on which aesthetic immediacy founders. But it encounters its own other and founders on the discovery that the self is both good and bad. When ethical seriousness leads to self-examination and thence to the confessional, the Ethical is indeed beyond itself (CUP, p. 376). This is why suffering, as the essential expression of existential pathos, culminates in guilt as the decisive expression (CUP, p. 468).

Reference to the confessional makes it clear that this guilt is before God. It is not the finite, quantitative guilt that is relative to human tribunals but the infinite, qualitative guilt that is relative to the absolute, divine tribunal. Thus, as the neighbor comes into existence with the passing of aesthetic immediacy, so God comes into being with the passing of ethical immediacy. Ethico-religious subjectivity stands in direct correlation with Jesus' summary of the law in terms of love of God and neighbor (Matthew 22:34–40).

As presented in *Either/Or* the Ethical is not without reference to God. But the God we meet there is rather like a magician's assistant, setting up tasks and leading the applause at my accomplishment of them. Now he becomes a genuine other upon whom I am essentially dependent, not merely for my being-there, as in speculative objectivity, but for the meaning of my existence in the sense of the term that ties existence to subjectivity and inwardness.[11] This genuine otherness of God is the annihilation of the human self in both its aesthetic and ethical immediacy, and the consolation to be found in religion is inseparable from this annihilation (CUP, pp. 436–437, cf. pp. 475, 488). The only escape from this linkage is to be found in bad faith. The life of genuine faith has suffering as an essential mark or sign of its presence (CUP, pp. 404–406, 412).

Our reflection has advanced to that stage of faith that Johannes Climacus calls Religiousness A. But even before the extended phenomenology of its existential pathos in the *Postscript,* Johannes lays the foundation for the deconstruction of this religious immediacy in the

Philosophical Fragments. The immediacy of Religiousness A is not at first moral but epistemological. At this stage the believing soul has undertaken the lifelong tasks of acknowledging that it cannot preside over either its happiness or its goodness. But it has not yet resigned its wish to preside over its own truth. This is the meaning of the Socratic assumption in the *Fragments* that the Truth is within us and needs but to be recollected, just as it is the meaning of the term immanence as a description of Religiousness A in the *Postscript*.

In the *Fragments, the Postscript, and Training in Christianity* Kierkegaard presents Christian faith as revealed religion in the traditional sense of the term and in opposition to Hegel's attempt to give it a persuasive redefinition. To speak of the faith as revealed is to say that in faith I acknowledge a truth that I recognize as beyond my powers to discover or validate. To say that I lack the condition and must receive it from the Teacher is to say that even if the Truth were staring me in the face I would not be able to recognize it as such, to pick it out of the lineup in which all the theories of the day present themselves to my view.

A thought that thought cannot think, a truth that reason cannot discover, or even recognize—this is the revealed mystery in the presence of which Religiousness A turns out to be another mode of immediacy. The move to explicitly Christian faith involves acceptance of a truth that is genuinely other to the unchecked vitality and unconditioned self-sufficiency of human reason. This is the meaning of the concepts of absurdity, paradox, contradiction, and madness that Kierkegaard's pseudonyms link so inextricably to the concept of faith. A close reading of the texts will show that these are relative terms. In the eyes of human understanding that takes itself to be the ultimate criterion of truth, the ideas of incarnation and atonement are absurd paradoxes and contradictory madness.[12]

This view of reason's limits is partly Kantian; but it is more fundamentally Lutheran and Pauline.[13] That is to say first of all that reason is here understood to be finite in its natural and historical conditionedness. Kierkegaard shares with subsequent existential and hermeneutical phenomenologists an understanding of the knowing subject as essentially situated. Accordingly we can say that Kierkegaard has a situation epistemology. But more basic than the limits of situation are those of sinfulness. If the moral dimensions of sin drive us from the Ethical to the Religious, then the epistemic dimensions drive from the religion of immanence to the religion of transcendence. Because the deepest obstacle to recognizing the Truth is sin and not finitude, the Teacher must also be the Savior.[14]

This God who must be both Teacher and Savior is the other before whom the immediacy of Religiousness A comes to light. Here we encounter a new dimension of faith's suffering, dying away from the immediacy of epistemological self-sufficiency, from the "unchecked vitality" of a Socratic reason that thinks it has the truth within itself and needs but to recollect, and from a Cartesian reason that makes its own clear and distinct intuitions the ultimate standard of truth.

It seems we have arrived at Religiousness B and have learned what is involved in becoming a Christian. As the culmination of the pseudonymous authorship, the *Postscript* presents Kierkegaard's alternative to the absolute knowing of Hegel's *Phenomenology,* the absolute faith of paradoxical Christianity. But, although it might be nice if this were so, it simply is not. Kierkegaard's dialectical phenomenology of faith as suffering has its most dramatic move yet ahead. We will be helped in our understanding of this final move if we pause long enough to ask why it might be nice if it were not necessary.

Religiousness B is a pretty good deal, as can be seen from the parable told in the *Fragments* about the king who loved the lowly maiden (PF, pp. 26–36). The believing soul is the maiden who by the loving grace of the king is to be married to him and taken to live happily ever after with him in his palace. What happier solution could there be to the problem of my infinite passionate concern for eternal happiness than the gift of eternal salvation granted to me by grace through faith?

There is a price to be paid, to be sure: namely, the threefold suffering involved in dying to the immediacy of the Aesthetic, the Ethical, and Religiousness A. But three considerations make this price seem a bargain indeed. First is the thought of the eternal happiness I thereby attain. An infinite blessing of a finite price is a bargain in any market. Second, the moves I have to make may well be moves I have made habitually from childhood. Unless I was raised by hippie parents I was born to the Ethical and learned by teaching, example, and punishment the meaning of ethical categories. If I was born in a religious family I may have been taught the moves of Religiousness A and even those of Religiousness B from childhood. They have become second nature to me. Third, the suffering involved is all but entirely inward. This is not to say that it is not real or that it might not involve some very painful battles of the soul. But it does mean that my outward life is essentially unchallenged. I cannot be a libertine and I will have to go to church instead of reading the *Times* on Sunday morning, but as long as I am a respectable member of the society in which I find myself I can proceed with business as usual. I can be like the Wall Street broker who, when asked how his Christian faith affected the way he did business responded, "I don't allow any cussing in this office."

You can easily find such a Christian broker for yourself and assure yourself that he (it was in fact a man and not a woman) accepts the primacy of ethical over aesthetic categories, that he recognizes his need of forgiveness and is no ethical triumphalist, and that he believes that we know about the incarnation and the atonement through which this for-giveness has been made available only because the Bible has revealed them to us.

Had the writings of Johannes Climacus remained the culmination of Kierkegaard's phenomenology of spirit, uncompleted by the work of Anti-Climacus and the "second" authorship that clusters around his work, Kierkegaard would have remained a rival of Hegel's. But the title for which they would have been competing would have been that of ideo-logical champion of Christendom. This is not to say that there are no seeds of the attack upon Christendom in Kierkegaard's pseudonymous authorship. That is hardly the case. Rather it is to say that Religiousness B as such has no resources for developing such an internal critique of or-thodox piety. On the other hand, the possibility of Religiousness B as the civil religion of a complacent Christendom is not hard to envisage. In our own time it has served both as the official faith of the New Right and as an extremely popular religion with many others as well. *Die Reganzeit* is inconceivable without its role as the would be civil religion of a large and crucial segment of the American public.

But Kierkegaard's phenomenology of faith as suffering does not end with Johannes Climacus, and before it is finished Religiousness B has also turned out to be an immediacy from which true faith is the dying away. It is an immediacy of cheap grace and, often enough, respectability and social security. Its other is God in human form, Jesus as the one who essentially appears in the form of a servant. God incarnate was the crisis for Religiousness A as well, but in a different sense. *There* the issue was epistemic and Jesus in the form of a servant, the putative God who does not look very much like God, was a paradox for belief. *Here* the issue is practical and Jesus in his humiliation is the Paradigm and Pattern for the believer's behavior.[15] For "the disciple is not above the master," from which it follows that "Christianity is not [merely] a doctrine" (TC, p. 108). *There* to be contemporary with Christ meant to have to judge whether or not he was the divine Teacher and Savior without being able to see the divine majesty that would make the answer obvious. *Here* to be contemporary with Christ means to be one who shares in his sufferings, not only the inward sufferings of the spirit but the outward sufferings of social opposition and even possibly martyrdom.

The difference between Religiousness B and what for the sake of convenience we can call Religiousness C is dramatically expressed with reference to Acts 5:40–42, where it is reported that the disciples were flogged for speaking in the name of Jesus, but that they went out "rejoic-ing that they had been found worthy to suffer indignity for the sake of the Name." In the *Postscript* (CUP, p. 405) we read that this "is not a case of religious suffering." The reason is that here the individual "is secure in his God-relationship and suffers only outwardly." What we are dealing with is a case of misfortune, a merely aesthetic concern. But during the period of the "second" authorship this passage is a repeated touchstone for the suffering that is the mark or sign of faith (JP, vol. 4, 4617; GS, pp. 146–147). Now, far from treating this outward suffering as a matter of fortune or misfortune, Kierkegaard constantly stresses that it is voluntary, something that can easily be avoided if we choose to do so. But true faith, following Jesus on the way of the cross, willingly accepts the outward suffering that normally greets true witnesses to the Truth.

Kierkegaard's phenomenological journey reaches its climax, then, not at the end of the *Postscript* but at the end of *Training in Christianity*. In the sixth exposition of its Part III, Anti-Climacus develops the distinction between two kinds of believer, the admirer and the follower of Jesus. He makes it explicitly clear that to be a follower is to make Christ the "Pattern" for one's life, to seek to "resemble" and to "imitate" him in his earthly sufferings. But this is to be publicly and outwardly at odds with Christendom. For Christendom will do its best to do away with "Christ's requirement of self-denial and the renunciation of worldly things . . . by endeavouring falsely to transform the Christian life into hidden inwardness, kept so carefully hidden that it does not become noticeable in one's life" (TC, pp. 245–246). In short, the strategy of Christendom will be to bring the dialectic to an end with Religiousness B and to bask in the "unchecked vitality" of this mode of faith.

Kierkegaard describes two modes of carrying out this strategy. One is to crowd out imitation by emphasis on doctrine. After noting that Christianity is no longer persecuted, he writes, "Well, no wonder, since men have completely abolished Christianity as a way of existing, a life of imitation, and have made it into nothing but doctrine" (JP, vol. 4, 4661). This is why, in a discussion of the disciple sharing in the suffering of the master, he also writes, "Christianity is not a doctrine" (TC, p. 108), suggesting that turning everything into a doctrine, even the paradoxical doctrines of the incarnation and atonement, is a way of seeking to avoid the offense of Christianity. "All the talk about offense in relation to Christianity as a doctrine is a misunderstanding, it is a device to mitigate the shock of offence at the scandal" (TC, pp. 108–109). Or again, "Thus men are willing enough, when it is proper, to *learn by rote*, but when it is necessary to *learn* by the aid of suffering, then it becomes so hard, since apprehension does not help . . . "[16]

The call to imitation of the sufferings of Christ can also be drowned out by emphasis on redemption and grace. Here the consolation of salvation is cut off from the annihilation of the call to suffering. Christianity is heard to say, "Because you are a sufferer, therefore God loves you," but one becomes so relaxed at this good news that one does not hear a second word, "Because you love God, therefore you must suffer" (JP, vol. 4, 4688). By this selective hearing, this editing of the text of the gospel, grace is cheapened.

Something very strange happens when the believing soul says, in effect, "No, no, away with every thought and reminder of 'imitation'—we have grace." This means that I assume "the right to plunge aggressively into preoccupation with finite interests and enjoying life" (JP, vol. 4, 4700). In this way Chrisitanity is transformed into "a refined epicureanism, *using eternity to give a flavor to the enjoyment of life*" (JP, vol. 4, 4725 –27). Cheap grace turns out to be sanctified epicureanism.

Ironically, when Religiousness B is treated as the end of the line, the religious life easily falls all the way back into aestheticism and learns to live its life, externally at least, in the pre-ethical categories presumably long since dethroned. Kierkegaard's phenomenology of faith as suffering reaches its final stage only when the inward journey developed in the pseudonymous writings is *aufgehoben* in the outward journey developed in the "second" authorship under the heading of the imitation of Christ. Religiousness C is the whole of which the previous stages on life's way are but parts. They are parts of the truth, to be sure, but for Kierkegaard as for Hegel, only the whole is true. This means that in isolation and apart from the setting provided by Religiousness C, the "earlier" stages on life's way, including Religiousness B, are abstract and false. The existential correlate of this epistemological situation is the suffering in which the satisfaction and security of each partial stage are undermined in the discovery that we must die to their self-sufficiency.

The time has come to explore the implications of this reading of Kierkegaard for the interpretation of his writings and for philosophy in general, leaving for another occasion questions relating to the philosophy of religion. I wish first to discuss two issues concerning the interpretation of Kierkegaard, both of which revolve around an awareness of how differently the pseudonymous authorship (especially the *Postscript*) and the "second" authorship speak about suffering. This difference is symbolized by Kierkegaard's two radically different readings of Acts 5 with reference to the flogging of the apostles. The question concerns the significance of Kierkegaard's change in attitude toward outward, public suffering.

The first suggestion comes from a splendid essay by John Elrod contrasting the writings of Johannes Climacus and Anti-Climacus on suffering. With reference to the exclusiveness of Climacus's concern for inwardness, Elrod writes:

One must wonder how Climacus can so casually dismiss the pain inflicted upon the individual by both natural causes and human agency external to himself. Climacus calls this pain misfortune, and he appears to regard concern with it as being beneath the dignity of the individual who has elevated himself to the ethical-religious stage of human existence. One suspects that Climacus' neglect of misfortune — the sort of pain suffered by the vast majority of humankind — stems from his own version of an idealistic ontology. . . . It should not be surprising to us that misfortune is so completely neglected by Climacus since the only real objectivity over against the subject is the subject's own reflected and idealized version of himself.[17]

The charge is clear. In his concept of the world and the worldliness whose primary concern is good fortune, Climacus has fallen into the romatic trap of isolating subjectivity from objectivity. Even if one insists that Climacus's subject has God over against itself, and not just its own idealized self-image (CUP, p. 391), the world of objectivity has been given such short shrift that the charge of a romantic or idealistic ontology seems well founded.[18]

Elrod cites an autobiographical passage from Kierkegaard to confirm this charge and to provide a biographical interpretation of the trasition from Climacus to Anti-Climacus (from Religiousness B to Religiousness C).

Well acquainted as I was with the suffering of inwardness in relation to the task of becoming a Christian, and strictly brought up as I was in this apprehension, the other side of the matter almost escaped me . . . for at the decisive instant when I was radically altering my existence-relationship on account of *Concluding Postscript,* I had an opportunity to observe what one will never believe until he has experienced it, namely, this Christian truth that love is hated.[19]

Elrod takes this, no doubt correctly, to be a reference to the *Corsair* affair in which Kierkegaard became the object of public ridicule and scorn. "This encounter helps him to see beyond Climacus' limitations to the social dimension of ethical-religious suffering. It is Anti-Climacus who develops this view."[20]

Elrod's book, *Kierkegaard and Christendom,* is our most helpful guide to Kierkegaard's "second" authorship, the writings that come after the *Postscript,* and the essay in which he focuses on the differences between Climacus and Anti-Climacus on suffering is an invaluable supplement to it. But in the light of Kierkegaard's phenomenology of faith as suffering, I do not believe we can leave the interpretation of those differences as he leaves it. For, as Kierkegaard himself insists in *Point of View*, there is an integrity to his writings as a whole that is not the product of his conscious intentions and that needs to be understood, not biographically but in terms of the substance, *die Sache selbst*. It is the clue from *Point of View* that I believe best illumines the move from Climacus to Anti-Climacus on suffering.

In the first place, as the discussion of Job in *Repetition* makes clear, Kierkegaard was aware of the ethico-religious significance of misfortune prior to the *Corsair* affair. If this theme is ignored in the *Postscript*, there is a better reason than the autobiographical one suggested by Kierkegaard himself and cited by Elrod. A primary task of the *Postscript* is to distinguish existence lived under the categories of fortune and misfortune from existence lived under ethical and religious categories. If, as Elrod rightly insists,[21] there is an "ethical and religious significance" to the sufferings rightly called misfortune that needs to be acknowledged, this is possible only where life has come to mean more than seeking to maximize fortune and minimize misfortune. For those who have progressed to ethico-religious subjectivity, it is not the pain of misfortune as such that dehumanizes our life, but rather the inability to interpret that pain in any but aesthetic categories and the corresponding inability to see in it any "ethical and religious significance."

Second, and perhaps more important, what is at issue in the move to Anti-Climacus is not misfortune at all. It does not concern "the sort of pain suffered by the vast majority of humankind." Unlike misfortune, the suffering upon which Anti-Climacus focuses our attention is voluntary, a point that Kierkegaard repeats again and again. The flogging of the apostles in Acts 5 is a suffering from which they could easily have escaped. All they needed to do was cooperate with the power structure. The suffering that is constitutive of Religiousness C, to be sure, has an external and public character. In this respect it resembles misfortune. Outwardness is taken seriously once again. But this outwardness is not that of immediate, pre-ethical human existence. Rather it is the outwardness of specifically Christian existence, trained in the severe disciplines of inwardness and, on the basis of that training, willing to confront the public world as a witness to the truth. Far from being the suffering common to "the vast majority of humankind," it is not even common to the vast majority of professing Christians. For this reason its theory and practice represent not just a critique of secular modernity but an attack upon Christendom as well.

Shall we say then that the *Postscript*'s preoccupation with inwardness represents a lapse into a romantic view of the self? Does its abrupt dismissal of the public suffering of the apostles betray an "idealistic ontology''? This would be appropriate if the *Postscript* were to be taken as standing alone. But, in the phenomenology of faith as suffering presented here, the *Postscript* does not stand alone. Even more important, it is not the terminus of the journey that defines the whole within which all the parts are to be understood. It is itself a part still in quest of the whole to which it properly belongs. Seen in this perspective, the incompleteness of the inwardness of both Religiousness A and Religiousness B is there for all to see, not as a biographical defect of the author but as an existential defect of certain modes of human existence, crying out for completion.[22] If the journey to inwardness and subjectivity is absolutely necessary so that aesthetic and speculative immediacy may be overcome, it results in an immediacy of its own, the self-sufficiency of inwardness, which must in turn be overcome.

This essential incompleteness of the pseudonymous authorship leads directly to a related issue in the reading of Kierkegaard's writings. To what extent do his writings hold together coherently and to what degree is the theory of the stages a key to any such coherence? Some of the most helpful interpreters of Kierkegaard have argued against finding diversity without unity in his works. For example, Mark Taylor argues for coherence as a middle way between finding no unity and finding systematic unity in the writings. Moreover, he views the theory of the stages as central to this coherence.[23] But he qualifies this claim considerably by making it apply only to the pseudonymous writings. Between these and the later writings, especially those that make up Kierkegaard's attack upon Christendom, he finds considerable tension, calling special attention to the changed significance of suffering in the later writings.[24] He thinks the theory of stages will not be of any help in bridging the gap between Kierkegaard I and Kierkegaard II.

A similar view is expressed by Stephen Dunning. He finds the formal dialectic of inwardness in the pseudonymous authorship to provide a strong unity to those writings.[25] He finds a similar dialectic giving unity to the writings of Anti-Climacus, drawing *Sickness unto Death*[26] and *Training in Christianity* into closest unity.[27] But, between the later works and the theory of the stages in the pseudonymous writings, he finds no clear link. Rather, "the question of the relation between these late works and the dialectical structure of the theory of stages as such is more difficult. There is no obvious way in which *The Sickness unto Death* and *Practice in Christianity* [TC] illuminate that theory."[28] Nor, presumably, vice versa.

If one takes the theory of stages to be simply a matter of the Aesthetic, the Ethical, and the Religious categories for existence, it is hard to quarrel with these conclusions. This remains true even when, with the *Postscript* in mind, the religious stage is subdivided into Religiousness A and B. As developed within the pseudonymous authorship itself, the theory of stages is inadequate to illuminate the unity of that authorship with the later writings. But if we allow the later writings to show us the essential incompletness of the pseudonymous theory of stages and to lead us beyond Religiousness B to what I have been calling Religiousness C, not only is the theory of stages itself enriched; it also becomes the key to the coherent unity of virtually all of Kierkegaard's writings. It becomes possible to build a bridge between Kierkegaard I and Kierkegaard II. And, given the *triple* subdivision of the original religious stage, it becomes possible to incorporate all the religious, edifying discourses into the authorship as a whole. That Kierkegaard himself did not explicitly articulate this unity to his work would be an objection to the reading I am suggesting only on the assumption that an author is the definitive interpreter of his or her own work.

Finally, I want to suggest that this reading of Kierkegaard is not just a matter of Kierkegaard scholarship, but is of general philosophical interest. For it not only helps to unify the Kierkegaardian corpus; it also places his thought in relation to contemporary discussion of the "end of philosophy" and the attempt to deconstruct the metaphysics of presence.

John Caputo has argued that especially in *Repetition* Kierkegaard is already beyond Heidegger I and in his contrast between repetition and recollection is already evoking the foundering of the metaphysics of presence. Recollection orients itself to eternity as the realm of the eternal now, where there is no past or future and thus no absence but only sheer presence. From the perspective of recollection, such an eternity is a lost possession. But this means that in recollection sheer presence is regained. What more dramatic expression of what Derrida means by presence is there than the account of recollection in the *Phaedo*? In recollection we apply our "pure and unadulterated thought to the pure and unadulterated object." To recollect "we must get rid of the body and contemplate things by themselves with the soul by itself."[29] What is at issue is the unmediated possession of the unconditioned object: in Derrida's language, the transcendental signified. In *Repetition,* because Kierkegaard finds Hegel's mediation to be but a variation on the theme of Platonic recollection, he seeks to develop repetition as an alternative to both. In this way he seeks to defer presence, to affirm the incompleteness of temporal experience against those who would escape from time by the back door of recollection in order to enjoy the presence of completion.[30]

I believe the reading of Kierkegaard I have suggested supports Caputo's reading, though it is drawn from different texts. It may seem strange to portray Kierkegaard as in any sense an ally of Derrida, for he passionately believes in God, who is for Derrida the paradigmatic transcendental signified. Moreover, he talks as if he shares the Pauline hope that he will some day see God "face to face" and know him as he has been known by him (I Corrinthians 13:12). This sounds like the unmediated possession of the unconditioned object, the metaphysician's dream of removing meaning from *difference*.[31] But Kierkegaard takes it for granted that under present conditions such presence is not ours, and he spends little time talking about what it would mean to see God "face to face." He surely has no theory about it. On the other hand, he talks a great deal about the fact that the existing individual, now and for the entirety of this present life, sees "in a mirror dimly."[32] About this he does have a theory, one short summary of which reads as follows:

> Reality itself is a system—for God; but it cannot be a system for any existing spirit. System and finality correspond to one another, but existence is precisely the opposite of finality. ... Anyone who is himself an existing individual cannot gain this finality outside existence which corresponds to the eternity into which the past has entered. If a thinker is so absent-minded as to forget that he is an existing individual, still, absent-mindedness and speculation are not precisely the same thing. (CUP, pp. 107–108)

With Hegel, Kierkegaard denies to the existing individual the "immediate immediacy" of the sheer, intuitive presence envisaged in the *Phaedo*. Against Hegel he denies to the existing individual the "mediated immediacy" of totality and systematic finality. As an existing individual my reach always exceeds my grasp. The task is never completed, there is always work to be done, and there is always more to be said.

Derrida's critique of the metaphysics of presence occurs in the context of a highly abstract theory of language as writing. His claim that language and meaning always have the form of writing means that "the signified always already functions as a signifier. ... There is not a single signified that escapes." This means that there is no "full speech that was fully *present* (present to itself, to its signified, to the other ...)." Nor is there "an originary speech itself shielded from interpretation."[33] To deconstruct the transcendental signified is thus to give up hope for "a reassuring end to the reference from sign to sign" and thus to the need for further interpretation.[34] To see things "in a mirror dimly" is to see them, not as they are in themselves, but as incomplete presences that point beyond themselves. In the words of his translator, "all conclusions are genuinely provisional and therefore inconclusive."[35]

When Derrida speaks of the hoped for but impossible escape from this hall of mirrors as "reassuring," he implies that we are dealing with more than semantic inevitabilities. Existential interests are also on the scene. The metaphysics of presence has never been simply a mistake. It is gounded in longing and is, in the Freudian sense of the term, an illusion. These extrasemantic aspects of the issue regularly come to light in Derrida's diction. For example, Derrida speaks of our epoch as one in which "language itself is menaced in its very life, helpless, adrift in the threat of limitlessness, brought back to its own finitude at the very moment when its limits seem to disappear [Is this a reference to Husserl?], when it ceases to be self-assured, contained, and *guaranteed* by the infinite signified which seemed to exceed it."[36] When he speaks of Heidegger's inability to escape from the onto-theo-logical assumptions he seeks to expose, he notes:

> in Heidegger's discourse, the dominance of an entire metaphorics of proximity, of simple and immediate presence, a metaphorics associating the proximity of Being with the values of neighboring, shelter, house, service, guard, voice, and listening. As goes without saying, this is not an insignificant rhetoric. . . . It is within a metaphorical insistence, then, that the interpretation of the meaning of Being is produced. And if Heidegger has radically deconstructed the domination of metaphysics by the *present,* he has done so in order to lead us to think the presence of the present. But the thinking of this presence can only metaphorize, by means of a profound necessity from which one cannot simply decide to escape, the language that it deconstructs.[37]

In short, the longing for presence, whether as metaphysics or as linguistics, is an existential longing to be finished with the tasks of life, to get on with the "and they lived happily ever after" part of it. It is the desire of Ulysses to be at home by the fire with his wife and dog. The desire of language to be semantically secure or, as Derrida puts it, "*guaranteed,*" is the desire for the language game of life to have completed its journey, to be able to rest.

Kierkegaard's phenomenology of faith as suffering tells the existing individual that it is always too soon to rest. For, in the first place, short of Religiousness C every stage on life's way is at best penultimate. Nor is Religiousness C the ultimate stage because there one can rest and live happily ever after. On the contrary, at this stage those who hear that because they suffer, God loves them, hear most clearly the rest of the message: that because they love God, they must suffer. Furthermore, at this stage the call to suffering is most intense because most complete, uniting the outer with the inner. The lack of epistemic guarantees that characterizes Religiousness B is here subsumed in a lack of existential guarantees that leaves one constantly open to hostile rejection, even and sometimes especially by those who profess to profess the same faith.

But this does not sound very much like Derrida, it might be objected. Granted. However, this critique of the metaphysics of presence is at least as radical as his. It differs most conspicuously in the spirit of ethico-religious seriousness that pervades its central concept of faith as suffering. But, then, who said that playful nihilism is the only spirit in which the metaphysics of presence can be challenged?

6

Where There's a Will There's a Way: Kierkegaard's Theory of Action

C. Stephen Evans

One of the most enduring philosophical myths of our time is the view that Kierkegaard was a glorifier of the notion of "radical choice." According to this myth, Kierkegaard, as the father of existentialism, is supposed to have invented a radically new concept of choice in which human agents make their most fundamental and crucial decisions for no reason at all. Such choices must be made without criteria, and they are therefore in a crucial sense arbitrary and absurd.

This myth has been accepted by both friend and foe of Kierkegaard. Probably its most powerful statement comes in Camus' essay "An Absurd Reasoning."[1] The myth however, is not simply a popular or literary notion, but survives in the works of serious philosophers. A recent influential example is Alasdair MacIntyre's *After Virtue*.

As MacIntyre sees it, Kierkegaard's project in *Either/Or* is to provide a foundation for morality or ethics. The Enlightenment project of giving a rational justification for ethics had failed and Kierkegaard had clearly seen the failure as irremediable, given the premises of the project. The solution he devised was to abandon the whole notion of a rational justification of morality and substitute for reason a radical act of will as the foundation for morality:

> Kierkegaard and Kant agree in their conception of morality, but Kierkegaard inherits that conception together with an understanding that the project of giving a rational vindication of morality has

73

failed. Kant's failure provided Kierkegaard with his starting-point: the act of choice had to be called in to do the work that reason could not do.[2]

MacIntyre correctly sees that *Either/Or* is designed to force the reader to choose between two ways of life. The first volume presents the reader with the papers of an aesthete who lives for the moment and orients himself around the category of sastisfaction, albeit in a refined, reflective manner. The second volume contains letters from an older married man to the aesthete arguing the superiority of a life of ethical commitment. Both volumes are edited by one Victor Eremita; Kierkegaard nowhere appears in his own persona. The reader must decide which kind of life is superior, with no external result or conclusion to influence the choice.

Why should MacIntyre think that Kierkegaard intends this choice to be a radical, criterionless decision? After all, both the aesthete and the married man provide reasons of a sort for their perspectives. His central argument goes like this:

Suppose that someone confronts the choice between them (the ethical and the aesthetic lives) having as yet embraced neither. He can be offered no *reason* for preferring one to the other. For if a given reason offers support for the ethical way of life—to live in that way will serve the demands of duty *or* to live in that way will be to accept moral perfection as a goal and so give a certain kind of meaning to one's actions—the person who has not yet embraced either the ethical or the aesthetic still has to choose whether or not to treat this reason as having any force. If it already has force for him, he has already chosen the ethical; which *ex hypothesi* he has not. And so it is also with reasons supportive of the aesthetic.[3]

I believe this argument is weak. An analogy may help us to see this. Suppose that in an ethics class I provide the students with arguments for rival positions on a contemporary issue such as abortion. Their assignment is to analyze the arguments and choose a position. I am careful not to tell the students which position I hold or which arguments I regard as cogent, because I want them to do some thinking on their own.

One might think that in this situation the student who has not yet decided which position to hold "can be offered no reason for preferring one to the other." For when analyzing one of the reasons for holding a position, the student must decide whether that reason has any force. If it does have force, then the student is not truly undecided; if it does not, then the choice appears arbitrary.

The fallacy in this line of thinking lies in the assumption that the student must choose to regard a reason as having force before it has any. Normally, reasons given for a position strike us as forceful or they do not, and whether they do is not subject to our voluntary control. So a student who has not yet chosen a position on the moral issue in question could conceivably find an argument for a position convincing in making the choice.

Perhaps MacIntyre might respond at this point that the two situations are not strictly analogous. My illustration concerns an intellectual issue where *beliefs* are being formed. Because it is often claimed that beliefs are not under our direct, voluntary control, perhaps no issue of choice really arises here. If the individual finds the argument compelling, his or her belief will follow accordingly. So an uncommitted student may well be swayed by an argument.

The case Kierkegaard is presenting is quite different, MacIntyre might claim. Kierkegaard is analyzing not the formation of a belief, but a decision to live a certain kind of life. And Kierkegaard evidently sees this decision as a free choice for which the individual is responsible. If the decision is determined by reasons then the choice is not really free.

The argument could be put in the form of a dilemma. Reasons either determine a choice or they do not. If a choice is determined by reasons then it is not free (given certain controversial incompatibilist assumptions about the nature of freedom and its relation to determinism). If a choice is not determined by reasons then it is arbitrary.

If *that* is the argument then it seems to me that the problem does not lie in Kierkegaard's concept of free choice, but rather in the very notion of free choice. The argument of the previous paragraph is a perfectly general one that implies that every truly free choice is arbitrary and any choice that is performed for a reason is for that reason not free. A full response to the common charge that Kierkegaard urges on us a doctrine of radical choice will therefore require us to give a fuller treatment of Kierkegaard's theory of action *and* look once more at the whole question of the relationship of reason to free action.

THE ARISTOTELIAN UNDERSTANDING OF ACTION

Kierkegaard conducts a running polemic in his authorship against intellectualistic theories of action. He is terribly concerned with the Hegelian doctrine of the "unity of thought and being," mainly because he takes this as eliminating the distinction between thought and action. He wants to argue that to "think that A is good" or to "judge that A is good" is by no means identical with having done A. Nor does doing A follow as a matter of course from such a judgment. (Later I shall attempt to show that this intellectualistic view of action is by no means absurd and in fact has a vigorous following in contemporary philosophy.)

This polemic of Kierkegaard's has obscured the fact that thought has a significant role to play in his understanding of action. Kierkegaard's theory, in fact, is a variation on the traditional Aristotelian picture of action as the result of choice that is itself the product of deliberation.[4] By "the traditional Aristotelian view" here I do not mean to refer strictly or even mainly to the views of Aristotle alone, but to a tradition, traceable to Socrates, developed in the Middle Ages, and represented in our day by such outstanding philosophers as Donald Davidson and Alan Donagan.[5]

Donagan traces this tradition to the remarks Plato puts in Socrates' mouth in the *Phaedo* (98c – 99a), where Socrates criticizes Anaxagoras for claiming to explain the universe as the work of mind, while in fact giving a physical explanation. Such a view is comparable, in Socrates' eyes, to ascribing his being in prison to the processes and states of his "bones and sinews." Socrates claims that the true cause of his being in prison is "that he decided that it was best for me to sit here, and that it is right for me to stay and undergo whatever penalty they order." If his opinions about this were different, his behavior would be different as well, with his bones and sinews following suit.

Aristotle developed this Socratic insight in a powerful way. For Aristotle, the distinctive aspect of human beings lies in our power to represent the world to ourselves in propositional form. Human beings do not merely have immediate desires for an object. We can desire *that Jim have a turn with the toy* or *that Susan move the car out of the driveway*. Propositions are the object of our beliefs, hopes, fears, wishes, and a host of what Bertrand Russell termed *propositional attitudes*.

On the Aristotelian view human action begins when a person has a wish, an intellectual appetitive attitude toward some possible state of affairs. This leads to deliberation about how to bring about that possible end, a process that culminates in a choice, which directly explains the action.

Obviously this general account leaves many points of detail open to development in various ways. One crucial point concerns the relationship of the process of deliberation to the choice that issues from it. Kierkegaard himself raises the crucial question in an early journal entry: "In what relationship does the will stand to the last act of understanding; does the will follow necessarily the final cognition of understanding?"[6] If one accepts the Socratic dictum that virtue is knowledge, it will appear reasonable to answer the question by affirming that the will does indeed necessarily follow the final "cognition of understanding." The person who knows what is right or good, or even correctly believes what is right or good, will do what is right or good. On such a view where the will simply follows the dictates of the intellect, it is tempting to simply eliminate the will altogether, and explain human actions as the product of appetitive attitudes and thought. Deliberation leads directly to action.

This view is precisely the intellectualistic theory of action Kierkegaard so vigorously opposes. However, this intellectualistic theory is merely one version of an Aristotelian theory, and Kierkegaard's opposition to it should not obscure the fact that his own theory is also Aristotelian. Other thinkers have insisted that the last intellectual judgment an individual makes does not necessarily determine an action. It is possible for an individual to will what he or she knows is not the best. The phenomenon of incontinence or weakness of will presents a severe challenge to any intellectualistic theory of action. (More on this later.) In what follows I will try to sketch the major outlines of Kierkegaard's understanding of action.

KIERKEGAARD'S THEORY OF ACTION

Although Kierkegaard rejects the notion that action follows as a matter of course from reflection, he nevertheless sees reflective deliberation as a necessary condition for action. This is sometimes hard to see because he is continually criticizing the rival view, but even his criticisms of intellectualistic theories clearly presuppose that the intellect plays a crucial role in action. For example, Johannes Climacus, in the *Concluding Unscientific Postscript* (whose views on this issue are clearly Kierkegaard's own, I think), says that "the ethical is not merely a knowing; it is also a doing that relates itself to a knowing."[7] The assumption is clearly that no one would deny that "the ethical" (which in this context means the arena of responsible action) involves the intellect.

Kierkegaard lived before the day of eliminative materialism, and the idea that human action could be explained apart from the propositional attitudes that are an essential part of our "folk psychology" is foreign to him. The problem for him lies rather in those who think that "knowing" is sufficient to account for action. In this case "the intellectual would swallow the ethical."[8] Against such an intellectual theory Climacus appeals to the Aristotelian concept of movement or change. The realm of reflection is possibility, and the transition from possibility to actuality is never automatic or necessary. It involves a "leap."[9] This concept of the leap is obscured if it is immediately brought into connection with the choice to become a Christian. Thus, one should not necessarily associate the leap with the concept of the absurd. Rather the leap is simply Kierkegaard's general term for decision or choice. In claiming that choice involves a leap he is claiming that choice involves an act of will that is not determined by an act of intellect.

Kierkegaard sees a distinct act of will as necessary to explain action because the intellect alone has a kind of infinity about it. The intellect cannot bring itself to closure. This can be seen in Climacus's critique in the *Postscript* of the problem of "the beginning" in the Hegelian system. As Climacus interprets Hegel, the system begins with a skeptical process of self-reflection that continues until it "cancels itself."[10] From the perspective of Climacus, this means that the system cannot get started at all, as reflection cannot bring itself to a close. This can be seen in the phenomenon of doubt. Doubt cannot bring itself to a close or overcome itself. It is true that underlying doubt is a basic certainty, but this certainty cannot be gained through more doubting because "doubt is continuously deserting this certainty in order to doubt."[11]

This point is crucial to Kierkegaard because his basic objection to Hegel is not to the conceptual relationships that the Hegelian system embodies, but to the notion that such an intellectual enterprise provides the highest task for human existence. It is the Hegelian claim that speculative understanding provides a *telos* for human existence that draws his unrelenting opposition. And this Hegelian claim he sees as logically tied to the intellectualizing of action.

The insight that underlies Kierkegaard's view is clearly expressible in relation to ordinary action. When we are deliberating about an action, from the point of view of deliberation itself there is no way to bring the process to a close. I think about a possible action A and the reasons for performing it or not performing it. I review those reasons and evaluate their relative merits. But how do I know I have reviewed all the relevant evidence which bears on the issue? Should I not think some more? And could I not review my assessment of the relative force of the reasons I have considered? Perhaps I have made a mistake somewhere and new insights would come with further reflection.

Of course for ordinary, sane people this process of deliberation (sooner or later) is brought to a close. We do not go on thinking about what to do forever. But *how* is it brought to a close? By thinking that I have thought long enough about the problem? But this is itself a conclusion that could be debated. Why is it that we have thought long enough? Surely, it is because there is a difference between thinking and acting, and life consists in acting. To the extent that we want to live and not merely think we must care enough about some proposed action to close off the process of reflection. Granted, we run the risk of premature closure and failure to do the right thing. But without running such a risk we cannot act at all.

Action therefore requires something more than deliberation. One might think that this something more would simply be affective. To bring the process of reflection to a close one must want something or care about something badly enough to stop thinking and act. Kierkegaard does think something like this is necessary. We must care in order to act. The notion of a *liberum arbitrium* in the sense of a totally disinterested and indifferent will he denounces as a myth.[12] To exist is to be interested, because for Kierkegaard all actuality is an *inter-esse*.[13] However, the unique and fascinating thing about human life is that the passions and cares that move us are not simply things that befall us. Kierkegaard rejects the Kantian assumption that "inclinations" are always things for which we are not responsible and therefore morally neutral.

Certainly we are not responsible for what might be termed our *original impulses*, and many people do live what Kierkegaard termed an *aesthetic life*, which consists simply in trying to satisfy such impulses. However, it is possible for someone to develop and form these "raw materials." In fact, that is just what the ethical life consists in. Climacus cites with approval the words of Plutarch: "ethical virtue has the passions for its material, reason for its form."[14] The fact that we are responsible for the formation of our passions means that something like the will is essential to understand human action. Not all passions are originally present; many of them are formed precisely through repeated action. If we are responsible for the formation of our passions, then we must have some freedom with respect to the actions that form those passions. Our actions are not simply the inevitable products of forces acting within us. Thus Kierkegaard consistently attributes to humans the power to will or not to will an action. In fact, he comes close to simply identifying action with an act of will.[15] "The real action is not the external act, but an internal decision in which the individual puts an end to the mere possibility and identifies himself with the content of his thought in order to exist in it."[16] This theme of the true action as an inner action is one of the more well-known and interesting elements of Kierkegaard's understanding of action, and it deserves closer examination.

THE DEPRECIATION OF RESULTS

Johannes Climacus claims that the moral significance of an action lies wholly in what is intended by the agent. In the final analysis all a person can do is will what is right; the results are really in God's hands.[17] This Kantian depreciation of the consequences of action actually leads Climacus to assert that a truly ethical personality would choose, if it were possible, to be ignorant about the consequences of his actions. He would not thereby be tempted to desert the purity of ethical resolve for the delights of "world-historical significance," which for Climacus is not a thing that can be gained merely through ethical striving.[18] "The true ethical enthusiasm consists in willing to the utmost limits of one's powers, but at the same time being so uplifted in divine jest as never to think about the accomplishment. As soon as the will begins to look right or left for results, the individual begins to become immoral."[19]

These claims of Climacus appear exaggerated at best and outrageous at worst, on first reflection. It hardly seems possible seriously to will a certain end and at the same time be so indifferent as to whether that end is realized that one would choose to be ignorant of the results of the action. And it certainly seems strange to say that the results of one's action are merely a matter of fortune or providence. If there were not some regular connections between willing a certain end and achieving certain results, it would in fact be impossible to act at all, as such causal regularities seem to be one of the things we presuppose in acting.

However, although there is certainly a touch of hyperbole in Climacus's discussion on these points, a serious and defensible point is being made. Of course, a person could not be regularly ignorant of the results of his action and go on acting. Hence, it is charitable to read a touch of irony in Climacus's remark that a truly ethical person would choose to be ignorant in this way "*if* it were possible." And, of course, a person could not will to move his arm were there not a regular causal connection between his so willing and his arm going up. (This is mainly because the agent must believe that there is a causal connection between the two in order to will the action.) Climacus could hardly be ignorant of such a fact.

Still, it is literally true that a person cannot by willing guarantee that he will not be struck by paralysis at the very moment he wills to lift his arm, however unlikely this may be. To be reminded of this fact is to face one's finitude squarely and recognize that one is not God. In the final analysis what happens in the world depends on many factors which are not within our control. This is particularly true when we move away from simply bodily movements to those external happenings that are connected to our bodily actions by remote causal chains.

Climacus actually gives an example of an action that helps make his real meaning plainer. In a variation of the Good Samaritan story, he describes a repentant Levite who first passes by the poor wounded man, then later regrets his decision and hastens back to give assistance. Unfortunately he arrives too late; the good Samaritan has already taken care of the victim. Climacus then raises the question as to whether the Levite has performed an action and answers it affirmatively: "Certainly he had acted, and that in spite of the fact he had no opportunity to act in the external sense.''[20] Both the question and the answer seem odd, because it seems so obvious that the man had acted, and that he had done something "in the external sense"; namely, return to the scene of the crime where he had initially passed by the victim. Clearly, by *external action* Climacus does not merely mean "some physical change in one's body or elsewhere in the world." In saying that the repentant Levite had no opportunity to act in the external sense he means that the Levite had no chance to effect a meaningful or significant change, one with "world-historical significance." Here it seems quite reasonable to remind ourselves that such changes cannot be regarded as results that are solely in our power and that the temptation to take a moral short-cut to produce a desirable result is indeed a moral temptation.

I am discussing this point at some length, not merely because it is an interesting one in its own right, but because it sheds light on Kierkegaard's general view of action. Why is it that the true action must be seen as "inner?" I believe that the answer is pretty clear. Kierkegaard shares the standard intuition that underlies libertarianism: persons are only truly responsible for that which is within their power. To the extent that results are not within our power, to that extent we are not responsible. This means, if there was ever any doubt about the matter in anyone's mind, that Kierkegaard must and does reject determinism, including "soft-determinist," compatibilist versions. Persons are responsible only for what they have the power to do or not to do; an act must be completely within our power if we are to be correctly ascribed moral responsibility for it.

In an interesting way, Harry Frankfurt calls attention to the importance of these intuitions in an attempt to call them into question.[21] Frankfurt raises doubts about the libertarian claim that in the case of a free action I must be able to say truthfully, "I could have done otherwise." This principle is in turn rooted in the libertarian intuition, shared by Kierkegaard as we have seen, that we are responsible only for what is in our power. Frankfurt constructs counterexamples to the "could have done otherwise" principle, which he calls the *principle of alternate possibilities,* along the following lines. Suppose that Joe hates James and is planning to shoot him. Though Joe does not know it, a third party, Jerry, also wants James dead. Jerry is delighted to find out about Joe's intentions. On the off chance that Joe should change his mind, however, Jerry has a contingency plan. In that case he will cause Joe to shoot James, and there is nothing Joe can do to prevent this.

Suppose that Joe does not change his mind and in fact shoots James. Surely we would say in that case that he did so of his own free will, and that he is responsible for the act. Yet he could not have done otherwise, because if he had not freely decided to shoot James, then Jerry would have caused him to do so. So he did not have the power to shoot James *or not*.

I believe that what these Frankfurt-type counterexamples show is not that the principle of alternate possibilities is false. A free, responsible action is one where an individual had the power to perform the action or not. Rather, they show that strictly speaking Kierkegaard is correct when he insists that the true action lies in the inner resolution of the will. Regardless of what Jerry does, Joe does have the power to freely will to shoot James or not. He does not, in this case, have power over the external result. Regardless of what he decides to do, he will in fact shoot James. But so long as Jerry does not control his will, he can determine whether the shooting of James is a free act for which he is to be held responsible. If Jerry does control his will, he is not responsible for the action. Jerry can cause him to shoot James, but he cannot cause him to shoot James of his own free will.

WEAKNESS OF WILL

The significance of a concept of will in the theory of action can be seen clearly by comparing Kierkegaard's account of weakness of will with that of an influential twentieth century account of the phenomenon. Donald Davidson, in an essay entitled "How Is Weakness of the Will Possible?"[22] gives an explanation of the phenomenon that Kierkegaard would certainly regard as entailing an intellectualistic view of action. Davidson holds that one must have a reason for any action, because actions are events caused by reasons. The problem in cases of weakness of will is not that we have a reason for acting as we do, but that we have better reasons for not doing so, or for doing something else.

This is possible, says Davidson, because there are two types of reasons to be distinguished. In the process of deliberation, reasons are prima facie reasons. It occurs to us that x is a good reason for doing A, but of course we realize that y may be an even better reason for not doing A. As a result of reflection, we try to make the best possible overall assessment of what it is best for us to do, "all things considered." The difficulty is that we never in fact consider all things. Judgments of this sort must be regarded as conditional and hypothetical, for we realize that further reflection might modify our judgment. They have a form like this: "Insofar as I have considered the relevant evidence available to me, it looks like I should do A."

Davidson points out, however, that one cannot deduce from this judgment that A *is* in fact the best thing to do. Action requires a different kind of judgment, a judgment that A is the thing to do, where this judgment is an "all-out" or unconditional judgment. Therefore persons who act against their better judgment have not necessarily acted from contradictory premises. Such persons are irrational, says Davidson, because in inductive reasoning it is rational to rely on the total evidence available.[23]

However, it is possible without contradiction to hold that A seems the best action, insofar as I have considered all the relevant evidence available to me, and also judge unconditionally that B is superior to A.

From Kierkegaard's perspective this discussion is interesting in several respects. First, Davidson's discussion illuminates and supports Kierkegaard's claim that the intellect by itself has a kind of infinity that prevents closure. In another essay, Davidson puts this point very nicely: "It is a reason for acting that the action is believed to have some desirable characteristic, but the fact that the action is performed represents a further judgment that the desirable characteristic was enough to act on — that other considerations did not outweigh it."[24] This further judgment however, cannot be conclusively demonstrated. The fact that I want something sweet, and that a particular food is sweet cannot deductively warrant that I should eat the food in question, because "there are *endless* circumstances under which I would not eat something sweet, and I cannot begin to foresee them all."[25]

This is precisely Kierkegaard's point when he claims that reason alone cannot lead to action. What *does* enable an individual to make the transition from such a conditional, insofar as I have considered the matter, judgment to action with its all-out, unconditional character? For Kierkegaard this is precisely where the will comes into play.

How does Davidson answer this question? In cases of rational or continent action, I take it his view is that the reasons a person has simply cause the action in a straightforward way. (Though, of course, he is careful to insist that this does not mean that any causal laws connect the reason as a reason to the action.) Hence, in these cases his view looks intellectualistic to Kierkegaard. It is not of course that Davidson wants to reduce action to thought, but that the transition from thought to action occurs as a matter of course.

But is this really so? After all, Davidson recognizes that there are cases of incontinent action, where a person's overall judgment does not determine his or her action. So it seems that reasons do not lead automatically to action. What does bridge the gap between the tentative, never-to-be-completed process of reflection and action in those cases? Here, Davidson's answer is that no rational answer can be given:

> Why would anyone ever perform an action when he thought that, everything considered, another action would be better? If this is a request for a psychological explanation, then the answers will no

doubt refer to the interesting phenomena familiar from most discussions of incontinence: self-deception, overpowering desires, lack of imagination, and the rest. But if the question is read, what is the agent's reason for doing *a* when he believes it would be better. all things considered, to do another thing, then the answer must be: for this, the agent has no reason.[26]

In cases of weakness of will, then, Davidson says no explanation can be given of how an agent moves from a process of deliberation to action. Or, to be more precise, no *rational* explanation can be given, only an explanation in terms of nonrational causes. Actually, given Davidson's view that reasons are neurophysiological events and that the ultimate causal laws in this area connect intentions as physiological events to bodily movements, the ultimate explanation must surely come from the neurophysiologist.[27] And this explanation is certainly nonrational.

But that seems to me to imply that in these cases the agent is not really responsible for the action. If no reason can be given why reasons are not effective in moving me to action in incontinent cases, except that nonrational causes block their operation, then it is hard to see how the agent can be held responsible for cases of continent action, either. Surely one is just fortunate that in those cases ones reasons are causally effective, because there is no indication that one has effective control over the nonrational causes that sometimes block the efficacy of reasons. Sometimes reasons cause one to do things but they do not do so *qua* reasons.

When the concept of will enters the picture, the situation is quite different. One can acknowledge the force of reasons and also the power of nonrational causes. Agents are responsible for their actions, however, only to the extent that they can through their will choose to act or not to act on those reasons, will to oppose or not to oppose those nonrational causes.

PUTTING MYSTERY IN ITS PLACE

I believe we now have the resources for understanding why the interpretation of Kierkegaard as a proponent of radical choice is so appealing, and why it is nonetheless mistaken. In Kierkegaard's view, actions are neither arbitrary nor determined. They are not arbitrary, because agents can well have reasons for their actions. They are not determined, because reasons can provide a basis for action without causally determining that action. Besides having a reason for an action, an agent must will an action to perform it, and such an act of will does not follow automatically from an intellectual judgment that the action is worth doing.

Nevertheless it is easy to see why Kierkegaard's view looks like a doctrine of radical choice when looked at from a certain perspective; namely, the perspective of the determinist. Kierkegaard's view of action makes actions appear arbitrary and capricious to the determinist, simply because Kierkegaard's theory is a version of libertarianism, and this is how libertarian theories of action always look to determinists. And we must admit that there is something mysterious about human action if libertarianism is true, a mystery that is named but not dispelled by such notions as "agent causation." In saying that human action is genuinely free, libertarians are saying that humans have the power to perform an action or not, even given the past and present conditions of the agent.

This means that agents really are "first causes," at least first causes of the "relative" type Johannes Climacus discusses in *Philosophical Fragments*.[28] Nothing in the past guarantees a free action; it is in no way a necessary unfolding of processes already in motion. Such an action really does bring something new into the world, and it seems appropriate to indicate this by designating the process by which the action comes into being as a leap.

To the determinist, however, this is simply reveling in mystery, an admission that free actions cannot be explained. The argument of course begs the question, because the only explanation that will satisfy the determinist is precisely a deterministic one, and the libertarian will insist that this kind of explanation will simply eliminate freedom. Kierkegaard himself, for example, through his pseudonym Vigilius Haufniensis, denies that sin can be explained by any science.[29] The reason for this is surely that sin involves free, responsible action, and such actions cannot finally be explained as the necessary outcome of pre-existing conditions.

I am under no illusion that I have resolved the issue in dispute between libertarians and determinists here. My purpose is to understand Kierkegaard's theory of action, and I have succeeded if I have made action on Kierkegaard's view no more mysterious or arbitrary than action is in the views of such philosophers as Thomas Reid, Roderick Chisholm, and Peter Van Inwagen.

It is worth noting that the banishment of mystery carries a price, however. We saw earlier that in Davidson's theory of action, it looks as if no explanation can be given of why reasons are sometimes effective and sometimes not except in terms of nonrational causes. Either we are left with the unsolved mystery of how we move from hypothetical, open-ended deliberation to all-out action or else the mystery is dispelled by denying that reasons have power to move us as reasons. Whether we are moved by reasons depends not on ourselves but on nonrational causes that affect us. To me this avoiding of mystery seems a high price to pay, for it is tantamount to abandoning agency in any really significant sense.

And if we avoid this explanation that dispels mystery, the mystery of will seems preferable to simply saying that we can give no account of how the transition to action is made.

That we can and do move from reasoning about what is good, all things considered, to action seems to me to cry out for an explanation. It is not the sort of thing that just happens. That there should be something mysterious and unexplained in human agency does not appear strange, however, because it certainly appears that it is precisely its originative character that makes human agency so distinctive.

CAN A FREE ACTION BE MOVED BY REASONS?

There is one other respect in which actions on the Kierkegaardian model may appear arbitrary. I have argued that Kierkegaardian free choices may be done for reasons. But are those reasons really *reasons*? Does Kierkegaard really think that rational considerations could justify a choice, even if we agree that this could be done without determining the choice?

The problem is a genuine one, I think, because Kierkegaard does not regard deliberation about actions as a neutral, disinterested affair. By contrast, on reading Davidson's account of practical reasoning, one almost gets the feeling that practical deliberation is something that could be carried on by a computer. Weakness of will is irrational because it violates a principle of good inductive reasoning, which is to base one's judgments on the total evidence available to one.

From a Kierkegaardian perspective, this is naive. It assumes that the evidence is "out there," in some objective way, independent of my inclinations and passions. But of course this is not so. A typical reason for doing some action is that the action will satisfy some desire of mine. Though some philosophers may have assumed that my desires are objective occurrences over which I have no control, this is certainly not true of many of them. I can at least control many desires indirectly over time, and this is even more true of those long-term caring involvements Kierkegaard termed *passions*. So very often the "evidence" that I should pursue a certain course of action, in the sense of the reason why I should perform the action, is something that is affected by my emotional life.

It is thus even more evident why "reason" by itself is powerless to motivate action. In the practical sphere reason "by itself" is an abstraction; it does not exist. It is analogous to that "pure thinking" that Climacus denounces as a mirage in the *Postscript*.

So, are the proponents of radical choice right after all? If the notion of an objective reason that could justify choice is a mirage, then actions appear arbitrary in the end. Or so it would seem if we are classical foundationalists in our epistemology.

I believe that the temptation to throw in the towel and admit that choices are ultimately arbitrary stems from residual classical foundationalist strains in our everyday epistemology: surely for a reason to be a good one it must be one that could be justified before a neutral, objective audience. Reasons tainted by subjectivity could not be good reasons.

To expose this line of thinking, I believe, is to call it into question. The history of twentieth century epistemology and philosophy of science suggests that the ideal of a reason untainted by any whiff of commitment and subjectivity is a myth. But this lack does not prevent us from reasoning and holding justified beliefs, and it is not at all evident that it should prevent us from acting in justified ways.

The way Alasdair MacIntyre sets up his case against Kierkegaard in *After Virtue* suggests to me that a touch of this residual classical foundationalism may be at work in his account despite the fact that he seems to reject classical foundationalism in his concluding chapter. He claims that the reasons given by Judge William for the ethical life in Volume 2 of *Either/Or* are no good because they will be acceptable only to one who already is committed enough to the ethical life to feel its attractiveness. Now the judge certainly gives many arguments that he hopes will appeal to the aesthete who is the author of Volume 1. For example, he argues that marriage is superior to the casual love affair, even when judged on aesthetic criteria. You might say that marriage actually realizes the ends that are implicit in the aesthetic romantic project. The judge even gives an argument against the aesthete, focusing on the unity of the personality over time, which is remarkably like an argument given by MacIntyre himself.[30]

It is possible, of course, that this argument will fail to be convincing, even if it is a good argument. It may well be that the aesthete will not be convinced, because he is determined to remain an aesthete. Does this fact show that the judge's reasons are not good reasons? I think not. What would an argument have to accomplish to provide a good reason for choice? Must it be able to convince anyone and everyone? If so, no philosophical argument of any substance is a good argument. The idea that an argument must be convincing to anyone, regardless of the assumptions and values they bring to bear on their evaluation of it, seems to me to be one that would be attractive only to a classical foundationalist. For such a foundationalist can at least put forward as an ideal that people should be able to set aside all assumptions and commitments and think in a neutral, objective way about the question. On the assumption that people are capable of at least approximating this ideal, rational arguments should in principle be convincing to all who enter the arena of thought.

If, however, we reject the notion that reason requires the jettisoning of all commitments and values, and instead explore the idea that reasoning is in part an attempt to test such values by developing their implications and seeing how well they function when integrated into our theoretical and practical lives, then the picture looks different. There surely must be something between the radical, arbitrary choice and the algorithmic decision-process that a properly programmed computer can execute. Somewhere in that expanse lies the Kierkegaardian leap, which can indeed be informed by reasons, but must in the end be created by passionate willing.

III   Toward a Sartrean Ethics

7

Love and Perfect Coincidence in a Sartrean Ethics

Linda A. Bell

PROLOGUE

To limit the scope of this essay, I have concentrated on what Sartre has to say in his plays, novels, short stories, and some of his less well-known philosophical writings about relations with others. Because what he says in *Being and Nothingness* about love and relations with others is quite well known in circles like the one I am addressing, I assume adequate familiarity with that discussion.

Some of the other assumptions with which I begin may not be so uncontroversial. One such assumption is that *Being and Nothingness,* as Sartre later says,[1] is a discussion of consciousness in bad faith and not an exhaustive analysis of relationships with others. I have argued elsewhere[2] for this and the other assumptions I make; in this paper I shall endeavor to show, from Sartre's own examples and analyses, that scattered throughout his writings are at least three different kinds of love and that each was recognized early as well as late in his career.

A final but crucial assumption is that critics like Marcuse and Merleau-Ponty are wrong when they depict Sartrean freedom as absolute, subjective, and isolated. In an early essay, "Materialism and Revolution," published in *Les Temps Modernes* in 1946, Sartre rejected, as Marcuse acknowledged, such "inner freedom that man could retain in any situation" as "a pure idealistic hoax," reducing freedom, as it does, to "the autonomy of thought" after "separat[ing] thought from action."[3] To speak, as Merleau-Ponty does, of Sartre as "a good Cartesian" and of his philosophy as the "Philosophy of the pure subject"[4] is to ignore what

Sartre says even in his earliest writings about facticity, one's being for others, and one's inability ever to escape one's past. Marcuse discovers a "radical conversion" in Sartre's later work only by dismissing as "idealistic mystifications" and "mere ideology" much of what Sartre said earlier.[5]

THREE VIEWS OF LOVE IN SARTRE'S WRITINGS[6]

In *Being and Nothingness,* Sartre affirmed that all actions are equivalent: "thus it amounts to the same thing whether one gets drunk alone or is a leader of nations."[7] Many of Sartre's critics and even some of his admirers have concluded from this remark and from other aspects of *Being and Nothingness* that Sartre's notion of authenticity is totally individualistic and compatible with any and all behavior toward others. Unfortunately, this misinterpretation is supported by many of Sartre's own analyses — for example, his circle of concrete relations with others, and by his many plays, novels, and short stories the central characters of which are loners, individuals cut off from others, usually by their own doing.

Whereas these examples and analyses reinforce the view that Sartre's position allows only what Mary Warnock calls a "perpetual hopeless struggle of each against the other,"[8] other depictions of relationships challenge this view and indicate more positive possibilities for human relationships. These other examples include the relationships of Eve and Pierre (*The Chips Are Down*), of Hoederer and Hugo (*Dirty Hands*), of Hilda and Goetz (*The Devil and the Good Lord*), of Lucie and Henri (*Men without Shadows*), and of Anna and Kean (*Kean*).

From analysis of these relationships as well as of the more familiar aspects of Sartre's writings, three quite different views of love emerge. There is first the game-of-mirrors view of love, as presented in *Being and Nothingness*. A second view might be called the common-enemy view. And a third, the most important and least recognized, is a depiction of a kind of love that affirms human freedom, that is lucid yet nonetheless joyful, and that seeks perfect confidence and coincidence only as a regulative ideal.

The first view of love is the view with which readers of *Being and Nothingness* are quite familiar. At this level, "Sadism and masochism are the revelation of the Other," as Sartre said in *Cahiers*. But, he added, this sadism and masochism "have meaning . . . only before the conversion."[9] In this type of relationship, the lovers are in bad faith and seek to use each other in trying to hide their freedom and responsibility from themselves.

Such lovers seek solitude, Sartre says, because the look of a third party effectively destroys the game they play with one another. Such love requires sequestration.

Second, there is the sort of love that exists between or among those who, as it were, are comrades in arms. This is the sort of love produced by terror, according to the *Critique* ("a practical bond of *love* between the lynchers [of traitors]"),[10] and that Goetz has in mind when he affirms, "To love anyone is to hate the same enemy."[11] Similarly, when Mathieu, in *The Age of Reason,* imitates Ivich's gesture and stabs his own hand, their common definace of others' opinions brings them momentarily to a sense of intimacy that they have not previously experienced and do not experience again.[12]

It is in terms of this sort of love that Henri and Lucie (*Men without Shadows*) are drawn closer through their tortured shame and suffering even as they are separated from Lucie's former lover Jean. Jean and Lucie are imprisoned with several of their comrades. Jean, the leader of the insurrectionary group, was captured separately, and the captors do not suspect that he has any connection with the others. In fact, the others are being tortured for information concerning him. A triangle of sorts develops as Henri, one of the comrades, confesses his love for Lucie "because it doesn't matter any more." Lucie allows Henri to kill her young brother François who, they fear, under torture will reveal Jean's identity. Their shame and suffering bring Lucie and Henri together and separate them from Jean. When Jean reminds Lucie that their love was their whole life, she responds:

> Our life, yes. Our future. I lived in an external expectation. I loved you in expectation. I was waiting for the end of the war. Waiting for the day when we could be married in the eyes of the world. Each night I waited for you. Now I have no future. I expect nothing but my death, and I shall die alone. . . . Leave me alone. We have nothing to say to each other. I am not in pain and I have no need for consolation.

Like Pablo Ibbieta in "The Wall," Lucie lived in an illusion of immortality. When that is destroyed, all she has is her pride. She says, "All that I want is for them to come for me again, and to beat me, so that I can keep silent again, and fool them and frighten them."[13]

Apparently Sartre sees opposition as central to love because, in discussing *The Devil and the Good Lord,* he says: "Broadly speaking this is what I mean. First, every love is in opposition to God. As soon as two people love each other, they love each other in opposition to God. Every love is in opposition to the absolute because it is itself absolute. . . . If God exists, man does not exist; and if man exists, God does not exist."[14] Though love may be always in opposition to God, it is clear from Sartre's examples that it need not be always in opposition to anything else. Pierre and Eve (*The Chips Are Down*) love each other but they neither have nor hate the same enemy. In fact, they are members of different classes and have different enemies and different loyalties that pull them apart and prevent them from loving each other "with perfect coincidence and with all their . . . might."[15] They must achieve this love, or they must return again to the netherworld of the dead. Similarly, Hoederer's love for Hugo seems not to be connected with hatred of enemies; in fact, even though both are communists and active in the party it is not at all clear that they hate the same enemy.

What can be seen in the love of Pierre and Eve is the recognition of a third sort of love, of human relationships that strive in a positive and authentic way for a perfect coincidence, a perfect confidence. Such coincidence with another, like that of an individual with herself or himself, cannot be achieved. Although they do love each other, when they rejoin the living they are torn by other loves and loyalties. Pierre tries to save his comrades from staging an insurrection that in fact will be only a trap for them. Eve is concerned about her sister Lucette whom André, Eve's husband, is trying to win over so that, after Eve's death, he can marry Lucette for her dowry just as he earlier married Eve for hers.

Unable to love each other with perfect confidence and not even the slightest of misgivings, Eve and Pierre return to the dead. There they meet two young people, who like Eve and Pierre earlier, have discovered they were made for each other and who also seek the opportunity to live their lives over. They eagerly ask Pierre and Eve if they really can try to live their lives over. Pierre and Eve respond with funny looks and gentle smiles, "'Try,' Pierre advises. 'Try it anyway,' murmurs Eve."[16]

Although Sartre admits that he was having fun here with a nonexistential determinism (in which the chips are down and lovers are meant for one another),[17] the play itself suggests a couple of points with respect to love. First, a love of perfect coincidence, of perfect confidence and no misgivings, is presented as an impossibility given the ambiguous creatures human beings are. This recognition should surprise neither Sartre's critics nor his admirers. What may surpise is the additional affirmation of the attempt to love with perfect coincidence, an affirmation that emerges in Eve's and Pierre's responses to the young aspiring lovers. There is a wistfulness in their responses, but there is more: in their urging is a recognition of the importance of the attempt even though it cannot succeed. Ambiguity and a tension of opposites are an ineradicable part of the human condition, yet the effort to harmonize and unify the inharmonious and disparate may well be vital to human striving, particularly, as we have seen, to authentic striving.

Hoederer's relationship with Hugo is quite revealing as well. At his own peril, Hoederer recognizes Hugo's difficulty in growing out of his middle-class childhood and into a revolutionary. Hoederer respects Hugo's freedom and risks his own life to help Hugo grow up. Realizing that Hugo has been sent as an assassin, Hoederer nevertheless gives Hugo numerous opportunities to complete his mission. Hoederer trusts Hugo even though it may—and eventually does—mean Hoederer's own death. It is only when Hugo finds Jessica and Hoederer embracing that Hugo shoots Hoederer. Even then Hoederer tries to protect Hugo by telling the guards that he had been sleeping with Hugo's wife.

At each point, Hoederer's efforts backfire. Hugo feels insulted, humiliated, made fun of, rather than loved and respected. When Hoederer intervenes and tries to resolve the antagonism between Hugo and Hoederer's bodyguards, Hugo is outraged to find himself defended by Hoederer. Similarly Hoederer's trust of Hugo, even to the point of giving Hugo the opportunity to fulfill his assignment by assassinating Hoederer, evokes from Hugo the response, "I hate you."[18]

In the plays *The Devil and the Good Lord* and *Kean*, Sartre develops two other characters who, like Hoederer, love without being loved in turn and who also love clear-sightedly, nonpossessively, and without bad faith. Hilda recognizes Goetz's misery, stays with him, and later confesses to Heinrich that she loves Goetz, acknowledging only that Goetz has loved her "as much as he has loved himself."[19]

Against Goetz's fear of "coupling in public" ("under the eyes of God"), Hilda responds that love is a "deep night" that hides lovers from God's regard: "when people love each other, they become invisible to God." In response to Goetz's horror of sexual love ("how can I desire to hold in my arms this bag of excrement?"), she assures him that "If you die, I will lie down beside you and stay there to the very end, without eating or drinking; you will rot away in my embrace, and I will love your carrion flesh; for *you do not love at all, if you do not love everything*" [emphasis added].[20] Finally, she loves without idealizing: she recognizes that Goetz "will never be like other men. Neither better nor worse: different."[21]

Joseph H. McMahon proposes that Anna in *Kean* is "a new kind of character in Sartre's work." From the previous analyses of Hoederer and Hilda, it is clear that the kind of character Anna represents is not especially new in Sartre's work; McMahon is correct that she represents "a significant development in Sartre's theory of love." However, unlike McMahon, I see her as *part* of a significant development and I am a bit wary of his claim that "she represents a kind of feminine force" heralding this "significant development."[22]

In the play, Anna has fallen in love with the actor Kean whom she has observed through many performances. When Kean, assuming he has

wowed her with his performance, seeks to shock and disillusion her by
informing her that he was "drunk as an Irish lord," she indicates that she
was quite aware of that fact and acknowledges his various errors: calling
other actors by the wrong names, inserting moving soliloquies from other
plays. Mystified that she knew he was drunk and yet "applauded all the
same," Kean is told that she applauded to encourage him and because she
knew he must be unhappy.[23]

Anna sees Kean quite clearly and responds to what she perceives as
his need somewhat as Hilda does to the suffering of the peasants and later
to Goetz's misery: "So I made enquiries, and I found you were a drun-
kard, a libertine, crippled with debts, melancholy and mad by turns, and
I said to myself: 'That man needs a wife.'" When she recognizes that Solomon, Kean's prompter, also loves Kean, she resolves that "nothing will
be changed" and that Solomon should live with her and Kean after they
are married; like Hilda, Anna seems unafraid of the eyes of the other. Finally, as she prepares to leave for America, she seems to accept with good
grace the conclusion that Kean does not love her. Although she lies, as
she says, to "make" Kean marry her, she nonetheless seems to be as
clear-sightedly aware of Kean's freedom as she is of his character.[24]

In Hoederer's love for Hugo, Hilda's for Goetz, Anna's for Kean,
and in the unsuccessful love of Eve and Pierre, Sartre exemplifies what
he recognizes in *What Is Literature?* namely, "that is is quite impossible
to treat concrete men as ends in contemporary society." As in the cases
of Hoederer and Hugo and of Eve and Pierre, the injustices of the age,
classes, racism, and so on, Sartre argues, inevitably will intervene and
vitiate "at the roots" the good that one strives to accomplish.[25] Similarly,
Goetz remains the unlovable bastard, unable to accept himself and desiring only "to be a man among men."[26] He moves from feeling more alone
the more he is loved[27] to acknowledging Hilda's love by incorporating her
into himself and admitting her to his loneliness: "You are myself. We
shall be alone together."[28]

Kean may appear more optimistic inasmuch as it ends with Kean
linking arms with Anna and Solomon and saying, "My true, my only
friends."[29] However, it is difficult not to imagine the future Kean as he
tries to make a living in America, whether by acting or not, once again
wondering if his action was truly an action or merely a gesture[30] and once
again struggling with his existence as a bastard in the eyes of others.

Although it may be impossible today to treat men as ends, nonetheless, according to Sartre in *What Is Literature?* the writer strives, as does
Hoederer, to hold in tension the affirmations of revolution and the kingdom of ends. In the loves exemplified by Hoederer, Hilda, Anna, Pierre,
and Eve, ambiguity prevails. Failure is inevitable; nevertheless they
reach beyond such failure.

THE POSSIBILITIES OF AUTHENTIC LOVE

What these analyses indicate about the possibilities of love is to have been expected, given Sartre's view of man, freedom, and authenticity. There is a kind of love that recognizes and affirms the freedom of the beloved as well as one's own. Whatever the features of the human condition or of the social structures created by human activity that render problematic or impossible the expression or realization of such love, the authentic individual must affirm and actively support the freedom of others. Such love goes beyond the sado-masochistic dialectic of enslaving freedoms to a "deeper recognition and reciprocal comprehension of freedoms" — a dimension that Sartre noted in *Cahiers* was lacking in *Being and Nothingness*. This sort of love "requires the *tension*: to maintain the two faces of the ambiguity, to retain them in the unity of the same project."[31] It is a "completely different thing than the desire to appropriate."[32] Authentic relationships with others, like other authentic activity, must maintain a tension between what is sought and what is achieved, between coincidence and inevitable alienation and separateness, between treating the other as an end and treating him or her as a means. Like the writer, though, an authentic individual can approach the other with a confidence concerning human freedom.

Such love may involve all the joy and some of the sorrow depicted in the account of love in *Being and Nothingness*. There Sartre notes "the basis for the joy of love when there is joy: we feel our existence is justified."[33] This joy bears a strong resemblance to the aesthetic joy Sartre described in *What Is Literature?* — "It is identical, at first, with the recognition of a transcendent and absolute end which, for a moment, suspends the utilitarian round of ends-means and means-ends."[34] Aesthetic joy involves a recognition, on the part of the reader, of his or her freedom and "a consciousness of being essential in relation to an object perceived as essential." Sartre calls this aspect of aesthetic consciousness "the feeling of security," notes that it "stamps the strongest aesthetic emotions with a sovereign calm," and affirms that "it has its origin in the authentication of a strict harmony between subjectivity and objectivity."[35]

Although Sartre loses the illusion that identified him with Roquentin—that through writing he could justify his life and become essential—nevertheless he continued to write and, I presume, to experience aesthetic joy. Surely one can say the same thing about love. The authentic individual has lost any illusions of being justified and made essential by another. This individual recognizes her or his own freedom and thereby, if Sartre's analysis in *What Is Literature?* is right, already experiences a kind of joy. Like the writer, the authentic lover can approach the other with confidence in freedom and with a trust and generosity.[36] Aesthetic

joy and the joy of love may be momentary, but nonetheless they are intimations of that harmony sought. As momentary, they may bring sorrow
and negate the aspirations of those who sought therein to be justified and
essential and to escape their freedom and responsibility. But for the authentic, such intimations may be taken in stride as temporal albeit fleeting
and ambiguous embodiments of the ultimate but impossible goals toward
which they strive. Once again, what is sought does not change when one
becomes authentic, but the way it is sought does change.

Such love is not part of a morality that fuses individuals into a single
consciousness. Sartre warned against this in *Cahiers* and against a kingdom of ends that recognizes each consciousness only in its Kantian universality. Rather, the morality he approves would take each individual in
its "concrete singularity."[37]

In *Cahiers,* Sartre sheds a bit more light on authentic love when he
discusses how in aiding another one not only comprehends the other's
end but also makes it one's own. Although, he says, there is a preontological comprehension of the original structure of all ends, a preontological
comprehension of the other's freedom by my freedom, this is not an intuitive comprehension, but rather "it presupposes an active original intention that is the basis of its revelation. The end of the other is able to
appear to me as end only in and by the outlining of the adoption of this
end by myself." I engage myself but nonetheless recognize that the end is
not mine. To will this end authentically, I must will "that the end be realized by the other." In choosing to aid another, I will that

> the world have an infinity of free and finite futures of which each
> would be directly projected by a free will and indirectly sustained
> by all the others, insofar as each wills the concrete freedom of the
> other, that is to say, wills it not in its abstract form of universality
> but, on the contrary, in its concrete and limited form. Such is the
> maxim for my action. To will that a value realize itself not because
> it is mine, not because it is a value, but because it is a value for
> someone on earth.

In the other's appeal and in the aid I offer in response, there is "refusal
to consider the original conflict of freedoms by the look as something impossible to overcome."[38]

Sartre's example of "the human relation of aid" illuminates both
the appeal and the aid. Sartre's example is a familiar one: "A runs toward
the bus; B, on the platform, extends his hand. . . . In grasping it as an instrument, [A] contributes to realizing his own project." Yet, A becomes
instrument for B, because A serves as a means to realizing B's end (in this
case, that of himself serving as an instrument). A's hand is grasped and

pulled; A becomes an object that is seen, appraised, and pulled, a passivity. Thus A "feels himself in question in his own freedom." Yet this does not happen against his freedom as he becomes an instrument precisely in pursuing his own end. He discovers the other's freedom, not as opposed and threatening his freedom, but rather "he discovers it at the heart of his freedom as a free movement of accompanying [him] toward his ends. . . . [E]ach freedom is totally in the other."[39]

Here, with each freedom totally in the other, there seems to be the kind of transparency of which Sartre writes elsewhere. This is different from relations where individuals have a *common project* in the sense, for example, of having the same enemy. Rather, in the relation of appeal-aid, the one who assists adopts the other's end in such a way that *it remains the end of the other and to be realized by the other*. One who aids responds to the appeal not because the aid-giver happens to share the other's end but rather just because the other has this end. There is gratuity in the appeal as well; and this, Sartre says, is in fact that which makes morality[40] — "From the beginnning I recognize that my end ought to be conditional for the other as it is for me. That is to say that it ought always to be possible for the other to refuse aid if the utilized means of aid alter his own ends."[41] In appealing to the other, one adheres to the ends of the other: "I sustain them in their concrete content by my approbation."[42] This is why the appeal is a "promise of reciprocity" and why one does not demand aid from those whose ends one cannot approve, from those whom one would not oneself aid.[43]

In the relation appeal-aid, each discovers and wills the other's freedom and each is totally in the other. This is why Sartre sees in the appeal a sketch of a world that he previously called a utopia ("where each treats the other as an end, that is to say, takes the enterprise of the other as end") — "a world where each person will be able to appeal to all the others." This is why Sartre sees an authentic appeal as necessarily "conscious of being overcoming of all inequality of condtion toward a human world where all appeals of one person to another might be always possible."[44]

If what Sartre says about the ideal of total transparency is combined with what he says elsewhere about human relationships, his late analysis of fraternity[45] emerges as a viable ideal, vital, as he says, to a moral system: "Fraternity is what human beings will be in relation to each other when through all our history they will be able to say of themselves that they are all bound to each other in feeling and in action."[46]

8

Authenticity, Conversion, and the City of Ends in Sartre's Notebooks for an Ethics

Thomas C. Anderson

Everyone knows that *Being and Nothingness* concludes with Sartre's promise to devote a future work on ethics. More precisely, he promises to answer a series of questions that he posed in the final paragraphs:

1. Whether it is possible for freedom to "turn its back on" and "put an end to the reign of" the "value or the ideal presence of the *ens causa sui*"? That is, can human freedom choose as its "ideal of being" something other than God?

2. As an alternative to God, can freedom "take itself for a value as the source of all value"? And if so, "what would this mean?"

3. If freedom "takes itself for an end," is it "a question of bad faith or of another fundamental attitude [elsewhere called *authenticity*]'?"

4. If freedom does "take itself for an end" will it escape all situation or be all the more concretely situated "as an existent by whom the world comes into being?"

Sartre then concludes, "All these questions which refer us to a pure and not an accessory reflection can find their reply only on the ethical plane. We shall devote to them a future work." Parts of that unfinished future work were published by Sartre's daughter three years after his death under the title *Cahiers pour une morale*. These are two of approximately a dozen notebooks written in 1947–1948.[2] Published with these notebooks are two brief appendices, one written in 1945 and the other undated.

The almost six hundred pages of the *Cahiers* contain a wealth of material of uneven clarity and significance ranging from passages that treat one topic or a collection of related topics extensively, to entries of only one paragraph, sentence, or phrase. I will not attempt here to give a comprehensive overview of the work, rather I will concentrate on some of its central concepts, especially those that will enable us to ascertain Sartre's responses to the questions he posed at the end of *Being and Nothingness*. I will first focus on Sartre's notions of pure reflection or conversion, authenticity, and the God project, and then discuss his ideal of human relations, the city of ends. Before I begin let me say that in my opinion these *Cahiers* do not offer a totally new and unexpected version of Sartrean ethics. Rather, they supplement some features of the ethical theory whose fundamentals were outlined in Sartre's and de Beauvoir's published works of this period, especially his *Being and Nothingness* and *Existentialism Is a Humanism,* and her *Pyrrhus et Cinéas* and *The Ethics of Ambiguity*.[3] Because I have argued elsewhere that Sartrean ethical theory is far more coherent than most critics recognize and that it generally flows from, and is consistent with, the ontology of *Being and Nothingness,* I will not repeat myself here.[4] In what follows, I will, however, occasionally indicate which positions taken in these unpublished notebooks can also be found (often more cryptically) in the published works of the 1940s. I will conclude this paper by mentioning Sartre's own criticisms of the ethics contained in these early notebooks.

PURE REFLECTION, CONVERSION, AUTHENTICITY

Taking our cue from his concluding remarks to *Being and Nothingness,* let us begin by examining Sartre's discussion of pure reflection in the *Cahiers*.[5] Note at the start that he insists that reflection is not contemplation, not a passive observation of the unreflected. All reflection is a project; it has a consciously chosen goal. Pure reflection and its goal can best be seen in contrast to impure, or as Sartre more often designates it, "complice" (accessory) reflection that, he says, is far more common. By calling reflection *complice* he means that it goes along with (is an accomplice of) the natural tendency of the prereflective dimension of human consciousness (being-for-itself). As Sartre explained in *Being and Nothingness* and repeats here, this natural tendency or nonthetic project of the for-itself is to be God. It wants *itself* to be a totally self-identical substantial being that would be the cause of itself, one that would be the necessary foundation of its being and so exist by right, not gratuitously. According to Sartre because reflection is necessarily posterior to and "takes birth in, the unreflected" it naturally tends to arise at first as an effort to achieve that goal which the for-itself prereflectively seeks. But because attaining this goal is impossible, accomplice reflection is doomed to the same failure as the nonthetic project from which it arises. Every attempt (through money, power, virture, and so on) to achieve a necessity in being by becoming the foundation of ourselves (*causa sui*) is in vain. In the memorable line of *Being and Nothingness,* "it amounts to the same thing whether one gets drunk alone or is a leader of nations."[6]

However, this very failure, Sartre now says in the *Cahiers,* coupled with the fact that human beings are always prereflectively conscious of their freedom,[7] can motivate an individual to undertake a pure or nonaccomplice reflection. This reflection, which Sartre explicitly identifies here with conversion,[8] refuses "to have anything to do with" the God project. It "renounces being as en-soi-pour-soi, i.e. as cause of itself," and so is not an accomplice of man's nonthetic project. In the following passage Sartre clearly distinguishes the two reflections in terms of their projects: "it is evident that accomplice reflection is only the prolongation of the bad faith that is found at the heart of the primitive nonthetic project [to be God], whereas pure reflection is a rupture with this projection and the constitution of a freedom that takes itself as end."[9]

Note that pure reflection, conversion, not only breaks with the God project, it substitutes freedom for that unattainable goal. Recall that this is exactly what Sartre suggested at the end of *Being and Nothingness.* Thus he answers affirmatively to his first two questions: can freedom choose as its goal something other than God, and can freedom take itself for an end? These answers also indicate how we should interpret most of *Being and Nothingness.* Except for its last few pages, where Sartre mentions the possibility of pure reflection, all of this work describes human existence either on the prereflective level or on that of *complice* reflection! Although he distinguishes between *complice* and pure reflection in *Being and Nothingness,* he states that he intends to, and does, discuss only the former.[10] The notebooks, on the other hand, emphasize the latter. Lest there be any doubt about this interpretation of his ontological work, on the third page of the *Cahiers* Sartre asserts, "*Being and Nothingness* is an ontology before conversion."

Let us turn now to the third of Sartre's questions at the end of that work: if freedom does take itself for an end is this a fundamental attitude other than bad faith? Again the *Cahiers* answers unambiguously: yes. Pure reflection results in a "new way of being to oneself and for oneself, an authentic way, which transcends the dialectic of sincerity — bad faith."[11] The authentic individual is one who undertakes the conversion of pure reflection, then, one who "refuses" and "renounces" the inauthentic quest to be God and instead chooses human freedom.

In the *Cahiers* Sartre further describes the authentic person's pure reflection as recognizing that the for-itself is intrinsically a failure (to be God) and assenting to it as such. The authentic individual reflectively seizes her existence as free, gratuitous, and unjustified and yet wills it. She accepts the fact that it is precisely because she is not totally self-identical or substantial, precisely because she is not necessary, precisely because she is a contingent failure, that she is free. She consents to the fact that insofar as she is free no transcendent, a priori values bind her, nor justify her existence. In other words, the meaning of her life is always in question and it is entirely up to her (and other human beings) to justify it. Thus, pure reflection, conversion, authenticity involve, Sartre says, "a radical decision for autonomy."[12]

Moreover, it is precisely because pure reflection involves the acceptance by the person of her contingent freedom that it also involes, according to the *Cahiers,* the recovery of her unjustified existence and its justification. This means that human existence is not for Sartre an irretrievably "useless passion" or "doomed to failure," for its desire for justification can be met (to some extent). Now to justify something, he explains, is to give it an intentional foundation so that its reality is not a gratuitous, meaningless fact but has a raison d'être, a purpose, a *sens* (meaning or direction).[13] Of course, in the Sartrean universe, which lacks all transcendent or objective values, human beings alone are the irreducible source of all the value and *sens* that any being, including themselves, possesses. Because pure reflection recognizes and accepts this fact, it acknowledges that it has "only itself to justify itself."[14] Its choice of human freedom and autonomy confers *sens* on it and thus gives human reality a foundation, a justification. Thus, Sartre writes, "it is me, that nothing justifies, that justifies myself."[15] He even observes that by doing so I become, in a (weak) sense God (*causa sui*), for I am the cause or foundation of the meaning-*sens* of my being. (I call this a *weak* sense because human beings can never cause themselves to be necessary beings that possess *sens* and being by right rather than contingently.)

There is more. Not only does the authentic individual in pure reflection choose her freedom as the foundation of all values, she also, Sartre says, grasps creation as a, or "the," fundamental ontological structure and destiny of her freedom. We have already noted that human beings are the sole creators of meaning and value in the universe. But it is not just that human freedom creates meaning in an already existing world. For as *Being and Nothingness* has shown, and the *Notebooks* repeat, human reality alone causes there to be the interrelated *Weltangshauung* of objects that we call the world in the first place![16]

It is not that human beings choose to be creators of the world, rather we are such in our "original ontological structure," Sartre says. Insofar as we are condemned to be free, just so are we "condemned to create."[17] The authentic individual by pure reflection, or conversion, accepts and wills his creativity. He accepts the fact that his "task" and "destiny" (Sartre's words), is to freely reveal Being, by giving it meaning as a world.

To speak of creation as the human being's task, or destiny, however, is strange. For who or what other than man himself can give him a task? Sartre's explanation is interesting for he partly resorts to what he himself labels a *myth*. (In *Being and Nothingness* it was called *metaphysics*.) Being-in-itself is radically contingent because it is in itself for no reason, for nothing and no one. Like human reality it lacks a foundation because it does not proceed from a conscious intention, and so there is no explanation or justification for its being. At this point Sartre introduces the myth. Borrowing from Hegel he observes that it is as if the in-itself produces being-for-itself to found and justify itself by giving itself a *sens* or raison d'être. It is as if Being-in-itself "calls" human consciousness to reveal it by becoming more and more conscious of it, and thus to give it value and meaning as world. Actually, this myth admits of a rather straightforward ontological interpretation. In truth human reality itself wants its world and Being to have a foundation and justification. For if they have none, neither ultimately does man himself because he is fundamentally a being-in-the-world, ontologically grounded in Being. Thus human reality gives itself the task or destiny to create the world and justify and found it by giving it *sens,* for doing so is essential to its own self-justification.[18]

The authentic individual, Sartre adds, finds joy in his generosity as creator. He delights in "losing himself" as being (i.e., in ceasing his attempts to be self-identical substantial being) in order to accept himself as the freedom by which Being, and his being, is saved from meaninglessness. For him "there is no other reason to be then to give."[19]

To conclude this section, I should point out that Sartre has offered in the *Cahiers* not simply a description of the authentic individual and pure reflection, but a persuasive argument for undertaking the latter and becoming authentic. (An argument that, by the way, seems to be cryptically presented in *Existentialism and Humanism*.)[20] If one grants Sartre's ontological claim that only human beings, or more precisely human freedom, can be the foundation of all meaning and value and that these same beings seek to justify their existence along with Being's, then it follows that the most logical way for them to attain justification is to do what Sartre suggests, reflectively accept and value their creative freedom. One should choose to value this freedom because one thereby fulfills one's "destiny" (desire) to bring justification to Being, including one's own being. However, what this means in the concrete order is unclear. Apart from his suggestion that human beings should "maximize" the amount of being they create and that they create more when they clearly face their concrete situation than when they seek to escape into some imaginary realm, Sartre never spells out what the authentic person should do to be more of a free creator.[21] In fact he admits that *all* human actions and attitudes are creative and that whatever happens to a person allows that person to create more. Perhaps some content can be furnished to the choice of free creativity, if we consider how the authentic individual is said to relate to other human beings in the *Cahiers*.

THE CITY OF ENDS

Even though Sartre is often inconsistent in his use of key terms (such as objectification, alienation, oppression) in the notebooks, he is clear that the authentic individual not only wills her own freedom, she also recognizes and wills that of other human beings. Yet this does not mean Sartre has totally retracted his statement in *Being and Nothingness* that "conflict is the original meaning of being-for-others." For in the *Cahiers,* too, he portrays the original and most common relationship of one human being to another quite negatively.[22] Thus, he says, that my first and most basic relation with others involves objectification, and this in two senses: (1) the other by her look inevitably reifies me, that is, sees me as a thinglike object; (2) every action and every creation of mine is inevitably exteriorized in the world, which means that it escapes my freedom and becomes the prey of others' free evaluations and actions that are beyond my control. Of course, both types of objectification befall me throughout my life, but because they occur in childhood, Sartre says, they have as their normal result that I take the other's view of me and my actions as ontologically primary. Sartre calls this our "original fall' and our alienation. It is alienation, of course, because I do not explicitly recognize myself as the free autonomous source of my own life and values, but see myself as a dependent, even inessential, object of the essential other who supplies the values and tasks I must accept if my life is to have significance. In one place he even labels this alienation *oppression*: "oppression is when my free subjectivity is given as inessential, my freedom as epiphenomenon, my initiative as subordinate and secondary, when my activity is directed by the Other and takes the Other as end.[23]

Of course, oppression can take many more overt forms: masterslave, capitalist-worker, colonizer-colonized, male-female, and so on. Nevertheless, what is common to all of them, according to Sartre, is objectification; in fact, it is the ontological condtion that makes oppression possible. Yet this ontological condition is not in and of itself oppression, he insists, for oppression is basically a human decision.[24] This must mean that although objectification of my self, actions, and products by the other is an inevitiable part of the human condition, it is not absolutely necessary (though it may be "normal," due to childhood) that I, in addition, take the other as ontologically primary and thereby become alienated, oppressed. Nor is it necessary or inevitable that I or others choose to inflict the degrading kinds of reification involved in the more obvious types of oppression just mentioned. Though one can never avoid being objectified by others, the authentic individual, Sartre says, by "nonaccomplice reflection totally escapes the category of alienation."[25] This is because in pure reflection not only do I accept my freedom, "I accept my being-object," as an inevitable part of my human condition. Human reality, Sartre writes, "can and should in authenticity assume the objective transformation of itself and its metamorphosis in destiny."[26] The authentic person is able to accept her objectification precisely because she has by her conversion renounced the God-project. She is not attempting to be in total control of her own being like a *causa sui*.[27] Thus she accepts the fact she is "at risk" in the world of the other, that her exteriorized action and product, not to mention her objectified subjectivity, will be "stolen" by the other. Indeed, because authenticity involves valuing my creativity, and because real creativity must result in something coming to be in the in-itself whose being is independent of its creator, authenticity must entail valuing the ontological objectification of my creative act in Being.

However, this does not mean that the authentic person accepts every subsequent kind of objectification beyond these inevitable ontological ones. Quite the contrary, for Sartre states that authenticity involves fighting against all oppression that is an obstacle to the coming of the city of ends. The latter is his term for the ideal society, one in which oppression is overcome because each individual takes both the other and himself as his end. It involves, Sartre says, "the conversion of all," "an absolute conversion to intersubjectivity," which he calls the *Apocalypse*. In this "city" no one has the goal of being God and hence of using or destroying others to attain that impossible objective. Each recognizes and wills his own freedom and that of others as well.[28]

Unfortunately Sartre does not describe his ideal in any detail, in fact he says that we cannot do so from our present alienated and oppressed situation. He does label it *socialism* and say it includes: "suppression of classes and of the State," "emancipation of the proletariat," and "radical transformation of the economy."[29] He also repeatedly exhorts authentic human beings to act concretely by taking full account of their historical situation. The "era of freedom," he states, will be achieved only through concrete means that take their cue from the present oppressive obstacles to be overcome; for example, the capitalist class structure. Accordingly, he advises us to go to the oppressed themselves and discover from them the particular violence that we must together change in order to bring the utopian ideal closer. At the present time, he writes "the realm of ends is precisely in the preparation for the realm of ends."[30] Still, the *Cahiers* provides no concrete analysis of post-World War II conditions or particular suggestions or plans of action for postwar Europe. (I mention this because one of his later criticisms of the *Cahiers* was that is was too abstract and lacked an adequate sense of history.)

But even if authenticity means to will each other as ends in a classless society, a question remains as to just how it is possible given Sartre's epistemology. As we have seen, Sartre believes that each subject inevitably reifies others, and not even pure reflection can overcome this. Thus he says, "Whoever would take in particular his freedom or that of others for an end would substantialize it." (The same point is made in *Being and Nothingness*.)[31]

One suggestion he makes is that a subject not focus explictly on the other's freedom and make it her direct object, but rather make it "an object of a lateral realization" by focusing on a particular project of the other. (This is like the we-subject relation in *Being and Nothingness*.) For example, if we direct our attention to assisting another to obtain food, employment, or, more important, power over the economic forces of society, we "in the bargain" aid him in becoming more free for we help open a wider field of possibilities for him and we do not in the process objectify or substantialize him.[32]

However, a more significant response by Sartre in the *Cahiers* comes in his discussion of comprehension, a notion only briefly mentioned in *Being and Nothingness*.[33] Unlike knowledge, which inevitably objectifies the other, comprehension is described as a sympathetic conscious "engagement" in the other's freedom. And the authentic individual not only comprehends, but *adopts,* the other's free project as his own by willing its realization. Though I thereby become in a sense an instrument of his freedom, "I am not transcended [objectified] by it since I freely adopt his end," Sartre says. Likewise the other that I help is not objectified by me. For he "discovers by comprehension and passion the other's [i.e., my] freedom, but he does not discover it as a transcended-object opposed to his freedom, nor as a transcendence-subject which conceals it [he] discovers it at the heart of his freedom as a free movement of accompaniment toward his ends."[34]

Sartre even calls this nonobjectifying intersubjective relationship *authentic love* and claims that it results in a certain kind of unity, "a certain type of interpenetration of freedoms." He insists that this is not an ontological fusion of subjects nor a merging of them into a superindividual reality. On the other hand, the individuals involved are not totally distinct either. They constitute he says, a "synthetic totality," "a unity of diversity," for there is a "sameness" among them that overcomes radical separation and otherness: "otherness is recaptured by unity, even though it always remains ontically." This is a unity on the plane of will and action, he explains, that is not possible on the plane of being.[35]

One of the interesting results of this unity or sameness is a radical modification of whatever objectivity we still possess when we are looked at or known by the other. Not even the pure reflection of the authentic person can eliminate the fact that I am still at times an object for him. But, Sartre claims, this is not a "troubling objectivity" if he also comprehends and wills my freedom. If he does so, I am positively enriched by the new dimension of being he gives me. Sartre's words here in the *Notebooks* are a significant advance over the degrading concept of objectivity that pervaded the "ontology before conversion" set forth in *Being and Nothingness,*

> by the other I become object. And this is not a mishap or peril in itself. It only becomes so if the Other refuses to see in me also a freedom. If, on the contrary, he makes me exist as existing freedom as well as being-object, ... he enriches the world and myself, he gives a meaning to my existence in addition to the subjective meaning I myself give it.[36]

In other words, because the other wills both my freedom and my facticity, his objectification of me is not oppressive or a degradation, nor a source of conflict, but an enrichment of my existence. For it is not objectification caused by an alien other, but by one who is the "same" as me, one who is united to me in love. (I should point out that although its portrayal of objectification and of human relations is extremely negative, *Being and Nothingness* itself does indicate that positive human relationships are possible after the conversion—which it does not intend to discuss).[37]

Of course, even if it is possible to comprehend and will the other as freedom, and at the same time remove the degrading side to objectivity, as Sartre proposes, another question remains that is probably even more important for his moral theory. Even if I *can* do so, why *should* I will the freedom of any human being other than myself? As all values are creations of human freedom for Sartre, no one's freedom has any intrinsic value. If I freely choose to will only my own freedom, it will thereby possess a value that no one else's has. To be sure, Sartre would call me inauthentic, but then authenticity itself has value for me only if I choose it to. The question remains, even if rephrased, why should I choose to be authentic? In my opinion, nowhere in his published work does Sartre offer an adequate answer. This is also the case for the *Cahiers*. The *Notebooks* contain some suggestions as to why the city of ends, the mutual comprehension and willing of freedoms, should be every authentic person's goal, but none are elaborated in fully formed arguments. I will concentrate here on the *Cahiers'* most significant suggestions.

As part of an extended treatment of the call or appeal for help, Sartre appears to offer three reasons why I should will the freedom of others and assist them in achieving their goals:[38]

1. If I refuse to do so by preferring my own freedom and its ends, this implies that in the spirit of seriousness I take my values and goals as unconditional absolutes. Sartre implies that, as no freedom possesses any intrinsic value that would make it superior to any other, all freedoms must be willed equally. (However, as I noted earlier, this implication simply does not follow. By preferring my freedom and goals to others I need not imply that it possesses an objective value. I may simply recognize that *my* freedom is the ultimate source of all my values and thus that if I freely select it over others' the result will be that, by my very choice, it does receive a value that others lack.)

2. Sartre also seems to argue that the natural result of one's comprehension of another is assistance of that other. In a very uncharacteristic statement he maintains that human beings "first of all have the tendency to help someone pursue and realize his end," whatever it may be. The "operative principle" of this initial helpfulness, which is more prevalent than we think, he says, is that "every end is good as future realization of value, until the contrary is proven." Sartre's reasoning here seems to be that, because comprehension itself, as we saw, is a sympathetic engagement in the free project of the other, it naturally (but not inevitably) tends to result in an adoption of this freedom and its project. (Though this reasoning has force, it ultimately rests on a very non-Sartrean notion of the presence of an original natural sympathy in human beings. I have difficulty reconciling such a notion with his repeated position that man initially encounters his fellow human beings as others who objectify and reify him, and that this normally results in alienation of his free subjectivity and its actions and products.)

3. By far the strongest argument is offered by Sartre when he points out that by choosing to help others' freedoms I thereby will that Being be disclosed and given meaning from multiple perspectives. Because each freedom is in its own unique way a creative

source of the world, to aid others' freedoms is in effect to will the maximum creation of meaning. Recall that we noted earlier that the *Cahiers* propose that in pure reflection we choose to value our free creativity in order to justify our existence and its creations and we so choose because our freedom is the source of the meaning and value of our existence and of the world. But, of course, other freedoms also confer meaning and value on my life and world and, if the meaning they confer supports my freedom and its projects, this certainly enriches the solitary justification I have given myself. Though Sartre does not actually say so, I presume that he would agree that my desire for justification is a desire for as much meaning as possible for my life; that is, for as much positive approbation by as many free subjects as possible. If this is the case, then it follows that I should value the free creativity of others from which comes their valuation of me and my world. (Indeed, if I do not value their freedom, their evaluation of me, even if positive, would be meaningless to me.) Furthermore, if I value their freedom and creativity rather than ignore or oppress it, it is far more likely that they will reciprocate with a favorable valuation of me and mine. Most important, Sartre suggests that I want a meaning and justification that comes from those who *freely* choose to affirm me.[39] Recognition from a vassal or slave is worth something, but not nearly as much as authentic love freely given by another free human creator. Thus, I should will the other's freedom and goals so that the meaning she in turn freely gives to me and my world will be favorable and will be from a source that I myself consider signficant.

Let me repeat that this third argument is not found in the *Cahiers* exactly as I have put it together, though its elements seem to be there. I might add that it is present in detail in a marvelous little book by Simone de Beauvoir, published in 1944, *Pyrrhus et Cinéas,* almost universally ignored by Sartre scholars.

CONCLUSION

I will conclude my treatment of the *Cahiers* with a glance at the criticisms Sartre himself later offered of it. No doubt part of the reason he refused to see these two notebooks published in his lifetime was that they were part of a larger whole (ten to twelve notebooks) the rest of which was lost. In addition, the *Cahiers* comprise only the first of three moralities that Sartre worked on and apparently he had difficulties with this initial attempt that led him to abandon it. He eventually referred to it as a "failed attempt,"[40] and specifically criticized it as too abstract (or idealistic) and too individualistic. By the first complaint he meant that this morality failed to adequately take into account human reality's concrete historical situation. It was too removed from the socio-political-economic realities of its time. I have indicated earlier, in my discussion of his notions of authentic creativity and the city of ends, my general agreement with this criticism.

The morality of the *Cahiers* was later considered too individualistic by Sartre inasmuch as at this early stage of his development he viewed individuals and their freedom as radically independent of each other ontologically and psychologically. He later felt that at this time he did not adequately understand the influence of others on what an individual is and can be, even on his very freedom and self-awareness. I personally think this second criticism is too harsh in the light of the *Cahiers'* discussion of the call and the authentic response to it, its admission that objectivity need not be oppressive and that oppression itself is not inevitable and should be overcome, and its treatment of comprehension and authentic love. Certainly, the *Notebooks* offer something of a counterweight to the generally negative, individualistic portrayal of human relationships in *Being and Nothingness*.

Whatever the accuracy of his criticism of this early morality, it in no way implies a wholesale rejection of everything in the *Cahiers*. For Sartre himself stated in interviews toward the end of his life that he was returning to this first morality—enriched by a thorough reconsideration of the ontological intersubjective bond among human beings.[41] In my opinion Sartre never totally abandoned much of the ontology set forth in his early work. The *Notebooks* provide invaluable assistance in interpreting this ontology and its relationship to morality. They show unquestionably that *Being and Nothingness* was never intended to portray the definitive human condition, but rather its state "before conversion." The discussion of authenticity, pure reflection and conversion in these notebooks clearly presents Sartre's alternative to his portrayal of bad faith and accomplice reflection in his phenomenological ontology. Thus they leave no doubt about his responses to the questions he posed at the end of that work about its "ethical implications." The *Cahiers* give no support to those who maintain that nihilism is the inevitable outcome of the positions enunciated in *Being and Nothingness*. For they show that, even in these early years, Sartre's belief was that if persons fully accept their free contingency and all that it entails, they can create a life that overcomes despair and conflict, one in which human beings, united in mutual respect and love, act to justify each other's existence.

9

"Making the Human" in Sartre's Unpublished Dialectical Ethics[1]

Elizabeth A. Bowman and Robert V. Stone

Sartre's *Notes for the 1964 Rome Lecture* begin with the striking sentence: "Our meeting proves that the historical moment has come for socialism to rediscover its ethical structure, or, rather, to unveil it." Sartre made three assaults on the problem of morality. The first, in the late 1940s, a sequel to *Being and Nothingness*,[2] resulted in the recently published *Cahiers pour une morale*[3]—an effort Sartre renounced as a failure.[4] In the middle 1960s he tried again and the *1964 Rome Notes*—an ethical sequel to the *Critique of Dialectical Reason*[5] — were part of the result. Though he declared himself satisfied with this second project,[6] which he never renounced, he set it aside for his work on Flaubert[7] and did not resume it. In the middle 1970s, after his blinding stroke in 1974 reduced him to "writing" with a tape recorder, he planned yet a third effort with the young ex-Maoist, Benny Lévy.[8]

We are concerned here with the "second" or "dialectical" ethics of the mid-1960s, as Sartre variously referred to it.[9] In addition to *Notes for the 1964 Rome Lecture*, there are two other manuscripts in the dialectical ethics: his *Morality and History*[10]—notes for lectures of that title to be given at Cornell University in April 1965—and unorganized notes of 1964 for these lectures. Thanks to several of Sartre's associates, we have photocopies of the three typescripts—totalling 776 pages.[11] The subject matter of the three writings overlap, but there is little repetition.

We shall reconstruct a conception that figures importantly in the *1964 Rome Notes*, the most finished if not the most important of the three

111

writings in dialectical ethics. Sartre was preparing to address a group of European and American left intellectuals at a conference on "Ethics and Society" to be held at the Italian Communist Party's Gramsci Institute.[12] His program was to uncover an ethical structure occluded by Stalinist faith that altering production arrangements would automatically solve all ethical problems—"sending ethics on vacation" as Sartre put it. Yet he also sought to avoid returning to the moral idealism of pre-Marxian socialism. The body of this work is divided into three titled sections: "The Experience of Morality," a phenomenological ontology of everyday social norms; "The Roots of Ethics," a grounding of morality in need that uses the Algerian Revolution as an example; and "The Morality of Praxis and Alienated Moralities," a discussion of the moral problems of revolutionary action. The result is an account whereby "morality has its roots in the exploited classes and in their struggle against the dominant classes." The argument is tightly woven and of the greatest interest. Simone de Beauvoir described the *1964 Rome Notes* as "the culmination of Sartre's ethics."[13]

Our topic will be "humanity" or "the human" or "man" (all interchangeable terms for Sartre) and how this conception functions as an end of conduct without being an ideal or a value. But we shall, with Sartre, back into our subject by analyzing an example: the infanticide of "thalidomide babies" in the Belgian town of Liège in the late 1950s. A sleeping pill, thalidomide, caused severe deformities in newborns — in particular, short, flipperlike limbs — and several mothers responded by killing their offspring and announcing that fact.

In bourgeois society, Sartre remarks, the organic life of children of both the favored and the unfavored classes is not an end but a means. For the unfavored it is a means to the end of work, for the favored to the end of inert reality—inasmuch as even favored children are born to serve the things they inherit. All serve "the system" and all are consequently "subhumans." A world awaits in which the newborn will have two out of three chances of being born to malnourished parents, and the infant who survives will have four out of five chances of belonging to exploited classes. A human future—one in which all newborns have all chances to be fully human—is possible, but it is "impossible" in our era; a fully human future may later become realizable. Within this context, the Liège mothers suffer in anguish a specific moral conflict between the peasant-feudal valorization of organic human life itself, and the bourgeois valorization of the content of human life. The bourgeois "maxim" forbids prolonging any life that is deprived at the start of all the chances of being fully human. But because stopping all such lives would entail humanity's suicide due to the present impossibility of a fully human life—even for the most favored newborn—Sartre concludes that the bourgeois maxim is self-cancelling.[14]

A second reason the bourgeois maxim is impracticable today is that it rests on our defining what a fully human life might be. We cannot do this, Sartre claims. We know only what the fully human person is not: "What he certainly is not *is ourselves*." Although knowing we are sub-human is motive enough to move beyond that condition, such knowledge, Sartre contends, does not positively determine what is needed to be fully human. That determination is the unpredictable end of praxis, not a predictable inference from one's situation.[15] Humanity cannot be conferred upon us by any system, Sartre insists. If we become human it shall be because we will ourselves have made us so, in effect inventing ourselves.

Now because universalizing a maxim in Kant's sense calls for a definite conduct in light of some determinate rule and because the pertinent end here—full humanity—is posited only generally as the negation of the present state of affairs, it follows, according to Sartre, that the act of the Liège mothers is not comprehensible in Kantian terms. More to the point, they intended no exemplary practice, captured in a maxim, to be repeated in similar situations, as Kant requires of acts that conform to the moral law.

Despite failing by the Kantian criterion, Sartre insists the infanticides *were* normative. Kant erred in taking the normative to be restricted to the repeatable. The acts of the Liège mothers lacked the "tranquility" of justification available when one behaves in the light of or in creation of a value. These acts were instead "anguished" because historical; that is, dated and unique. For Sartre, their nonuniversalizable-yet-normative maxim is "I kill my child today so that tomorrow no mother will be tempted to kill hers." This is of course the opposite of the repeatable action given in a maxim that satisfies the categorical imperative. The act's normative character issues from the fact that, though singular, it aimed at *making way for* the universal. In attempting to realize this "unknowable" future human plenitude, the mothers reconnect the polar opposites of good and evil that had been artificially separated by the existing dominant moralities.

If it would be mistaken to ask whether the infanticides are *justified* —because this presupposes some transhistorical moral principle valid in advance of any action, and Sartre persistently denies there are such[16]— we can still ask just how he proposes to account concretely for this normative element in the example. For him, the infanticides were a "revolt" against the present in the name of a yet-to-be-constructed "human future" for all newborns. Against the structuralism then in ascendancy on the Left,[17] Sartre insists that the mothers creatively overcome, and are not merely prisoners of, the conflict between peasant and bourgeois moralities at war within them: "*yes* [Sartre interprets their act as meaning], *human life is an absolute value,* but only as the possibility of realizing in itself and for (and by) others, *integral humanity.*" Medicine *can* avoid such accidents, the infanticides were affirming. But, because this is today technically impossible, Sartre interprets them as demanding just such "a human technology" of the future that greater vigilance in the present can help bring about. In sum, the act of sacrificing the chemically deformed newborns had three dialectical aspects or moments: a revolt against an inhuman technology; a demand for an era when humans will *generally* produce humanity, rather than subhumanity; and, finally, a first practical step in bringing that era about. The normative character of the infanticides therefore lies, for Sartre, not in obeying a rule immanent in contemporary society nor in positing a transcendent and unattainable ideal or value, but in coinciding with history's own movement as struggle for humanity — a transcendent yet attainable future society in which all newborns shall in fact have every chance of enjoying full humanity. This "nonrepetitive" end, which *is* "morality" for Sartre, is native to "unfavored classes." That middle-class women pursue it in this case shows that morality can "penetrate" more privileged strata.

We shall pause over this rich and central notion of making the human, examine its components and roots, situate it in the ethical tradition and in Sartre's *oeuvre,* and examine an objection ot it. First, let us place it among "norms," which Sartre calls "the objects of everyday moral experience."

The human is implicit as an end not only in norms that prescribe a "pure future" where "man is his own product" (as in the Liège cases), but also in "alienated" norms that prescribe a limited future. All imperatives and values are norms under their alienated aspect because in them humanity is vainly posited as attainable only by first repeating some class-divided system.[18] But even actions prescribed in the most rigid of such "alienated moralities" — Sartre's example is the medieval morality of family honor — imply a pure future, humanity. This is because such actions, for example saving honor by battling an opponent, are always "unconditionally possible." This means that such battling is capable of being done even if one dies in the act.

Moralities are "inhuman" when they inveigle agents into freely valorizing an exploitative system over their own pure future. Thus, the pure future, though original, can be "imprisoned" in the limited future, such that "the representation of my freedom is the motive impelling me to effect my fullest alienation." The inhuman here is not humanity's absence, it is rather "a mutilation of humanity giving itself as a value." The human, that is the pure future — life-risking action against the existing exploitative system *itself* — is therefore presupposed in the inhuman, not as an inevitable future event (as posited by official Marxism of the era), but as an inescapable possibility. Sartre's point is that implicit in obeying even the most alienated of everyday imperatives is the possibility of at any time making ourselves human.

So far "making the human" has been characterized largely by what it is not. What can be said positively about this end of conduct? We can distinguish two essential features.

First, autonomous action— "praxis" — if for Sartre central to humanity as an end of conduct. The major normative distinction for the dialectical ethics is not between favored and unfavored classes, but between praxis and the "practico-inert" — the imprint of past praxis upon things, causing that praxis to appear to present agents as natural and permanent.[19] Sartre likens our present situation to that of the Lyon silk workers who rebelled in 1848 with the slogan: "Live working or die fighting." (Indeed, he calls this "the norm of all morality"!) Like them, we know only "that history has no reality except as the unconditional possibility for man to realize himself in his full autonomy; that is, as praxis dissolving the practico-inert in its very bosom in proportion as it produces it. Or, if you prefer, as the praxis of all men in association.[20] *Autonomy,* for Sartre, means producing ourselves through our own action, not merely bringing our action under a norm—even a norm chosen by us. Such self-productive action is autonomous only when (1) direct rather than indirect (i.e., unmediated by interiorized imperatives or values); (2) its intention is recognizable in its end-result; and (3) it is part of a group rather than a serial endeavor.[21]

To briefly explain this last point, contrary to the bourgeois conception of autonomy as predicable only of serialized "private individuals," Sartre says autonomy is elusive precisely "as long as [such agents] will not unite in an autonomous praxis which will submit the world to the fulfillment of needs." In his *Critique of Dialectical Reason* volume 1, of four years earlier, Sartre had argued that group praxis alone is capable of autonomy. Otherwise (given class divisions) the practico-inert will divert the praxes of serialized agents from their several intentions into "counterfinalities"; that is, those unintended but inevitable consequences of an act that frustrate its intended consequences and render it unrecognizable to its agent.[22]

Second, need is the other central feature of this conception. Sartre calls it "the very root of ethics, its gushing forth at the deepest level of materiality." Need, he contends, "is never an alienation," by which we understand him to mean that one is never made subhuman by the mere fact of being needy. On the contrary, satisfaction of need enjoys normative primacy as an end of conduct because "it is by itself adequate justification for its satisfaction." Obviously, thus favoring need undercuts capitalism, for which only "effective demand"—need that happens to be joined to money—is entitled to satisfaction. Need is not a blind *vis a tergo* but a felt lack. Its object is not present. The future arises as the dimension in which the lack may or may not be filled. Initially, need is experienced as the negation of human life: we apprehend our impending death *in* feeling this lack—if it continues unfilled. But, because need is always felt by a *practical* organism, Sartre holds that "need produces elementarily praxis as autonomy." As a power to satisfy needs, praxis thus comes to us from our need-constituted future as an alternative to death. Praxis is productive agency that materially alters the world to satisfy need. Mediating between need and world, praxis negates and reaches beyond the world's present negation of us by fashioning out of the given world a future, integral, satisfied agent. A novelty thereby emerges dialectically; namely, *the human qua humanly made life*. The initial lacking world that threatened us is reconstituted by praxis as an "unconditioned future," a field in which something *ought* to be done, and therefore *can* be done, to meet our needs. In responding to this exigency through group action, the practical agent literally produces himself; that is, *he acts autonomously,* in Sartre's sense.

This convergence of satisfied need and autonomy is significant. Much debate in moral and social philosophy assumes that both cannot be realized at the same time. But for Sartre, the moral "ought" first appears precisely to the practical agent in need: "The root of morality," Sartre contends, "is *in need,* that is to say in the animality of man. It is need which posits man as his own end and praxis as domination of the universe *to be affected through work.*"[23] Making humanity our goal implies no conflict between choosing our satisfaction and choosing our autonomy; on the contrary, autonomy and satisfaction are identical. Usually we aim at humanity *through* systems—which are therefore inherently inhuman just because humanity for them is a mere indirect result. But need unconditionally posits ourselves as directly satisfied through our own collective efforts. In Marx's terms, which Sartre frequently uses, we can be the product of our own labor instead of being merely the product of our product.[24] The "man of need" lacks something. What he lacks is integral humanity or himself as satisfied in the future. But because need thus posits oneself as integral and as having been made so by one's own (part in collective) activity, this end is one with autonomy. For the dialectical ethics, then, self-produced human life *is* autonomy and obeying imperatives is its antithesis.

Now, when our praxis, and hence our need, is blocked by others oppressively confining our unconditional future in a system, "subhumanity" characterizes our oppressor as much as ourselves. Each is bound—the oppressor by interest, the oppressed by raw need—to repeating the hellish system by which they reproduce themselves and their alienation. Humanity, which is "beyond all system" (even socialist ones), will therefore be the end for anyone who is a subhuman. Whereas for Sartre *all* are subhuman in capitalist society, "humanity" is preeminently the end of the "exploited" or "oppressed" or (Sartre's favorite term) "unfavored" classes, as need moves them most directly.

The Algerian Revolution of 1954–1962 is Sartre's example. The colonized come to realize that the true object of their need — themselves as autonomous, satisfied — cannot be attained either by assimilationist acceptance of the sated colonizer as model of the human or by return to a preimperialist Muslim past. After World War II it became clear that a novel future beyond both systems must be produced. Not even paid enough to reproduce their labor power ("superexploitation"), the Algerian masses' alternative to starvation became independence. As with the Liège infanticides, humanity is invented as the only way out of an impossible fix. Of course, in practice "independence" may mean only moving from de jure colony to de facto economic colony. It does not follow that humanity is unattainable, only that praxis is always situated, and that — idealistic humanisms to the contrary notwithstanding — the practico-inert can at best be dissolved as it arises. This is Sartre's "realism." It envisions a kind of permanent revolution submitting all problems as they come up to collective decision. "Humanity" here is neither an a priori moral imperative nor an eternal ideal. It is constructed piece meal in revolutionary praxis as the negation of the negation. It cannot even be known a priori because it is both discovered *and* invented in the act of throwing off one's subhumanity. Though Sartre does not quote Marx, it is clear that this conception of humanity, as a spontaneous creation of liberating struggle, is the *existential* recuperation of Marx's point that "communism is not an . . . *ideal* but the *real* movement which abolishes the present state of things."[25] In the dialectical ethics, this point becomes: "Humanity is the end — unknowable, but graspable as orientation — for a being that defines itself by praxis, that is, for the incomplete and alienated humans that we are."[26] We can make an alienated humanity by obeying imperatives derived from systems, or we can directly make humanity together.

According to Sartre, "revolutionary praxis" — a "meta"-praxis aimed at recovering the ability of *any* praxis to satisfy need — directly gives rise to the human. Thus, we can presently begin making ourselves by taking action against the system that makes us subhuman. Indeed, he holds that we thereby already *partly bring about* the end of humanity; that is, we partly make ourselves. "Humanity" is in this sense attainable now. Because there is no higher end, everything at our disposal is a means to it. If we hold onto life at all costs, we limit our choices of means and, correspondingly, our capacity to overcome our subhumanity. For "pure praxis," which is always revolutionary, there are only two alternatives: either the system is ended or one's life is. In either case one's subhumanity ends and humanity is born.

This conception of "making the human" is a major development that sheds new light on earlier Sartrean projects. Perhaps most important, in it, the early ethics of freedom is married to the dialectic of need in his post-1958 philosophy of history. But we also see in this conception of 1964 a deepening of themes initiated a dozen years earlier in his biographical study *Saint Genet*,[27] and especially in his play, *The Devil and the Good Lord*.[28]

Our reading of this play is informed by *Saint Genet*, whose discussion of Manicheism prefigures and provides a paradigm case of the *1964 Rome Notes'* account of alienated moralities. Manicheism, Sartre claims in *Saint Genet*, is the dominant ideology of our era; it would subsume all human acts and thoughts under the categories of Good and Evil. It is born when "right-thinking men" collectively expell their own negativity by projecting it upon others, thereby constructing the vacant social role of pariah. When an individual like Genet consents to fill the vacancy, he confirms the right-thinkers in their self-definition as Good. But their "Goodness" is strictly speaking reactionary: they are "Good" solely because the other, the pariah, is designated "Evil." In fact, "Good" and "Evil" come to "right-thinking men" from the practico-inert as imperatives to repeat the past and embrace themselves in their socially privileged subhumanity as the model of the human. Living out such Manicheism means artificially sundering *in the same act* both society and that synthesis of Being and Nothingness that is free praxis.[29] To naively pursue "Good" under such circumstances is to be gulled into repeating as "natural" the punishment of an oppressive and exploitative system. Manicheism, like all alienated moralities, thus conceals (and perpetuates) the gap class society opens between the intentions and the objective results of one's actions—a gap that renders the human impossible.

In this situation morality as virtue—being Good by doing Good—is simply "impossible," as Sartre remarks in a major footnote.[30] Genet seems to transcend this impossibility by playing the "loser wins" game; that is, declaring this impossibility as his victory. But for Sartre this glorification of failure is a deficient response to being made a pariah.[31] Genet initially accepts society's definition of him as Evil, imagining he *does* Evil because he *is* Evil. But because wanting Evil ultimately entails doing Evil to Evil, that is betraying Evil, Genet eventually subverts Manicheism. Although this begins "humanity," the results of *Saint Genet* are pessimistic: all morality is impossible. By contrast, in positing the present attainability of the human in the *1964 Rome Notes* Sartre embraces a new Promethean optimism.

In *The Devil and the Good Lord*, we see this optimism. The bastard Goetz, like Genet, is a pariah committed to fulfilling society's definition of him. He chooses in stages Evil, Good, and asceticism before discovering humanity as a way out of an impossible fix. Initially, Goetz thinks destroying is doing Evil; he succeeds only in killing miscellaneous people. By playing "loser wins" he could label this failure a victory. However, Heinrich announces that God wants Good, not Evil, to be impossible. Goetz, tempted to prove on the contrary that Good is possible, switches from devilry to sainthood. In trying to do Good, however, "his" peasants are killed and his ideal community is annihilated. Such contradiction of intentions by accomplishments expresses, and cannot be explained by, Manichean moralism. Goetz protects himself by next ascetically internalizing his Evil project. As in Genet's sainthood, Goetz becomes both judge and judged, high priest and sacrificial lamb, a self-punishment already implicit in doing Evil.

　　Goetz could again play "loser wins" and, by declaring as triumph the impossibility of either Good or Evil, thereby remain inauthentically at the ascetic stage. But Heinrich again interrupts, this time to judge him in God's name. Good, Heinrich contends, is a farce objectively indistinguishable from Evil. Not only does God want Good to be impossible, He also wants "man" to be abject, to be "nothing"[32]— yet He expects all humans, Goetz included, to choose Him. Heinrich thus forces Goetz to choose between accepting an abject subhumanity and starting from nothing to make the human. So Goetz confronts the impasse of alienated morality: either God—"Good" and "Evil"—does exist and the human is forever *impossible*, or God—"Good" and "Evil"—does not exist and there is a possibility of *making* the human.

　　Goetz declares that God does not exist and kills Heinrich. He thereby chooses the human as a project. In terms of the *1964 Rome Notes* Goetz has chosen "the possibility beyond the impossibility" of the human. Goetz's awakenings to the contradiction of his intentions by his accomplishments had compelled him to change course at each stage. Humanity, qua autonomous action, seems to have been made impossible by this God-imposed flaw, this fissure between morality and history. As Goetz determines, however, it is made impossible by other humans like Heinrich. Having failed as a bastard in doing Evil and as a saint in doing Good, Goetz finally recognizes that his underlying problem—loss of autonomous agency—issues from his own acceptance of an objective origin for the all-too-human categories of Good and Evil. Reconciled to their human origin, Goetz makes a radical conversion, for the first time, to what the *1964 Rome Notes* call "a revolutionary morality" whereby recovery of autonomous agency takes moral precedence over merely doing Good. Goetz is now free to undertake the daily endeavor of human liberation. Consenting to do what is called "Evil" *in order to* bring about so-called "Good," he joins Nasty's peasant army in their struggle against their subhumanity. He uses means that directly contribute to the goal of full humanity, regardless of whether they are categorized as "Good" or

"Evil." By thus rejoining Good with Evil, he reincorporates the negativity of human freedom into pure praxis. The play concludes with Goetz's comment: "The reign of the human begins with a murder."[33]

The *1964 Rome Notes* provide a structure for grasping Goetz's profound moral-political conversion. Instead of seeking salvation in repetition of alienated norms, one can act upon a new or pure norm: the possibility of agency as direct self-production. This "radical conversion" issues from pursuing the negative side of Manicheism, the will to Evil, to its logical consequences — a liberation whose possibility is already inscribed in alienated morality.

We have reviewed the context, features, origins, and methodology of "making the human," and we have seen its usefullness in illuminating two of Sartre's published works. We shall conclude by briefly situating this conception in the tradition and entertaining an objection to it.

Given the central modern tradition of ethics, it is noteworthy that Sartre joins autonomy and satisfaction in his conception of the human. Contrary to the Reformation-Enlightenment view, according to which need (sometimes renamed *inclination*) is opposed to autonomous doing of duty (and hence to the normative dimension itself), Sartre holds that the normative enters our experience precisely through actions aimed at satisfying need. The unconditional exigency of the normative arises, he holds, from the unconditional exigency with which needs press for satisfaction. For the modern tradition, autonomy usually requires either suspending or mastering all needs — suppressing "the internal worker" as Sartre puts it[34] — for the sake of a higher rationality. In asserting need's moral primacy and its identity with autonomy, the dialectical ethics moves radically beyond this tradition.

Sartre's conception is pertinent to the debate within Marxism over morals. One current strain of Marxism treats *all* morality as mere ideological apology for the status quo,[35] another acknowledges and assimilates the normative force in Marx's own call for workers' self-liberation.[36] Sartre's conception may help resolve the tension: for him the human is posited not only in pure, but in alienated moralities, though in the latter case as a "deformed" image, an ideology imposed by a system. Thus for Sartre, the normative embraces *both* ideological apologetics and workers' self-liberation. No fatal voluntarism is implied in saying of needy subhumans that they can choose between alienated and revolutionary morality, between colluding in their own oppression and resisting, or between renewing their subhumanity and inventing humanity. The human— "the pure norm of morality" — is the terrain of both mystification and liberation and hence of the choice between them.

Let us stand back from the conception of making the human developed up to this point and entertain the following objection: "Making the human" is an incoherent end of conduct, the objection might run, because the future it envisions is composed of incompatible elements. On the one hand, this future is "pure" and "unconditioned," a sort of clean slate on which acts spontaneously stipulate the nature of humanity. On the other hand, because satisfying needs is a central part of that pure future and because such satisfaction requires definite social and productive procedures, the future projected is in fact not "pure" at all but determined in broad outline and hence conditioned. Not everything will satisfy human needs. Moreover, if satisfying human needs has "primacy," there can be *only* conditioned futures. So if "making the human" implies a future combining of these elements, then it does not make sense, because they are mutually exclusive.

We offer the following defense on this point:

1. An "unconditioned future" is one in which obedience to a norm requires the agent to undertake some action. Such an action presents itself to him as "unconditionally possible" in that it *can be done regardless of conditions*. Now this is not the same as saying that it can be done successfully. Nor, more to the point, does it mean that the future doing of it will not also be "conditioned" in the sense of being *situated*, because that doing will unfold at a particular place and time, with certain means available, and so on. Sartre has consistently held that all actions take place within a determinate situation and constitute a (sometimes deficient) transcendence of it.[37] Thus, there is no incompatibility here: actions can be both "unconditioned" and "conditioned" in the preceding senses of these words, because those senses are not mutually exclusive. A medieval knight must "save the family honor." This act is given as "unconditionally possible" and the future in which it unfolds is "pure." Saving honor does not require vanquishing the opponent, on the contrary it may require the offended knight's death should he find himself weaponless and tempted to flee. Victoriously or not, the required act *can* be accomplished, but obviously only within the *conditions* of the situation, that is, with the given weaponry, armor, and terrain. So self-determination, a pure future, is possible on the basis of determinate conditions; indeed, it is possible only on their basis.

2. Sartre nowhere denies that satisfying human needs requires definite production procedures, but he calls these procedures only "partly foreseeable" as they will be determined by collective decision. Needs for Sartre contain no imprint of their satisfying object; we cannot specify a priori which objects are and are not

needed. The "serious" view is that there is such an imprint, an essentialism of needs that Sartre criticizes in both its left and right formulations.[38] Even pervasive fundamental needs — the kind Sartre is speaking of in these *Notes*—do not externally *determine* human conduct like Freudian instincts because, in pointing beyond the present toward a future satisfaction, they partake of human freedom itself.[39] That humans can themselves collectively meet all their needs is their unconditioned possibility, and because this end is the "synthesis" of the means to it, neither are those means determined a priori. They are invented; but inventing them *is* inventing the end.

3. The objection fails to appreciate the novelty of Sartre's thesis. It assumes, and does not prove, that satisfying needs and autonomous action are incompatible. Sartre holds that satisfaction of needs has moral primacy over other ends, but for him, and perhaps even for Marx,[40] satisfying needs does not historically precede autonomous action. Nor does one found the other logically. They are in fact *identical*: to satisfy needs directly and to make the human autonomously are one and the same. This is what Sartre means when he says morality is not merely a part of the social superstructure but is already present in the productive infrastructure, indeed, in the very act of reaching for a tool.[41] If he is correct in describing autonomous action as the collectively determined productive processes by which humanity literally produces itself, then there is no incompatibility between the conditioned and the pure futures.

Additional questions might find their answers in Sartre's companion work, *Morality and History*. Although these notes for the Cornell lectures do not directly deepen the *Rome Notes'* treatment of making the human, they undertake to: expand the phenomenology and nomenclature of the normative, show how such phenomena arise in interaction with the practico-inert, demonstrate the effective force of morality in history, show how the agent becomes subject of interiority in order to act upon the unconditional possibility implicit in fulfilling norms, and bring out "the ethical paradox" of praxis as basis of both alienation in imperatives and liberation beyond them. Clearly, though, the *1964 Rome Notes'* account of making the human already signals a novel and powerful approach to moral phenomena. We are certain that the *Notes for the 1964 Rome Lecture* and *Morality and History* will renew discussion of the foundations of morality when they appear, which we hope will be soon.

10

*Woman's Experience: Renaming the Dialectic of
Desire and Recognition*

Patricia J. Mills

To discuss "the question of woman" is to make an axial turn, as
Adorno would say. For centuries the question has been posed as "the
woman question"—a question asked by man about woman. Today "the
question of woman" is a question of self-understanding posed by woman
herself. I would suggest that it is a question concerning the dialectic of
desire and recognition in terms of female identity formation that is most
clearly illuminated through the work of Horkheimer, Adorno, and
Marcuse, the first generation theorists of the Frankfurt School of critical
theory.

The two versions of memory in critical theory that articulate the significance of suffering and happiness in human experience have a parallel
in the two civilizing myths used to explicate the dialectic of desire and
recognition. For Horkheimer and Adorno there is an account of the development of self-consciousness provided by Homer's *Odyssey* that reveals reconciliation as mythic deception. Homer's tale of alienation, ad-
venture, and "return" is appropriated in the *Dialectic of Enlightenment*
to show the limits of recognition rooted in a process of the subjugation of
desire through self-denial, suffering, and pain; the ego is defeated by a desire for self-preservation. In contrast to this depiction, Freud's myth of
the primal horde is reappropriated by Marcuse in *Eros and Civilization* to
elucidate the dialectic of desire as familial and incestuous: in it the memory of happiness remains tied to the memory of the mother. Marcuse ar-

123

gues for a dialectical regression based on the Oedipal desire for gratification; he argues for a "return" to the mother through the sexual craving
for mother as woman. In reclaiming these two myths the Frankfurt
School appropriates Freud and simultaneously moves behind Marx to an
appreciation of Hegel. Both Hegel and Freud analyze the relation between civilization and desire by focusing on desire as fundamental to the
formation of self-consciousness: both trace the formation of self-consciousness as an ontogenetic (individual) and phylogenetic (historical)
process.

The attempt by critical theorists to appropriate both Freud and Hegel raises a fundamental question concerning the arena of ego development. Although the mechanism is desire in each case, for Freud incestuous desire within the family is the mechanism that, in direct
intersubjective relations with others, is repressed and forms the basis for
civilized life. For Hegel, desire (initially for objects and then for others)
within civil society is central to the development of self-consciousness,
and the master-slave dialectic prepares the way for intersubjective recognition through object creating as productive activity. Freud's intersubjective situation is not the same as Hegel's understanding of intersubjectivity, which requires that two consciousnesses *first* confront each other
as equals. The inequality of the master-slavee dialectic is a *result*, not the
ground, of the encounter. The slave, by risking death for recognition, enters the dialectic as an equal who has the potential to recognize the Other.
The master and slave positions are not predetermined—only in the conflict does one person concede and *become* the slave. Conversely, the par-
ent-child relationship *begins* as a relationship of inequality: the Freudian
child does not enter the Oedipal conflict as an equal Other able to confer
recognition. The parent and child are predetermined in their relation. The
question that must be addressed is whether ego development is a process
that occurs primarily in the family, as Freud claims, or between strangers
in civil society, as Hegel claims. We must further ask if there is a relation
between the two arenas that has yet to be articulated.

Paul Ricoeur attempts a comprehensive analysis of the relation between the Hegelian and Freudian models of ego development. The civilizing project that these models share and that gives credence to the attempt
to unite them is explicitly outlined in his book *Freud and Philosophy: An
Essay on Interpretation*.[1] Most important for Ricoeur is the relation between desire and intersubjectivity that is rooted in the infinite character
of desire in both theories. He attempts to place Hegel's master-slave dialectic at the heart of the Oedipal complex by claiming that in both accounts the division of consciousness is nonegalitarian. But this entire
project is grounded in Ricoeur's confusing an intersubjective situation
with Hegel's concept of intersubjectivity. In a later work, "Fatherhood:

From Phantasm to Symbol," Ricoeur examines in detail the concept of fatherhood (as differentiated from simple biological fatherhood).[2] He acknowledges some of the difficulties that emerge from the confusion concerning intersubjectivity in his earlier work, and he sets limitations on the attempt to place the Hegelian reduplication of consciousness at the center of the Freudian drama. Here, he places the master-slave dialectic *after* the Oedipal drama as the content of the latency period in Freud. However, this comes up against the same dilemma that is at the heart of the appropriation of Hegel and Freud by critical theory: which is the arena of ego development, the family or civil society? What is the relation between the two arenas? Ricoeur's later essay changes the basis of the original analysis by introducing a contractual relation into the father-son relationship; this effort introduces a relation of civil society into the familial tie and negates his earlier analysis.

In critical theory, Freud's theory of ego development within the family is seen as crucial, but the Hegelian paradigm of intersubjectivity, as a relation between free and equal Others outside the family, is the goal. The exact nature of the intersection between the two theories is not clearly defined. The implicit assumption is that no difficulty is created by using the two models together to describe ego development. This assumption is certainly questionable and becomes even more so when we focus on the differing processes of ego development for males and females within the two accounts.

Hegel and Freud both try to develop a theory that gives full due to the nonidentity of nature and history, but in each case the theory collapses back into identity due to an internal failure to come to grips with woman's experience. In Hegel, natural immediacy is overreached by the dialectic of recognition in society: nature collapses into history. In Freud, society or history is ultimately reduced to nature because sexual difference is collapsed into a signal polarity: the absence or presence of a penis. For both, female experience is a moment in male experience, which is reckoned to be fully human.

Woman is confined to the family in the thought of Hegel and Freud and consequently is confined to the family in critical theory's appropriation of their civilizing myths. She is not an equal Other; she does not attain intersubjective recognition or an independent ego. Her desire remains subject to and defined by male desire. Woman is dominated both by *recognizing* her difference and confining it within the family and by *denying* this difference within civil society. This situation raises the Hegelian problem of the relation between identity and nonidentity, which is central to the tradition of critical theory.

Although the theorists of the Frankfurt School acknowledge woman's domination, there are significant oversights and assumptions concerning woman in their appropriation of the civilizing myths of Odysseus and the primal horde. Both myths fail to understand woman as an historical actor and fail to analyze the specificity of the female psyche in terms of desire and recognition. They focus on the relations between men and on the relations between man and woman from the perspective of the man. Neither addresses the relations between women or the relations between woman and man from woman's perspective. The reappropriation of the myth of Odysseus by Horkheimer and Adorno is concerned primarily with male recognition; female desire is discussed only insofar as it is seen as promiscuous heterosexual desire that represents the domination of nature. For this reason their use of the myth distorts an understanding of woman's desire and her role in the process of recognition. The myth of the primal horde as reappropriated by Marcuse is a myth of male homoerotic bonding in which the question of female desire is simply ignored. Female difference is written out of the myth, although the heterosexual couple is seen to be in conflict with the male group. The insufficiencies that result from the omission of woman's self-experience of desire reveal that neither of the civilizing myths can be universalized; the myth of male desire and the myth of male recognition cannot be used to describe female desire or female recognition.

MOTHERHOOD AND SISTERHOOD RECONSIDERED

The analysis of the dialectic of desire and recognition is central to critical theory, both as theory and as emancipatory project. The omission and distortion of woman's experience of this dialectic calls for a consideration of woman's *self*-experience of desire and a consideration of the relations between women. Feminists have pointed to the importance of sisterhood and motherhood as female-female relationships. However, within the contemporary woman's liberation movement there has been a shift from a focus on sisterhood to a focus on motherhood.[3] My analysis of critical theory makes it possible to understand this shift in a way that gives new form to the diverse strains of feminist theory. This task is achieved by clarifying and making explicit what has remained, up to now, only implicit in the feminist project: within the feminist critique of society, female desire, as a desiring relation between daughter and mother, is seen as the origin or ground of woman's experience, whereas recognition between women (sisterhood) is the goal or telos.

Woman's desire has been written out of the modern emancipatory project of critical theory except as promiscuous heterosexual desire that has been dominated by man to establish heterosexual monogamy. Because of woman's identification with nature as immediacy, her desire, considered from the male perspective, has been seen as not fixed on a specific (love) object. From a feminist perspective, the motive for marriage and monogamy is revealed as the male need to contain female desire, to limit desire that is not merely a moment of male experience. Woman's active heterosexual desire is feared by man, as we see in the myth of Medea. As active lover and mother, as a combination of vagina and womb, woman is perceived as deadly by the male. She is then psychically castrated in a form of reversal: fearing castration, man proceeds to "castrate" woman. This psychic castration is accompanied by social domination through rape and incest. The male assertion of power that is not manifested in direct, overt violence against woman turns into a male assertion of power through the threat of withdrawal from the male-female union. Through this analysis patriarchy is revealed as a system of domination in which woman's desire is repressed, distorted, and denied fulfillment.

To understand woman's self-experience of desire, feminists have turned to an analysis of the development of the female psyche in terms of the Freudian and neo-Freudian accounts of incestuous desire. However, the reconsideration of female desire from the daughter's perspective has not led to a new theory of heterosexual desire insofar as the focus in on female relations (daughter-mother); the father is either ignored or remains understood as the "third" Other who enters the mother-infant dyad to break the oceanic consciousness. No *new* account of the daughter-father relation, based on the transformed understanding of the pre-Oedipal relation between daughter and mother is articulated. This psychoanalytic analysis culminates in a reconsideration of homosexual desire as female-female desire, but it leaves in place the Freudian account in which female heterosexual desire can be interpreted only as a desire for the authoritarian father. There is, in this respect, no basis for a redefinition of heterosexual *desire* from the daughter's perspective as a female-male relation. Woman's desire for man, as anything more than the desire for domination, remains to be named.[4]

Within contemporary feminist theory, therefore, a paradigm shift occurs in the search for a libidinal union that cannot be broken. The concern with female desire from the mother's perspective has become a concern with a desire for the Other as a desire for the child. More important, though not always explicit, this is a desire for the child as daughter. Thus, the pre-Oedipal mother-daughter relation has been substituted for the man-woman love relation and becomes the basis for an analysis of lesbian desire. From the perspective of the daughter, this paradigm replaces the focus on the triad of mother, infant, father, within the Oedipal drama.

The analyses of desire as familial incestuous desire between daughter and mother are analyses of desire within a relation of inequality, a vertical relation in which who is daughter and who is mother is predetermined. Yet this vertical relation of inequality has become the implicit ground for the analysis of relations of equality, of horizontal relations between women. Where the analysis of woman's desire has become a reclaiming of motherhood, it is important to remember that women came together in the movement not as mothers but as sisters. Hence, the telos of the movement has been, and remains, sisterhood as recognition.

Sisterhood is a concept taken from the private realm, the realm of the family; it was initially used in the public world by the women's liberation movement to *challenge* the family by pointing to the fact that women have a bond that, like the family, is a bond not chosen.[5] From a shared social position of domination women created a solidarity and a vision of liberation through consciousness-raising. Sisterhood, in this context, represents a relation of mutual recognition outside the family, civil society, and the state. It is not a true blood-tie; it is not mediated by a process of object creating; and it is not based on each woman being free and equal. Sisterhood represents, rather, a nondesiring relation of recognition between women that focuses on the political potential of a universal community of women.[6]

This concept of sisterhood has been confronted with the desiring relationship between women—lesbianism—not only as a personal preference but as a political choice. It moves the concern with the nondesiring relationship between all women to the desiring relationship between two women. The eroticization of feminism by lesbianism assumes that free intersubjective relations require an Other that is the "same as" the self and obscures the problem of nonidentity. Freedom of sexual choice is a necessary part of feminism; nevertheless, lesbianism is not the same as feminism, and the analysis of lesbian desire is not a comprehensive response to the question of female desire.

From this brief consideration of the relation between motherhood and sisterhood we find that a feminist inquiry into the development of the female psyche, in terms of the dialectic of desire and recognition, is a necessary corrective to the male focus and perspective on the relations between men and the relations between man and woman. However, significant problems in feminist theory emerge with greater clarity when they are seen within the context of critical theory's analysis of the civilizing process.

First, the relation between motherhood and sisterhood implies the same problem made explicit in my analysis of critical theory concerning the arena of ego development. The attempt to ground the dialectic of desire and recognition in both Freud and Hegel remains problematic in critical theory. No passage from Freud to Hegel has been articulated that can ground the enterprise of using Freud's theory of desire as a theory of origin and Hegel's theory of intersubjectivity as the goal. This problem has an analogue in the feminist enterprise in which motherhood as a theory of desire is the origin and sisterhood as a theory of intersubjectivity is the goal.[7] Is female identity formation or ego development a process that occurs primarily in the vertical incestuous relations of the family, as Freud claims, or is it a process that occurs in horizontal relations between strangers in the public world, as Hegel claims? Or, is there a relation between these two accounts that has yet to be articulated? The "answers" to these questions imply different political strategies centering either on the family or civil society as the arena for social change. Put somewhat simplistically, they become either a politics of childhood socialization or a politics of equal opportunity–affirmative action.

Second, we find that nothing new is said about heterosexuality as a relation of female *desire* insofar as the Freudian father as the "third" remains in place or is simply ignored. Feminist theory often attempts to ground the intersubjective recognition of the Other in "identity"; that is, the intersubjective paradigm is based on female-female relations as daughter-mother or sister-sister relations. Within this analysis relations between females are the basis for defining and restructuring female-male relations. The desiring relationship between women is seen as important to the development of the group, but there is no analysis of the relation between homosexuality and heterosexuality. If the group is founded on homoerotic desire between women, how does that relate to the question of heterosexual desire and the formation of the heterosexual group? The underlying question in feminist theory emerges here as the underlying question in critical theory: the question of the relation between identity and nonidentity in the dialectic of desire and recognition.

IDENTITY, NONIDENTITY, AND NAMING

To criticize the domination of nature, Marcuse retains the Hegelian notion of identity-in-difference as a utopian vision. The redemptive vision of the reconciliation of nature and history, subject and object, provides the motive and ground for his critique. Thus, he supports the movement for women's liberation in a political sense, but can provide no theoretical conception of woman as historical actor based on the specificity of the female psyche. Woman remains a "principle" or representation of liberation:

> Patriarchal society has created a female image, a female counterforce, which may still become one of the grave-diggers of patriarchal society. In this sense too, the woman holds the promise of lib-

eration. It is the woman who, in Delacroix' painting, holding the flag of the revolution, leads the people on the barricades. She wears no uniform; her breasts are bare, and her beautiful face shows no trace of violence.[8]

The reconciliation of identity and nonidentity in Marcuse's work ends by romanticizing woman and swallowing her into an identitarian framework that privileges male experience.

The Hegelian problem of the relation between identity and non-identity is central to the feminist project of creating a free and equal society. Theorists search for a form of intersubjective recognition (a relation between self and Other) that allows for concrete differences but does not, on that account, render women unequal. However, as Adorno has shown, Hegel's notion of reconciliation presents us with a false identity of subject and object, nature and history, particular and universal. The ontological and epistemic claims of universality and the reconciliation with the Other have always meant the domination of the particular. Adorno argues that identity philosophy is animated by a hostility to the Other and necessarily excludes certain forms of experience; feminists argue that woman has been "feared, idealized, and negated" as the Other: she has been defined as different from man, and as the ontological principle of difference itself, to be dominated and excluded.[9] Thus, a theory of nonidentity is a prerequisite for a theory of women's liberation. Adorno presents such a theory in *Negative Dialectics* where the non-identity of nature and history, subject and object, particular and universal, does not mean an absolute dualism but a dialectic whose "reconciliation" avoids the annihilation of the Other: "The reconciled condition would not be the philosophical imperialism of annexing the alien [the Other]. Instead, its happiness would lie in the fact that the alien, in the proximity it is granted, remains what is distant and different, beyond the heterogeneous and beyond that which is one's own."[10] Here, the recognition of nonidentity, which would allow for the rescue of woman as Other, as the particular, the different not to be dominated, seems most firmly grounded. Whereas he formulates a critique of abstract equality ("equality in which differences perish secretly serves to promote inequality"[11]), he also rejects direct access to difference, which would simply confine woman to her "own" sphere ("The illusion of taking direct hold of the Many would be a mimetic regression . . . a recoil into mythology"[12]).

For Adorno access to the nonidentical comes indirectly through the construction of "constellations." These constellations are philosophical "texts" that are not constructed arbitrarily but juxtapose concepts around the object such that no single concept is identical with the object.

"Properly written texts are like spiders' webs: tight, concentric, transparent, well-spun and firm" in which the object, the concrete particular, is interpreted through its many representations.[13] It is an infinity caught in the web of everyday life, and Adorno's metaphor recalls woman's weaving as an act of creation.

The question that emerges here is how the concern with conceptual thought, which relies on such an indirect route to the nonidentical (the weaving of constellations), relates to the project of the historical actor. Adorno rejects the notion that there is a given class or group that is necessarily the source of liberation: any group can be ideologically corrupted under the prevailing system of domination, no matter how much its social location may point it to truth. In his schema the domination of woman has created her as a symptom and representation of distorted nature. As actor she would either be destructively regressive by emphasizing her difference, which is the "scar tissue" of repressed nature, or she would be dominating, by accepting the identitarian logic that *denies* her difference in the name of abstract equality. The social component of Adorno's theory is removed from the realm of politics to the aesthetic realm. It is in autonomous works of art that a liberatory moment is to be found: "It is now virtually in art alone that suffering can still find its own voice, consolation, without immediately being betrayed by it."[14] Thus, Adorno's negative dialectics saves nonidentity by severing it from a historical actor.

What emerges from my critique is a polarity between the work of Adorno and the work of Marcuse, which is a polarity between the project of universal reconciliation and a defense of nonidentity. Whereas the nonidentical is secured in the philosophy of Adorno, the historical project of liberation is lost: it is removed to the aesthetic realm, severed from the realm of action. But where the historical project of liberation is secured in the work of Marcuse, the philosophical grounding in Hegelian reconciliation undermines the project of women's liberation. In the last analysis, Marcuse and Adorno both fail to provide an analysis for woman as historical actor. In their recognition and denial of woman's experience of difference they reduplicate the problem of woman's domination. For Marcuse the vision of woman formed within the family is the ideal of civil society insofar as woman represents freedom for man. This solution, however, rests on woman's confinement to the family in order to secure her difference. According to Adorno woman represents not freedom but the domination of nature. Her representation as "Other" secures her domination such that any attempt to act only reinforces domination, either through the emphasis on difference or its denial.

From woman's perspective it is simply not enough to be the aesthetic or psychic representation of liberation for man (Marcuse) or to be the conceptual representation of the domination of nature (Adorno). The dilemma for woman is that she must find herself as historical actor without denying her nonidentity; this dilemma lies at the heart of critical theory. It calls for a move beyond the polarity of Marcuse and Adorno to understand the dialectic of civilization as a dialectic of identity and nonidentity. Thus, we find an initial basis for renewing the critique of the domination of nature within critical theory by reflecting on and articulating woman's experience.

Woman's experience is to be found in the traces of memory reformed through the process of "naming." Although naming can never capture the immediacy of the experience — what is articulated is never *the same as* the experience — we must name experience to understand it; without naming, experience is simply passed through or endured. When concepts are linked to experience so that experience is understood and not just undergone, we are led to a rediscovery of philosophy as critical theory. The importance of naming is underscored by Horkheimer: "Philosophy is the conscious effort to knit all our knowledge and insight into a linguistic structure in which things are called by their right names."[15] The philosophical articulation of domination rescues the particular, the nonidentical, and initiates a vision of liberation and historical action: it gives an image to the name that transcends the present to become the future.

The civilizing myths that explicate the philosophical ground of critical theory attempt to name woman's experience, and yet they remain silent on the relations between women and on woman's self-experience of desire. In this way, woman's experience is distorted and denied. Woman's voicelessness reveals reification as silencing. By giving voice to her experience, by naming the unnamed for herself, woman challenges the reification of the name through silence, and she initiates the political project.

The effort to find the right names for woman's experience has been central to the women's liberation movement from the very beginning. In the 1960s woman's domination was described as "the problem with no name."[16] Soon after this, radical women began meeting in consciousness-raising groups to articulate and analyze the ubiquitous but amorphous sense of male domination. Along with the new political practice of naming one's experience for oneself, the traces of memory reformed through naming created feminist theories of domination and liberation. The feminist critique of the male-female relations embedded in a patriarchal-capitalist system of power expresses theories of liberation in the naming of motherhood and sisterhood. But the feminist theories of motherhood and sisterhood are only partial: they focus on relations between women and woman's self-experience of desire. As vital as this new naming is to the political project of liberation, it may become reified into new mythologies that themselves obscure aspects of woman's experience; mythologies are names subjected to a reified universal that obstructs the necessity to *name for oneself*.

Critical theory has occluded woman's experience within its analysis of the domination of nature; nevertheless, within this tradition the attempt to find the right names, to name woman's self-experience, is not an arbitrary intrusion but a self-reflective turn called forth by the theory itself. Critical theory discloses and dismantles reified universals by tracing them back to the experiences from which they arise; simultaneously, it carries partial insights forward into a universal reflection. As the contemporary expression of the critical and civilizing task of philosophy, critical theory makes it possible for woman to rename her experience of motherhood and sisterhood as experiences of the dialectic of desire and recognition within the civilizing process.[17]

11

Literature and Philosophy at the Crossroads: Proustian Subjects

Christie McDonald

Besides, with these particular feelings, there is always something in us that strives to give them a larger truth, that is to say, to absorb them in a more general feeling, common to the whole of humanity, with which individuals and the suffering that they cause us are merely a means to enable us to communicate. What mixed a certain pleasure with my pain was that I knew it to be a tiny part of universal love.[1]

Marcel Proust, *The Guermantes' Way*

Marcel Proust wrote in a notebook: "At bottom, my philosophy, like all true philosophy, comes down to justifying, to reconstructing what is."[2] As the articulation of a set of systematic laws, speculative thought might appear as a discourse different from or independent of the narrative, but, as it turns out in *Remembrance of Things Past*, nothing could be less sure than the status of these generalities when it comes to their *working through* in the literary text. At issue was not so much whether Proust should write a novel or a philosophical study, but whether he would be a writer at all, and if so, what that meant.

The paths of literature and philosophy, as ways of making the world intelligible and giving meaning to it, like the paths that diverge in the beginning of the novel (Swann's way, Guermantes' way), so intertwine as to become almost inseparable. Still, Proust's project can be initially divided in two: on the one hand, it is the mediator of rational thought, in the

135

search for a total work and a totalizing theory of the artistic subject; on the other, it is the operator of linguistic movements that, without being classifiable as simply irrational, escape the logic of rationality. Totality here as elsewhere corresponds to a principle of intelligibility. This identification of thought with the totality means, for Proust, that the total work emerges only as it produces and contains its own genesis: recounting throughout the novel the discovery of his vocation as a writer, the narrator ends at the very moment that he is about to undertake the writing of the book. The question is whether the last pages recapitulate the book that we have just read or begin a book not yet—and yet always already— written.

Proust transformed the philosophical question, How does one think? into the question, How can one write? or How can one become a writer? He was able to break from the traditional opposition between perception and reflection and understood that the dualisms of binary thought could or had to be superseded by some kind of revolution in thought. He sensed—as Freud and Saussure were to be discovering simultaneously —that psychology and language, as consequences of philosophical positions, would be the focal domains of thought. Thought would no longer be perceptive or reflexive, conscious or unconscious, direct or oblique. Proust would call the intertwinings of these dualities "The rectification of an oblique interior discourse."[3]

"Every day, I set less store on intellect," he writes in the *Contre Sainte Beuve* in a sketch of what is to become *Remembrance of Things Past*. Next to the truth of art and the revelations that it brings, the truths of intelligence flatten and pale. At the point in his life where he finds himself, when his hours are numbered (isn't that our common lot? he queries), it is perhaps frivolous to embark upon an intellectual work. The paradox is that if the intelligence is inferior to affect, *only* the intelligence can comprehend and reveal this inferiority.

The initial project as it is set out in the Preface to *Contre Sainte Beuve* is totalizing. It is a project in which the end as the beginning must lead to the completion of understanding and meaning in writing; that is, a hermeneutic project. The preface contains a sketch of the experiences of involuntary memory that will be described in the first volume, juxtaposed with those that will be found in the closing volume. The initial project in four parts was finished in 1914; over the next several years a proliferation of writing was to bring the addition of interim volumes—*The Guermantes Way,* Parts I and II; *Cities of the Plain,* Parts I and II; *The Captive, The Fugitive (Albertine disparue)*—in which the original structure no longer dominated. It was as though an autonomous grafting operation was to take place from "within," much of it concerning the narrator, Marcel, whose love for and jealousy of Albertine comes to occupy the center of the later volumes of the novel. The marked shift in tone and inability to enclose meaning into the frame of the original project suggests that the text first posits its own conditions of possibility only to then exceed them in a compelling way. By changing the project from within, a new "style" emerges in the search for the self in time, and displaces art as absolute truth through sequences leading to associations and repetitions without end.

The "two sides" of Proust's work can be grasped through the critical methods that have been deployed to analyze the novel. Criticism written prior to the mid-1960s tended to concentrate on the phenomenology of mind inscribed in the project. During the period of structuralism within literary studies, in the 1960s and 1970s, critics tended to concentrate on the rhetorical structures and strictly semiological aspects of the work. The phenomenological studies dealt with the concept of the object (Poulet, Richard) and analyzed consciousness and time in relation to it. The rhetorical studies (Genette) traced and described linguistic patterns at varying levels. Through the explicit displacement of rhetoric as traditionally conceived, these latter sought to establish a form of systematization that ensured, at a linguistic level, the coherence of the work of art. Schematically described, neither of these approaches is alone adequate to the model of Proust's project: the phenomenological studies risked leaving aside, as a central preoccupation, the problem of language and the unconscious, whereas rhetorical studies left the problem of the subject and the truth of the structure unquestioned. Deleuze would be able to write that *Remembrace of Things Past* was not about memory and time but truth and signification.

This project diverges from the phenomenological, the structuralist and the so-called post-structuralist models, yet attempts to combine aspects from each: that is, to examine the constitution of the writing subject as that which both furthers and questions the tradition that puts reason at the center. For Proust, the notion of totality and the concept of an englobing theory were at some level synonymous. The narrator's quest for the general laws of love and emotion frame — in rational terms — the desire to write. The work of art, as a coherent project, is a philosophical endeavor that tolerates neither lack nor excess. To discover what the nature of the creative and creating subject is, in its essence, constitutes the goal of the quest. Although Proust was searching consciously for the invariant, the generalities of art and life, these were not the grounding for his project.

Proust writes: "A work in which there are theories is like an object which still has its pricetag on it" (vol. 3, p. 916).[4] The conceptual use of language in the writing of theory, with its already formed expressions, leaves no place for what is unique and constitutes "the temptation for the writer to write intellectual works—[which is] a gross impropriety." The narrator continues, and this is what is crucial, that "a writer reasons, that is to say he goes astray, only when he has not the strength to force himself to make an impression pass through all the successive states which culminate in its fixation, its expression" (vol. 3, p. 916). This is because "the impression is for the writer what the experiment is for the scientist, with the difference that in the scientist the work of the intelligence precedes the experiment and in the writer it comes after the impression" (vol. 3, p. 914).[5] The force of moving through these states is the strength of the work, and this force, both exhausting and inexhaustible, establishes another space: the space of the theoretical. By this, I mean an economy of thinking that seeks through intelligence to grasp the laws that determine thought and necessitate a practice that can only come out of a principle of individuation in the affect.

As a writer attempting to make sense out of impressions, Proust addresses the relationship of the singular idiom to the universal in what may seem to be the ongoing quarrel between poetry and philosophy; that is, on the one hand, the separation of poetic effort into the achievement of individual or self-creation by the recognition of contingency, and, on the other, the traditional philosophic effort to achieve universality by the transcendence of contingency — the epiphanic moments of involuntary memory and metaphor. Generalities may be consoling: "to think in terms of general truths, to write, is for the writer a wholesome and necessary function the fulfillment of which makes him happy, it does for him what is done for men of a more physical nature by exercise, perspiration, baths." But clearly that does not suffice for the description of creation as an innovative process.

Innovation must link together private obsession with public need, in which the great work shows the line between weakness and strength. It must show the line between use of a language that is familiar and universal and production of a "new" language that, although initially unfamiliar and idiosyncratic, strikes one as inevitable. Our Proustian impressions abound; they are now integrated as part of our ordinary experience. More important, what Proust shows is not so much literature as the successor to philosophy, that is, as the place in which one can find anecdotal illustrations of abstract principles, but literature as the place where traditional philosophy is de-formed and then re-formed otherwise.

The polarities of essence and contingency can be initially located in the oppositions between art and life, man and woman. Art presupposes a revelation and the unveiling of essence, whereas life presents itself in an endless sequence of changing perceptions. Nowhere does this become more apparent and yet inscrutable than in the suffering of the jealous lover. In the Proustian scheme, love requires a *final truth* to come through the other; yet this truth can be attained only through the interpretation of signs. The "essence" of love is presumed to be found in the hermeneutic work of meaning because the truth of woman remains captive, dreamed in the form of a physical possession: a pure and "immaterial" love.[6]

For this reason, contingency is reserved for women in the original project: woman is the second born. In the very first pages of the novel, a woman is born from a dream:

> Sometimes, too, as Eve was created from a rib of Adam, a woman would be born during my sleep from some strain in the position of my thighs. Conceived from the pleasure I was on the point of consummating, she it was, I imagined, who offered me that pleasure. My body, conscious that its own warmth was permeating hers, would strive to become one with her, and I would awake. The rest of humanity seemed very remote in comparison with this woman whose company I had left but a moment ago; my cheek still warm from her kiss, my body ached beneath the weight of hers. If, as would sometimes happen, she had the features of some woman whom I had known in waking hours, I would abandon myself altogether to the sole quest of her, like people who set out on a journey to see with their eyes some city of their desire, and imagine that one can taste in reality what has charmed one's fancy. And then, gradually, the memory of her would dissolve and vanish, until I had forgotten the girl of my dream. (vol. 1, pp. 4–5)[7]

Who is Eve? She is the one, second in the order, who, in aspiring to knowledge of good and evil, transgresses the law of God. As Adam's double, Marcel becomes the possibility of becoming woman already within man (the "devenir-femme de l'homme"). Later, Marcel again identifies himself with a suffering and weakened Adam: "The mist, from the moment of my awakening, had made of me, instead of the centrifugal being which one is on fine days, a man turned in on himself, longing for the chimney corner and the shared bed, a shivering Adam in quest of a sedentary Eve, in this different world" (vol. 2, p. 358).[8] Like an androgynous amputee, Marcel feels the painful lack in his body of the one whom he no longer possesses in his waking life: "O mighty attitudes of Man and Woman, in which there seeks to be united, in the innocence of the world's first days with the humility of clay, what the Creation made separate, in which Eve is astonished and submissive before Man by whose side she awakens, as he himself, alone still, before God who has fashioned him!"[9]

The narrator discovers secondariness as the condition of primacy through the relation of man to woman. As the search for an absolute, love constitutes an effort to identify the singular being with a region of the transcendent being. Just as he will use the intelligence to prove its own inferiority, so love will prove that discovery of the truth of self cannot come through the feminine other. This is why the question of truth, and particularly the truth of and for woman, as the presumed object of love and secondary being, is not just a question in passing; it is the condition of being itself. Abandoning hope in love, the narrator finds that only reminiscence can restore the identity of the subject to himself in time and provide the basis for the creative act. Even before this final discovery that occurs in *Time Regained* the opposition between man and woman, as a product of binary thought, ceases to be pertinent.

The shifting sense of truth and the corresponding lack of definition in gender is revealed initially through the discourse of women's lying. The lover and ultimate wife of Proust's character, Swann, in *Swann's Way* is Odette. Into every fabricated story she tells Swann, she inserts a small, innocuous — but also incongruous — truth. This little true fact, which is meant to authenticate the fiction by anchoring it in "reality," ends up by having the opposite effect: it betrays her. No matter how true the fact, it is like excess material that detaches itself from the logic of the fiction and draws a line between truth and falsity: the recourse to truth, intended to authenticate the lie, marks its difference within the story. What Swann understands when his mistress Odette lies to him is not only that she is lying, but that there is a truth hidden behind the lie. The hermeneutics of Odette's discourse places truth in a hierarchy in which falsehood can be demarcated from it.

Albertine lies differently. Plausibility is what counts for her, and truth emerges only involuntarily: her ruses are impenetrable. As the seeker of truth and as her lover, Marcel is devastated over and over by his inability to "know" Albertine totally and hence to possess her "truth." Always in search of meaning, Marcel learns from Albertine not to look further for "true life and thought [. . .]" in the direct statements that others "voluntarily supply him with." His jealousy is as insatiable as her ruses are inexorable: both are without end. She lies by "inadequacy, omission . . . or from a surfeit of petty details" (vol. 3, p. 179). Proust writes that jealousy is born before the intellect, that intelligence cannot understand it and is incapable of consoling man. The necessity of possession as that which is not partial, but total and exclusive makes love possible; yet this very condition makes love impossible from its inception. Proust writes: "How many persons, cities, roads jealousy makes us eager thus to know! It is a thirst for knowledge thanks to which, with regard to various isolated points, we end up by acquiring every possible notion in turn except the one that we require" (vol. 3, pp. 80–81).[10]

According to this postulate, love is a function of what is unknown and beyond reach: one can love only the one in whom there is something inaccessible. One can love only a person who by definition one does not possess.[11] In this view, happiness and suffering are irremediably linked and lead to an untenable epistemological position, because all love, like all theory, states the narrator, "requires to be stated as a whole" (vol. 1, p. 606).[12] This means that even though love demands totality, it can emerge and subsist only if some little part remains to be conquered.[13]

The unknown person, so goes the hypothesis and the dream, is Beauty it- or herself. It is the sequence of incomplete perceptions, in fortuitous encounters, that suggest the possibility of finding the essence of beauty. Behind each person who makes us suffer a divinity hovers, of which the person is only a fragmentary reflection. This divinity is called the Idea (in the Platonic tradition) and causes our joy or suffering.[14] Love seeks thus to attach itself not to what is fragmentary and heterogeneous, or to what in the other changes, but love attaches itself rather to the reconstruction of that invisible person behind the perceived object, the one who puts everything into motion.[15] A paradox emerges, however: although the desire and the need for knowledge are congenital in love, it is imperative *not to understand,* because events related to love seem to be guided by magic rather than rational law.

Nevertheless, the formal structures governing the functioning of love may be described. The language of love has not been created for any specific creature; born in the past, as it will again be born in the future, the language of love has served and will again serve for others. Woman is not unique; she is "innumerable." She may be evoked by a million "elements" of tenderness, existing in fragmentary segments, but love is always greater than any single woman, in that it envelops but cannot know her. The totality of love emerges neither from the sum of successive "selves" remembered, nor from the sum of successive women that the narrator has loved; it emerges from the portion of the soul that is more durable than the selves that die successively in us. This part of the soul must detach itself in order to restore the generality and the comprehension of love to a sense of universal spirit.[16]

In a fragment isolated from the rest of the narration in the *Time Regained* the narrator writes: "Jealousy is a good recruiting-sergeant who, when there is a gap in our picture, goes out into the street and brings us in the desirable woman who was needed to fill it"[17] (vol. 3, p. 955). There follows a vignette on the rhythm, the functioning, and the provenance of jealousy. The narrator produces a hypothesis according to which jealousy comes about to fill a gap, and this can happen just about any time or place by chance, though it need not come from the usual gestures: a look, or anecdote, or retroflection. The example evoked comes out of a directory, called *Tout-Paris* for Paris and for the country *l'Annuaire des Chateaux.* The narrator writes

We had heard, for instance, but without paying any attention, some beauty to whom we have become indifferent say that she would have to go and see her sister for a few days in Pas-de-Calais, near Dunkirk; we had also, in the past, but again without paying any attention, thought that perhaps the beauty had formerly been pursued by Monsieur E——, whom she had ceased to see, since she had ceased to go to the bar where she used to meet him. (vol. 3, p. 956)

The narrator assumes that the sister is a housemaid. This presupposition brings several possibilities to mind. First, suppose that Monsieur E—had "taken her sister into his employment as a housemaid" to please the young woman. The narrator reasons that, as the two no longer see each other at the usual bar, this means that they meet at his home, either in Paris or in the Pas-de-Calais; he concludes that they cannot do without one another. However, if this hypothesis were false, it would not be inconceivable. The second hypothesis is that he had recommended "her sister to a brother of his who lives all the year round in the Pas-de-Calais" simply "wanting to help her." In this case, one would conclude that the two are indifferent to one another. Or, a third possibility, what if the sister were not a housemaid near Dunkirk or anywhere else but simply had relations in the Pas-de-Calais?

Our anguish of the first moment gives way before these last hypotheses, which calm our jealousy. But it makes no difference. Jealousy, concealed between the leaves of the *Annuaire des Châteaux,* came at the right moment, and now the space that stood empty in our canvas is filled to abundance. And the whole composition takes shape, thanks to the presence, evoked by jealousy, of the beauty of whom already we are no longer jealous and whom we no longer love. (vol. 3, pp. 956–957).[18]

Jealousy repeats the ternary structure that characterizes love: from indifference one passes to desire, which, when calmed once again, becomes indifference. The sad conclusion is that there is no desire without anxiety and no certainty without indifference.

Proust attached a great importance to this scene; he wrote in the margins: "capitalissisme." Not only is the scene framed by a beginning and an end, intended as an exemplary experience of jealousy, but it shows how unimportant the place of any "real" woman is in the structure of desire.[19]

They are, these women, a product of our temperament, an image, an inverted projection, a negative of our sensibility. So that a novelist might, in relating the life of his hero, describe his successive love-affairs in almost exactly similar terms, and thereby give the impression not that he was repeating himself but that he was creating, since an artificial novelty is never so effective as a repetition that manages to suggest a fresh truth. (vol. 1, p. 955)[20]

It is not the woman who is important, but *the means of knowing her*. Woman is only an accomplice to the structure. The whole scene is neatly finished as though the narrator could remain a spectator, as though the objectivity of the presentation could exemplify a general theory. Within the narrative structure, however, such a speculative endeavor is doomed because the subject, here the narrator, can never take his distance: he plays a role and, whether or not he likes it, is a part within the whole.

Here the ability to know truth becomes coextensive with the question of Albertine's sexual nature and habits. Marcel becomes obsessed with the question of whether she is or is not a lesbian. The reconstitution of the so-called facts of her life test the limits of perception, recollection, and the ability of the narrator to find truth. The inability to achieve (perceive) sexual definition of the other, here in Albertine, proves to be intolerable. The description of homosexual love constantly confirms, through examples, the general laws that govern Proustian love; that is, all love is torture in the failure of the subject to know the other. In the well-known scene of the first volume entitled "Montjouvain," the narrator watches a seduction scene between two women: Mlle. Vinteuil, daughter of the composer whose work is to become the quintessential model of the work of art, and her friend. Mlle. Vinteuil is described as having both male and female traits, in the same way that later on the Baron de Charlus will remind the narrator of a woman in the encounter with his lover, Jupien.[21] Albertine assumes all the roles: mother, father, child, and tender mistress. It becomes formally impossible to fix the positions of the characters in this scene. The narrator is driven wild in later volumes because he remains unsure whether the friend was or was not Albertine, even though he himself was present at the scene.

As long as homosexuality is considered a deviation from the norm, knowledge of Albertine's sexual mores, as the revelation of a meaning, preserves sexual difference in a hierarchy. But such a hierarchy cannot be maintained. Homosexuality is the truth of love, not because it divides normal from abnormal but because it is a function of a law of inversion that runs throughout the novel. There is an initial hermaphroditic state that becomes "the law of the diverging series,"[22] laying the basis for all future inversions and reversals:

> In this respect the race of inverts, who readily link themselves with the ancient East or the golden age of Greece, might be traced back further still, to those experimental epochs in which there existed

neither dioecious plants [having male reproductive organs in one individual and female in another] nor monosexual animals, to that initial hermaphroditism of which certain rudiments of male organs in
the anatomy of women and of female organs in that of men seem still
to preserve the trace. (vol. 2, p. 653)[23]

In hermaphroditism, one can see the superimposition of contraries, Man
and Woman, as defined biologically.

Hermaphroditism and androgyny come to signify, not the completion of the whole through the union of its parts, but indeterminacy as it is
inscribed in binary thinking. Sexual inversion is the most fundamental
type of the inversion, but the social world operates according to the same
principle. Swann, for example, moves from an aristocratic to a bourgeois
language, and Roland Barthes points out that neither of the polarities in
the seesawing back and forth between opposites is more true than the
other.[24]

Within nineteenth-century thought, two types of androgyny can be
traced that succeed each other and are confused: androgyny as synthesis
and totality (theorized by F. von Baader and present in the works of Mich-
elet, Balzac, and Wagner), and androgyny as it becomes the central figure
within the arts and literature (from Swinburne, Peladan to G. Moreau and
S. Georg) as ambiguity, hesitating between the two poles of erotic and sa-
tanic provocation. Proust's work straddles the dominant patterns of two
centuries: the nineteenth century in which fragmentary thought was to be
subsumed into the notion of a totality and the twentieth century in which
the notion of the thinking subject and totality were to encounter resistance and become effects of an irreparable division. The questioning of
the relationship between man and woman, masculine and feminine, in the
narration of love as an unending process of interpretation, would be indications of that change.

What the narrator "learns" through his experience of love and jealousy of women (and women can learn with women as well as men with
men) is that the abandoment of love, in the search for truth and the creative process (writing the book we have just read and yet will never read),
does not lead to the completion of meaning in art. For life is a book already written within, and the narrator will be tortured both by his inability to grasp truth—through the infinite truths of woman (here Albertine)
—and his insatiable desire to write *his* book of the self. Shortly before the
end of the novel (or was it from the beginning?) he decides that it is with
"her" that he would create his total work of art. The alternative between
life and art collapses, not only in the passage from memory to art, but because, as the narrator writes, "As there is no knowledge, one might almost say that there is no jealousy, save of oneself" (vol. 3, pp. 392–393).[25]

12

Philosophy Becomes Autobiography: The Development of the Self in the Writings of Simone de Beauvoir

Jo-Ann Pilardi

INTRODUCTION

This essay on the development of the self in Simone de Beauvoir's writings is concerned with her notion of the self in the directly philosophical writings as compared with her presentation of self in the autobiographical writings. The major difficulty with such a project is that Beauvoir, as an existentialist or existential-phenomenologist, is part of a tradition that almost never discusses the "self" by that term. When the term is discussed, it is for the purpose of denying that it exists, affirming that it, the self, *is not*.

Beauvoir's notion of the self has been a difficult one to develop, because she herself does not methodically develop or argue for any concept of the self; the idea of the self she used in *The Ethics of Ambiguity* and elsewhere is derived from the more elaborate idea developed by Jean-Paul Sartre.

The Sartre-Beauvoir connection poses particular difficulty for the scholar because of the personal relationship of the two principals. It is well known that she and Sartre discussed ideas together continuously and that they read and edited each other's writing before it went into print.

The Beauvoir-Sartre mutual influence may be unique in certain ways, but it sharply reveals many of the problems that have haunted and will eternally haunt scholarship, problems by now familiar to the contemporary philosophical-critical landscape. We have the problems of (1) authorship and originality (i.e., intellectual inheritance, ancestry, inspiration, and ownership); (2) the displacement or acknowledgment of influences of patriarchs like Nietzsche, Freud, Husserl, Heidegger, and now Derrida (who has been criticized for too minor an acknowledgment of his own philosophical ancestry) and (3) "purity," of the word and of the doctrine. This last difficulty was faced by Sartre (toward Husserl, in *The Transcendence of the Ego*), Merleau-Ponty (toward Sartre's phenomenology, in "Sartre and Ultra-Bolshevism" in *The Adventures of the Dialectic*), and Simone de Beauvoir (toward Merleau-Ponty's "fake" Sartrism, in her essay, "Merleau-Ponty et le pseudo-sartrisme").

THE SARTREAN ANALYSIS OF CONSCIOUSNESS

For the early Sartrean school of existential phenomenology, the definition of the self is tricky. Simply stated, if one claims that the self, that is the "true self," is immediate, prereflective consciousness, the self does not exist because immediate consciousness is an emptiness, a nothingness. If we say that the self is what is distilled by a reflective consciousness, the self would be seen as a past self, as in autobiography. The self, then, would not exist, as it would exist no longer. The future self, insofar as it is an ideal project, would exist as a "not yet." Thus, it does not exist either.

In Sartrean terms, therefore, the autobiographer presents two types of self. The past self is that person being described both through events that "happened" to her and through her own past behavior: choices, statements, and actions of all sorts. In addition, the narrative voice of the autobiographer is also a self, an abiding presence that may intrude into the story to comment upon it. Beauvoir's third volume of autobiography, *Force of Circumstance*, provides an example of this narrative voice: "In Madrid, I could not find my past ... here, the thread of time had been mended, but it was not my time, mine had been broken, forever."[1] Beauvoir the narrator, writing this circa 1963, tells us of an experience in 1944 in which she could not find her own past, the "self" that had preceded her there by several years (1931) but that no longer existed, because of drastic changes in her "self." The narrator is that presence, that narrating-consciousness-1963, watching that remembered-consciousness-1944, which revisited Madrid and watched the earlier-consciousness-1931, the original visitor to Madrid. This system may continue in complication as new volumes of an autobiography are published with introductions that comment on previous volumes, or with commentary in the text that also comments on previous volumes. (Beauvoir herself did this.) The narrative presence is the immediate consciousness of the writer: a consciousness by definition empty in and of itself but that gains its content from the objects it encounters. In the case of the autobiographer, the object, chosen for its immediate consciousness, is the person's own past experience, her past "self." For the purposes of this chapter, then, *self* may mean either the "for-itself" of consciousness (the self as nothingness) or the ego (the substantial self, the remembered or reflected-on self).

THE ETHICS OF AMBIGUITY

In *The Ethics of Ambiguity,* published in 1947, Beauvoir's intent is to go beyond the Sartrean ontology of *Being and Nothingness,* using its categories to create an ethics. As in Sartre, the for-itself is characterized here by nothingness. Another way of defining nothingness, which is especially relevant to an ethics, is as freedom, for "to will freedom and to will to disclose being are one and the same choice."[2] The for-itself is free, that is, is defined in its core as freedom, because it is nothing and therefore is not determined. In choosing and pursuing its future projects as well as in choosing to reflect on the past and create a past "self," the for-itself becomes more than what it was; it transcends or surpasses itself; each goal achieved or failed becomes a new point of departure for a new surpassing and for a new moment of the self.

THE SECOND SEX

The notion of the self in *The Second Sex* in some respects follows closely to that within *The Ethics of Ambiguity,* but there are important additions. The for-itself is a free, surpassing, transcendent being — a subjectivity that exists through projects and that is distinguished from being-in-itself. This being-for-itself, a subject, is an individual and as such is sovereign, autonomous, and unique.

The fundamental problem posed in *The Second Sex* touches directly on the issue of the for-itself; woman, being human, is a subject. She is being-for-itself. Thus, she is sovereign, a unique individual, and she carries the "essential" quality that all subjectivity carries. Her being is freedom in the mode of negativity, in the mode of transcending. But woman's situation makes her "inessential," because the for-itself has been automatically divided according to gender. In the language of *The Ethics of Ambiguity,* the freedom of the for-itself has been abridged, and facticity has been encouraged by "parties of oppression" who maintain woman in a perpetual situation of oppression. Woman, being human, is a subject:

that is, a free and autonomous existent with the ability to make choices. Yet this transcendence in woman is burdened with a situation that requires her to be a nonsubject, a nonautonomous existent: "The drama of woman lies in this conflict between the fundamental aspirations of every subject — who always regards itself (*se pose*) as the essential — and the compulsions of a situation in which she is the inessential. How can a human being in woman's situation attain fulfillment?"[3] That is, how can a for-itself that is forced to be a nonintentional being, an in-itself, a nonsubject, survive? What kind of a self does a self have that is a for-itself perpetually demeaned to the status of an in-itself?

In an important article carried in *Feminist Studies,* French scholar Michèle Le Doeuff claims that, to use existentialism in *The Second Sex,* Beauvoir had to overcome certain aspects of it that were limitations to her project.[4] *The Second Sex* is a book that details the oppression of women, placing great emphasis on the situation and condition of women. Thus, she ran the risk of being accused of validating the theory of determinism that runs counter to the existentialist notion of the human being, particularly the early form of Sartrean existentialism; "man is free, man is freedom," Sartre had written in "Existentialism Is a Humanism," in 1946.[5] Her analysis insists on the enforced condition of immanence, or facticity, to women by "man the subject." By claiming that such conditions exist and that they are part of a situation of coercion external to women's own choices, Beauvoir shifts the weight of the subjectivity of the female toward the pole of determinism. In so doing, as Le Doeuff points out, she greatly weakens the existentialist ontology that she herself continues to call upon throughout the book.[6]

The simplicity of the distinction between the for-itself and the in-itself in *The Ethics of Ambiguity* becomes greatly complicated in *The Second Sex.* Beauvoir, moving on from Sartrean existentialism with the help of Hegel's and Levi-Strauss's ideas, uncovers a "plot" in all history, one might say, to objectify a for-itself — woman. Unlike members of other oppressed groups, women under the situation of patriarchy have been systematically forced into being objects. They have been forced into "the brutish life" of things and relegated to immanence not transcendence, the being of the *en-soi,* not the *pour-soi.*[7]

"MERLEAU-PONTY AND PSEUDO-SARTRISM"

Several years later, in a 1955 essay, "Merleau-Ponty et le pseudo-sartrisme," Beauvoir categorically rejected Merleau-Ponty's reading of Sartrean philosophy, a reading that Beauvoir labeled a "flagrant" falsification.[8] The long article, never translated into English and cursorily discussed by the English-speaking commentators who mention it, provides her clearest remarks on the self.[9]

The title of the essay is formed from a word-play on Merleau-Ponty's piece, "Sartre et l'ultra-bolchevisme," Chapter 5 in Merleau-Ponty's *Les Aventures de la dialectique,* also published in 1955. *Les Aventures de la dialectique* was Merleau-Ponty's critique of the U.S.S.R. and the role assigned to the Communist Party. "Sartre et l'ultra-bolchevisme" constituted a public attack on Sartre by the former de facto political editor of *LTM* and Sartre's and Beauvoir's long-time friend and colleague.[10] Merleau-Ponty's piece, in its turn, was "provoked" by the publication of Sartre's work, *Les Communistes et la paix.*[11] Beauvoir tells us that Merleau-Ponty's attack on Sartre served the extreme Right, so that her defense was political as well as philosophical in motivation.[12]

Pseudo-Sartrism is a "philosophy of the subject"; that is, a philosophy that mistakenly equates "consciousness" with "subject" and that emphasizes the importance of the subject over the world and others. "True Sartrism," on the other hand, is a philosophy of consciousness, not of the subject. Pseudo-Sartrism assumes that there is a sense given or imposed on things by a decree of consciousness and that the world and the things of the world hold no meaning other than what consciousness provides to them. In addition, it holds the existence of the Other as unimportant, because the Other is seen as just another object under the "gaze" of the subject.

Merleau-Ponty had claimed that Sartre thought that the subject was exactly what it thought itself to be; in other words, as subject, one held a mastery, a sovereignty, over reality (the world), rather than a partnership with it. When she refutes this belief, Beauvoir insists that, for Sartre, the subject is not within consciousness but an object to it: "transcendent" and not a "transcendental." The subject, then, is an object that can be surpassed or transcended through the freedom of consciousness. One is "stuck" with one's consciousness but not with one's subjectivity and not with one's self.

Beauvoir calls on Sartre's phrase "the circuit of selfness" to continue her explanation of true Sartrism: [13] there is in the Sartrean ontology a reciprocal conditioning of the world and myself *(le moi);* "without the world, no selfness, no person; without selfness, without the person, no world."[14] In calling attention to the importance of this circuit, Beauvoir points out how, in a number of ways, in a number of texts, Sartre's notion of consciousness holds that consciousness is surpassed by "the menacing and sumptuous opacity" of the world. It does not maintain that consciousness has mastery over or "surpasses" the world.[15]

According to Beauvoir, Sartre had insisted that the for-itself is necessary to the world but is not constitutive of meaning. Sartre's famous example of the gaze (*le regard*) is only one way he claimed that we encounter the Other, that is, through such a confrontation that shocks each individual, the "I" and the "Other." But Sartre never claimed that the gaze, the relationship of *"je"* and *"l'Autre,"* exhausts the possible ways of encountering the Other.

In this piece Beauvoir claims that Merleau-Ponty set up a straw man in his attack on Sartre. He and Sartre agree — as does she, we can assume — on the secondary importance of the *subject* (its nonoriginary nature), on the equal status of the world and consciousness, and on the notion that the world and not consciousness produces meaning. Thus it was "with a useless good sense" that Merleau-Ponty pointed all of this out to "correct" him, when he attacked Sartre.[16]

BEAUVOIR'S AUTOBIOGRAPHY

The second part of this project, a comparison of Beauvoir's notion of the self with the self as presented in her autobiographies, is interesting because of the questions it raises. The obvious question to be explored is whether a particular thinker narrates her own life by means of the philosophical vocabulary and ideas she has developed or defended. This could be framed as a question about consistency: does the thinker envision her life in the same terms and under the same principles in which she envisions human life in general, or does she judge it by the standards she claims to value philosophically, that is, ethically, aesthetically, or politically? But we *might* want to view this question — mistakenly — as one of authenticity. We could ask not simply whether she carried out her philosophical vision, or remembered it when she turned to the autobiographical page, but if she really believed it enough to formulate her own life within her own philosophy. How deep did the philosophy go? This question, although probably the more interesting one, is unfortunately the less answerable of the two, because it questions the author's internal psychic structure, which is no more accessible to the author than to anyone else.

I will view consistency here directly on the level of the text. Consistency between the philosophy and the autobiography simply tells us how the writer chose to *write* about the life she lived. No judgments will be made above and beyond the level of the text as to the writer's own internal psychic condition, existential authenticity, or moral integrity.

The second question this project raises concerns the connection of gender to philosophy. Beauvoir, a woman, produced in *The Second Sex* a text of major theoretical importance to the feminist movement. She is the only example of a French existentialist who wrote a copious autobiography and the only one who wrote feminist theory. My questions become then, specifically: (1) what is such a thinker's conception of the self? (2) how did such a thinker choose to narrate her own self, to present her self? and (3) was there any apparent change after the writing of the feminist work, *The Second Sex,* either in the notion of the self or in her presentation of her own self?

In studying autobiography (Beauvoir's, in this case) we are clearly studying two aspects. First, we look at the "announced content," that is, her personal history in terms of family, economic condition, life experiences, work, and so on. But we are also studying how the writer *chose* to make herself public — to present herself. Any work of history is a selective retelling of the past; certain things are mentioned; others are not. This reality holds true in autobiography, biography, and in history per se, especially public history. Thus, the study of autobiography is an ideal locus from which to study the practice of writing; it also is an ideal locus from which one can explode the notion of the objectivity of any narration of events, whether it is called "history," "biography," or "autobiography."

Written over a period of sixteen years, Beauvoir's autobiography — that is, the four volumes, *Memoirs of a Dutiful Daughter, The Prime of Life, Force of Circumstance,* and *All Said and Done* (of which I'm considering only the first two in this paper) — forms a very large body of work, nearly 2200 pages in the original French: one of the longest autobiographies in any language by a woman, as one recent commentator stated.[17]

When we look at the specific content of Beauvoir's autobiography to question whether she as narrator presents her self as she philosophized the self to be, the two notions of self mentioned earlier must be included. They are (1) the existentialist-phenomenological notion of the self inherited from Husserl and Sartre and used in *The Ethics of Ambiguity,* that is, the self as a for-itself that is free, has projects, is a nothingness, and performs as a subjectivity by making choices; and (2) Beauvoir's "feminist notion of the self" (what I call the "gendered self"), that is, a substantial self based on the condition of woman with a new emphasis on facticity and situation (this notion was developed in *The Second Sex*). In this more empiricist notion of the self, Simone de Beauvoir parts with the most extreme forms of her existentialism to "radically historicize the self."[18]

The tone of the first volume, *Memoirs of a Dutiful Daughter,* is often ironic, a feature more than one reader has commented on. The reader is made to understand that the narrator takes a certain distance from the protagonist; that distance is marked sometimes by amusement — an almost comedic detachment — and often by impatience or smugness, that is, in general a critical attitude.[19] Even the book's title points to this ironic detachment: *Mémoires d'une jeune fille rangée*. The title of the work is an announcement of a genre; these are "memoirs." But it is impersonal; no name is given; this is not *The Autobiography of . . .* or *Memoirs of Simone de Beauvoir* but of *"une jeune fille,"* a young girl. The English translator used the word "daughter," whereas a more literal translation of the French title would have been *Memoirs of A Dutiful*—or *Steady*—(or *Ordered, Well-Brought Up*) *Young Girl. Rangée* can even mean "ranked," and, in another context, "pitched," as in a "pitched battle," a meaning that is suitable at many places in this text.

When we relate the formal philosophy of Beauvoir to the autobiography, we are relating it to the narrator, not to the past self; that is, not the child Simone, but the narrator's description (which is often ironic), selection, and judgment of the protagonist, the child Simone. The subject, the past, historical Simone, like the content of a dream, is given only through the narration of the past (the dream); the child Simone is a phantom summoned up only through the voice of the narrator.

In *The Ethics of Ambiguity*, Beauvoir had in effect claimed that human existence is developmental; existents move from "the serious world" of the child in which the world and values are experienced as givens to the contestation of that in adolescence, with perhaps an actual escape from it. We could say that *The Ethics of Ambiguity* offers a kind of genealogy of morals; unlike Nietzsche's *Genealogy of Morals*, however, it does not explain the development of morality vis à vis the human race but rather through the development of the individual. The individual may move from acceptance of the given (as a child) to a challenge of and perhaps escape from the given (as an adolescent) into an adulthood in which her newly achieved freedom may be engaged in a variety of ways, of lesser and then higher ethical value (see Beauvoir's "types" of the human being in *The Ethics of Ambiguity*). The individual may go even to the highest ethical mode of responsibility for others as well as self but always in the acknowledgment of the negativity of the for-itself; that is, its state of nonfixity, tension, and existential struggle.

By the book's title itself, then, as well as by the content, Beauvoir alludes to the contest that characterizes the first volume of her autobiography. The contest is that of Simone as child, young girl, and young woman, against her parents: a self gradually demanding its sovereignty against the "divinities," the adults; that is, accomplishing its freedom against the world of givens. In *The Ethics of Ambiguity* Beauvoir had described the "serious world" of the child as one in which all values are seen as already given, not chosen, and in which adults are like gods: "He [the child] takes them for the divinities which they vainly try to be."[20] This world reveals itself as one of *force* and not benign divinity when the child begins to discover her or his own subjectivity; with this recognition the collapse of the serious world begins.

To compare this book with *Memoirs,* we can recall a passage in which Beauvoir relates her tendency toward tantrums as a child. A perfectly bright and well-liked little girl starts rebelling to the point of hysteria:

> I had fits of rage during which my face turned purple and I would fall to the ground in convulsions. I am three and a half years old . . . I am given a red plum and I begin to peel it. "No," says Mama; and I throw myself howling on the ground . . . I have often wondered what were the causes of these outbursts, and what significance they had. I refused to submit to that intangible *force*: words. The arbitrary nature of the orders and prohibitions against which I beat unavailing fists was to my mind proof of their inconsistency; yesterday I peeled a peach; then why couldn't I peel a plum? I knew myself beaten; but I wouldn't give in. I fought my losing battle to the bitter end . . . I was engulfed in the rising dark of my own helplessness; nothing was left but my naked self (*ma présence nue*) that exploded in prolonged howls and screams.[21] (italics mine.)

In this passage, the serious world described in *The Ethics of Ambiguity,* the child's world in which the adults are divinities, is realized as one of force. With the beginning of the development of the child's subjectivity in the desire to choose for one's self (e.g., to peel a plum), what seemed like givens are exposed as actions of force, as wills of other individuals subjecting the child Simone's will to their own. With the realization that her own will is in contest with another's, her "naked self," that is, the intentional for-itself, emerges, making its own choices, but it does not have the power yet to carry them through. The tantrums, the little battles, were battles of and for the self as for-itself. But these excursions into selfhood were terminated—or sublimated?—about the age of six, when finally Simone metamorphosized into a good little girl for many years. "And so I said goodbye to the independence which I had tried so hard to preserve in my earliest years. For some time, I was to be the docile reflection of my parents' will."[22] On a close reading of the *Memoirs,* we might want to dispute her claim of docility, but in any case, the bulk of *Memoirs* is meant to be a narration of that self which is a "docile reflection" of the will of others, a self not yet able to assume its freedom.

Beauvoir claimed that certain times in the life of an individual are most conducive to the assumption of freedom. Adolescence is such a privileged time. An important passage from *The Ethics of Ambiguity* attests to this belief: "it is adolescence which appears as the moment of moral choice. Freedom is then revealed and he (the adolescent) must decide upon his attitude in the face of it."[23] *Memoirs* ends in 1929 when Beauvoir is twenty-one; it is a year that marks her escape from the fate laid out for her.[24] It also is the year of the death of her best friend Zaza, Elizabeth Mabille. Zaza died the victim of a battle she fought with her proper bourgeois family to marry the man she loved, Merleau-Ponty. One's comrades may fall in battle, underscoring the life and death struggle that freedom entails, its precious and costly nature. The last sentence of *Memoirs* asserts an existential partnership — Simone and Zaza: "we had fought together against the revolting fate that had lain ahead of us . . . "[25] In the Preface of the next volume, *The Prime of Life*, the English translation reads, "What new direction would the course of my life take as a result of this . . . pitched battle that had culminated in victorious release?"[26] Beauvoir the narrator chooses to end these first memoirs with the claim of a battle being fought and won (we will recall, she chooses to use in the book's title the word *rangée* that is descriptive of the protagonist as both embattled and orderly), and she begins her second volume with the reminder that indeed it was a battle—for life, in her case, and to the death, in the case of Zaza. Not all of those who fight against their fate would gain a "victorious release." Having achieved her freedom from "a revolting fate" designed for her by her family and her class, Beauvoir in *The Prime of Life* tells us she turned toward the future in the realization of freedom, the freedom of the for-itself, we might add. "Freedom I had — but freedom to do what? What new direction would the course of my life take . . . ?"[27]

We are to understand that Beauvoir is taking seriously her claim in *The Ethics of Ambiguity* that freedom is not a state inherited or given: " . . . freedom will never be given; it will always have to be won."[28] It is what a self, a for-itself, may achieve only if that self fights against thinghood by asserting that it *is* freedom, with a future of its own choosing: not a thing with a "fate" created by others nor a thing determined by conditions.

Because we are studying Beauvoir's early philosophy from a work of ethics rather than of metaphysics, her formulations of the self constantly move between an "is" and an "ought." In *Force of Circumstance*, Beauvoir relates that *The Ethics of Ambiguity* was the result of her opinion that one could base a morality on *Being and Nothingness* if one converted the simple desire to *be* into an assumption of existence; that is, a choice consciously and responsibly made by the self.[29] In *The Ethics of Ambiguity* itself, she put it this way: "To will oneself free *is* to effect the transition from nature to morality by establishing a genuine freedom on the original upsurge of existence."[30] The "ought" begins with the claim that one must will freedom by positively assuming the freedom that the for-itself is and has. By the book's middle, however, and up to the end, a new and important point is added to her analysis of freedom—the willing of one's own freedom is intricately bound up with that of others: " . . .

this kind of ethics . . . is not solipsistic, since the individual is defined only
by his relationship to the world and to other individuals; he exists only by
transcending himself, and his freedom can be achieved only through the
freedom of others."[31]

The philosophical proposition that the individual achieves her freedom only through the freedom of others, that is, the assertion of the interconnectedness of human freedom, may be what led Beauvoir to make
the last haunting remark of *Memoirs*: " . . . for a long time I believed that
I had paid for my own freedom with her [Zaza's] death."[32] Beauvoir
wrote this about an event that took place in 1929, before she published
The Ethics of Ambiguity. We have no way of knowing when she began believing this statement nor when she came to the opinion of the interconnectedness of human freedom. Indeed, we cannot know which "caused"
which. The death of Zaza and Beauvoir's own sense of guilt because she
was both alive and free may have been significant in leading her to her
claim of the interconnectedness of human freedom. When reading (in *The
Ethics of Ambiguity*) the claim that the individual achieves her freedom
only through the freedom of others, one tends to think of struggles of
masses on the national and international front against oppressors, not of
a struggle on the individual level. This passage does not seem to suggest
that one who achieved freedom may have felt some guilt if her friend
failed to, as if freedom were a limited quantity, with individual pieces of
it cut from a finite pie, but this may here have been the case. Beauvoir's
guilt is particularly strange, as she had made a clear decision, in advance
of Zaza's death, that she would do all she could to support her friend's
attempt to escape; "I had decided to fight with all my strength to prevent
her life becoming a living death," she said.[33] (Instead, it became an actual
death.) Thus, the narrator of *Memoirs* presents evidence that, years prior
to her own extension of the Sartrean notion of the self into an ethics, the
young Beauvoir had exhibited, in her concern and care for Zaza, a notion
of the interconnectedness of human freedom; that is, of her later claim
that "to will oneself free is also to will others free."[34] Furthermore, the
emphasis upon this point in the *Ethics* went beyond Sartre's thought.

Beauvoir's use of her notion of the gendered self in *Memoirs,* published in 1958 almost ten years after *The Second Sex,* is intriguing. In the
work she obliquely acknowledges a gendered self by her specific denial
that she had any awareness that being a girl, a female self, made any difference to her growing up. Though she acknowledges that her "feminine
condition" existed, she denies any consciousness of it: "I had no
brother; there were no comparisons to make which would have revealed
to me that certain liberties were not permitted me on the grounds of my
sex; I attributed the restraints that were put upon me to my age. Being a
child filled me with a passionate resentment; my feminine gender,

never."[35] And yet (as noted earlier) she was becoming more and more docile, in spite of her original independent spirit, so that by the age of eight, she was "a well-behaved little girl . . . "[36]

Embedded in her self gendered as feminine (as perhaps it is in all women) was a feminist self. Even in so *rangée* a self as this one, Simone had her significant rebellions against the creation of her feminine self. A case in point is provided in the description of the type of play in which she and her sister Hélène (nicknamed Poupette) engaged. In playing with their dolls, they assumed the roles of mothers without fathers; that is, their husbands were always "away." The domestic feminine condition even then seemed so odious to her that in formulating her own future she decided she would have no children.[37] This anti-marriage-and-mother-hood attitude continued far beyond the time of doll play.[38] She later also had a conscious sense of the sexism inherent in the double moral standard and had a strong reaction to it: " . . . I insisted that men should be subject to the same laws as women. . . . Therefore, despite public opinion, I persisted in my view that both sexes should observe the same rules of chastity and obedience."[39]

Along with and in spite of this sense of basic fairness, Beauvoir had for many years an attitude of strong ambivalence toward her own gender. This is best perceived in some remarks made much later in *Memoirs*. As a brilliant young university student befriended by the best male students (a list that included Merleau-Ponty, Levi-Strauss, Jean Hippolyte, as well as Sartre), she says she never regretted being a woman. Her acceptance of the common belief that the female sex was intellectually inferior to men made her own intellectual success all the more satisfying, because it meant she was an exception to her gender: "Far from envying them [men], I felt that my own position . . . was one of privilege . . . [yet] I did not renounce my femininity," she says.[40] Beauvoir was both feminine and a member of a male elite, a woman who intellectually, at least, very nearly "passed" as a man.

In her next volume, *The Prime of Life* (published in 1960), when she narrates the story of the early years of her relationship with Sartre, she insists again on feeling she had an exceptional status. "Just as previously I had refused to be labeled a 'child,' so now I did not think of myself as a 'woman.' I was *me*."[41] This comparison, that the child is to the self as the woman is to the self, is striking. Beauvoir refused categorization in both cases, sensing that such a categorization was a condemnation to a secondary status. Yet in the case of Beauvoir as woman, as in the earlier one, she was condemned to categorization anyway. For the story she tells of the early years she and Sartre spent together is full of details that lend themselves to the interpretation that Simone was not only a female self, but one whose feminine condition may have been intensified by being in the relationship with Sartre. To put it in the terms she used in *The Second Sex,* she was becoming more of a "relative being;" she lost interest in philosophy and began to take her self less seriously philosophically, as she came under the shadow of Sartre. In the following remark, Beauvoir quite consciously provides a textbook example of one woman's relativity and her reactions to it:

> Though I was less wholeheartedly committed to literature than Sartre, my thirst for knowledge rivaled his. Even so he pursued the truth far more persistently than I did. I have attempted to show, in my book *The Second Sex,* why a woman's situation still, even today, prevents her from exploring the world's basic problems. I longed to know the world, to find a way of expressing that knowledge; but I had never envisaged tearing its final secrets from it by sheer brain power. In any case I was too full of the novelty of my experiences during this year to devote much time to philosophy. I restricted myself to debating Sartre's ideas with him.[42]

In this example and in numerous other places in *The Prime of Life,* the book dedicated to Jean-Paul Sartre, Beauvoir shows us, inadvertently, herself as the "woman in love," the being whose existence becomes restricted through her total identification with her lover and her voluntary surrender of her freedom; she becomes the being she discusses in Chapter 23 of *The Second Sex.* At one point, she tells us that Sartre's mere existence justified her world, though the same was not true for him in regard to her.[43]

Within a year or two after the relationship began in earnest, Beauvoir experienced a kind of despair, losing interest in her own work and losing her pride. The intimidation she felt due to Sartre's friends and himself was a major factor in this unproductive, "lazy" period. "You used to be full of little ideas, Beaver," Sartre said.[44] The condescending tone of this remark is intensified in the original French, a more literal translation of which is, "But before, Castor (Beaver), you thought a *lot* (or a *heap*) about *little* things" (italics and translation mine).[45] In spite of her announced insistence to herself that she was her self and not a "woman," it seems that she became more and more a "woman," that is, a being whose existence is relative to a man, by directly comparing herself to Sartre and devaluing herself. Thus we read her harsh summary statement of this period: "I had ceased to exist on my own account, and was now a mere parasite."[46]

Later in the book we learn that she dissociated herself from the field of her training, philosophy; still acknowledging her own philosophical critical skills and her deep interest in the field, she no longer wanted to think of herself as a philosopher; to be a philosopher required both an originality of thought and an "obsessional attitude," a certain "lunacy" that she claimed does not *naturally* develop in women.[47] Such an insistence on "natural" abilities was anathema to the existentialists.

The direct confrontation with the issue of women's condition and the production of what she calls "femininity" in *The Second Sex* occurred through her listening to the testimony of other women, specifically those friends of hers over forty years old, for she continued to insist that the problem of women's condition did not directly concern her.[48] Thus, the issue of women's condition is presented to the reader as having come from *outside* Beauvoir, from others who felt discrimination, as she did not. She continually maintains in *The Prime of Life* that she was never the victim of discrimination by Sartre and his friends. The evidence she presents, however, allows the reader to conclude that indeed she was.

The repeated use of the pronoun *we* in *The Prime of Life* to indicate the couple, Beauvoir and Sartre, is a strong marker of the change in self that Beauvoir underwent at this period of her life in the direction of loss of autonomy. The self that she presents in the early part of the book is often not individualized; the *we* occurs and recurs in regard to an extensive variety of states, actions, and thoughts they shared — from their health and disposition, to their lack of limitations, to their emotions ("we were furious"), their expectations, their acceptances, their life choice ("we were writers"), their rejections, and their successes.[49] She continually calls attention to both the similarities between herself and Sartre and their differences. He was her superior as well as the perfect fellow traveller, because they were "marked by an identical sign."[50]

This notion of the self as "we," as she uses it in *The Prime of Life*, appears to be opposed to the existentialist notion of the self as a subject marked by individual choice, responsibility, and freedom. A particular contribution of Beauvoir is that through her own life story she indirectly shows us how the two notions of the self we have been looking at, the existentialist notion and the feminist notion, come together in the merging of the "I" into a "we" — into what I will call the "companionate self." The particular experience in which this happened was that of Beauvoir's being a "woman in love." Her own story has a certain universality to it. As the woman in love, she is marked by her self-surrender; that is, by the subordination of her own existence to that of another. Beauvoir lost the autonomy with which *The Prime of Life* began, for it had begun with the excitement over her hard-won freedom — never to be disputed, never in doubt — of which she spoke in the highest existentialist terms: "I had established my autonomy once and forever, and nothing could deprive me of it."[51] For a person who was never content to be either a "child" or a "woman," but who insisted on being "me," herself, that is, who insisted on a radical individuality, this fusion to a "we" was an extreme change.

Beauvoir applies direct criticism to the "companionate self" at one point, and in regard to disagreements with Sartre, yet even there she does not greatly assert the sovereignty of the individual, as we might expect from the writer of *The Ethics of Ambiguity*. She merely allows that *some* experiences are lived through alone.[52]

By the end of *Force of Circumstance,* the next volume of her autobiography, Beauvoir carefully and defensively explains her choice to follow and be overshadowed by Sartre. She made the choice, she claims, because "he led [her] along the paths [she] wanted to take" being the more suited for the role of leader, she argues, because he was the more creative thinker, both philosophically and politically. In response to the critical remarks of some feminists on her choice to follow Sartre, she neatly if unconvincingly insists that it was indeed a use of her freedom to acknowledge his superiority and *freely* follow him philosophically and politically; that is, to accept his ideas. In spite of such a straightforward acknowledgment of intellectual ancestry, there are questions to be asked.[53]

One could ask if and how, even prior to the writing of *The Second Sex,* she managed to live outside of the boundaries of the gendered self. In addition, how did she minimize her own contributions while acknowledging Sartre's? In what ways was she, too, philosophically and politically creative, as she describes Sartre to be? Further, in what ways did her own thinking lead his along new paths? These last questions can be asked against Beauvoir's own protestations.

In the second volume of the autobiography, *The Prime of Life,* the reader finds a tone similar to that of *Memoirs,* by turns judgmental and amused; this tone prepares the reader for her important claim at the end of Part One that her life was divided into another part, as it had been in 1929; the person being narrated is no longer her self. The understanding of "History" changes her life from 1939 on. So important is this change that she questions the value of the early part of her life; because of its ignorance of History, she says, she is strongly tempted to reject it as "false," though she eventually overcomes this temptation.[54]

As History entered her life, she became aware of more than her own life and concerned with more than her own happiness. She understood both that she herself was a historical being and that her life, any life, is part of a world and flow of activity that is not entirely in one's own control.[55] In the terms of the existentialist notion of the self developed in *The Ethics of Ambiguity,* Beauvoir was claiming that with this part of her life she began an ethical life: "There we have an irreducible truth. The me-others relationship is as indissoluble as the subject-object relationship.

... To will oneself free is also to will others free.''[56] She credits this change to the process of the writing of her first novel, *L'Invitée* (*She Came to Stay*). The years during which she wrote it, 1938 to 1941, also marked the beginning of World War II in Europe. In writing this novel, partly a roman à clef, she began to distinguish that past self she described — in the character of Françoise — from her then present self. The past self, having an autonomy with regard to her parents, was concerned with her own personal happiness and individual relationships exclusively. Then, she changed. ''Then, suddenly, History burst over me, and I dissolved into fragments. I woke to find myself scattered over the four quarters of the globe, linked by every nerve in me to each and every other individual,'' she states.[57] She reiterates the critical nature of this point much later in the book, referring to the change as the beginning of her ''moral period.''[58]

In the path of destruction wrought by World War II, Beauvoir's own self became historicized and socialized, aware of its mortality.[59] With this change, perhaps because of it, came the acknowledgment of the human condition: its ambiguity and its mortality, both of which are themes we find in *The Ethics of Ambiguity*.[60] By the end of the war, the change in her was complete. In a sense, and without yet knowing it, she was on the way to becoming the ethical person she would write about in *The Ethics of Ambiguity* two years later. She describes herself at this period in the following manner: ''Events had changed me; what Sartre used to call my 'divided mind' had finally yielded before the unanswerable arguments that reality had brought against it. I was at last prepared to admit that my life was not a story of my own telling, but a compromise between myself and the world at large.''[61] Here she obliquely points to a statement she made in *Memoirs* when, by contrast, she said: ''My life would be a beautiful story come true, a story I would make up as I went along.''[62]

Beauvoir's new knowledge of History, that is, that the world and the self are constituted by others as well as by external events, spills over into the notion of the self and the practice of writing autobiography. In her important reflective passage at the end of Part One of *The Prime of Life*, she provides a sort of manifesto of her own special type of feminine genderization (ever insisting on her special status, her intrinsic individuality). This explanation is followed by the only direct explication in the autobiographies of her notion of the self. Amazingly, she states her belief still in ''the theory of the 'transcendental ego''' (the translation here is faithful to the original), a theory that Sartre repudiated in *The Transcendence of the Ego*.[63] Had she forgotten? Most likely, she meant to say ''transcendent ego.'' She also claims that the self (*''le moi''*) is grasped through ''profiles.'' (Because the English translation renders *''profils''* as ''outer edge,'' this statement loses the phenomenological tone that runs throughout the passage.) Alluding to Husserl's notion that any object is delivered over through its profiles, Beauvoir, in discussing the self, says that it is an object with profiles—albeit a "probable object"—because the self is an object with an "inside"; it is, so to speak, the transcendental ego. As an object and therefore as something seen through its profiles, the self, she states, is seen more easily and better by others; that is, from the outside. An actual cognizing of that special object, the self, by the self, is impossible; hence, she claims, "One can never know oneself but only tell about [or narrate] oneself" (translation mine).[64] Unlike the Cartesian move by which consciousness, the thinking power, becomes the self, Beauvoir here continues the phenomenological insistence that the self is a by-product of consciousness, an object for it. Yet for some reason, she reintroduced that thorn in the side of phenomenology, the transcendental ego.

At the end of the first part of her next volume, *Force of Circumstance,* Beauvoir provides us with a description of a life that is also a poetic explanation of autobiography itself. To a writer of autobiography from the existential-phenomenological tradition, the self presents itself as a life to be narrated at the same time as it is an object to be known and a freedom to be appreciated. But the self/life is no ordinary object:

> A life is such a strange object, at one moment translucent, at another utterly opaque, an object I make with my own hands, an object imposed on me, an object for which the world provides the raw material and then steals it from me again, pulverized by events, scattered, broken, scored yet retaining its unity; how heavy it is and how inconsistent: this contradiction breeds many misunderstandings.[65]

The autobiographical writer's task is to show both the contradiction and the unity, in whatever ways possible. Beauvoir progressed from the writer of *Memoirs,* who neither made introductions nor needed an epilogue; to the writer of *The Prime of Life,* who required a preface and several long, reflective, "intrusive" passages at the end of each of the book's two parts; to the writer of *Force of Circumstance,* who required an introduction and an interlude as well as an epilogue. In such formal structural ways, as well as in passages like that just quoted, she presented to the reader an increasing problematization of the process and practice of autobiography, the labyrinthine narration of the unknowable self.

This study, a comparison of Beauvoir's notion of the self with the self presented in her autobiographies, began by showing that Beauvoir's analysis in *The Second Sex* problematized the original existential-phenomenological notion of the self she had used: the self as for-itself. In *The Second Sex,* Beauvoir showed that the self was also "gendered."

Consequently, Beauvoir's existentialism gave way, to some extent, to empiricism. In the autobiographies, both conceptions of the self are evident. Beauvoir's selection and narration of events in her life and her reflection on her life in various retrospective passages bear the mark of a thinker who wanted to preserve the tension between freedom and determinism inherent in her brilliant work, *The Second Sex*. Though she was a woman and hence oppressed by patriarchy, when discussing this issue in the autobiographies, she denied its personal relevance. Assuming her liberty, she continually judged herself to be free.

Part Two

Writing Differences in Continental Philosophy

13

Dialogue and Discourses

Bernhard Waldenfels

The idea of dialogue that plays such an important role in Western thinking continues in phenomenological concepts such as intersubjectivity, sociality, Mitsein, intercorporeity, otherness. What I want to offer is an example of what Merleau-Ponty called 'coherent deformation.' Deforming an idea does not mean denegrating it. Nevertheless, such a deformation does violence to established orders of thinking and behaving whatever they might be. The process of deforming at stake here is provoked by a *crisis of occidental rationality and subjectivity* that long ago was announced by Husserl and others and that nowadays finds its rather helpless expression in the *paroles de guerre* of *modernity* and *postmodernity*. In this chapter I shall intervene not straight on but from the side, starting just from the concept of dialogue.

THE AMBIGUITY OF DIALOGUE

What, since Plato's time, has been called *dialogue* and what we use to distinguish from simple and ordinary conversation is originally infected with something ambiguous, something that goes against the grain. This is even more true of a dialectic that starts from the art of διαλεγεσθαι that seeks to surpass this crosscurrent.[1] Why speak of ambiguity? The prefix *dia-* points to a process of *division*. This process creates an intermediary realm or common ground (*Zwischenreich*) wherein *logoi* come and go, meet or miss each other. But this process of division

will be counterbalanced by a process of *collection*. Every dispute seems
to be rooted in an initial accord and oriented toward a final consent that
would put an end to every form of dissent. The apple of discord that the
goddess Eris throws into the arena is eaten up by Logos. The common
Logos (κοινὸσ λόγος) constitutes the vivid medium wherein all differences are to be decided and settled. Nothing is excluded from this community of Logos but what excludes itself: thus the idle talk of the rhetor
who suns himself in his own opinions or the vain skirmish of the eristic
who tries to win at any price, and finally pure violence that leaves all
words behind — all these are excluded. Nevertheless it does not follow
from this exclusion that dialogical and antilogical, dialectical and eristic
agents live in different worlds. Even dialogical truth has to fight against
being decomposed from the outside. But what weapons should it use —
are they pure arguments? Do not even syllogisms turn into "knife-stabs"
when employed against the forces of untruth? Plato knew well that the
voice of the enemy sometimes sounds "out of one's own house"
(οἴκόθεν) (Sophocles 252c), and traces of such internal revolt are to be
found throughout his dialogues.[2] From the very beginning, dialogue and
dialectic do not present themselves in an unclouded light. But this does
not seem to affect the idea itself, that is, the idea of a place where we are
on a common path to the "things themselves" (αὐτα τὰ πράγματα) —
where to settle disputes nothing is accepted but arguments — where even
contradiction and opposition bring us nearer to the goal — where everybody is admitted, Menon as well as his slave — where our being engaged
in things makes us free for ourselves and urges us to the recognition of
others — where detours and delays are tolerated and the rhythms of conversations are not determined by the trickling sands of an hourglass —
and last, but not least, where agreement is expected from nowhere but
dialogue itself: such an open and flexible form of reason is truly not something to be despised. The artifices of dialectics may be left to their adventures, but who would be daring and cunning enough to be opposed to
such an idea of dialogue without himself making use of it?

Nevertheless, it cannot be denied that this great idea depends on a
large presupposition. It presupposes that Logos is the central and final
instance in which all differences might be bridged and where all plurali-
ties might be gathered. When the realization of this idea finds its limits,
then these remain factual limits to be overcome in the long run. As long
as this presupposition holds, dialogue as a whole presents itself as a
monologue with distributed roles. And from a dialogical dispute between
persons to the dialectical mediaton of positions, there is only one further
step: to filter out the contingency of particular circumstances. The unity
of unity and plurality or the identity of identity and difference will inevitably be dominated by the respective first term of the opposition, and so

there will be no place for irreducible diversity and plurality. The presumed reconciliation, or even atonement or at-one-ness, assumes aspects of violence if the presuppostion just mentioned fails. Now, it fails indeed if the central instance of Logus dissipates and if dialogue itself ramifies into the crosscurrents of a polylogue. The crisis of reason, which is largely connected with the question of reasons's unity, casts its shadow over dialogue and the position of the partners and "subjects" in dialogue.

These are the issues from which I want to thematize the concepts of dialogue and dialectic, subjectivity and intersubjectivity, ownness and otherness. I shall try to reveal certain junctures where the unity of a great dia-logue splits into different dis-courses. We shall have to ask how these discourses are preserved from running hither and thither, loosing all contact. But this question should not be answered all too quickly by conjuring up an imminent chaos. It is quite possible that modes of union are to be found that differ from the old mode of logocentrism. The role of the subject raises similar questions. The alternative of the salvation or the abdication of the subject leaves out the possibility of the transformation of the subject. Finally, linking together the issue of the *subject* with the issue of *reason,* we shall try to prevent the revival of a pure immediacy of life under the catch-word of a new subjectivity or intersubjectivity that would be quickly enough overtaken by the old agencies of mediation. Linking together as well the issue of *intersubjectivity and sociality* with the issue of *reason,* we shall avoid resorting to a mere change of paradigm; that is, replacing the paradigm of subjective consciousness by a paradigm of mutual understanding, all other things being left as they are. Passing from dialogue to a variety of discourses requires changing the ground-plan of subjectivity, intersubjectivity, *and* rationality — otherwise nothing significant is achieved.[3]

FROM GLOBAL DIALOGUE TO REGIONAL DISCOURSES

The Irruption of Questioning

Questioning is marked by its opening a more or less extended field of understanding, acting, and encountering. It breaks through the walls of what is taken for granted or seems to be obvious, and it marks out points of reference with which answers can link up. It is not the state of ignorance that is decisive in questions but their treatment of knowledge and ignorance. This is an old topic that has persisted since the wakening of Socratic questioning through to the interrogative thinking of Heidegger or of Merleau-Ponty and in the dialogical unfolding of texts in Gadamer's hermeneutic.[4] In what follows I shall focus on the irruptive character of dialogical questions about states of things.

First, it should be said that questioning is an especially refractory event from which the usual validity claims glance off. Contrary to statements, questions do not *claim truth* and they are not connected with other linguistic events in such a way that they could be deduced from others or functions as the premise in such deductions. Thus, they resist any attempts at *universalization* and *systematization*. Contexts of questioning look more like a landscape than a building.

But does not questioning at least *strive after some kind of knowledge* that brings us nearer to truth? Does not questioning consist in a seeking that is not solely for the sake of seeking but for the sake of finding, as Aristotle tells us (Eth. Nic. X, 7, 1177a26f)? Against this objection, I would argue that such a finalization of questions presupposes that every question can be integrated into an all-encompassing and -pervading movement of questioning — be it the interest of reason or whatever. But this would entail that questions are only awakened, not posed. Such a restriction does not go together with the choosing of what is interrogated or consulted and with the difference between what is interrogated (*Befragtes*) and what is asked about (*Gefragtes*). This selection of a certain what and how includes alternatives that do not fit together as a whole.

At last, the posing of a question seems to call for subjective *responsibility* so that we are free to pose or not to pose questions. But even at this point we are stopped. Questions are not only posed *by us* but also *to us*, and often they *arise* without being posed by anybody. If the questionability is part of being itself, and not only part of the deficiency of human being, then we fall into questions as we fall in love, and we get into a maelstrom of questions just as we get into trouble or danger. Otherwise questions could be ordered like actions.

Consequently questioning appears as an unruly event within the drama of dialogue that cannot be mastered and that can hardly be steered. If we consider that each statement that has to be *made* or *enunciated*, has something questionable not covered by a validibility claim, we see that it is not only a marginal problem that confronts us. Questioning perforates the great spheres of truth, justice, and authenticity unfolded in Habermas's theory of communicative action and validated in specific discourses.[5] It seems to me obvious that every dialogue begins with an openness and readiness that precedes logic.[6] To say it more simply, without diction there can be no contradiction.

But if the divergence of questioning does not amount to a great logic of truth, one must not expect that questioning to come out of the blue and disappear back into it. Questions certainly allow for qualification. They may be senseless, flat, stupid, unimportant, incomprehensible, misplaced, or importunate. Questioning itself may be suppressed or defended, and the desire for questions may die. There is a variety of order functions that even questioning cannot escape.

Orders of Speech

There is no simple and pure dialogue, as there is no simple and pure case of a moral action or a love affair. Dialogical utterances arise in the framework of medical examinations, parliamentary debates, juridical interrogations, confessional avowals, and everyday conversations or, finally, in philosophical disputes that are not totally *hors de série*. Such variable and various orders, which are not at all restricted to speech but extend to all kinds of behavior, may be discussed from different points of view.

First, I mention the organization of speech fields. Husserl's and especially Aron Gurwitsch's theory of thematics, enriched by the results of Gestalt theory, are to be applied here. Every question asks something about something. In doing so, it gives the key note of a certain *theme*, it opens a *thematic field* and it pushes other utterances to the *margin* as being impertinent and inappropriate. Already, this elementary way of organizing involves selection as well as exclusion and presses dialogue into the limits of a more or less circumscribed field of activity. Here, the contrast of figure and ground resists any simple coordination of perspectives.

Such fields of speaking are stabilized in different ways. Here we should mention the process of *typification* largely described by Alfred Schütz. Recurrent features and contexts are privileged against what is atypical, and this privilege does not depend on unshakable, essential laws but on *relevancies* corresponding to certain interests. In such a way spaces of acting and speaking grow up as examined in Goffman's frame analysis or in Hannah Arendt's open places. They are further articulated in the way of normalization; for example, by a certain *style* of speaking. Finally, we find *institutional* or *quasi-institutional rule systems* such as orders of parliament, legal proceedings, or rules of examination by which speaking is regulated and the chances of speaking are distributed.

But it could be argued that by focusing on these regulated discourses we totally neglect the free dialogue that Plato had in view and that is still present in the form of a well-instructed public. To this objection I would like to answer in the following way: there may be different degrees and forms of regulation, but there is no free place where nothing is asked except the truth. Conditions of conversation overtake every utterance, conditions of truth frame every truth. There is no gap between dialectic and rhetoric, between truth and efficiency. Therefore, I prefer to follow

Foucault who speaks of *discourses* whose positive orders include the processes of thematization, typification, normalization, and norm-giving, that is to say, that include procedures of selecting, excluding, and controlling. There is no global discourse that allows for saying anything whatever. A discourse that looks for nothing but truth tends to be used as instrument of exclusion in referring to a "veritable being" or to "veritable interests."[7]

Contradiction and Conflict

The variety of competing orders leads to an important consequence. Contradiction functions as a "fountain" (*Springquelle*) of dialectic as long as we stay within an homogeneous field with the effect that the exterior may be the result of exteriorization and the alien the result of alienation. With respect to dialogue, contradiction presupposes that the partners of dialogue refer to the same thing, or else they would be at cross-purposes. Contradiction, however, will lose its central role as soon as the formation of fields of discourse produces by itself an outside that accompanies the discourse like its shadow. Where alternative orders of discourse clash, there we find forms of difference, of *différend*[8] that are not put right by any final award because no pervasive rules or measures can fill the gap. The famous dispute over the "incommensurability" of paradigms has to be placed on the level of the realization of experiences, not on the level of claims of validity (*Geltungsansprüche*). Thus, Thomas Kuhn and Paul Feyerabend compare the change of paradigms to the Gestalt switch that precedes predicative truth. It may be objected that the variability of orders does not contradict first data and final rules. This may be true in a certain sense. But going in this direction one sidesteps the issue. One will find only some kind of under- or over-agreement that does not resolve the problem of *concrete or specific agreement*. The conflict between incompossible orders is not to be reduced to contradictions between incompatible statements. Contradiction functions as long as it is supported by the normality of an existing agreement and of a well-established discourse. Contradiction loses its power when the running agreement begins to fracture.

From Governor of Reason to Functionary?

If the logos of the dialogue changes, the quality of the "between" and the status of the partners of dialogue change, too. As long as dialogue tends toward a monologue with distributed roles, the partners are expected to *complete* each other as to the particular and to *replace* each other as to the universal. Taken as sensible being, everybody is one body among others; taken as reasonable being, everybody is as good a body as the other. The dialectic of mutual recognition attributes to forming a circle between the particular and the universal, and this would consist in the "turn from the appropriation of the other into the alteration of the own."[9]

What happens to the subjects, to these governors of reason, when reason dissipates into the various forms of polylogue? Without doubt the selections and exclusions that penetrate the orders of discourse affect the status and the mutual relations of the partners of dialogue. The face-to-face relation acquires the features of a masked play, but does it turn into a pure masque?

Here we come to a critical point. If the subject were nothing more than a variable destined to occupy a vacant place it would degenerate into a pure functionary within a system. Nothing would be left of Husserl's "functionary of mankind." The macrology of reason would cede to a micrology of systems, and even Foucault's theory of discourse sometimes tends toward this direction.[10]

INTERCONNECTION AND TRANSGRESSION OF DISCOURSES

A remedy against fixating on established orders consists in the practice of genealogy, which keeps alive the genesis of orders. The intruding question from which our reflections started is indeed subjected to certain conditions but it refuses incorporation in a certain order. An ordered question would cease to be a question. This means that we never completely enter into an order and that we never will be absorbed by it. Every discourse exceeds itself in a double way; namely, by *interdiscursivity* and by *transdiscursivity*. The former does not resemble a universal language but rather the relation between the mother tongue and a foreign language, whereas the latter resembles the relation between what can be said and what cannot be said in a certain language. First, a few words about *interdiscursivity*. The lines that circumscribe certain orders intersect with each other in multiple ways; the pure and simple own (*das Eigene*) as well as the pure and simple alien (*das Fremde*) are mere constructs. There is a lot of overlapping, consonances, resonances, equivalents, and so on. Second, a remark on transdiscursivity. What is excluded by an order does not simply turn into nothing, it remains as excluded. Without referring to an *être brut* or an *être sauvage,* as the later Merleau-Ponty calls it, cultures would be walled up in their orders. So interdiscursivity presents itself through horizontal interconnections like series, networks, textures, or circles of similarity. These all belong to what Merleau-Ponty calls a "lateral universal."[11] On the other hand, transdiscursivity presents itself in oblique modes such as deviation, deformation, estrangement, and excess. These forms allow one to think the transition from one order to another without relying on a preliminary or final form of synthesis. The forms of an open, incarnate or negative dialectic, such as is found in Merleau-Ponty or Adorno, stake everything on an excess that cannot be seized and integrated.

In this way, perspectives arise that point to a new kind of dialogue or even dialectic. To make this clear, I shall briefly outline some problems of intersubjectivity, subjectivity and speaking.

Intertwining of the Own and the Alien and the Otherness of the Other

There are different models of intercourse such as the communicative model of sender and receiver, the social model of the reciprocity of perspectives, the genetic model of an increasing reversibility of standpoints,[12] or, finally, the ethical model of the golden rule. These all come together in taking for granted the following two presuppositions: first, that the own and alien are to be clearly separated from each other; second, that the symmetrical distribution of the own and the alien amount to a maximum of rationality and sociality. Remove the first presupposition and you will destroy responsibility, take away the second one and you will undermine justice. Logos and ethos seem to join here in a most convincing manner. Nevertheless, these presuppositions are not beyond doubt.

Let us begin with the separation of the own and the alien. Both can be separated all the more one partner in a dialogue disposes of what he will say before he really says it, as when somebody transmits a message and the other merely receives it. The common "code" completed by contextual conditions allows for normal understanding. Things change if the common presuppositions of mutual understanding are themselves at stake; that is, if the dialogue not only obeys an order of discourse but also changes it. In this case, nothing is to be simply transmitted but something is going to be coproduced, and in the case of this coproduction you cannot say where the own ends and the alien begins. We might speak of a sort of dialogical "principle of uncertainty." This holds true for talking, where one word leads to another, as well as for reading, where the work, as Proust puts it, creates its own posteriority and changes the reader himself.[13] Following Merleau-Ponty, we might speak of an interlacing or intertwining of the own and the alien behavior taking hold in a sphere of "intercorporeity." Now let us take the second presupposition; namely, the claim of symmetry. This claim, too, arises *post festum* when I step out of the relation to the other, when I compare my own position with the position of the other and *put them on a par*. Already, the structural difference between I and Thou escapes such comparing and equalizing. In my relation to the other, the other arises before me in the form of an otherness that constitutes a *nonreciprocal relation,* as Levinas has shown.[14] The otherness shining forth in the human face marks something exterior that does not result from exteriorization. "The absence of the other is just the presence of him as another."[15] Within communication something appears which *cannot be communicated* (see also Adorno, who took it from Kierkegaard). We transgress the discourse without arriving elsewhere. The one is only on the other's *track.*

The Otherness of the Ego

The otherness of the other could be added to my own experience only if it did not announce itself in the otherness of myself. The classical path from *ego* to *alter ego* reverses itself because the ego, following Ortega y Gasset, shows aspects of an *alter tu.* Doubt arises about the conception of a cogito that goes out of itself and, having encountered the adventures of otherness, returns to itself. Here it is also true that the identity of the ego, of the speaker or actor, is the less problematic the more it is considered within the framework of an existing order. Identity becomes problematic on the borderlines of the discourses, where the authority of office ends. From different points of view, it can be demonstrated that the eclipse of logocentrism casts its shadow over egocentrism. The unity of the ego goes to pieces, the reflexive self-contact ends in a short circuit.

Allow me to call on some prominent witnesses. George Herbert Mead divides the Ego into I and Me, and even the most rigid theories of roles are unable to fill up this fissure. Social psychologists like Vygotski have tried to show that language develops from the social form of public language (*äussere Sprache*) through the child's stage of "egocentric" speaking to the individuated form of inner language (*innere Sprache*). From this it follows that the "the inward dialogue carried on by the soul with itself," in spite of its own rules, preserves something of an interiorized dialogue. The process of individuation does not come to an end. In his studies on verbal hallucinations, Daniel Lagache explains the phenomenon in a highly significant manner. The estrangement of the patient's own voice is to be explained by the fact that the intersubjective segregation of I and Thou, and the intrasubjective scission into *je* and *moi,* stems from a process of differentiation that can be revoked under certain conditions. The "I say" has always something of an "it says," and I am no more the proprietor of my speech than I am the proprietor of my body. Merleau-Ponty speaks of a "kernel of depersonalization" that is immanent to the ego as ego.[16] These reflections are confirmed by psychoanalytic theories of human development. René Spitz takes dialogue to be anchored in the symbiotic relation of mother and infant, which is settled by common rhythms of life. Donald W. Winnicot refers to an "intermediary field" where we find "transitional phenomena" that are half real, half symbolic like puppets and stuffed animals. These transitional beings allow for a gradual loosening of the mother bond. But the intermediary field does not disappear in the adult's life. It returns as a place for imagination and play. In Lacan the process of detaching and differentiating amounts to a fission or splitting of the subject that constitutes itself in the detour of imaginative mirror reflections and symbolic orders. Here also otherness appears already in the intrasubjective sphere, so in the infant's identification with its own mirror image in which it recognizes (*erkennt*) and — so to speak — misrecognizes (*verkennt*) itself.

These and similar investigations are backed by an insight into temporality developed by Levinas and Derrida in the footsteps of Husserl and Heidegger. The temporality of our own being means that self-consciousness as the original dwelling of sense is always for itself in delay. Presence is always penetrated by nonpresence, the same is always affected by the other. Husserl already attributed a residue of anonymity to the functioning ego,[17] and Merleau-Ponty speaks in a similar context, using Homer's words, of an *outis*, a non one.[18] Here we reach a point where the subject, integrated in discourses, tends to transgress itself, but in the direction of the nameless.

Does it still make sense to speak of a "subject" who would be more than a *subject* in the political sense of the word, that is, a subordinate? Even if we hesitate to follow Lacan's verbal alchemy, there is not much left of a *hypokeimenon,* of something underlying all things or a central instance. And actions and speeches are just as little to be ascribed to a clearly circumscribed actor and speaker — to this simple author that Nietzsche includes among the superstitions of grammarians and moralists. To avoid gliding into a pure "it speaks" or "it acts" there are other remedies. Actions and speeches should be taken as prescribed mixtures of doing and happening, of what is one's own and what is alien. These mixtures could be articulated not by disjunctive but by accentuating conceptions. As Husserl says, actions are staged (*inszeniert*)[19] and there is no need for a stage director overlooking and dominating the scene.

Plurivocality of Speech

Finally, the change in our conception of subjectivity and intersubjectivity is confirmed by the findings of a theorist of literature who, more than everybody else, has focused on the multiple forms of dialogue. I refer to Michail Bakhtin to whom Kristeva's concept of the polylogue is indebted.[20] The "inner dialogicity" ascribed to the word (*Wort*) by Bakhtin does not begin only when we address others. This dialogical quality depends on the fact that the "word ray" by means of which our intentions turn to the object is multiply refracted in the medium of alien words, valuations, and acccents that are incorporated in the object itself. The speaker's word moves "on the frontier of the own and the alien. The word is a half alien word," it is "charged with alien intentions, even overcharged."[21] Thus Bakhtin interprets the manifold speech of the novel as a play with the frontier between the own and the alien. The author's speech and the speech of represented persons, alternatively combined by Plato in the mixed genus of the epic (Politeia IV, 392c ff), overlap in a hidden or hybrid way. An author not only speaks *in* a certain language but also *by* it, and so is enabled, "to say something of his own in the alien language and something alien in his own language."[22]

What we called the *intertwining* of the own and the alien is thus exemplified by literature. Finally, in his methodological reflections Bakhtin opposes the constructs of an ideal author or an ideal reader and offers something like a dramatic movement that is kept going by an excess of otherness. The "overcoming of the alienness of the alien without transforming it into a pure own"[23] points to an "endless dialogue where neither a first nor a last word is to be found."[24]

The intermediary realm of such a dialogue should be located in the transition from one discourse to the other, in the margins and blanks of the different discourses where the carnival culture of peoples and the satirical arts of artists like Rabelais or Gogol find their place and where — even if in a fragmentary style — something like Barthes's lover's discourses (*discours amoureux*) might emerge. Finally, what about the subject? Perhaps we should content ourselves, like Nietzsche, with "one smile and two question marks."

14

Beyond Signifiers

M. C. Dillon

Far from possessing the secret of the being of the world, language is itself a world, itself a being — a world and a being to the second power, since it does not speak in a vacuum, since it speaks of being and of the world and therefore redoubles their enigma instead of dissipating it. *The philosophical interrogation concerning the world therefore does not consist in referring from the world itself to what we say of the world,* since that interrogation repeats itself again within language. To philosophize is not to cast the things into doubt in the name of words, as if the universe of things said were clearer than that of brute things, as if the real world (*le monde effectif*) were a canton of language [and] perception a confused and mutilated speech.[1]

"The philosophical interrogation concerning the world . . . does not consist in referring from the world itself to what we say of the world." Here, in a phrase, is the thought that separates Merleau-Ponty from those of his contemporaries who are currently in vogue. As stated here, it is a critical thought, a negative thought: it says that it is a mistake to put language in the place of the world as the ultimate theme of philosophical interrogation. The positive thought that is its correlate is the well-known thesis of the primacy of perception: "the perceived world is the always presupposed foundation of all rationality, all value, and all existence."[2] The issue centers on the question of foundations: either language is

177

founded on something prior to it that serves as its ground, origin, measure, and referent — or language refers only to itself and any appeal to a
foundation that would serve as its ground, origin, or measure is an appeal
to onto-theology.[3]

The question of foundations is crucial, on it depends the nature and
validity of philosophical interrogation itself. To abandon the foundations
of philosophical discourse is, *ipso facto,* to project oneself into relativism
and skepticism with regard to truth and value. And relativism, no matter
how guarded, how sophisticated, how virtuosic its expression may be,
has always the same consequence — rhetorical noise accompanied by
philosophical silence — for, although one can always attack, one can
never defend: without foundations of some sort, there can be no grounds
for espousing one viewpoint rather than another, and one can lay claim
only to consistency, never truth.

To forestall confusion, let me point out here that I espouse a conception of "foundation" that makes no appeal — overt or covert — to the
divine in any of its traditional guises. *Foundation,* then, does not here refer to an absolute, nor does it betoken a sphere of immutability, atempor-
ality, or finality. As already noted, Merleau-Ponty says that "the perceived world is the . . . foundation," and the perceived world, in its widest
generality, is a sphere of becoming. The ground on which we stand and on
which we build the edifices wherein we dwell, speak, and think is a mutable ground: it moves in space and changes in time. There is no sense in
which its ends can be clearly seen. For all that — because of all that — it
is still the ground: the unthematizable context that reveals and conceals
itself throughout our days, and underlies all the alphas and omegas we
generate in the open-ended attempt to understand.

In recent work, I have defended the claim that Merleau-Ponty's
phenomenology of language is a direct consequence of his phenomenological ontology and, as such, provides a response to the two forms of the
retreat to immanence that I shall describe here: post-hermeneutic skepticism and semiological reductionism. *Post-hermeneutic skepticism* is my
term for the standpoint, consequent upon a certain reading of Heidegger,
that Being is forever imprisoned within the house of language, that there
is no access to either Being or beings not mediated by language. *Semiological reductionism* is my term for the position that has grown out of a certain interpretation of Saussure and holds that signifiers refer exclusively
to other signifiers, that there is no signified that is not itself within the
chain of signifiers.[4] Beneath the differences between these two standpoints is the common result: from neither vantage is it deemed possible
to pass beyond the immanent sphere of language to a transcendent (i.e.,
extralinguistic) reality. And this means that there is no conceivable *terminus ad quem* that might be reached by disputants in a controversy, no

transcendent ground that could serve to substantiate one view and discredit the others: discourse could lead only to further discourse and terminate, if at all, by fiat of violence or fatigue.

POST-HERMENEUTIC SKEPTICISM

The problem posed by Heidegger in the section of *Being and Time* devoted to "Understanding and Interpretation" is essentially a variant of the problem of truth that emerges from the thesis of subjectivity: if the world, as I understand it, is necessarily the world-as-I-understand-it, and if my understanding of the world is necessarily an interpretation biased by presuppositions, then truth becomes a problem. The truth, as I understand it, is always only my interpretation, and the biases that structure that interpretation undermine its claim to objectivity, its claim to express what is as *it* is.

In *Being and Time*,[5] these biases are explicated in terms of the "forestructure" of fore-having [*Vorhabe*], fore-sight [*Vorsicht*], and fore-conception [*Vorgriff*]: understanding is biased by a structure of pro-jection or anticipation that is inherent to it. This projection of pre-suppositions is explicated in terms of the "totality of involvement" [*Bewandtnis-ganzheit*] that informs the primordial sphere of readiness-to-hand [*Zuhandenheit*]. The telic nature of our involvement with things thus results in a projection of meaning that constitutes the intelligibility of things or our understanding of them. This, in turn, produces a circularity intrinsic to understanding: we understand things in terms of a prior interpretation; what we seek to understand thematically is always already caught up in a prethematic context of understanding. The hermeneutic circle is a result of the fore-structure intrinsic to understanding; that is, it is a result of the inherent structure of understanding that it always projects a context of meaning or involvement ahead of itself.

In *Being and Time*, this problematizing of truth consequent upon the projective structure of understanding is not directly associated with language. Later, however, Heidegger makes the connection between truth and language that recasts the problem posed by the hermeneutic circle in a linguistic framework. In "The Origin of the Work of Art" (1935–36), Heidegger concludes that "art is by nature an origin: a distinctive way in which truth comes into being, that is, becomes historical."[6] Art brings truth into being by fixing it in place, by thematizing it. This act of thematization is ποιησισ, poetic creation. "*All art,* as the letting happen of the advent of the truth of what is, is, as such, essentially poetry."[7] Heidegger grants to poetry—"the linguistic work, the poem in the narrower sense"—a "privileged position in the domain of the arts" because "language alone brings what is, as something that is, into the Open for the first time."[8] This thought had been expressed earlier (in 1935) in *An Introduction to Metaphysics*: "it is in words and language that things first come into being and are."[9] And it reaches culmination later (in 1946) with Heidegger's statement in "What Are Poets For?" that "language is the precinct (*templum*), that is, the house of Being."[10] Truth happens in art, above all in poetry, where the thematizing of language brings things into being. Truth is αληθεια—unforgetfulness, unconcealment—and it is in language that the unconcealment of things happens.

Yet, every disclosure, every revelation, is, at the same time, a concealment; language covers things over in the very process of thematization or unconcealment. Furthermore, we live in a time of fallenness, a time of spiritual decline, a time when "language in general is worn out and used up."[11] Our time is characterized by a "flight of the gods": [12] the gods who "bring us to language"[13] have fled, and the poet—the one who stills himself, listens, and turns to the gods for his measure — faces an abyss.

We live in a time when language has become exhausted, when "Being has become little more than a mere word and its meaning an evanescent vapor."[14] We live in a time of "idle talk [that] destroys our authentic relation to things."[15] Idle talk dissembles, conceals things, and dissembles that dissemblance, conceals that concealment, by its very taken-for-grantedness. And this fallen, exhausted, dissembling language that subverts our relation to Being has taken us over. "Man acts as though he were the shaper and master of language, while in fact language remains the master of man."[16]

The problem of truth posed by the hermeneutic circle of projective understanding has now become a problem of language. We are mastered by a fallen language that dissembles our relations to things, conceals Being, and covers over its dissemblance by the very quality of ordinariness that betokens its exhaustion. Language, which grounds our understanding of things, is itself grounded in an abyss, an *Ab-grund,* an absence of ground: the gods, to whom the poets, the original speakers of truth, listen for their measure, have fled, and darkness prevails. Truth is grounded in language, but the ground of language has fallen away leaving an *Ab-grund*.

If this were the totality of Heidegger's teaching on the subject of language and truth, he would be rightly seen as a skeptic, even a nihilist: this view, as set forth here, imprisons man within a dissembling language and denies him any relation to Being independent of language by means of which that dissemblance can be rectified. If one attributes all meaning to the transcendental function of language — if one regards language as entirely centrifugal, as the sole ground of constitution and the source of all *Sinngebung* or projection of meaning—but denies that language originates in this world to which it refers, then one has severed language from any transcendent ground and foreclosed the possibility of measuring its truth.

Heidegger, however, is neither skeptic nor nihilist. Language, for him, remains a grounded phenomenon. One may dispute the legitimacy of his appeal to Being or to presence. Or one may find in his later elaboration of the concept of appropriation (*Ereignis*) a promising answer to the question of the ground of the "Saying of language."[17] I favor the latter, but this is not the place to argue the point. The issue at hand is that of post-hermeneutic skepticism. And the point I hope to have made is that, if one fastens upon the *problem* of truth posed by Heidegger's hermeneutic understanding of language and, at the same time, rejects the legitimacy of his or any other *solution*—if any appeal to a ground is *ipso facto* discredited as a relapse into traditional metaphysics and onto-theology— then one is committed to both skepticism and nihilism. I have characterized this position as *post*-hermeneutic skepticism to signal the fact that it is a position taken, not by Heidegger, but by those who have followed the path of his thinking to a crucial juncture and then departed from it.

SEMIOLOGICAL REDUCTIONISM

Semiology is the science of signs. Semiological reductionism is the attempt to reduce all science to semiology. This is a radical formulation of the position, but the position is itself necessarily radical—so radical as to be untenable—although its adherents have avoided direct confrontation with its ultimate consequences. It is difficult to defend the claim that the laws of physics, biology, psychology, sociology, and so on are reducible to the laws governing the relations of signs within societies,[18] but that is an ineluctable implication of the position currently dominating mainstream continental thought.

The premise that transforms semiology into semiological reductionism is the premise that signs refer exclusively to other signs, that signs cannot refer to extralinguistic realities; for example, phenomena to which we have cognitive access in non- or prelinguistic modes, preeminently in the mode of perception. Or, to state this premise in a positive form, semiological reductionism holds that all cognitive modes are thoroughly permeated by and conditioned on language and that this is because meaning or significance, the object of cognition, is generated exclusively in and by sign systems; that is, by language, broadly or narrowly conceived.

Note that this premise does not entail denial of the existence of things independent of language, nor does it entail denial of our ability to perceive these things: it contends only that our cognition of things is inextricably mediated by language or, again, that human cognition is imprisoned within the immanence of language.

Although Saussure did not explicitly espouse the standpoint of semiological reductionism, his influential *Course in General Linguistics,*[19] for the most part, is compatible with that standpoint[20] and might justly be regarded as its primary antecedent. Saussure was a linguist, not a philosopher; he chose to speak as a scientist and avoid the domain of metaphysics. Except for a brief critique of "the superficial notion" that language is "nothing more than a name-giving system,"[21] in which he argues that "the linguistic sign unites, not a thing and a name, but a concept and a sound-image,"[22] we find little in Saussure that betrays an ontological commitment. Indeed, elements of scientific realism — "the social fact alone can create a linguistic system,"[23] "language is a social institution"[24] — are unselfconsciously mixed with elements of a language-based transcendental idealism: "no individual . . . could modify in any way the choice [of a given signifier for the idea that it represents]; and what is more, the community itself cannot control so much as a single word; it is bound to the existing language."[25] Saussure writes of both the "internal" and the "external" elements of language — for example, the systematic relations among phonemes operative within the organism of language, and such influences impinging on language from without as political history, geography, ethnography, and so forth — but he does not discourse on the relation of word and thing.

However, three fundamental tenets in Saussure's thought lend themselves to the development of semiological reductionism. First is the thesis of cognitive dependency, the thesis that thought is dependent on language.[26] The second is Saussure's renowned definition of the primary linguistic entity, the sign, as the association of signifier [*signifiant*] (sound-image) and signified [*signifié*] (concept).[27] And the third tenet is the thesis of opposition or difference; this is the basis for Saussure's diacritical theory of language, and it maintains that the delimitation of a linguistic unit (or isolable sign) requires the differentiation of a signifier from all others in the chain of sound-images together with the concurrent and correlative differentiation of the signified from all others in the chain of concepts.[28] Here Saussure stresses the point that this identity by opposition can be established *only* through the correlation of signifier and signified: the "slice of sound" in a spoken chain is identifiable only if it is correlated with a discrete concept and, vice versa, a given concept is isolable only if it is correlated with a discrete signifier or sound-image (whence follows the first tenet, the thesis of cognitive dependency).[29] The correlation of a given signifier with a given signified is entirely arbitrary (i.e., not grounded in onomatopoeia or some concatenation of natural signs) and depends on linguistic "values that owe their existence solely to usage and general acceptance" within a community.[30]

These three tenets alone do not entail semiological reductionism, although they take us to its brink. Their cumulative effect is to assert that cognition depends on language and that the signs constituting the linguistic system cannot be divorced either from that system as an organic whole or from the communal values that establish themselves within the system. The premise that must be added to arrive at the reductionist position is the premise that signs refer only to other signs within the system and do not depend upon any grounding in an extralinguistic reality that would account for their origin, measure, and ultimate reference.

This premise does not appear in Saussure's theorizing. Indeed, it is excluded by the central notion of linguistic value, which stipulates a social grounding as necessary for langugage.[31] This, as noted earlier, is the scientific realism of Saussure at work.

But the reductionist premise that confines cognition within the immanence of language finds a hospitable host in Saussure's theory, specificially, in the operative equivocity of his notion of the signified. Following the convention of the use-mention distinction, it is the case that, for Saussure, *tree* signifies tree. He states this in two ways.[32]

[A]   *arbor* signifies tree.

[B]   *arbor* signifies 🌳.

Now *tree* and 🌳 in [B] function as signifiers for tree; neither is a tree, but both represent the concept, one by means of a word, the other by means of a picture. Trees cannot appear in texts, in written (or spoken) discourse. Suppose, *per impossibile,* Saussure could have included a real tree in his text. Or, suppose it occurred to him to use an indexical term; for example, *this page* signifies this page, the one on which these words are written. Would he have done so? I think he would have. I think that is why he used the picture, 🌳. But I must leave the point moot. The point that is not moot, however, is that the signifiers *tree* and 🌳 in [A] and [B] are ambiguous, *essentially ambiguous,* because they can be taken to refer either to a concept or to a thing. There is no way, within discourse alone, that one can resolve this ambiguity.

Of course, one can say

[C]   *this page* signifies this page, the one one which these words are written.

But the reductionist can always point out that the words "this page, the one on which these words are written" are themselves signs and not this page, the one on which these words are written. Indeed, that is the ploy employed by semiological reductionism. It underlies the claim that there is no egress from the claim of signifiers, no access to a transcendent reality, because signs are necessarily defined by reference to other signs and derive any meaning they can have therefrom. Even ostensive definitions such as [C] remain locked within the chain of signifiers according to the reductionist claim.

The question of semiological reference is at least as old as the medieval dispute over nominalism and realism — anticipations of it are evident in *Cratylus* (386 ff) — and one might expect contemporary philosophers to have realized that neither of the traditional standpoints is defensible: nominalism cannot account for the origin of signs, and realism cannot account for the transcendental function (or sedimentation) of language; some third alternative is required. Yet semiological reductionism is but thinly veiled nominalism. What gives the version current in continental thought its appearance of novelty is the synthesis of neo-Husserlian transcendental idealism with neo-Saussurean semiology. And that, simply stated, is the synthesis of Saussure's thesis of cognitive dependency with Husserl's thesis that all meaning originates within the sphere of immanence. The result is the attribution to Language, as a transpersonal, historically evolving agency of cultural constitution, all the functions of sense-bestowing Husserl attributed to the transcendental ego.

Language thus takes on the character of a groundless ground. It is a ground because it is the origin of all meaning or value and the ultimate object of cognition. But it is, itself, groundless — because the meaning bestowed by a given sign is arbitrary, cannot be read off the signifier, but must be defined by reference to other signs, which in turn require definition by reference to yet other signs, and so on: no sign is meaningful apart from its inclusion within the entire system. Yet the system, itself, has no referent, no source of meaning. The signs refer only to each other, but each signifier is itself devoid of meaning: where then does the system acquire its meaning? Saussure posited a social ground for language with his notion of communal value — which, one may assume, is a mediate reference to the world through the structures of social praxis. However, this ground has been forsaken in the reduction to immanence that reverses Saussure's ordering of priorities by positing language as the source of all value, including communal value. This leaves the sign system with no appeal except to itself, and gives it the character of a groundless absolute: a self-generating system that can speak only about itself. Furthermore, because the system, itself, is historically evolving, each synchronic slice must be understood diachronically, in the context of its antecedents, and this projects the search for grounds back into a linguistic prehistory where darkness necessarily prevails. The sign system, hence every individual sign within it, is adrift in what Anaximander called το απειρον.

This conclusion runs contrary to the beliefs of Saussure, who outlined a method of retrospective induction that could produce positive results in the search for historical grounds.[33] From the standpoint of semiological reductionism, however, "true reconstruction" is an impossibly optimistic conception. Given the absence of genuine foundations, there can be only partial de-constructions; that is, the dismantling of a linguistic structure held to be a priori within the present synchrony to reveal the accidents influencing its genesis. De-construction thus typically functions to produce an exposé, a scandal, a nexus of fissures in the edifice of received belief. Unlike its Heideggerian predecessor, destruction,[34] de-construction does not offer even a qualified promise that the clearing away of intervening assumptions (i.e., the history of Western ontology) will open the way for a disclosure of truth. Destruction is pointed toward the revelation of grounds; de-construction seeks to reveal their absence.

The question of the relation of language and history is central to the problematics of both hermeneutics and semiology. If one answers that question with the model of a closed circuit in which the nature of language is determined by historical accident and our understanding of history is determined by the vagaries of language, then one has locked oneself within a groundless immanence with no opening on truth and no possibility for any accumulation or refinement of knowledge. As Merleau-Ponty puts it,

> history cannot be our only approach to language, because language would then become a prison. It would determine even what one could say about it[35] and, being always presupposed in what is said about it, it would be incapable of any clarification. Even the science of language, enveloped in its present state, would be unable to reach a truth of language, and thus objective history would destroy itself.[36]

Post-hermeneutic skepticism and semiological reductionism — these are alternate routes to a neo-Socratic ignorance: a position that defends no position, but attacks from whatever vantage is expeditious at the moment. Indeed, because even in this philosophical counterpart of guerilla warfare every attack must originate somewhere, because every exposure of falsity betrays the latency of truth, those who engage in it must be careful to shift ground, to obscure their bases of operation, to betray their allies as a matter of principle, to erase the signs of having occupied some position, however momentarily. It is a dance that requires a level of virtuosity worthy of Socrates at the height of his casuistical power.

But just as Socrates's profession of ignorance was a rhetorical device that could not withstand critical scrutiny, so does the skeptical retreat to the abyss display its own bad conscience with regard to the impossibility of referring beyond the chain of signifiers. The statement that denies the possibility of referring within language to things lying beyond language must make the reference it denies is possible—and then put that reference under erasure.

This is a path that has already been investigated — perhaps most carefully by Wittgenstein, in his *Tractatus*. At the end of that book, he finds that he has spoken of things that cannot, according to his own theory, be expressed in language. And so he puts his words under erasure. "My propositions serve as elucidations in the following way: anyone who understands me eventually recognizes them as nonsensical, when he has used them—as steps—to climb up beyond them. (He must, so to speak, throw away the ladder after he has climbed up it.)"[37] Later, in the *Philosophical Investigations*, Wittgenstein realizes that the ladder cannot be thrown away. If his theory requires him to erase what it forced him to say, then it is the theory that must be thrown away because it embodies a contradiction. In the case of the *Tractatus*, the theory held that "*the limits of [my] langauge . . .* mean (*bedeuten*) the limits of my world."[38]

But the theory required Wittgenstein to speak of the relation between language and world to explain what it means for any proposition (including the one just cited) to be true.[39] And that requirement entails a reference beyond language to what language shows. The showing of language, its ownmost function, requires a passage beyond the chain of signifiers, a reference beyond the immanent sphere of language: the showing of language depends upon a cognitive, but prelinguistic, opening upon the world; it depends upon the perception of phenomena. "There are, indeed, things that cannot be put into words. They *make themselves manifest*."[40] "What we cannot speak about we must pass over in silence."[41] This is Wittgenstein's concluding proposition in the *Tractatus*. But the silence of which he speaks there is broken in the *Investigations* where it becomes the theme of his inquiry. And it is to this silence before speech, this silence within speech, this realm that transcends language and provides its enabling context, that Merleau-Ponty turns in his interrogation of language.

To summarize and conclude, I have presented a series of arguments designed to demonstrate the fallacies inherent in the retreat to linguistic immanence, which I have characterized as post-hermeneutic skepticism and semiological reductionism. These arguments sought to show (1) that the skeptical-reductionist position is self-referentially inconsistent (as, in conceiving language as effectively *causa sui,* it both deifies language and forecloses the possibility of accounting for its own genesis), and (2) that the position entails a species of relativism tantamount to philosophical suicide (because it denies the possibility of even that open-ended kind of truth necessary to the rational adjudication of competing cognitive claims).

The proposition that engenders the skeptical-reductionist position is succinctly expressed by Heidegger: "We human beings remains committed to and within the being of language, and can never step out of it and look at it from somewhere else."[42] This is not a version of the thesis of linguistic immanence — although it approaches its threshold — because, for Heidegger, language is also extrareferential: it speaks of things and shows things that lie beyond itself. In this context, then, I think the proposition is largely true. And this truth lends a spurious credibility to the thesis it engenders. Engenders — not entails: this is a crucial point, and with it I will conclude.

We cannot step outside language and look at it from somewhere else. Nor can we step outside our bodies. Or our genders. Or our cultures, histories, families, and the psycho-socio-economic-etc. infrastructures informing them. Nor can we step out of the archaisms that subtend our conscious lives. And each one of these parameters of human existence has its own "ism," its own all-inclusive reductionist premise, its own exclusive claim on the genesis of meaning. Each "ism" purports to explain all the others "at a deeper level." Each one was born amidst the optimism of discovery—here lies *the* key, *the* master hypothesis, *the* unifying theory—and each one has earned its place in the gaggling pantheon of academic disciplines—although none has won the throne it sought.

Is it not time to perform the simple induction? History fails when myopia transforms it into historicism. And the same is true of logic and logicism, psychology and psychologism, experimentation and empiricism, constitution and transcendentalism. Did we of the continental tradition repudiate positivism[43] only to generate our own language-based reductionism?

The point here is the point with which I began. We cannot step out of our language, our bodies, our histories, and so forth. Nor would we want to. Each one is an opening on to the world. And if, *per impossibile,* any one could be forsaken, the result would, indeed, be a simpler world —but simpler by virtue of impoverishment.

The world is permeated by language. As it is permeated with the structures of sexuality, power, consciousness, and so on. Everywhere we look, these structures precede us and work their transformations. This is the insight that took Heidegger beyond Dilthey into the general theory of hermeneutics. But the insight of hermeneutics is the recognition of immanence as a problem — and it degenerates into pessimism when that problem is skeptically misconceived as a solution.

Merleau-Ponty is often quoted as saying that "the most important lesson which the [transcendental] reduction teaches us is the impossibility of a complete reduction."[44] This, too, should be generalized. The most important lesson to be learned from all of the reductions, all the "isms," is that none will ever be completed exactly because they are all reductions.

"The philosophical interrogation concerning the world . . . does not consist in referring from the world itself to what we say of the world." Nor does it consist in reducing the world to the categories of sex, power, material, and so on. Once thought locates itself within any of these categories to the exclusion of the others, it becomes engulfed. This is the problem of immanence. Generalized to all such categories, categorical thinking, itself — or, more to the point, linguistically confined thinking, itself—becomes the problem of hermeneutics. The solution is transcendence.

POSTSCRIPT

When I have presented these thoughts to various forums, no one has attempted to defend the positions I attacked. But I have been vociferously chastised for my attribution of the skeptical-reductionist standpoint to Derrida and his school. Let me go on record here as saying that I would be entirely content and philosophically fulfilled were I convinced that neither Derrida nor his followers subscribe to the thesis of linguistic immanence. That statement, however, is voiced in the subjunctive because it names a state of affairs contrary to fact. That is, I remain unconvinced.

When Derrida writes "there is not a single signified that escapes . . . the play of signifying references that constitute language"[45] he invites the interpretation I have labeled *semiological reductionism*. This interpretation is reinforced in other texts where he enters such assertions as "there is no presence before and outside semiological difference."[46] I acknowledge that other interpretations of these passages differ from the one I have set forth. For example, one might evade some of my critical challenges by interpreting the *différance* that "produces" the "differences without positive terms"[47] that constitute language as the articulation intrinsic to phenomena — but then one would have either ceded the antifoundational standpoint or obscured an important distinction between sign and thing (and neither of these strikes me as acceptable to Derrida).

Derrida is notoriously (and, in my judgment, reprehensibly) obscure, evasive, circumlocutious on the questions I have raised concerning the origins, referentiality, and truthfulness of language. Not so the enthusiasts among his followers and critics: semiological reductionism is widely practiced by the former and lamented by the latter (although not by the name I have given it). And yet, so far as I know, Derrida has maintained an ambiguous silence—except, as I have recently been informed, to label the questions stupid.

Here is the labeling passage:

There have been several misinterpretations of what I and other deconstructionists are trying to do. It is totally false to suggest that deconstruction is a suspension of reference. Deconstruction is always deeply concerned with the "other" of language. I never cease to be surprised by critics who see my work as a declaration that there is nothing beyond language, that we are imprisoned in language; it is, in fact, saying the exact opposite. The critique of logocentrism is above all else the search for the "other" and the "other of language." Every week I receive critical commentaries and studies on deconstruction which operate on the assumption that what they call "post-structuralism" amounts to saying that there is nothing beyond language, that we are submerged in words—and other stupidities of that sort. Certainly, deconstruction tries to show that the question of reference is much more complex and problematic than traditional theories supposed. It even asks whether our term "reference" is entirely adequate for designating the "other." The other, which is beyond language and which summons language, is perhaps not a "referent" in the normal sense which linguists have attached to this term. But to distance oneself thus from the habitual structure of reference, to challenge or complicate our common assumptions about it, does not amount to saying that there is *nothing* beyond language.[48]

Derrida here equates the charge that his theories imprison us in language (by asserting the thesis of linguistic immanence) with the claim that these theories assert that there is nothing beyond language. By discounting the latter claim he dismisses the former charge. The equation, however, is spurious. As noted in the main text of this essay, the premise of semiological reductionism does not entail denial of the existence of things independent of language, nor does it entail denial of our ability to perceive these things: it contends that our cognition of things is inextricably mediated by language or, again, that human cognition is imprisoned within the immanence of language. The spurious equation allows Derrida to transform the challenge to his position into a straw man and, thereby, to obscure a legitimate question.

The question is whether his conception of the "'other of language'" is strong enough to do some necessary work. Can it account for the prescriptive and delimiting force of the phenomenal world, the force that requires language to accommodate itself to what is the case? (We no longer say that the earth is flat — because the earth has shown itself not to be flat.) Can it account for the possibility of adjudicating the conflicting claims to truth among competing theories? Can it account for the emergence of novelty in language and the growth of our cognitive enterprises? These questions ask whether Derrida's "'other of language'" refers to a world that transcends language and is *meaningful* apart from language. There is, I think, a dilemma for Derrida here.

Either our apprehension of the "'other'" is always and necessarily mediated by the kind of opening provided by language—in which case (1) the answers to the questions just posed must be negative, and (2) Derrida is committed to the current vogue of skepticism outlined earlier.

Or there can be some apprehension of this "'other'" that is not in every case mediated by language — in which case (1) we are open to a domain of meaning beyond signifiers, and (2) Derrida must acknowledge our presence within a world that transcends semiological difference.

To say that the perceptual world affords a measure to cognition is not to deny the sedimentation of culture and language in that world: it is to say that the world has demands of its own, demands that call for language and respond to language in varying degrees of acceptance and rejection, revelation and concealment. Not all discourses and cultures are equiviable: if they were, there would be no point to debate, no rationale to dialectic.

Derrida does, indeed, speak of an other "which is beyond language and which summons language." So far, we are in accord. But now must silence prevail? Or may we ask about this other: how it issues its summons, whether it allows us to measure the validity of responses to its summons, whether, in short, it has a discernible shape of its own or readily conforms to whatever significance the signifier of the moment would put upon it. What, in truth, can Derrida say of this other?

I have looked for this saying in Derrida's writing on "the trace." And there I find him asserting that "the trace is never as it is in the presentation of itself. It erases itself in presenting itself."[49] Again, "the trace is not a presence but the simulacrum of a presence that dislocates itself, displaces itself, refers itself." And, a few sentences later, "the present becomes the sign of the sign, the trace of the trace."[50]

This text that asks "how to conceive what is outside a text" quite deliberately and self-consciously erases itself (or so it seems to me) in order to remain consistent: what is beyond language we cannot finally name. So far, I would agree: in my terms, it is a mark of transcendence to elude the grasp of any putatively exhaustive chain of signifiers. Ockham knew that, as did Aristotle before him.

Love, for example, has had many names, but still remains to be named: the final baptism will be indefinitely deferred. That is half the story. The other half provides work for poets and philosophers, psychologists and anthropologists. Those who try to say what needs to be heard in the midst of the babble and confusion. Love calls for a saying that is better than what we have heard so far. Better, truer, more just to the other. And how will we measure this saying? By any and all means at our disposal, to be sure, although none will be final and exhaustive. Knowing this, we still work at the saying, and, in all deference to the evolving phenomenon, try to say the partial truths, try to displace the impartial errors, guided by what we can sense in the presence of love.

To reduce this presence to the sign of a sign, the trace of a trace, is to close ourselves off from the presence of transcendence. It is to make the act of contrition and resignation that has been the solace of the skeptics of all ages: *tu quoque,* my friend, cannot have the final truth, but I, at least, know that. Committed to finality—and, for that reason, in despair—I have the wisdom to quit. And content myself with displaying the futility of the search. With demonstrating the fact that your words, like all others, are but signs of signs, that your discourse alludes to nothing but the trace of a trace, reveals but another absence. I resign myself to the indefinite play of signifiers, because, beyond them, there is nothing that can be said.

There is always more to say about this other language—precisely because it is elusive, mutable, and responsive to our saying. But the response of the other is not always the same: acquiescence to any and every denomination (and hence to none). Love presents itself differently to each different appellation; to some it dissembles, from others it withdraws, in rare cases it resonates. Each response is, nonetheless, a revelation as well as a concealment. There is no finality here, but there is an opportunity to learn. No grand Truth, but a massive accumulation of partial truths that amounts to a historical unfolding. Of something beyond signifiers. About which it is well to know as much as we can. This is not the end of philosophy; it is its perennial renewal, its *telos.*

15

Merleau-Ponty and l'Écriture

Wayne J. Froman

The problematic of language is a link between phenomenology and work in other areas of contemporary thought. Clearly it is a link between phenomenology and "l'écriture," a crucial theme in the work of Jacques Derrida, insofar as Derrida finds that "l'écriture" is the other of metaphysics and metaphysics is the mode of thought predominant in the West since its beginning. Most juxtapositions of Derrida's writings with those of other writers, including phenomenologists, have made the "metaphysics of presence" the point of contention. Can this original offense be hunted down in the other writer's works once one has unburdened oneself in the reading-writing of Derrida's? Or, has Derrida appropriated the ability to de-construct from a predecessor in such a way as to be guilty of the "metaphysics of presence?" There are a number of variations. Here, my point of departure will be otherwise. I will examine the link between the phenomenological investigation of language and "l'écriture" by asking what happens when "l'écriture" is juxtaposed with Merleau-Ponty's interrogation of speech.

In "The End of the Book and the Beginning of Writing," the first section of Part I of *Of Grammatology,* we read:

All appearances to the contrary, this death of the book undoubtedly announces (and in a certain sense always has announced) nothing but a death of speech (of a *so-called* full speech) and a new mutation in the history of writing, in history as writing. Announces it at a distance of a few centuries. . . . "Death of speech" is of course a met-

193

aphor here: before we speak of disappearance, we must think of a new situation for speech, of its subordination within a structure of which it will no longer be the archon.

Where Derrida would unfix or liberate writing, Merleau-Ponty thought of a new situation for speech in a "structure" of which it is no longer the archon. First of all, in *Phenomenology of Perception,* in displacing objectivistic features from an unwarranted dominating role in the content of perception, Merleau-Ponty located language that is spoken in the field of perception and found that language that is spoken has meaning in a way that other elements in the field of perception have meaning. That is to say, meaning in language is "structure" — already described in *The Structure of Behavior* on the basis of a reinterpretation of the notion of "gestalt" — "structure" that is radically contingent. The shift from "structure" in *The Structure of Behavior* to *sens* in *Phenomenology of Perception* emphasizes that radical contingency. This radical contingency precludes thinking of language as a closed or total system — as at any point in the past having been a closed or total system, or as closeable or totalizable in the future. This is made explicit in the essay "On the Phenomenology of Language," where Merleau-Ponty demonstrates that language cannot be understood exclusively in terms of diachrony, nor exclusively in terms of synchrony, nor in terms of a combination of the two. Recalling the shortcomings of both empiricist accounts and idealist accounts of perception identified in the Introduction to *Phenomenology of Perception,* both of which amount to missing language in the field of perception, Merleau-Ponty demonstrates that language resists conceptualization as a closed or totalized system of signifiers, one that would signify things and relations of things or independently subsisting ideal meanings. Language also resists conceptualization as a system of signifiers that would signify places in a closed, totalized, or totalizable system. The "radically contingent structure" of language is "languagely meaning."

How does language that is spoken with its meaning "make its appearance"? Recall that the point is that Merleau-Ponty relocated speech in a structure of which it is no longer the archon. In the chapter "The Body as Expression, and Speech" in *Phenomenology of Perception,* Merleau-Ponty writes: "It makes its appearance like the boiling point of a liquid, when in the density of being, volumes of empty space are built up and move outwards."[2] It "makes its appearance" as do other gestures in the field of perception. Motility "makes its appearance" with the building up of sense or meaning in the phenomenal body's habituation of space. Speaking "makes its appearance" with the building up of sense or meaning in the phenomenal body's directedness in language in the field of perception. Merleau-Ponty writes:

It might be said, restating a celebrated distinction, that *languages* or constituted systems of vocabulary and syntax, empirically existing "means of expression," are both the repository and residue of acts of *speech,* in which unformulated significance not only finds the means of being conveyed outwardly, but moreover acquires existence for itself, and is genuinely created as significance. Or again one might draw a distinction between the *word in the speaking* and the *spoken word.* The former is the one in which the significant intention is at the stage of coming into being. Here existence is polarized into a certain "sense or meaning" (*sens*) which cannot be defined in terms of any natural object. It is somewhere at a point beyond being that it aims to catch up with itself again, and that is why it creates speech as an empirical support for its own not-being. ... Such is the function which we intuit through language, which reiterates itself, which is its own foundation, or which, like a wave, gathers and poises itself to hurtle beyond its own limits.[3]

It is a function then, one that is intuited through language that is spoken but that is operative throughout the "radically dynamic structure" of the field of perception. Is it a new situation of speech in a "structure" of which it is no longer the archon? The response might be that there is more here to be de-constructed than meets the eye. The root difficulty would seem to be that speech has been situated in this "structure" only by "stifling force under form" in describing how speaking "makes its appearance" with the building up of sense or meaning in the phenomenal body's directedness in language in the field of perception. Derrida writes in the essay "Force and Signification" that "force is the other of language without which language would not be what it is."[4] Add then: "Now, one would seek in vain a concept in phenomenology which would permit the conceptualization of intensity or force. The conceptualization not only of direction but of power, not only the *in* but the *tension* of intentionality."[5] And yet, "to stifle force under form" is precisely what Merleau-Ponty refrains from doing at this juncture. That is exactly why he speaks of the need to find this "function that subsumes both motility and intelligence" and identifies that function with an "irrational power" that might define the human being.

In "Force and Signification," Derrida calls for an attempt at emancipation from language in which the effort is made to articulate force in terms appropriate to form, language that Derrida identifies as what locates phenomenology within the most purely traditional stream of Western philosophy. He writes: "But not as an *attempt* at emancipation from it, for this is impossible unless we forget *our* history. Rather, as the dream of emancipation. Nor as emancipation from it, which would be meaningless and would deprive us of the light of meaning. Rather, as resistance to it, as far as is possible."⁶ Merleau-Ponty refrains from "stifling force under form" and resists the language in which an effort is made to articulate force in terms appropriate to form when he writes of the need to find "a function that subsumes both motility and intelligence," an "irrational power" that creates meanings and communicates them and might serve to define the human being. He writes of this need at a point where he encounters a critical difficulty in clarifying speaking.

What this difficulty is becomes clear in Part Three of *Phenomenology of Perception.* It is the difficulty of trying to maintain the perspective of a perceiver perceiving content of perception while describing a function that creates meanings and communicates them. In Part Three of *Phenomenology of Perception,* Merleau-Ponty examines three traditional strongholds of a subject that would be fully present to itself, or in other words, of a perceiver that would be somehow divorced from the field of perception, and in each case finds no self-coinciding subject. It is this difficulty in describing the dynamic of language that is spoken in the perceptual field that calls for a phenomenology of the perceiver-perceived phenomenon structure, or in Merleau-Ponty's words, a phenomenology of phenomenology.

We find a way forward in Merleau-Ponty's explorations of the field of painting, including "Eye and Mind." It is the dynamic of "reversibility" that Merleau-Ponty first discloses in vision, in that my seeing is as it is by virtue of my being located in the field of the visible. This reversibility is at work in touch. It is at work throughout bodily commerce with the world. The domain in which it takes place is named the *flesh* by Merleau-Ponty. The dynamic is the taking place of perception neither inside a "subject" nor outside a "subject." This is the clue for working through the difficulty of trying to maintain the perspective of a perceiver perceiving content of perception while describing a function that creates meanings and communicates them,⁷ for finding that function that subsumes both motility and intelligence without "stifling force under form." In the chapter "The Intertwining — The Chiasm" of *The Visible and the Invisible* we find that Merleau-Ponty begins to interrogate this dynamic. He writes there:

> To begin with, we spoke summarily of a reversibility of the seeing and the visible, of the touching and the touched. It is time to emphasize that it is a reversibility always imminent and never realized in fact. My left hand is always on the verge of touching my right hand touching the things, but I never reach coincidence; the coincidence eclipses at the moment of realization, and either one of two things always occurs: either my right hand really passes over to the rank

of the touched, but then its hold on the world is interrupted; or it retains its hold on the world, but then I do not really touch *it* — my right hand touching, I palpate with my left hand only its outer covering.[8]

And we note that the same *non*-coincidence, divergence, or differing that is never realized but is always imminent takes place with the reversibility of the voice:

Likewise, I do not hear myself as I hear the others, the sonorous existence of my voice is for me as it were poorly exhibited; I have rather an echo of its articulated existence, it vibrates through my head rather than outside. . . . But this incessant escaping . . . is not a failure. For if these experiences never exactly overlap, if they slip away at the very moment they are about to rejoin, if there is always a "shift," a "spread," between them, this is precisely because . . . I hear myself both from within and from without. I experience — and as often as I wish—the transition and the metamorphosis of the one experience into the other, and it is only as though the hinge between them, solid, unshakeable, remained irremediably hidden from me. But this hiatus between my right hand touched and my right hand touching, is not an ontological void, a non-being.[9]

It is this "hiatus" that is not a void, this "trace" that is strictly speaking neither visible nor invisible that is now to be interrogated. In the last paragraphs of "The Intertwining—The Chiasm" in discussing work that he describes as unsurpassed in investigating the bond between the visible and the invisible — the work of Marcel Proust — Merleau-Ponty identifies the "trace" as the clue to working through the most difficult point, the bond between the flesh and the idea, between the visible and the interior armature that it manifests and that it conceals. It is the clue to finding that "function" that creates meanings and communicates them, without "stifling force under form." It is the clue to working through the difficulty that Merleau-Ponty defines in Husserl's words at the end of the chapter "Interrogation and Intuition": "It is the experience . . . still mute which we are concerned with leading to the pure expression of its own meaning."[10] It is the clue to philosophy — "the reconversion of silence and speech into one another."[11]

The new situation of speech that Merleau-Ponty thought is its occurrence within the dynamic structure of "reversibility," a structure of which it is not the archon. What is the yield? If, as Derrida indicates in "The End of the Book and the Beginning of Writing," the "problem of language" has invaded the global horizon of the most diverse researches and the most heterogeneous of discourses, and if, by a slow movement whose necessity is hardly perceptible, everything that throughout some twenty centuries tended toward and finally succeeded in being gathered under the name of language is beginning to let itself be transferred to, or at least summarized under, the name writing[12] rather than a *"so-called full speech,"* it is Merleau-Ponty who worked a way through the problem of full speech to a new situation of speech within the dynamic structure of "reversibility" and the question concerning "the trace." The "trace" is the "hinge" that remains when the "noncoincidence" of reversibility is effaced in the establishment of an opposition between the visible and the invisible—the sensible and the intelligible—in an effort to recapture a self-coincidence of a subject before the sounding of the voice, one that has not ever been. That effort is what suppresses writing, in that writing is relegated to the status of a falling away further from the self-coincidence that is to be recaptured, in the domain of the purely intelligible, by way of full or pure speech. To put the matter a different way: the tension in the intentionality of speaking, the tension that takes shape in the effort to describe a "function" that creates meanings and communicates them builds up and moves outward into the margins of Merleau-Ponty's writings. "L'écriture" makes its appearance in those margins.[13]

Derrida affirms that we are not beyond the book. What "makes its appearance" in the margins does fall back within the book. After one has read *Phenomenology of Perception* — and one is aware that the thesis of the primacy of perception, which Merleau-Ponty describes in the 1946 address to the *Société française de philosophie* as a thesis that does not destroy rationality or the absolute but only tries to bring them down to earth, indeed does not confine the philosopher to a single current of existence but opens a way to each current of existence, there is a moment when one is struck by the possibility that to remain faithful to this thesis one would have to displace "the book" from an unwarranted dominating role in the reading perception in a way that permits describing the original content of this perception. Just as locating speech in the field of perception brings up the question of the origin of speech, the task of describing the original content of the reading perception brings up the question of the origin of writing. As with speech, a gesture is involved, and the inscription of that gesture has become the original content of the reading perception. The origin has been displaced. Direction and meaning are built up in the reading perception. "The book makes its appearance." Again the task is that of finding that "function" that creates meanings and communicates them, now by way of "the book." Again, the difficulty is that of trying to describe the dynamic of that "function" from the perspective of a perceiver perceiving content of perception. Again the perceiver-perceived structure must itself be displaced or put in play or at stake. The closure of "the book" is deferred. Reading that displaces "the book" from an unwarranted dominating role in the content of perception is writing. The question now concerns the "hiatus," the "hinge," the "trace" at work in the transition and metamorphosis between writing and reading, reading and writing, "the book" and "the book." In a working note dated November 1960, one finds that the question of the "hinge," the "hiatus," the "trace" that operates here did not escape Merleau-Ponty:

> Silence of perception = the object made of wires of which I could not say what it is, nor how many sides it has, etc. and which nonetheless is there . . .
> There is an analogous silence of language i.e., a language that no more involves acts of reactivated signification than does this perception—and which nonetheless functions, and inventively . . . it is it that is involved in the fabrication of a book—[14]

"L'écriture" makes its appearance in the margins of Merleau-Ponty's writings because it was already there within them. To extend Merleau-Ponty's observation in *Phenomenology of Perception,* the problem of "the book" consists in the fact that it is all already there.[15] The way to work through the problem is the interrogation of "the trace." Derrida does not silence this question. To be sure, he asks about a still illegible writing. The question is put at the end of the essay "Edmond Jabès and the Question of the Book":

> But what if the book was only, in all senses of the word, an *epoch* of Being . . . ? If the Being of the world, its presence and the meaning of its Being, revealed itself only in illegibility. . . . The dissimulation of an older or younger writing, from an age other than the age of the book, the age of grammar, the age of everything announced under the heading of the meaning of Being? The dissimulation of a still illegible writing?[16]

If the book is only, in all senses of the word, an *epoch* of Being, it is "the trace" that remains of the "epochal transition" that holds out a possibility of response to the question put at the end of this passage. Further, if "the trace" is operative in the fabrication of a book, however hidden it might be, is it to be found at work in a "still illegible" writing that might "precede" the book? In other words, this "trace" may be interrogated —it, too, along with the "configurations" between which it operates, is in play or at stake. After posing the question concerning a still illegible writing, Derrida proceeds to observe that writing would die of the pure vigilance of the question, as it would of the simple erasure of the question. Merleau-Ponty writes of a silence that may tempt the philosopher in the midst of the effort to state the philosopher's "contact with Being."[17] This silence is the vigilance of the question. It is not the silence that we are "concerned with leading to the pure expression of its own meaning in a language which, Merleau-Ponty writes, one has to believe would not be simply the contrary of the truth." And then Merleau-Ponty adds: "if language is not necessarily deceptive, truth is not coincidence, nor mute."[18] In the course of his approach to this language of truth, "l'écriture" makes an appearance in the margins of Merleau-Ponty's writings. Must "l'écriture" immediately upon making its appearance efface itself or be reappropriated by "the book" (in much the same way as the primordial motility that Merleau-Ponty discloses in the chapter concerning motility at the outset of *Phenomenology of Perception* appears almost inevitably to be reappropriated by objectivistically conceived space)? The problem is the problem of the book that consists in the fact that it is all already there. It is that problem that is at stake in the apparent necessity for Derrida *to initiate* the "de-construction" that is to result in "l'écriture," whereas the dynamics of "l'écriture" are understood to operate without such initiation, without an origination of this nature. When Derrida qualifies the use of the word *l'écriture* with "if there is any," this problem is indicated, aside from the issue of the suppression of "l'écriture." What would rule "l'écriture" out is the silence of the pure vigilance of the question (and that is a risk, after all, of "de-construction" that loses contact with the problem of "the book"). At the same time, simply erasing the interrogation that is initiated in *The Visible and the Invisible,* an interrogation of "the trace," would rule out "l'écriture."[19]

Derrida closes the essay in which he poses the question of an illegible writing "before" the book with the suggestion that literature perhaps has to be a "dreamlike displacement" of the question. The final piece in *Writing and Difference,* "Ellipsis," returns to *Le livre des questions* by Jabès. For a moment—perhaps that moment of hesitation between writing as decentering and writing as an affirmation of play, between anguish and something being at stake on the one hand and reassurance and appeasement on the other—*l'écriture* and a radical illegibility before the book come extremely close to one another. Derrida writes:

> If nothing has preceded repetition, if no present has kept watch over the trace, if, after a fashion, it is the "void which reempties itself and marks itself with imprints" [from Jean Catesson, "Journal non-intime et points cardinaux," *Measures,* no. 4, October 1937], then the time of writing no longer follows the line of modified present tenses. What is to come is not a future present, yesterday is not a past present. The beyond of the closure of the book is

neither to be awaited nor to be refound. It is *there*, but out there, *beyond*, within repetition, but eluding us there. It is there like the shadow of the book, the third party between the hands holding the book, the deferral within the now of writing, the distance between the book and the book, that other hand. Opening the third part of the third *Book of Questions*, thus begins the song on *distance and accent*:

> *"Tomorrow is the shadow and reflexibility of our hands."*
>
> *Reb Derissa*[20]

At this moment, "l'écriture," which makes an appearance in the writings of Jacques Derrida, and the interrogation of "the trace," which operates in the reversibility found in manual gestures (and phonatory gestures as well), come extremely close to one another. The title of this piece, "Ellipsis," is taken from the discussion there of the question of an apparently inevitable return to "the book" of whatever would remain beyond the closure of "the book," which is the discussion of the third volume of *Le livre des questions*. The return, Derrida writes, is elliptical, something is missing that would make the circle of return perfect. The "Ellipsis" also comes at the end of *Writing and Difference*, between *Writing and Difference* and other writings but also within *Writing and Difference*, marking where something is left out of the first essay devoted to Jabès. It also passes through each point in the circuit of *Writing and Difference* marking where something is left out between the book and the book, where something between "l'écriture" and an illegibility before the book escapes. At times one may get the impression that Derrida undertakes, precisely by not duplicating "the book" and by undoing any book that would make an appearance, to intervene where the lines that render his writings "sous rature" would cross, in such a way that together the writings would speak.

Derrida's writings speaking; *l'écriture* that makes its appearance in the margins of Merleau-Ponty's interrogation of speech—one would perhaps say that there is one voice too many here or, if one will, that there is one hand too many. Has a metaphor been formed? Are *l'écriture* and the reversibility of speech subjugated here to the Concept, which would amount to a reassertion of "the book"? I would suggest, rather, that in the moment of hesitation between writing as unlimited play and writing as displacement that puts at stake, speech makes its appearance in writing. Likewise, in the moment of hesitation between the silence that tempts the philosopher in the midst of the effort to state the philosopher's "contact with Being" and the effort to arrive at the language that would bring the experience still mute to the pure expression of its own meaning, writing makes its appearance in speech. Further, this marks reversibility at work between "the graphic" and the "sonorous substance" between interlocutors. The "hiatus," the "hinge," the "trace" at work here is yet to be interrogated. It marks the appearance of philosophy. This does not amount to a reassertion of "the book" because the philosophy that makes its appearance here is not an effort to recapture an alleged total self-coincidence, a metaphysics that will always appropriate what is other, but rather philosophy that was announced in Merleau-Ponty's unfinished work, an access to Vertical or Wild Being — a realm that "precedes" the "epoch of the book," an epoch that may dissimulate an older or younger, still illegible writing.

16

Docile Bodies, Rebellious Bodies: Foucauldian Perspectives on Female Psychopathology

Susan Bordo

Throughout his later work, Michel Foucault warns us that we must never underestimate the flexibility of a dominant discourse, its ability to swallow resistance, or darker still, to press resistance into its own service. In the modern era, the body has become the chief medium of such service. Through table manners and toilet habits, through seemingly trivial routines, rules, and practices, culture is *"made* body," as anthropologist Pierre Bourdieu puts it—converted into automatic, habitual activity. As such it is put "beyond the grasp of consciousness ... [untouchable] by voluntary, deliberate transformation."[1] Our conscious politics and social commitments, our strivings for change, may be undermined and betrayed by the life of our bodies — not the craving, instinctual body imagined by Plato, Augustine, and Freud, but the docile, regulated body, the body that is practiced at and habituated to the rules of cultural life.

We are what we eat, as Feuerbach noted over a hundred years ago — and also, in this era of compulsive dieting, what we do not eat. It is a dreadful irony that at a time when women are occupying more social space than ever before, we should be relentlessly, obsessively striving to contract the amount of physical space we take up. The obsession with slenderness[2] is, unfortunately, not anomalous. Women, as study after study shows, are spending more time on the management and discipline of our bodies than we have in a long, long time. In a decade marked by a reopening of the public arena to women, the intensification of such regimens appears as diversionary and subverting. Through the pursuit of an everchanging, homogenizing, elusive ideal of femininity (a pursuit that has no terminus, no resting point, and that requires that women be constantly attentive to minute and often whimsical changes in fashion) female bodies become what Foucault calls "docile bodies" — bodies whose forces and energies are habituated to external regulation, subjection, transformation, "improvement."[3] Through the exacting and normalizing disciplines of diet, make-up, and dress — central organizing principles of time and space in the days of many women — we are rendered less socially oriented, more centripetally focused on modification of self. Through these disciplines, we continue to memorize on our bodies the feel and conviction of lack, insufficiency, of never being good enough. At the farthest extremes, the practices of femininity may lead us to utter demoralization, debilitation, and death.

Viewed historically, the discipline and normalization of the female body—perhaps the only gender oppression that exercises itself (although to different degrees and in different forms) across age, race, class, and sexual orientation—has to be acknowledged as an amazingly durable and flexible strategy of social control. In our own era, it is difficult to avoid the recognition that the contemporary preoccupation with appearance (which still affects women far more powerfully than men, even in our narcissistic and visually oriented culture[4]) may function as a "backlash" phenomenon, reasserting existing gender configurations *against* any attempts to shift or transform power relations. Surely we are in the throes of such backlash today. In newspapers and magazines daily we encounter stories that promote traditional gender relations and prey on anxieties about change: stories about latch-key children, abuse in day-care centers, the "new woman's" troubles with men, her lack of marriageability, and so on. A dominant visual theme in teen-age magazines involves women hiding in the shadows of men, seeking solace in their arms, willingly contracting the space they occupy. In such an era we desperately need an effective *political* discourse about the female body, a discourse adequate to an analysis of the insidious (and often pardoxical) pathways of modern social control.

Here, I believe that a feminist appropriation of some of the concepts developed in Foucault's later work can prove useful. Following Foucault, we first need to abandon the idea of power as something that is possessed by one group and leveled against another and need to think instead of the network of practices, institutions, and technologies that sustain positions of dominance and subordination within a particular domain. Second, we need an analysis adequate to describe a power whose central mechanisms are not repressive, but *constitutive*: "a power bent on generating forces, making them grow, and ordering them, rather than one dedicated to impeding them, making them submit, or destroying them."[5] Particularly in the realm of "femininity," where so much depends upon the seemingly willing acceptance of various norms and practices, we need an analysis of power "from below" (as Foucault puts it): of the mechanisms that shape and proliferate (rather than repress) desire, generate and focus our energies, construct our conceptions of normalcy and deviance, and so on. Third, we need a discourse that will enable us to account for the subversion of potential rebellion, a discourse that, although insisting on the necessity of "objective" analysis of power relations, social hierarchy, political backlash, and so forth, will nonetheless allow us to confront the mechanisms by which the subject becomes enmeshed, at times, into collusion with forces that sustain her own oppression.

This essay will not attempt to produce a "theory" along these lines. Rather, my focus will be the analysis of one particular arena where the interplay of these dynamics is striking and, perhaps, exemplary. It is a limited and unusual arena—a group of gender-related and historically localized disorders: hysteria, agoraphobia, and anorexia nervosa.[6] I recognize, too, that these disorders have been largely class and race specific, occuring overwhelmingly among white middle- and upper-middle-class women.[7] Nonetheless, anorexia, hysteria and agoraphobia may provide a paradigm of one way in which potential resistance is not merely undercut, but *utilized* in the maintenance and reproduction of existing power relations.

The central mechanism that I will describe involves a transformation (or, if you wish, duality) of meaning, through which conditions that are "objectively" (and on one level, experientially) constraining, enslaving, and even murderous, come to be experienced as liberating, transforming, and life giving. I offer this analysis, although it is limited to a specific domain, as an example of how a variety of contemporary critical discourses may be joined to yield an understanding of the subtle and often unwitting role played by our bodies in the symbolization and reproduction of gender.

THE BODY AS A TEXT OF FEMININITY

The continuum between female disorder and "normal" feminine practice is sharply revealed through a close reading of those disorders to which women have been particularly vulnerable. These, of course, have varied historically: neurasthenia and hysteria in the second half of the nineteenth century; agoraphobia, anorexia nervosa, and bulimia in the second half of the twentieth. This is not to say that there were not anorexics in the nineteenth century — for many cases were described, usually within the context of diagnoses of hysteria — or that there are not still women who suffer from classical hysterical symptoms in the twentieth century. But the taking up of eating disorders on a mass scale is unique to the culture of the 1980s, as the epidemic of hysteria was to the Victorian era.[8]

The body is not only a practical locus of social control; it is also a cultural text, a surface on which the central rules of a culture are inscribed and reinforced through the concrete language of the body. Loss of mobility, loss of voice, inability to leave the home, feeding others while starving self, taking up space and whittling down the space one's body takes up — all have symbolic and *political* meaning within the varying rules governing the historical construction of gender. Working within such a framework, we see that whether we are looking at hysteria, agoraphobia, or anorexia, we find the body of the sufferer deeply inscribed with an ideological construction of ideal femininity emblematic of the periods in question. (That construction, of course, is always a homogenizing, normalizing one, from which racial, class, and other differences are erased.) Strikingly, in these disorders the construction of femininity is written in disturbingly concrete, hyperbolic terms: exaggerated, extremely literal, at times virtually caricatured presentations of the ruling feminine mystique. The bodies of disordered women in this way offer themselves as an aggressively graphic text for the interpreter—a text that insists, demands, that it be read as a cultural statement, a statement about gender.

Both nineteenth-century male physicians and twentieth-century feminist critics have seen, in the symptoms of neurasthenia and hysteria (syndromes that became increasingly less differentiated as the century wore on), an exaggeration of stereotypically feminine traits. The nineteenth-century "lady" was idealized in terms of delicacy and dreaminess, sexual passivity, and a charmingly labile and capricious emotionality. Such notions were formalized and scientized in the work of male theorists from Acton and Kraft-Ebbing to Freud, who described "normal," mature femininity in such terms.[9] In this context, the dissociations of hysteria, the drifting and fogging of perception, the nervous tremors and faints, the anaesthesias, and the extreme mutability of symptomatology associated with nineteenth-century female disorders can be seen to be concretizations of the feminine mystique of the period, produced according to rules governing the prevailing construction of femininity. Doctors described what came to be known as the "hysterical personality" as "impressionable, suggestible, and narcissistic; highly labile, their moods changing suddenly, dramatically, and for seemingly inconsequential reasons . . . egocentric in the extreme . . . essentially asexual and not uncommonly frigid"[10] — all characteristics normative of femininity in this era.

As Elaine Showalter points out, the term *hysterical* itself became almost interchangeable with the term *feminine* in the literature of the period.[11]

The hysteric's embodiment of the feminine mystique of her era, however, seems subtle and ineffable compared to the ingenious literalism of agoraphobia and anorexia. In the context of our culture, this literalism makes sense. With the advent of movies and television, the rules for femininity have come to be culturally transmitted more and more through the deployment of standardized visual images. As a result, femininity itself has come to be largely a matter of constructing, in the manner described by Erving Goffman, the appropriate surface presentation of the self. We no longer are told what "a lady" is or of what femininity consists. Rather, we learn the rules directly through bodily discourse: through images that tell us what clothes, body shape, facial expression, movements, and environment is required.

In agoraphobia and even more dramatically in anorexia, the disorder presents itself as a virtual parody — though a tragic one — of twentieth-century constructions of femininity. In the 1950s and early 1960s, when agoraphobia first began to escalate among women, domesticity and dependency as the feminine ideal was reasserted. *Career woman* became a dirty word, much more so than it had been during the war, when the survival of the economy depended on women's willingness to do "men's work." The reigning ideology of femininity, so well described by Betty Friedan, and perfectly captured in the movies and television shows of the era, was childlike, unassertive, helpless without a man, "content in a world of bedroom and kitchen, sex, babies and home."[12] The housebound agoraphobic lives this construction of femininity literally. "You want dependency? I'll give you dependency!" she proclaims with her body, "You want me in the home? You'll have me in the home — with a vengeance!" The point, which many therapists have commented on, does not need further explication. Agoraphobia, as I. G. Fodor has put it, seems "the logical — albeit extreme — extension of the cultural sex-role stereotype for women" in this era.[13]

The emaciated body of the anorectic, of course, immediately presents itself as a caricature of the contemporary ideal of hyper-slenderness for women, an ideal that, despite the game resistance of racial and ethnic difference, has become the norm for women today. But slenderness is only the tip of the iceberg, for slenderness itself requires interpretation. *"C'est le sens qui fait vendre"* said Barthes, speaking of clothing styles — it is meaning that makes the sale. So, too, it is meaning that makes the body beautiful. Meaning, of course, has varied culturally, ethnically, and historically. Even within a specified arena or culture, body ideals and practices have multiple meanings, some related to gender, some not. For the purposes of this essay an abbreviated, gender-focused reading will be offered. But it must be stressed that such a reading illuminates only partially, and that many other dimensions not discussed here — economic, psychosocial, and cultural — figure in strongly.[14]

We begin with the painfully literal inscription, on the anorexic's body, of the rules governing the construction of contemporary femininity. That construction is a "double-bind" construction, which legislates contradictory ideals and directives. On the one hand, our culture still widely advertises domestic conceptions of femininity, the ideological moorings for a rigorously dualistic sexual division-of-labor, with woman as chief emotional and physical nurturer. The rules for this construction of femininity (and I shall speak here in a language that is both symbolic and literal) require that women learn to feed others, not the self, and to construe any desires for self-nurturance, for self-feeding, as greedy and excessive. What is required is that women develop a totally other-oriented emotional economy.

Young women today are still being taught such a construction of the self. On TV, the Betty Crocker commercials symbolically speak to men of the legitimacy of their wildest, most abandoned desires: "I've got a passion for you; I'm wild, crazy, out of control" the hungering man croons to the sensuously presented chocolate cake, offered lovingly by the (always present) female. Female hunger, on the other hand, is depicted as needful of containment and control, and female eating is seen as a furtive, shameful, illicit act, as in the Andes Candies and "Mon Cheri" commercials, where a "tiny bite" of chocolate, privately savored, is supposed to be ample reward for a day of serving others. Food is not the real issue here, of course. Rather, the control of female appetite for food is merely the most concrete expression of the general rule governing the construction of femininity that female hunger — for public power, for independence, for sexual gratification — be contained, and the public space that women be allowed to take up be circumscribed, limited.[15] On the body of the anorexic woman such rules are grimly and deeply etched.

At the same time as young women today continue to be taught traditionally "feminine" virtues, to the degrees that the professional arena has opened up to them, they must also learn to embody the traditonally white "male" language and values of that arena: self-control, determination, cool, emotional discipline, mastery, and so forth. Female bodies now speak symbolically of this necessity, in their slender spare shape and the menswear look that is currently fashionable. Our bodies, as we trudge to the gym every day and fiercely resist our hungers, our desires to soothe and baby ourselves, are also becoming more and more practiced at the "male" virtues of control and self-mastery. The anorexic pursues these virtues with single-minded, unswerving dedication: "Energy, discipline, my own power will keep me going," says ex-anorexic Aimes Liu, recreating her anorexic days, "psychic fuel. I need nothing and no one else. . . . I will be master of my own body, if nothing else, I vow."[16]

The ideal of slenderness, then, and the diet and exercise regimens that have become inseparable from it, offer the illusion of meeting, through the body, the contradictory demands of the contemporary ideology of femininity. Popular images reflect this dual demand. In a single issue of *Complete Woman* magazine, two articles appear, one on "Feminine Intuition," the other asking "Are You the New Macho Woman?" In *Vision Quest,* the young male hero falls in love with the heroine, as he says, because "she has all the best things I like in girls and all the best things I like in guys"; that is, she's tough and cool, but warm and alluring. In the enormously popular *Aliens,* the heroines's personality has been deliberately constructed, with near comic-book explicitness, to embody traditional nurturant femininity alongside breathtaking macho-prowess and control. (Sigourney Weaver, the actress who portrays her, has called the character "Rambolina"!)

In the pursuit of slenderness and the denial of appetite the traditional construction of femininity *intersects* with the new requirement for women to embody the "masculine" values of the public arena. The anorexic, as I have argued, embodies this intersection, this double-bind, in a particularly painful and graphic way.[17] I mean "double-bind" here quite literally. "Masculinity" and "femininity," at least since the nineteenth-century (and arguably before), have been constructed through a process of mutual exclusion. One cannot simply add the historically "feminine" virtues to the historically "masculine" ones to yield a "New Woman," a "New Man," a new ethics or a new culture. Even on the screen or on television, embodied in created characters like the *Aliens* heroine, the result is a parody. Unfortunately, in this image-bedazzled culture, we have increasing difficulty discriminating between parodies and possibilities for the self. Explored as a possibility for the self, the "androgynous" ideal ultimately exposes its internal contradiction, and becomes a war that tears the subject in two — a war that is explicitly thematized, by many anorexics, as a battle between the "male" and "female" sides of the self.[18]

PROTEST AND RETREAT IN THE SAME GESTURE

In hysteria, agoraphobia, and anorexia, the woman's body may be viewed as a surface on which conventional constructions of femininity are exposed to view, through their inscription in extreme or hyper-literal form. They are also written, of course, in languages of horrible suffering.

It is as though these bodies are speaking to us of the pathology and violence that lurks just around the edge, waits at the horizon, of "normal"
femininity. It is no wonder, then, that a steady motif in the feminist literature on female disorder is that of pathology as embodied *protest* — unconscious, inchoate, and counterproductive protest, protest without an effective language, without voice, without politics, but protest nonetheless.

American and French feminists alike have heard the hysteric speaking a language of protest, even (or perhaps especially) when she was
mute. Dianne Hunter interprets Anna O's aphasia (which manifested itself in an inability to speak her native German) as a rebellion against the
linguistic and cultural rules of her father, and a return to the "mother-
tongue": the semiotic babble of infancy, the language of the body. For
Hunter, and for a number of other feminists working with Lacanian categories, the return to the semiotic level is both regressive and, as Hunter
puts it, an "expressive" communication "addressed to patriarchal
thought," "a self-repudiating form of feminine discourse in which the
body signifies what social conditions make it impossible to state linguistically."[19] "The hysterics are accusing; they are pointing," writes Catherine Clément in *The Newly Born Woman;* they make a "mockery of culture."[20] In the same volume, Hélène Cixous speaks of "those wonderful
hysterics, who subjected Freud to so many voluptuous moments too
shameful to mention, bombarding his mosaic statue/law of Moses with
their carnal, passionate body-words, haunting him with their inaudible
thundering denunciations."[21] For Cixous, Dora, who so frustrated Freud,
is "the core example of the protesting force in women."[22]

The literature of protest includes functional as well as symbolic approaches. Robert Seidenberg and Karen DeCrow, for example, describe
agoraphobia as a "strike" against "the renunciations usually demanded
of women" and the expectations of housewifely functions such as shop-
ping, driving the children to school, accompanying their husbands to social events, and so.[23] Carroll Smith-Rosenberg presents a similar analysis
of hysteria, arguing that by preventing the woman from functioning in the
wifely role of caretaker of others, of "ministering angel" to husband and
children, hysteria "became one way in which conventional women could
express—in most cases unconsciously—dissatisfaction with one or several aspects of their lives."[24] A number of feminist writers, among whom
Susie Ohrbach is the most articulate and forceful, have interpreted anorexia as a species of unconscious feminist protest. The anorexic is engaged in a "hunger strike," as Ohrbach calls it, stressing here that this is
a political discourse, in which the action of food refusal and dramatic
transformation of body size "expresses with [the] body what [the ano-
rexic] is unable to tell us with words" — her indictment of a culture that
disdains and suppresses female hunger, that makes women ashamed of

their appetites and needs, and that demands that women be constantly working on the transformation of their bodies.[25]

The very same gesture that expresses protest, however, also signals retreat. This, indeed, may be part of the attraction of the symptom. Kim Chernin argues, for example, that the debilitating anorexic fixation, by halting or mitigating personal development, assuages this generation's guilt and separation anxiety over the prospect of surpassing our mothers, of living less circumscribed, freer lives.[26] Agoraphobia, too, which often develops shortly after marriage, clearly functions in many cases as a way to cement dependency and attachment in the face of unacceptable stirrings of dissatisfaction and restlessness.

Although we may talk meaningfully of protest, then, we must stay clear about the fact that the protest written on the body of the hysteric, the agoraphobic, and the anorexic has a tragically self-defeating doubleness of meaning. Functionally, the symptoms of these disorders isolate, weaken, and undermine the sufferers, while at the same time turning the life of the body into an all-absorbing fetish, beside which all other objects of attention seem pale and unreal. On the symbolic level, too, the protest dimension collapses into its opposite and proclaims the utter defeat and capitulation of the subject to the contracted female world. The muteness of hysterics and their return to the level of pure, primary bodily expressivity has been interpreted, as we have seen, as a rejection of the symbolic order of patriarchy, and the recovery of a lost world of semiotic, maternal value. But *at the same time*, of course, muteness is the condition of the silent, uncomplaining woman — an ideal of patriarchal culture. Protesting the stifling of the female voice through one's own voicelessness, employing the language of femininity to protest the conditions of the female world will always involve ambiguities of this sort. Perhaps, this is why symptoms crystallized from the language of femininity are so perfectly suited to express the dilemmas of women living in periods poised on the edge of gender change, periods in which gender has become an issue to be talked about, where discourse about "The Woman Question," "The New Woman," "What Woman Want," "What Femininity Is," and so forth proliferates. The late nineteenth century, the post-World War II period, and the late twentieth century are such periods.

The language of femininity, too, is still the chief, if not the only, resource many women have to achieve power in this culture. In this connection, it is striking that anorexia and agoraphobia are chiefly disorders of middle- and upper-middle-class women. One needs material resources, time, and at least the *possibility* of success to pursue the norms of femininity as an avenue to power. (Obviously, too, hunger and food have very different symbolic meanings in the context of poverty, within different religious systems, and so forth.) Clearly, we need separate analyses of the effects of homogenizing feminine practice on various class and racial groups, and the different modes of protest that may be employed.

COLLUSION, RESISTANCE, AND THE BODY

The pathologies of female protest function, paradoxically, as if in collusion with the cultural conditions that produce them, reproducing rather than transforming precisely that which is being protested. In this connection, the fact that hysteria and anorexia have peaked during historical periods of cultural backlash against attempts at reorganization and redefinition of male and female roles is significant. Female pathology reveals itself here as an extremely interesting social formation; one source of potential for resistance and rebellion is pressed into the service of maintaining the established order.

How is this collusion established? Here, "objective" accounts of power relations fail us. For whatever the objective social conditions are that "produce" a pathology, the symptoms themselves must still be produced by the subject. That is, the body must be invested with meanings of various sorts. Only by examining this "productive" process can we see how the desires and dreams of the subject become implicated in the matrix of power relations. Here, examining the context in which the anorexic syndrome is produced may be illuminating. Anorexia will erupt, typically, in the course of what begins as a fairly moderate diet regime, undertaken because someone (often the father) has made a casual critical remark. Anorexia *begins,* emerges out of what is, in our time, conventional feminine practice. In the course of that practice, for any variety of individual reasons that cannot be gone into here, the practice is pushed a little farther than the parameters of moderate dieting. The young woman discovers what it feels like to crave and want and need, and yet, through the exercise of her own will, to triumph over that need. In the process, a new realm of meanings is discovered, a range of values and possibilities that Western culture has traditionally coded as "male" and rarely made available to women: an ethic and aesthetic of self-mastery and self-transcendence, expertise, and power over others through the example of superior will and control. The experience is intoxicating, habit forming: "The sense of accomplishment exhilarates me, [writes Aimes Liu] spurs me to continue on and on. . . . I shall become an expert [at losing weight]. . . . The constant downward trend [of the scale] somehow comforts me, gives me visible proof that I can exert control."[27]

At school, she discovers that her steadily shrinking body is admired, not so much as an aesthetic or sexual object, but for the strength of will and self-control that it projects. At home, she discovers, in the inevitable battles her parents fight to get her to eat, that her actions have enormous power over the lives of those around her. As her body begins to lose its traditional feminine curves, its breasts and hips and rounded stomach, and begins to feel and look more like a spare, lanky male body, she begins to feel untouchable, out of reach of hurt, "invulnerable, clean and hard as the bones etched into my silhouette," as one woman described it. She despises, in particular, all those parts of her body that continue to mark her as female. "If only I could eliminate [my breasts]," says Liu, "cut them off if need be." For her, as for many anorexics, the breasts represent a bovine, unconscious, vulnerable, side of the self.[28]

Through her anorexia, on the other hand, she has unexpectedly discovered an entry into the privileged male world, a way to become what is valued in our culture, a way to become safe, above it all (for her, they are the same thing). She has discovered this, paradoxically, by pursuing conventional feminine behavior (in this case, the discipline of perfecting the body as an object) to excess, to extreme. At precisely this point of excess, what is conventionally feminine "deconstructs," we might say, into its opposite and opens onto the world of what is coded as male in our culture. No wonder the anorexia is experienced as liberating, and she will fight family, friends, and therapists in an effort to hold onto it — fight them to the death, if need be. The anorexic's experience of power, of course, is deeply and dangerously illusory. To reshape one's body into a male body is *not* to put on male power and privilege. To *feel* autonomous and free while harnessing body and soul to an obsessive body practice is to serve, not transform, a social order that limits female possibilities. And, of course, for the "female" to become "male" is only to locate oneself on a different side of a disfiguring opposition. The new "power look" in female body building, which encourages women to develop the same hulklike, triangular shape that has been the norm for male body-builders, is no less determined by a hierarchical, dualisitic construction of gender than was the conventionally "feminine" norm that tyrannized female body builders such as Bev Francis for years.

Although the specific cultural practices and meanings are different, similar mechanisms, I suspect, are at work in hysteria and agoraphobia. In these cases, too, the language of femininity, when pushed to excess — when shouted and asserted, when disruptive and demanding — deconstructs into its opposite, and makes available to the woman an illusory experience of power previously forbidden to her by virtue of her gender. In the case of nineteenth-century femininity, the forbidden experience may have been the breaking out of constraint, of bursting fetters—particularly moral and emotional fetters. John Conolly, the asylum reformer, recommended institutionalization for women who "want that restraint over the passions without which the female character is lost."[29] Hysterics often infuriated male doctors for lacking just this quality. S. Weir Mitchell described them as "the despair of physicians" whose "despotic selfishness wrecks the constitution of nurses and devoted relatives, and in unconscious or half-conscious self-indulgence destroys the comfort of everyone around them."[30] It must have given the Victorian patient some illicit pleasure to be viewed as capable of such disruption of the staid nineteenth-century household. A similar form of "power," I believe, is part of the experience of agoraphobia.

This does not mean that the primary reality of these disorders is not one of pain. But if the symptoms did not offer, at the same time, what Susie Ohrbach has called "an attempted solution to being in a world from which at the most profound level one feels excluded" and unvalued,[31] the symptoms would not be taken up and clung to so fiercely. The literature on both anorexia and hysteria is strewn with battles of will between the sufferer and those trying to "cure" her; the latter, as Ohrbach points out, very rarely understand that the psychic values being fought for often are more important to the woman than life itself.

The "solutions" offered by anorexia, hysteria, and agoraphobia, I have suggested, present themselves out of the practice of femininity itself, the pursuit of which is still the chief route to acceptance and success for most women in our culture. Too agressively pursued, that practice leads to its own undoing, in one sense. For if femininity, as Susan Brownmiller has said, is at its very core a "tradition of imposed limitations,"[32] then an unwillingness to limit oneself, even in the pursuit of femininity, breaks the rules. But, of course, in another sense, everything remains fully in place. The sufferer becomes wedded to an obsessive practice, unable to make any effective change in her life. She remains, as Toril Moi has put it, "gagged and chained to [the] feminine role,"[33] a reproducer of the docile body of femininity.

This tension between the psychological meaning of a disorder (which may enact fantasies of rebellion and embody a language of protest) and the practical life of the disordered body (which can utterly defeat rebellion and subvert protest) can illuminate the arena of "normal" cultural practice, as well. A range of contemporary representations and images, for example, have coded the transcendence of female appetite and its public display in the slenderness ideal in terms of power, will, mastery, the possibilities of success in the professional arena, and so forth. Such rhetoric appears routinely on the pages of women's fashion magazines, diet books, and weight-training publications; it emerges most dramatically when contemporary anorexics speak about themselves. "[My disorder] was about power," says Kim Morgan in an interview in the documentary *The Waist Land,* "that was the big thing ... something I could throw in people's faces, and they would look at me and I'd only weigh this much, but I was strong and in control, and hey, *you're* sloppy."[34]

Yet, whereas the rhetoric and body symbolism is one of empowerment, for many women the material life of the body seeking that empowerment proceeds in the direction of "docility." Female bodies in the twentieth century, pursuing public power and authority, have often found themselves as distracted, depressed, and physically ill as female bodies in the nineteenth century, pursuing a feminine ideal of dependency, domesticity, and delicacy. Such contradictions are manifested not only by those who suffer from anorexia or bulimia. They ought to give pause to all of us who spend all day at the gym building up our muscles (working to emulate the toughness and tight bodies of the cool, macho heroines on the movie screen), or running compulsively, or dieting to distraction, increasingly disturbed by all reminders of "chaotic" female flesh. Recent statistics—for example, the recently publicized University of California study of fourth-grade girls in San Francisco — suggest that, at least in some American cultures, more and younger girls (perhaps as many as 80 percent of the nine-year-olds surveyed) are making dedicated dieting the central organizing principle of their lives. These fourth-graders live in constant fear, reinforced by the reactions of the boys in their classes, of gaining a pound and thus ceasing to be "sexy," "attractive," or, most tellingly, "regular."[35] They jog daily, count their calories obsessively, and risk serious vitamin deficiencies (not to mention full-blown eating disorders and delayed sexual and reproductive maturation). We may be producing a generation of young women with severely diminished menstrual, nutritional, and intellectual functioning.

One lesson that women might take from this is a Foucauldian one of caution regarding the workings of power, particularly in this period of cultural backlash against the second major feminist wave. We need to be especially cautious of those discourses that speak to us in the seductive language of freedom from the traditional constraints of gender, while demanding that we invest our time and energy in obsessive body practice. We need not (nor ought we to) abandon such practice entirely. Body building, for example, has obvious benefits for women living in a culture in which rape and sexual abuse are endemic; arguments can certainly be made, too, for the empowering and healthful effects of diet, exercise, and other forms of body "management." We must struggle, however, to keep these practices working in the service of resistance to gender oppression rather than in the service of "docility" and gender normalization. This requires a determinedly skeptical attitude toward the seeming routes of liberation and pleasure being offered by our culture, and awareness of the often contradictory and mystifying relations between image and practice, between rhetoric and reality. In the 1990s, such wariness may be difficult to maintain. Without it, we run the peril of ignoring important mechanisms, crucial to keep track of, in the politics of gender.

17

Sex, Gender, and the Politics of Difference

Eleanor H. Kuykendall

French philosophers of difference called *feminist* are often assumed by their English-speaking critics to defend a uniform position, called *essentialist,* equating biological sex with culturally defined gender. But such a generalization cannot be made because their positions are far from uniform, and some of their positions have changed during their careers. The political implications of these variations are complex.

For example, Annie Leclerc, widely known as an "essentialist," has more recently questioned essentialism. Leclerc's questions raise the more general questions whether women's bodies constitute or are constituted by language, what language is, what knowledge of language is, and how women ought to speak and write. To these more general questions Luce Irigaray, Julia Kristeva, Shoshana Felman, and Monique Wittig give conflicting answers whose complications, finally, are a matter more ethical than epistemological.

Annie Leclerc was criticized for her essentialist position in her 1974 *Parole de femme*[1] by the materialist feminist Christine Delphy.[2] In 1985, though, Leclerc's *Hommes et femmes* was published, in which she reconsiders her earlier position:

Doubtless one agrees a little too easily that they are women who struggle against or with men. Is women's business indeed with men? With those who have power? And the others, most numerous, who have no power, neither scientific, nor technical, nor economic, nor even sexual? Are they men or not? As soon as we leave behind

217

strictly biological reference, or a strictly physiologically referable sexual identity, it is difficult indeed to know what we are talking about.[3]

Whether they use the word or not — and they use the word *genre* rarely — by *gender* French feminist theorists like Leclerc mean a political critique of certain assumptions about biological sexual difference. This critique is unclear in English because the words *sex* and *gender* are interchangeable in common and accepted use. In French the critique is contradictory. French feminist theorists portray women's bodies as systems of signs continuous with language; yet women's bodies are also portrayed as continuous with language in that they are part of the individual unconscious, whose origins precede learning syntax and vocabulary. This contradiction yields the dilemma that either what we know of gender must create or constitute knowledge of language, or that what we know of language must create or constitute gender. In either case the meaning of *language,* as well as *gender,* is unclear. Controversies in the politics of difference, or political controversies about what difference is, may be perceived as a consequence of that unclarity, which in the end is a problem more ethical than epistemological.

I will address the epistemological problem first, by contrasting conceptions of knowledge of language assumed or argued by Irigaray, Kristeva, and Felman. I then turn to the ethical problem presented by contradictory analyses of a specific example — uses of the (exceptionally) gender-neutral pronoun *on* or "one" — given by Irigaray and Wittig. I conclude that the contrast between Wittig's and Irigaray's arguments displays, but does not decide, the ethical dilemma speakers of French face in choosing between gender-specific and gender-neutral reference.

The epistemology of French feminist philosophies of language is itself complex, for there are at least four conceptions of knowledge of language to which French feminist theorists appeal. The first is Chomskyan cognitive knowledge or competence in grammar as a rational system. This conception of knowledge of language, of course, has nothing to do with such concerns as "writing the body"; but neither is it totally dismissed by all philosophers of difference. Luce Irigaray, for example, whose earliest work was in psycholinguistics, acknowledges that competence is a useful category for distinguishing the deformed syntax of schizophrenic from normal speech.[4] The syntactical deformations of schizophrenia do not vary by the sex of the speaker, but those of senile dementia may.[5]

The Chomskyan conception of competence is explicitly rejected in the second conception of knowledge, as in Julia Kristeva's argument in "The Ethics of Linguistics."[6] There, without naming Chomsky, Kristeva proposes that phonology, as in mother-infant communication before the child learns word meaning or grammar, ought to be included in knowledge of language.

The third knowledge of language theory is knowledge of word meaning, including its analyses to disclose unacknowledged presuppositions. This is British ordinary-language philosophy, which rules out inquiry into unconscious presuppositions. The Austinian version of this inquiry is stood on its head by Derridean deconstruction, which seeks the unconscious origins of meaning in literary texts. Derridean deconstruction is overturned by such feminist philosophers of difference as Shoshana Felman. She points out that the Austinian example of promising, used to seduce and betray, undermines morality as it is conventionally constructed by speech-act theories of promising that presume the speaker's sincere intention to keep the promise. Felman also shows that the power to undermine conventional morality through insincere promising is gender-specific, in certain cases, as in the repeated seductions and betrayals of Don Juan.[7]

These three conceptions of knowledge of language — syntactic, phonological, and semantic-pragmatic — are set into opposition by the fourth conception of knowledge of language, implicit in Leclerc's distinction between sex, gender, and power and in Felman's critique of supposedly gender-neutral accounts of the speaker's power to both act and betray. This fourth conception of knowledge of language demonstrates unacknowledged presuppositions of gender in syntactic constructions that elude the usual semantic and syntactic tests for ambiguity. At times these demonstrations are presented in a manner reminiscent of Soren Kierkegaard's "indirect communication," as in Luce Irigary's "Ce sexe qui n'en est pas un" and "Quand nos levres se parlent."[8] These examples, which rely on pronoun reference and reflexive verbs specific to the French language to communicate their political argument, have to be translated into English as "This Sex which is Not One" and "When our Lips Speak Together."[9] (In English the communication cannot be carried by the verb but must be done by the pronouns and the adverb "together.") Nevertheless, in English as well as in French, such syntactic-pragmatic disclosure or "deconstruction" of unacknowledged presuppositions of gender can be communicated by example and translated.

Detailed analysis of the uses of certain syntactic constructions differently gendered in French and English offers clarification of the elusive distinction between biological sex and socially defined gender; it also discloses conflicting moral and political attitudes toward drawing such a distinction. This conflict is at the heart of the present confusion in French feminist philosophies of language — a conflict in ethical and political attitudes toward the written and the spoken language, and specific cases of its use. For example, I find in the writings of Luce Irigaray and Monique

Wittig conflicting commentaries on uses of the French personal pronoun *on,* which the English *one* does not begin to capture.

According to Wittig, writers, and by extension speakers, use *on* to express solidarity through gender-neutral, "indifferentiated" reference. For Wittig impersonal reference thereby empowers speakers and hearers of either sex, and particularly of the traditionally excluded female sex. But according to Irigaray, speakers, and by extension writers, use *on* to evade responsibility for what they say or write. Hence, they avoid responsibility for their own subjectivity. For Irigaray, then, impersonal reference — always disguised, dominating, and masculine — disempowers speakers and hearers of either sex, who cannot otherwise present themselves in serious discourse. These clashing interpretations of uses of *on,* offered by Wittig and Irigaray, demonstrate the present limits of feminist deconstructions of knowledge of language, which founder on clashing ethical conceptions of subjectivity as gender-neutral or as gender-specific solidarity.

The French *on* is used in speaking, though not in writing, quite differently from its English counterpart, *one.* Although *on* was historically masculine, it may be used to refer to people of either sex and may therefore be followed by a feminine adjective, as in "A soixante ans on est moins belle qu'à vingt ans."[10] In familiar speech *on* can be used for the first-person plural *nous* and for the second-person singular, according to Healey and Judge; in practice, both in Paris and in Canada, it can also be used for all three persons, singular and plural. In formal written French these other uses of *on* are not accepted; thus, there is a class issue involved in the very distinction between formal and colloquial, written and spoken, French.

Wittig's position is closer than Irigaray's to the ethical and political view feminist anglophones usually share. She uses the gender-neutral *on* to further the goal of eliminating a speaker's internal and unconscious division between covertly masculine and officially gender-neutral reference. This division presents a double bind in which a woman, such as a woman philosopher, cannot refer to herself unequivocally in gender-neutral or gender-specific terms. Although the English translation of her *L'Oppoponax* rendered *on* as passive, the substitute misses the point, Wittig argues in a recent article. Instead, Wittig interprets her use of *on* in the novel as an exercise of her feminine subjectivity — using the "indifferentiated" or gender-neutral *on* of colloquial speech as a writerly transformation of the language:

> With this pronoun, which is neither gendered nor numbered, I could locate the characters outside of the social division of sexes and annul it for the duration of the book ... *one, on,* here is a subject pro-

noun which is very tractable and accommodating since it can be bent in several directions at once. First, as already mentioned, it is indefinite, as far as gender is concerned. It can represent a certain number of people successively or all at once—everybody, we, they, you, people, a small or large number of persons—and still stay singular. It lends itself to all kinds of substitutions of persons. . . . One, on has been the pathway to the description of the apprenticeship, through words, in everything important to consciousness, apprenticeship in writing being the first, even before the apprenticeship in the use of speech. One, on, lends itself to the unique experience of all locutors who, when saying I, can reappropriate the whole language and reorganize the world from their point of view.[11]

Wittig's passage argues one side of a dilemma: if *on* is a genuinely indefinite pronoun, referring to people whose identity is unknown or irrelevant to the speaker, or indeed if it refers to everyone in general, then it cannot refer to anyone in particular; therefore it escapes the possibility of the speaker's making any serious ethical commitment. If, however, *on* actually is definite, because the identity of the referent is known and another pronoun may be found to substitute for it, then in formal written French it cannot be taken seriously. The *on* does refer either indefinitely or definitely. Thus, either unforeseen adverse ethical consequences result from Wittig's use of indefinite reference or the ethical consequence drawn by an analysis advocating specific reference in the feminine gender does not work.

This dilemma admits various resolutions. The indifferentiated *on* as a substitute for *nous* or *je* may be used to express solidarity, as Wittig suggests; but as a substitute for *tu, on* may also be uttered in condescension. As a substitute for *vous* with adults it may convey contempt, indifference, or powerlessness. For example, in "Alors, on s'en va?" the speaker transforms a straightforward "Let's go!" into a question that anticipates rejection at the same time that it attempts to evade its possibility.[12] Thus, the indifferentiated or definite *on* is ambiguous in its indication of dominance, in spoken French.

Though the indifferentiated or definite *on,* for which some other pronoun might be substituted, is stylistically unacceptable in formal French, its possible use in informal spoken French, as in the previous examples, raises a question of interpretation unresolvable by appeals to formal syntax. Either the definite *on,* which Wittig would substitute for *je* and *nous* in solidarity, may also be used to display a power over other speakers that is incompatible with solidarity; alternatively, as Irigaray argues, it may be used to defer to the other speaker's power to define the terms of the conversation and to mask the exercise of that power. For

Luce Irigaray, in contrast to Wittig, the use of *on* raises the serious ethical problem of denying a speaker's covert presupposition of masculine subjectivity:

> Masculine utterances are generally already transformed into the *third person*. The subject there finds itself masked in the word, in truth. But this universe is of the subject's construction. The *it (il)* is a transformation, a transformation of *I (je)*. A sort of effacing of the utterance in the edifice of language. Also a denial of whoever produced this grammar, this meaning, and their rules.[13]

Irigaray argues that transformation into the third person, be it the standard, ostensibly neutral but syntactically masculine *il* ("it") or the syntactically neuter *on,* masks any specifically feminine presence. Irigaray and Wittig agree that men, unlike women, unreflectively use *I* interchangeably with the masculine *il* or the syntactically neuter *on* to refer to themselves, and even to themselves only. They also use other constructions to this effect. For example, Irigaray reports a study of male and female university students in which the men repeatedly produced constructions such as the passive "*Est-ce que je suis aimé?*" or "Am I loved?" that refer only to themselves. By contrast women provided examples like "*Est-ce que tu m'aimes?*", or "Do you love me?" which presuppose another person to respond, creating a dialogue.[14]

Although the intimate second person is absent from English, what is striking about the contrast in French is that the speaker's gender determines whether the speaker will refer to himself, gender specifically, or address another person. This distinction persists in English. It is a distinction of gender rather than of sex because the use of these constructions is learned, and learnable by men or women, much as French is learnable by speakers of English.

What is learned and practiced has further ethical implications. Learning to love others as the same or "*meme*" gender specifically, which is Irigaray's project for solidarity,[15] cannot be assimilated gramatically with an indifferentiated *on.* Irigaray argues that women must first learn solidarity with other women before any other kind of connection or communication is possible; for in the indifferentiated *on,* the feminine subject is lost:

> Why would a subject not say: *I feel thus, I see such and such a thing, I want or I can do this, I affirm that?* That must be a question of time? A *brake* on discoveries? But this brake no longer is recognized as such and pretends to be the truth.

Now the "I" is sometimes more true than the "one" or the "it" *(il)*. It is more true because it speaks its sources. And, when science goes very fast, it is possible that the transmutation of "I" into "one" might no longer make sense. If not that of an imperialism which does not acknowledge itself.[16]

Irigaray concludes this passage with a much larger question that does not have to do with the syntax of *on* but with the more general boundary between sex and gender with which this paper began: "We end up today with this paradox: scientific studies prove the sexuality of the cortex; science maintains that discourse is neutral."[17] To pursue Irigaray's remark, as she herself does not, let us suppose that there really is something about the female body, such as the female brain, that distinguishes the female from the male in respects other than the reproductive organs. If speech and writing were to display this distinction phenomenologically through clashing syntactic constructions, clashing uses of syntax alone, such as the example of *on* considered here, would begin to help decide whether and how gender, subjectivity, and power are connected in specific acts of speaking and writing. But the ethical question of gender as creating the speaker's or writer's solidarity with others cannot be decided in this way.

18

Rationality, Relativism, Feminism

Terry Winant

If relativism is understood as an epistemological doctrine, I want to reject it. Still, there is something pressing in the question of the relativity of rationality. Indeed, epistemological perspectivism—the doctrine that all knowledge is conditioned by the perspective of the knower—may seem a commonplace. The burden of this essay is to show that, at least with regard to gender relativism, relativism about rationality need not entail epistemological relativism.

Although rejecting epistemological relativism, I want tentatively to endorse a variety of political relativism and a variety of methodological relativism. To render my position plausible requires two major departures from philosophical tradition. Philosophy must no longer be assumed to be epistemology-centered: it must be possible to envisage alternative candidates for the role of first philosophy. Gender theory is my candidate for this role. Moreover, the notion of "first philosophy" must be distinguished from that of a foundational inquiry; the claim that there might be some such inquiry as "first philosophy" must be separated from foundationalism. In making these departures from tradition, the account I give is inescapably metaphilosophical and feminist.

My account exhibits a tension that makes it confusing both to construct and to follow: it is both (and neither) a philosophical account about feminism and a feminist account about philosophy. The philosophical account about feminism takes its place in the project aimed at bringing unity and solidarity (sisterhood, if you will) to a movement (the women's movement) that draws its integrity and its prospects for success in large measure from the multiplicity of differences represented within it.[1] The women's movement needs philosophical analysis of feminism, if only because it is a specifically philosophical project through which we must find appropriate ways to theorize about sameness and difference, unity and diversity, among women as well as between women and men. Not surprisingly, the problematics of relativism are the site of much of this philosophical work.

Feminist accounts about philosophy, including the one I am telling, have in common a trait that has led many to suppose that feminist theory is a species of critical social theory, more or less in the tradition of the Frankfurt School: the upshot of a feminist story is to "point the finger" in a particular philosophical direction, saying, "Y'all missed something! Y'all missed something important!" The narative displays how what was left out was a gender issue and spells out how it came to be left out *because* it was a gender issue. I used to aspire to do this sort of work, pointing the finger at recent debates about relativism, specifically in the direction of those philosophers who hope to defend Reason against relativism. Just as Geneviève Lloyd[2] has been successful in pointing out that what has historically been missing is the way in which Reason has been male, I once hoped to spell out how the inclusion of debate about the gender of Reason would clarify and relax the animosity between rationalists and relativists. Such an account might parallel one Ian Hacking provides,[3] in which he charges that issues of historicity are missing from philosophical treatments of science, and that these issues raise questions that even the "arch-rationalist" should willingly address.

But my project turns out to be unstable in a way that critical-theoretical accounts are not. It so directly concerns the relationship between feminist inquiry and philosophical inquiry that my project becomes peculiarly sensitive to the constraint of reflexivity — that the account not entail the impossibility of its own articulation. The tension arises from attending to the contribution feminism can make to philosophy and leaving aside (for the time being) the philosophical project concerning feminism. But the splitting off of feminist aims from philosophical aims produces too great a distortion. It presupposes that specifically philosophical aims can be articulated gender neutrally in anticipation of a contribution (ostensibly from the feminist epistemologist) of strategies for recognizing, and avoiding or eliminating, gender bias in the procedures undertaken in view of these philosophical aims. From the feminist philosophical stance this presupposition is questionable.

So, as a feminist, I say that I am not a philosopher first and only then a feminist, nor am I a feminist first and only then a philosopher. My choice must therefore be to produce both accounts at once, integrating them into a single story, though a fragmented one. This story illustrates well the requirement, imposed by feminist-theoretical integrity, that we do *much* better than merely cope with our multiplicities of differences. It shows how it might be both rational and pleasurable to treat our feminist philosophical work as coalition building.

With all of its internal fragmentation, my story's integrity consists in this: I offer some of my reasons for giving up my long-standing conviction that philosophical and political positions are so inextricably intertwined that one does injustice in isolating their philosophical aspects from their political aspects. I held this conviction firmly and tended to apply it across the board, exempting no philosophical position, whether it be existentialism, computationalism, deconstruction, or feminism. This conviction now looks to have been a concomitant of traditional epistemology. In particular, it is a concomitant of the traditional epistemological commitment to the centrality of theory of knowledge to all theorizing. This essay explores what happens when specifically feminist pressures are brought to bear on epistemology's centrality.

I

Does feminism entail relativism? Feminists speak for women. Quite straightforwardly, we may thus be said to articulate women's perspectives. The fact that women's situations are distinctive — though they are not all distinctive in the same way — is enough to have led feminist theorists to view women as making our own specific contributions to culture. It is not controversial that women's own accounts of our situations as women have not been matched either for detail or for insightfulness. Even if it were the case that women's accounts were not more accurate than those of mainstream inquiry, they would nonetheless be distinctive. Sexism distorts, occludes, and confuses, so that, other things being equal, women and men have different relations to our common objects of inquiry, especially when those objects are directly related to institutions connected with gender.

To say this much is only to endorse a weak gender perspectivism. But for now this is enough. For if perspectivism entails relativism, and feminists articulate a particular perspective, then it would seem that whatever we know or say might be true only relative to that perspective: "true for women," as the expression goes, would not entail "true for men." In our sexist society the best we could expect is that "true for men" be taken to mean "true for people."

It is useful here to consider the epistemological position of certain sociologists of knowledge who, among others, have charged that antirelativism is usually held dogmatically or opportunistically. I want to explain this charge, and to say what about relativism troubles me as a feminist, ultimately showing how my response to the relativist provokes a shift away from traditional epistemology.

The relativism endorsed by sociologists of knowledge associated with the "strong programme" is a relativism about inquiry and its product: knowledge. The strong programme takes the acquisition of knowledge to be so thoroughly bound up with the inquirer's context — especially cultural and ideological context — as to make knowledge itself dependent, for its meaning and intelligibility as well as its truth, on the ideological and cultural projects from which it emerges. In short, knowledge is interest-relative. The relativist finds nothing to lament in this, instead hoping that the dependence of knowledge on processes and contexts of inquiry can make the study of inquiry — particularly of scientific and social-scientific inquiry — into a fruitful arena for cultural criticism and for the self-examination of epistemic subjectivity. No more Socratic an aspiration could be desired.

The hope is a false hope, however. What it proposes as a task of self-examination is actually a strategy for anthropologistic or psychologistic evasiveness about the ground for claims to know or to understand. According to the strong programme, justification would come down to appeals to some feature of us: "That's just how *we* do it." Thus, Barry Barnes and David Bloor write: "In the last analysis, [the relativist] acknowledges that his justifications will stop at some principle or alleged matter of fact that has only local credibility. The only alternative is that justifications will begin to run in a circle and assume what they were meant to justify."[4] Any request or demand for further justification is then met with evasion. Sometimes the demand is called unintelligible: "What could it possibly mean to ask whether current theories in chemistry describe events that occurred in prehistoric times?" Otherwise, such a request is treated as naive, self-serving, or naively self-serving. At the extreme, the charge of imperialism is leveled against those who expect more of justificatory discourse than description of some local epistemic practices. The strong programme treats the notion that genuine questions remain beyond the sociology of the practices of those we call *scientists* as nothing more than a symptom of traditional epistemology's project for hegemony over conceptual space.

It is ironic that this debate rarely turns to ask who the "we" is, and that on those rare occasions, the "we" is discussed as larger or smaller: "we humans"; "we anglophones"; "we North Americans"; "we academics"; "we scientists." In articulating our "we" what ought to count is not simply the acknowledgement of failure of universality, but the elaboration of difference in *kinds* of epistemic practices.

The anti-relativist stands accused of begging the question and doing so on self-serving grounds. The anti-relativist is said to reject relativism because it has skeptical consequences to which one ought not succumb. Nowhere is this more explicit than in the case of relativism about rationality itself. In this case, it is agreed that inference is exemplary rational behavior, and the debate turns to the question of psychologism in logic: are our inferential practices grounded in nothing more than contingent and historical features of the workings of our brains?

Even painstaking critiques of psychologism in logic, such as Husserl's, may then be written off by the relativist as opportunistic and fallacious. For suppose that among the consequences of psychologism is the assertion that the laws of logic might have been different or might not be binding. The sociologist of knowledge will claim that the logician ought to bite the bullet, because the nasty consequences are no *argument* against psychologism or relativism but a symptom of the logician's ideological situation.

Although I think these accusations unfair, this is not the place to attempt to settle the debate about psychologism in logic. I want instead to make two observations about relativism as psychologism. First, not merely logic — in the sense of the theory of inference — is at issue. The whole of the theory of rationality is at stake, for inference takes its place among other cognitive phenomena. Second, insofar as relativism about rationality is a psychologism, it is committed to naturalistic epistemology in Quine's sense: the explanation of our rationality is to be sought by empirical-psychological means. Questions about rationality fall into two classes: those that can be studied effectively within empirical psychology and those that are not worth asking. I return to Quine's naturalism in Section III, to contrast it with other naturalisms. What I say there about Quine applies as well to the naturalism of the sociologists of knowledge.

Before proceeding, I must clarify my feminist qualms concerning relativism about rationality. I did not deny that my qualms are politically motivated, and thus subject to the strong programme's charge. Indeed, mine is exactly the expected strategic worry, namely that relativism about rationality might legitimate a distinction between thinking like a man and thinking like a woman. Given the sexist circumstances in which we find ourselves, it is hard to imagine such a distinction contributing to the empowerment of women. Moreover, relativisms about rationality tend dangerously toward an excess of tolerance. The relativist babbles, seeming to say, "So what if we subscribe to disparate canons of inquiry — you do your thing and I'll do mine." The danger is that we might have no conversational context within which it is possible for me to formulate and defend my objection to the "research" that you claim shows I am not your peer. Let me fix the pronouns here. The danger is that we might have no conversational context within which it is possible for me — me, the philosophical feminist radical — to formulate and defend my objection to the "research" that you (or we) — we (or you) phenomenologists, existential Marxists, cognitive scientists — claim shows I am not your (or even my own?) peer.

These are my political qualms. The qualms, however, are not merely political. They are symptomatic of difficulties that arise in taking a position on any issue whatsoever without making clear where one is coming from. Deep ambiguities are associated with the contrast between *what* is asserted and *from where*. In particular, the contrast occurs differently along epistemic, political, and philosophical lines.[5]

As epistemic subject, where one is "coming from" is one's epistemological perspective — one's location in the space whose elements are all the members of one's community of inquiry. To take epistemological perspectivism seriously is to allow that this space is not homogeneous. It can happen that in matters of discovery, assertion, or justification one's accomplishments are partly a function of one's situation.

As political subject (i.e., citizen), where one is "coming from" is one's political standpoint — one's situation in relation to the causes to which one is committed. These commitments give rise to one's political choices — partisanships in the struggles through which one's community produces its future. To take the politics of differences seriously is to allow that no political community is — nor ought to strive to become — homogeneous, so that the political positions one takes depend on how one identifies oneself in relation to the multiplicities of differences that structure the pluralistic community.

In doing philosophy, where one is "coming from" is one's philosophical stance — one's location, as it were, in philosophical space. This shows up less in overtly endorsed views than in its (often unacknowledged) contribution to the style of one's philosophical activity. Most important, the way one formulates one's questions, the order in which one feels pressed to address them, and the urgency various issues have in one's work will all depend on one's philosophical stance.

Inasmuch as "where one is coming from" shows up in these ways as one's philosophical stance, political standpoint, and epistemological perspective, it is clear that the intimate connections among these three sorts of commitments need attention if we are to understand one another. Thus, the appreciation of our work can be helped along by articulating all three of these facets of the places we are coming from and working out the connections among them.

An illustration of such a tie between stance, standpoint, and perspective may be drawn from the literature of feminist relativism about science. Although stopping short of epistemological relativism, Evelyn

Fox Keller's work offers one of the strongest cases for the view that women and men practice science differently. Both epistemological perspectivism and methodological and political relativism are discoverable in Keller's analysis of the work of geneticist Barbara McClintock. Keller's *perspectivism* is evidenced by her careful discussions of the dialectical interactions between the social and political context of McClintock's work and the methodological commitments of her research program. Keller's *relativism* is evidenced by her discussions of the nature of the interaction between scientist and object of inquiry. The scientist relates concretely to specimens of chemical or biological species. This relation is structured in conformity with the metaphors that govern a research program, metaphors sustained in a culture more or less through mythological processes.

According to Keller's analysis of McClintock's location in the gender system of scientific research, men and women alike—including Barbara McClintock—aim to learn about the biological processes as they are objectively; that is, independent of what they are taken to be. McClintock pursued a research program that involved interacting with corn plants not disinterestedly but rather with a certain measure of emotional attachment. Keller's title, *A Feeling for the Organism,* names this attachment. Keller argues that this attachment enhanced the objectivity of McClintock's results. Nonetheless, McClintock's research was considered marginal for decades.[6]

I suggest that Keller's relativism is not merely a Quinean naturalistic epistemology or psychologism about rationality. Keller has taken her relativism about rationality beyond epistemology. Her feminist theory of science may well be relativistic and naturalistic, but it is distinguished from most sociology of science by the precedence Keller grants to questions about gender over questions about knowledge. McClintock's feeling for the organism is characteristic of McClintock's epistemological perspective. By examining McClintock's—and her own—political and methodological standpoints, Keller brings to light McClintock's epistemological perspective. In this respect, Keller is an exemplary philosophical feminist, for exactly as modern philosophy makes the epistemological turn when it grants precedence to questions about knowledge over questions about being, so contemporary and future philosophy makes the feminist turn when it grants precedence to questions about gender over questions about knowledge.

We now have feminist epistemology because we have not yet made this feminist turn, and the path to it goes by way of epistemology. Thus, feminist epistemologists are leaving few stones unturned in the perhaps doomed attempt to handle questions about gender within the framework of traditional epistemology.

II

One option open to feminist epistemologists is to build a "standpoint epistemology." Standpoint epistemologies ascribe the apparent relativity of epistemological perspectives to the phenomena of oppression themselves. This option is open quite generally to anyone who hopes to ground knowledge claims that arise out of a movement for social change and are articulated on the margins of the epistemic community.

According to standpoint epistemologies, illegitimate authority structures society so as to give subjected peoples a "consolation prize" of epistemic privilege. The perspective of the oppressed encompasses that of the oppressor; the perspective of the oppressor is blind to that of the oppressed. Although this commits standpoint epistemologists to epistemological perspectivism, it is not relativistic. Rather, it treats relativism as a phenomenon to be explained away. Indeed, it explains relativism as a paralogism due to injustice, and it claims that this explanation is an indispensable tool in political struggle. Hence, the standpoint epistemologist expects social change to transform what is now "true for the oppressed" into universal truth. It follows that, exactly to the extent of their antirelativism, standpoint epistemologies ultimately deny perspectivism, too: come the revolution, every epistemic subject will share in the universal perspective—the perspective now available only to the most completely oppressed. As Sandra Harding points out, *objectivity* is at stake for the standpoint epistemologist.

The trouble with standpoint epistemologies is this: the standpoint epistemologist is correct to say that the universalism characteristic of liberalism is false and deceptive, but misguided in continuing to aspire to this very universalism—setting it up as a goal to be achieved through the transformation of society, or perhaps as a regulative ideal to constrain our practice.

My complaint about relativism may now be formulated this way: relativism is a type of pure tolerance. It fails to discriminate among epistemic situations, treating them all equally, and as equally fallible. It is a virtue of standpoint epistemologies that they do not fall into this trap. Consider for a moment the way liberalism treats this problem. Embarked on a search for universality and objectivity, liberalism observes that the way to approximate (or, perhaps, to construct) a nonperspectival, universal knowing is to generate a multiplicity of perspectives. If this can be done in imagination, then it is possible, even from an armchair, to get from perspectival to nonperspectival knowing: objectivity is molded out of imaginary intersubjectivity. In this way, the liberal and the standpoint epistemologist offer two ways to reject both relativism and perspectivism. Furthermore, each treats both relativism and perspectivism as at once epistemological and political doctrines.

In separating epistemological perspectivism from epistemological relativism, I am hoping not only to accept but to celebrate perspectivism while nonetheless rejecting epistemological relativism. This option is important, I believe, because no epistemology is truthful if it claims that women or feminists share a unified epistemic situation, and no epistemology is politically or philosophically alert if it asks that women or feminists aspire to such a unified perspective. On the other hand, relativism with respect to philosophical or political commitments—inasmuch as it accurately acknowledges complexities of identity and difference—is the moral of my philosophical story about feminism.

In order to return to epistemological perspectivism (though not to epistemological relativism), it helps to recall a lesson that can be learned from Hannah Arendt. Contemplating a multiplicity of imaginary situations might be an important kind of thinking, but it cannot supply the needed practical wisdom. Our grasp on human plurality requires being buffeted about concretely, actually acting politically in a multiplicity of actual situations. Imaginary multiplicities are insufficient for developing political skill, and hoped-for unity cannot substitute for such skill. Our plurality is genuine, and an epistemology honest about the actual politics of differences must be a perspectivism.

III

Epistemological relativism is typically understood to be a type of skepticism, but it need not be. It can even be an extreme sort of anti-skeptical foundationalism, just as a radical relativism in ethics can be the claim that ethics has a foundation in private emotional life. These, at any rate, are positions within traditional epistemology. In the versions most attractive to students of politics and ideology, however, relativism can seem to have left traditional epistemology behind in favor of a naturalistic epistemology.

In this section I explain what I mean by traditional epistemology and then say something about the various ways relativism occurs as traditional epistemology. This leads me to distinguish, following P. F. Strawson, between a narrow and a broad sense of naturalism. The former turns out to belong to traditional epistemology after all; the latter serves (in Section IV) as a pathway for a genuine departure from traditional epistemology. My claim there will be that feminist relativism, insofar as it is plausible, must be outside of traditional epistemology, taking a philosophical stance that grants precedence to issues of gender over those of knowledge.[7]

Traditional epistemology not only grants precedence to questions of knowledge and justification over metaphysical questions, it also, in one way or another, is preoccupied with (and distressed by) skepticism. This means that the traditional epistemologist either makes the skeptical challenge, attempts to meet the skeptical challenge, or both. Naturalisms stand in contrast with traditional epistemology in that they neither make the skeptical challenge nor attempt to meet it, but rather they aim to resist, deflect, or deflate it.

Strawson, in his Woodbridge lectures, entitled *Skepticism and Naturalism: Some Varieties,*[8] distinguishes naturalisms like Quine's from naturalisms like Wittgenstein's. Naturalisms like Quine's resist the skeptical challenge by a reductive move; they replace epistemological problems with questions for empirical science. Naturalisms like Wittgenstein's are of a more dramatic type; they hope to stave off skeptical challenges by preventing them from getting started.

Strawson's distinction is vital for feminists. In light of this distinction, Quine turns out, after all, to be a traditional epistemologist. This suggests that the broad naturalisms are interesting in virtue of their departure from traditional epistemology. Such a departure is a part of the philosophical interest of feminist theory. Indeed, feminist theory serves as my main example of what the turn from traditional epistemology might be like. Heideggerian fundamental ontology provides another example of such a turn, so it will be helpful to explore the parallel between the two.

IV

What would it be like to have escaped traditional epistemology? What would it take to pursue theories of knowledge without the commitment to theory of knowledge as first philosophy? The key is to rework the notion of first philosophy. When epistemology plays the role of first philosophy, it is easy to see how first philosophy comes to be a domain of inquiry on which all other inquiries depend but which is itself not dependent on any of them. For inquiry aims at knowledge—all inquiry. The rejection of the autonomy of epistemology thus seems to precipitate the very circularity that the skeptical challenge has schooled the epistemologist to fear.

Quine's naturalism is exactly a rejection of epistemology's autonomy. And Quine's image of Neurath's boat, floating while being repaired, is meant to calm the resultant fears of circularity. Quine, however, takes himself to have rejected much more than the asymmetrical dependence of all inquiry on epistemology. He claims to have quit looking for any candidate for the role of first philosophy, and so, a fortiori, to have rejected epistemology's claim to be first philosophy. In supposing that all of these may be rejected in a single swoop of holism, Quine must be confusing epistemological foundationalism with the assertion that epistemology is first philosophy. Both views emerge as the doctrine that science (indeed all inquiry) has to have its adequacy certified in the "sub-basement" called *epistemology*.

Quine attacks foundationalism in epistemology. But in a certain sense, Quine's naturalism continues to grant epistemology the role of first philosophy. Once naturalized, epistemology is but a part of empirical psychology; for Quine it is a part of behavioristic empirical psychology. The explanations such a science constructs are ultimately causal explanations in terms of conditioned responses to sensory stimuli. These in turn are rendered respectable in terms of explanations drawn from physical science — physicalistic explanations of the causal processes that make up the psychological processes.

Still, there is no such thing as a domain of inquiry or a scientific investigation that can forgo specifically epistemological inquiry. This is so because, for Quine as for traditional epistemology, all investigations aspire to acquire knowledge. Even if knowledge is understood in utterly behavioristic-psychological and physicalistic terms, it is nonetheless the case that inquiry into the processes whereby we acquire knowledge (or some specific body of knowledge) will have a crucial place in any careful investigation. The point is not that epistemological investigation is in a logically prior sub-basement, or in any sense preliminary, nor that epistemology is autonomous or self-contained. The point is that the epistemological investigations are never beside the point. Although it may not be the only theory that is never beside the point, the theory of knowledge is central to all theory. In this sense it still counts as first philosophy, even for Quine.

Generally, then, say that a certain branch of inquiry, *X,* counts as first philosophy just in case inquiry belonging to *X* is central to all inquiry, in the sense that no inquiry, *Y,* is such that questions and problems from *X* are irrelevant to *Y.* This schema neatly fits Heideggerian fundamental ontology. Fundamental ontology counts as first philosophy, though any sense in which it should be taken to be a foundational inquiry is certainly not an *epistemological* sense. The hermeneutic circle requires exactly this contrast. Inquiry belonging to fundamental ontology is central to all inquiry in that inquiry cannot responsibly get along without drawing on fundamental ontology, for it is only in the analytic of Dasein that it is possible to find the resources for a response to the question of Being. Any attempt to do otherwise is thus a failure of responsibility to the question of Being.

Feminism is a philosophical stance that also fits this schema neatly. The feminist stance takes gender theory to be first philosophy in the sense that no responsible inquiry can shirk the question of gender. If there are inquiries that genuinely are gender neutral, it must be within gender theory that this is determined. Any attempt to do otherwise is a failure of responsibility to women.[9] Nonetheless, gender theory is not (and makes no claim to be) epistemologically foundational. It is not a body of inquiry with any special epistemological status. Rather, it is an area of inquiry that no responsible theorist can afford to ignore. Perhaps this is a fact about our historical position — I, for one, would be delighted to see the gender issues once again recede. Their centrality, and the precedence of gender theory, however, belongs to philosophy as long as sexism is the going social practice. What then becomes of traditional epistemology? Why would the centrality of theory of knowledge be incompatible with the centrality of theory of gender?[10] The feminist turn is a supplanting of epistemology's place as first philosophy, albeit by indirect means. Making gender theory central is not enough to oust epistemology, because nothing (except, perhaps, ruined hopes for certain types of foundations) requires first philosophy to be unique. Our feminist political standpoint, however, does not let us accept epistemological relativism, although it forces us to epistemological perspectivism. It is this conjunction, together with an attempt at a Quine-style naturalized epistemology, that provokes the sociologist of knowledge to the charge of question-begging opportunism. The move to make is toward a different style of naturalism, both in epistemology and elsewhere — a style that does not hang onto the centrality of theory of knowledge, and leaves the job of first philosophy to a more historically appropriate discipline.

V

At this juncture, it behooves me to elaborate more fully my vision of gender theory, for so far I have proceeded as if there were consensus about it. Just what sort of inquiry is gender theory? What does it study? What does it aim to produce? What are the desiderata for an adequate gender-theoretic account? What is the state of the art in the field? And, most important, how can I coherently envisage gender-theoretical research as aspiring to make itself marginal as the gender issues recede politically? Will I not thereby fall back into the universalistic false hope of the naive revolutionary?

To a point, I think we do have consensus about gender theory. Whatever else gender theory is, it is the discipline responsible for discovering and explaining gender bias wherever gender bias occurs. It is important to my argument that this responsibility already encompasses the responsibility for establishing gender neutrality wherever (and if ever) it occurs. In addition, there is consensus about the fact that some gender theory has already been done, and with a modicum of success, though there is no consensus at all about which accomplishments qualify. We do have consensus as to the existence of some somewhat successful gender theory.

For a time it seemed we had consensus about the distinction between sex and gender, but this consensus has been partially eroded by the increasing sophistication of feminist critiques of biologism and by the influence of psychoanalysis of the Lacanian variety. Perhaps the most salient consensus we now have concerns the importance of paying attention to classism and racism: oppressive social structures *other than* the gender system.

There is as yet no consensus, however, about how to envisage gender theory as such. As a stopgap, I offer my own idiosyncratic and provisional answers to the questions just formulated. Gender theory is an eclectic and multidisciplinary (often extradisciplinary) exploratory inquiry aimed at figuring out what gender is and at tracing the workings of gender throughout the world. In these global terms, gender theory does for gender what optics does for light. Unlike optics, though, gender theory does not yearn for an analogue to the theory of electromagnetic radiation. The goal is not to find a grand theory into a corner of which gender theory could nestle and feel well cared for.

What is more, I believe gender theory does not even yearn for so much as an analogue of geometrical optics. The enterprise is one of exploring gender by carefully surveying gender phenomena and making explicit "laws" of their reflections, refractions, intensities, and so on. This enterprise is well under way, but it is not an undertaking that ought to result in an axiomatic theory or in any neat self-contained collection of propositions. Rather, gender theory may forever remain a pastiche of descriptions of women's situations, narratives of women's experiences and emancipatory traditions, distinctions sexism tends to conflate, slogans aimed at cheering us on and at steering us away from pitfalls, and arguments offered on behalf of little theories of this and that.[11]

The kind of pastiche I have in mind is exemplified in the work of Barbara Smith.[12] Smith gives a theory of the kitchen table as an institution in African-American women's lives.

> More than anything, I wish Leila and I could go there, home. That I could make the reality of my life now and where I came from touch. . . .

> The front door would be open. . . . Aunt LaRue would be in the
> kitchen. Before I would see her, I'd call her name.[13]

Smith eloquently explores the power of this institution in explaining women's situation within the struggle against racism in the United States and in understanding black feminists' heritage. In this way, she not only proposes some ways of interpreting descriptions and narratives of some experiences specific to black women, but also alerts us — women of all races — to pitfalls we confront as we work to eliminate racism from the women's movement.

The theoretical pitfall ahead for us is the accusation that in welcoming and sustaining a non-totalizing — or only partially totalizing — theoretical practice, we are insufficiently ambitious, somehow settling for less than real theory. But this pitfall may itself be countered with a slogan: the most ambitious enterprise is the one that aims for the flourishing of our differences. This also, I believe, excuses my aspiration to make the gender issues recede without making gender theory obsolete. I envisage gender-theoretical inquiry continuing to provide ever-necessary resources for our sustaining of differences — ever-necessary resources even when they are no longer the sine qua non for first philosophy. Because the sexism that we suffer is ubiquitous, gender theory as well must become ubiquitous. But both sexism's ubiquity and gender theory's claim to philosophical centrality are historical and contingent. In our time, it is a betrayal of women to marginalize gender-theoretical inquiry. I can hope — perhaps a bit naively — that this will not always be so.

In summary, my position is this. To sever the tie between perspectivism and relativism, relativism should be formulated not as an epistemological doctrine but as a matter for politics. Toward this end, I distinguish between philosophical stance and political standpoint, and between each of these and epistemological perspective. These distinctions permit the formulation and analysis of the question about the relativity of rationality from three separate angles. I am thus enabled to respond to the question whether rationality is gender relative, sorting out what otherwise would appear as incoherencies.

So, is rationality relative? Am I rational? Is Man (not me) rational? On the side of epistemological perspective, any tension between rationality and relativism seems an artifact of an outmoded traditional epistemological stance. On the side of political standpoint, my rationality seems unshakable. It is only on the side of philosophical stance that I am at loose ends. Does rationality really demand that I commit myself to the view that there is such a thing as "first philosophy"? And, supposing I have succeeded at preparing myself to relinquish my traditional epistemological stance, how am I conscientiously to select among stances? Am I philosophically feminist? naturalistic? phenomenological? Might I adopt all these, and some others as well?

I suspect that individual philosophers are better at recognizing one another's philosophical stances than we are at making such choices for ourselves. Consequently, on the side of philosophical stance, it is mine to ask, but not to answer: am I rational?[14]

19

Modern Democracy and Political Philosophy

Claude Lefort

What is modern democracy? Is it a political form of society that we could specify in relation to other ancient and modern political forms, or do we live in a world the principal characteristics of which are now determined by economical or technological change? This is my first question, which calls for another one: are we allowed to attempt to carry on the long-run research initiated by the classical thinkers, even though we have to enter upon new ways to respond to new issues? Or should we admit that all the political tradition has become obsolete? These questions seem closely linked to one another. Nevertheless, they are distinct as I will try to show. Indeed, there is a way of claiming a return to political thought that renders less relevant the specific political features of our societies.

Before coming to terms with this apparent paradox, I would briefly cite recent tendencies that in France have marked a certain reevaluation of political judgment. At the origin of these tendencies, various events should be noted. I will limit myself to mentioning only a few of them. First is the deterioration of Marxist ideology linked to consciousness raising of the terror or the crude oppression in the United States that presented itself as socialist. Next, the collapse of the 1968 movement. Following this, the economic crisis that contributed to the dissolution of certain beliefs in an endless material progress. Finally, the unfortunate experience of the French socialist government in the beginning of the 1980s. The consequences of such events were distinctly different and their impact upon the opinion of the Left and the Right should not be confounded. However, they similarly suggested that, far from becoming irrelevant in the face of economic, technological, or strictly social transformations, human choices have not ceased to be decisive. On the one side, we have observed a new concern for civil liberties and, more generally, for human rights in response to the threatening power of state bureaucracies in the East and the West. On the other side, a lot of people in the ranks of the Left have become conscious of connecting the demands for social justice with realistic requirements, whereas in the ranks of the Right a new liberalism has emerged in close relation to the ideology of Reagan or Thatcher.

For my purpose, the most striking fact is the juxtaposition of a merely moralistic point of view and a merely realistic point of view in the face of national and international issues. Indeed, it seems to me that new philosophical trends have resulted from this changing intellectual climate. In postwar times, the philosophers involved in public debate were discussing dialectics, history, class struggle, and rational principles of the social order. Such a discussion came to appear increasingly more ideological. Beneath the banner of antihumanism, though from entirely different premises, the structuralist theories, on the one hand, and, on the other hand, the Heideggerian trends or the various currents devoted to the "deconstruction" of the Subject provoked a divorce between philosophy and history as well as between philosophy and politics. At present, we witness a double criticism of the thinkers of the first and the second periods I have just evoked. Whereas Hegelian and Marxist thought as well as phenomenology seem disqualified, the notion of the Subject has been strongly reaffirmed along with its supposed capacity for judging by itself what is the good and the evil and what is possible and unreal in each given situation. A new sort of rationalism, which is said to draw its inspiration from Kantian philosophy, claims to involve a return to politics. Nevertheless, I fear that the revival of political thought cannot proceed from such assumptions.

In the Preface of *Adventures of Dialectics* thirty-two years ago, Merleau-Ponty criticized what he called the *politics of understanding,* which seems to be celebrated anew by some philosophers today. Merleau-Ponty borrowed this denomination from Alain (a well-known thinker in the prewar period) who opposed such a politics to the "politics of the reason"; that is, to Hegelian and Marxist theories. For Alain, Merleau-Ponty says, "the politics of understanding . . . does not flatter itself with having embraced all of history but rather takes Man as he is, at work in an obscure world, resolves problems one at a time, attempting in each instance to infuse in things something of the values which Man when he is alone discerns without hesitation." Merleau-Ponty rightly objected that denouncing the illusions of the politics of reason was not dispensing oneself with replacing each singular event in a social and historical context, and interpreting this context in accordance with one's own values. I think we could say something more about this point, which Merleau-Ponty, curiously, left aside. It is not sufficient to free oneself from a theory that relates each event to the whole of human history or a theory that takes each event in itself to give it significance and provide the right answer for particular problems, here and now. History involves, at each period and through different periods, various kinds of political communities. These communities are differently articulated and differently instituted. Their mode of articulation implies a conception of the symbolic order, especially a notion of power, law, knowledge, and the relationships between individuals. In this sense, reflecting on political action in particular circumstances cannot be dissociated from reflecting on the principles upon which communities are founded and that justify or fail to justify such political activity. We cannot appreciate what is at stake in a conflict, either within or between different states, or appreciate the way of dealing with these conflicts without questioning the nature of the states we are considering. For instance, we can criticize the politics of a democratic government, but we must know whether we make this criticism in virtue of our attachment to democracy or if democracy is for us a facade beneath which private interests are solely determinant. We can criticize the way that a communist government represses a worker's strike, but we must decide whether such repression is the outcome of a particular crisis or if it results from the principles of a totalitarian state. Today, the supposed return to politics has hardly anything to do with a return to political philosophy in that it does not involve any reflection on the different political forms of society in the present world or, by the same token, any reflection on the best way of life.

I now return to my first question, which I would like to reformulate in these terms: does political philosophy offer a new approach to modern democracy?

I will begin by referring to Leo Strauss, a thinker who wanted obstinately to remind us of the teaching of classical philosophers and to call for a revival of political philosophy. In *Natural Rights and History,* Strauss observes that the moderns hardly understood the ancient notion of *politeia*. This notion, he says, ordinarily translated into a constitution, did not mean for the Greeks something merely legal. *Politeia* referred both to constitutional aspects and to a particular way of life (in the sense in which we speak of the "American way of life" today). The best modern equivalent seems, for Strauss, to be *regime,* provided that we give this word the same significance he does when he evokes *l'ancien régime.* In this sense, a form of government and a way of life would be interwoven in *politeia.* However, Strauss insists that, for the ancients, the way of life itself was supposed to depend on a certain understanding of the source of power and the particular exercise linked to it. According to him, the modern blindness to the ancient image of *politeia* would go along with the devaluation of political philosophy. Strauss notes that political philosophy vanished at the same time that social, economic, and cultural history became preponderant. Thus, modern thought no longer understands what politics meant for the ancients, but by the same token, it does not understand politics itself.

We are sometimes tempted to think that such a criticism aims only at the modern theoreticians. In a few passages of his work, Strauss notes that people continue to live in societies that are differently organized, guided by different principles, and that have to preserve their integrity and defend themselves against one another, so that they seem to retain certain political characteristics. Nevertheless, Strauss's criticism of modern thought can hardly be separated from his criticism of modern social practice, the background out of which such thought has developed for a long time. Consequently, both political philosophy and political life are vanishing. Needless to say, Strauss does not conflate modern democracy with totalitarianism. However, we must ask ourselves whether, for Strauss, totalitarianism represents more than the worst outcome of democracy? I ask, further, whether the main features of present society must still be related to a form of government.

Indeed, according to Strauss, the expansion of technology, founded upon a new scientific ideal, has radically changed human life. We are indubitably confronted with various sorts of social organizations, nevertheless what is called a *state* and what is called *society*, at present, constitute something deeply different from political communities in the past. To the extent to which I know Strauss's work, he was not particularly interested in the picture Plato drew of Athenian democracy in *The Republic*, although the witty and cruel description of Athenian democracy could have strongly sustained his own criticism of relativism and nihilism in modern societies. As one knows, democracy in *The Republic* was presented as the outcome of a corrupted regime: oligarchy. This last regime was supposedly derived from another corrupted political form, timocracy, which itself proceeded from the alteration of the best regime. Democracy in Book 8 appeared as the society in which all the norms required for the maintenance of the community (norms already subsisting in oligarchy and timocracy) had gradually dissolved. In sketching the portrait of the democratic city and the democratic man, Plato enjoyed portraying the children who no longer respect their fathers, the pupils who despise their teachers, the old men oblivious to authority kidding in order to seduce children. Plato described a topsy-turvy world wherein the donkeys themselves pretend to be independent and jostle people on the street, forgetting they are just donkeys. Conversely, Plato ironically praised this charmingly beautiful form of government that made it possible for each one to live and to speak freely of everything. Lastly, he compared democracy to a bazaar to which people were going to look for the junk that seemed to provide a good model.

Whatever attraction Plato's criticism retains for us, we feel that it cannot be seriously applied to modern democracy. Leaving aside the question of whether the criticism was justified at the time, we must admit that modern democracy has not come into being beneath the banner of license. At the source of democratic claims, we find a rejection of arbitrary power, an idealization of law and new demands for a rational social order. This, I think, is the reason why Strauss's arguments do not focus on license, even though we could point out moral disorders in many aspects of modern life. Strauss prefers to bring to light an extraordinary change in the relationship between Man and Nature. Instead of conceiving his insertion in Nature, Man has transformed it into a matter that must be dominated. Modern science and technology proceed from an artificial conception of the world, so that everything, including Man himself, seems open to indefinite improvement. In such a perspective, modern universalism, the modern view of human progress or equality and individual freedom depends on the new conception of rationality. Generally speaking, modern humanism is closely connected with the belief that the world was made for Man, adjustable to his operations and able to be fashioned in accordance with his needs. Strauss suggests that the ancient's theoretical questions concerning the best form of government have been replaced by the practical questions concerning the most efficient means of improving standards of life. This is the origin of the present relativism and nihilism, which apparently are in contradiction with universalism but testify similarly to the negation of human nature and the limits of human power. So relativism and nihilism do not proceed from license. They result from the loss of the notion of ultimate ends that determine the good way of life. License seems to be no more than a by-product of the new "world-view" initiated by the modern current of rationalization. Rationalization through scientific knowledge and technology in itself involves nihilism owing to its incapacity to clarify its own ends. Criticizing rationalization without being able to question the nature of the city and that of Man induces another sort of nihilism.

When Strauss notes that philosophy of history has replaced political philosophy, I think that he establishes a close correspondence between, on the one hand, the new idea of necessity that is included in the continuous progress of technology and the accumulation of the means of production capable of satisfying the evergrowing needs of population and, on the other hand, the theories formulating the history of humankind as one unique development from its origin to its end. It is true that Strauss insists on the role of the philosophers who paved the way to modern thoughts: Machiavelli, then Hobbes, and Rousseau and Nietzsche. However, modernity seems simultaneously characterized by the social change that resulted from the advent of a new scientific spirit. Hegelian and Marxist philosophy is said to be responsible for radically breaking with political philosophy and definitely blurring the distinction between the "is" and the "ought to be." However, modern society, transformed as it was by technology, had already come to ignore this distinction and to generate blind demands for progress.

Let me, in passing, pay attention to a criticism of the philosophy of history that is something of a paradox. From observation of the past, Strauss identifies a series of logically articulated transformations that lead to the present state of things. Wherever the point of departure of modernity may be, we should have to recognize one moment from which the chain of the great transformations of human life has become fully intelligible. The Straussian view of modernity is all the more remarkable in that it seems quite close to other approaches founded upon different theoretical premises.

For instance, the philosophy of Heidegger. He has radically criticized the concept of history and simultaneously pretended to deliniate the epoch during which the occulation of Being has become predominant by specifying the stages of this process. It is well known that Heidegger goes as far as finding the starting point of the occultation of Being in Plato's philosophy. Nonetheless, the advent of modern science and technology marks a turning point. From this time on, we are supposed to witness a rigorously determined development of the Western mode of thinking.

Precisely what Strauss's interpretation owes to Heidegger, I am not able to evaluate. In opposition to Heidegger, Strauss appeals to the readers to turn back to Plato, Aristotle, and Xenophon, the founders of political philosophy. For him, the essential issues depend on our notion of Nature, not of Being. Both of them, however, share the same appreciation of modern times. I will also mention Hannah Arendt, whose works are more relevant for my purpose. Although in this case we have no doubt about her relation to Heidegger, we must recognize that she worked out an original theory of politics, the inspiration of which has nothing to do with Heidegger's teaching. At the same time, this theory is deeply different from, not to say in contradiction to, that of Strauss, because Arendt assumes that there was a radical break between our way of thinking and all tradition. However, denying in turn any validity to the philosophy of history, whether spiritualist or materialist, Arendt attempted to overembrace the modern times by going so far as to sketch out the genesis of our present world. In *The Human Condition*, Arendt describes the rise of *homo faber* and his transformation into *homo laborans*. She points out the coming into being of the managerial state and the emergence of the society as such, something that had never existed before, whereas, according to her politics, that which is the domain of action tends increasingly to vanish.

I was speaking of a paradoxical relationship to history. In each of the points of view I have just mentioned, the concept of history seems similarly rejected. But what constitutes for these thinkers the constant target is the belief in a cumulative history of humankind. At the same time, we attend to a tacit restoration of history as a process that develops negatively, that is, by doing away with the reference to Nature, to Being and to Action (or Freedom). Each one of these thinkers connects main transformations from the seventeenth century to the present time, as though there were one unique direction for human history, independent from its various accidents. In such a theoretical framework, modern democracy is disqualified either implicitly or explicitly. To paraphrase Marx's criticism of ideology, democracy draws nothing from its source.

I would like to briefly posit a different thesis by holding that we cannot understand the characteristics of our way of thinking and living without taking into consideration what Tocqueville called the *democratic revolution*. Neither technology itself, nor economic change in itself suffice to account for our experience of the world, because their effects are widely determined by their inscription into one singular political form of society. This argument could be clarified by referring to the emergence of totalitarian states. First, the advent of fascism, Nazism, and Stalinism bear the marks of the modern belief in the capacity of the state to master scientifically the social order and create a New Man. However, this artificial project is closely connected with an organic project that proceeds from the furious negation of the democratic spirit. Above all, the democratic way of life appears as the absolute evil that the new ideology has to eradicate. Second, the totalitarian mutation is of a symbolic order, as is clearly revealed by the appearance of a kind of power supposedly welded to the social body, able to cancel any internal division, and presenting itself as the source of the law as well as of the knowledge of the ultimate ends of Man. Third, this kind of regime does not connect the technological development or the alleged economical rationalization with the satisfaction of material needs of the population: something that constitutes, for Hannah Arendt, the driving force of modern society.

Nevertheless, I prefer to leave aside the comparison between democracy and totalitarianism and to follow another way. Tocqueville entered upon this way when he attempted to explore the ambiguities, indeed the contradictions, that modern democracy carried within itself. He threw light on a new symbolic matrix resulting from the collapse of the *ancient régime*. No matter how strange this assertion may appear, I have long been convinced that Tocqueville has sketched out a phenomenological analysis of modern democracy. Perhaps Tocqueville became capable of paying attention to the ambiguities of democracy and became so much involved in the experience he was describing precisely because he did not seek to advocate some particular cause. As is well known, he was attracted to democratic liberty while remaining attached to an aristocratic ethics. Of more importance to my mind, however, is the fact that he was aware of being confronted with new, unsurpassable horizons, in such a way that he could inquire into the present social field without dreaming of another world.

Tocqueville holds that the democratic revolution is irreversible. In a certain sense, time itself is irreversible and each event bears the mark of irreversibility. But Tocqueville suggests that humanity as such has entered upon a road from which it can no longer escape. So the appearance of democratic institutions and democratic beliefs is not, properly speaking, a particular event within history or something localizable within the social space. We should rather admit that the image of society and the image of history as such appear for the first time, so that henceforth all that we could say or think about politics supposes a reference to the Universal.

When I was speaking of a phenomenological investigation into modern democracy, I remembered how Merleau-Ponty presented such a task in the preface of *Phenomenology of Perception* and in his last writings, which went beyond the limits of classical phenomenology. What I recall is the appeal for rediscovering the virtues of a questioning that does not anticipate the final result, the appeal for setting aside the concepts and the theoretical distinctions imported from science and the tradition of philosophy and the appeal to return to the as yet unreflected, precritical experience in order to deliver the questions that this experience carries within itself. Needless to say, such a description involves our awareness of being ourselves situated in the experience that we attempt to clarify. Indeed, proceeding so, we have some chance to free ourselves from the prejudices that prevent us from deciphering the signs of the new and from taking into account the most disconcerting facts.

Because I have just mentioned Hannah Arendt's work, which is so stimulating in many respects, I will point out that modern democracy remains beyond her reach because she holds preconceptions regarding the definition of power and authority, the significance of the distinction between the social and the political, between work, labor, and action, and so on.

To return to Tocqueville, one knows that in examining the democratic revolution, he thought he had discovered the primitive fact *(le fait generateur)* of the equality of conditions. However, the "fact" of which he was speaking differed from that which one used to call a *fact* in the ordinary sense of the word, as the difficulties in fixing its origin and limits clearly show. The process of equality of conditions cannot be separated from the appearance of a new image of Man. Beyond empirical transformations of relationships between individuals, it involves the recognition of the similar by the similar and, by the same token, it is associated with a new sense of law and the foundations of society as such. We could say that this fact is essentially symbolic. It is the reason why Tocqueville, in pointing out the equality of conditions, was lead to scrutinize the different aspects of change within each sphere of human experience. He came to search for new characteristics of social relationships, and of the individual, public opinion, the modern family, and the political institution as well as new ways of thinking, feeling, and speaking, whether in the religious domain or in the domain of literature, philosophy, or history. Tocqueville's purpose was not to reduce the entire democratic revolution to one unique meaning. We should rather understand that he wanted to practice a sort of exploration into the "flesh" of the social (I borrow this word from Merleau-Ponty), convinced as he was that each mode of human behavior, belief, representation, and each kind of social relationship bears the imprint of other phenomena and is imprinted on the others.

Proceeding so, Tocqueville became capable of discovering what remained most often hidden from a scientific, objective approach. Indeed, being aware of the depth of the social field, he did not limit himself to illuminating the meaning of each feature of democratic life. But from passing from the face to the reversal of the thing he was observing, he revealed the ambiguities of the new. On the one hand, he noted the new signs of human inventiveness, of the independence of the individual, and of the hold of Man on his institutions and, on the other hand, the new signs of passivity, of the dependence of the individual, of the establishment of the "social power" over men.

Is this, perhaps, a matter of the emergence of the individual? Tocqueville showed how he extricated himself from the old network of personal dependencies: this network in which each individual had always occupied a determined place in relation to another located above or below him. From this perspective, the independence of the individual involved a new capacity to live according to his own standards. However, freedom seemed to him to go hand in hand with weakness, loneliness and a growing attraction to the similar. It required an identification with others to compensate for the insignificance of the individual.

Or, perhaps, it is a matter of public opinion. On the one hand, its extension seemed truly positive. Based upon the new freedom of speech and the new concern for urban affairs, public opinion brought an essential limitation to an arbitrary government. On the other hand, one witnessed a coalescing of the consciousnesses, the rise of an invisible power relying upon a general conformism.

Or perhaps it is a matter of legislation. The same ambiguities clearly appear. On the one hand, law ceased to go beyond the reach of people. It became subject to the changing requirements of social life. On the other hand, under the banner of general equality, the legislation turned out to be more and more uniform, rigid, and abstract.

Tocqueville's approach did not reduce itself to the mere observation of the facts at the time. He proceeded from a philosophical reflection as the discussion about the nature of the democratic individual clearly teaches us. When he pointed out the new dependence of the individual upon public opinion or social power, the argument transcended the empirical data. Tocqueville noted that the individual was never a separate being, that each began to form thoughts of his own only after having incorporated the thoughts of others.

This was the reason why Tocqueville paid so much attention to the dangers implicit in the democratic revolution. According to him, the dissolution of the old bonds tying individuals within a hierarchic order had not resulted in the extinction of any form of dependence. After becoming incapable of investing authority in determined visible persons, the individual came to search for the image of the good in the similar, and so was increasingly taken with a game of reflection, without being able to rely upon nature or some reality out of the changing appearances. Authority tended to lie in similarity. At this point, we might be tempted to think that lateral dependency has replaced vertical dependence. However, this view is hardly satisfying. Similarity came necessarily to detach itself from the particular similars and to rule over them.

Instead of beginning with strictly defined concepts, Tocqueville, as I said, seeks to give his concepts new significance in the course of his investigations. In doing so, he frees the readers from a positivist view of social realities. Just as the nature of the individual depends on a view of oneself constituted by the social milieu, so the nature of society cannot be separated from the image that the individual forms of it.

Considering the relations between the individual and society, we observe that reality and fantasy are definitely interconnected. However, we must not forget the third pole of the analysis at which Tocqueville hinted: the discovery of the idea of Man, which undoubtedly cannot be actualized, but opens a new horizon for the individual and the society.

Tocqueville does not attempt to do away with the democratic ambiguities. His investigation tends rather to discover at each stage of the analysis the counterpart of what appears as a positive change without forgetting the virtues of this change. I concede that most often he insists on the negative side of the democratic process. However, the experience we have of history today should permit us to inquire further into the ambiguities that the democratic revolution has been gradually revealing.

On the one hand, we have experienced new forms of conformism combined with apparent social or intellectual progress and, generally speaking, a reinforcement of the "social power" that Tocqueville anticipated so clearly. On the other hand, in opposition to his picture, our modern society appears as more and more differentiated, heterogenous and conflictual. Concerning the first observation, the question Tocqueville announced at the time certainly remains fully relevant: is the power of no particular one the most beautiful sign of human emancipation, or beneath the cover of anonymity has not power gained an as yet unknown force?

Let us remark that Tocqueville did not need to refer to the rise of modern science, or the capitalistic development of economy to pose this critical question. Indeed, Tocqueville continued to belong to the tradition of political philosophy and so was capable of detecting new issues proceeding from democratic experience. Like the classic thinkers, he was convinced that the manner in which authority was conceived and practiced in a certain society determined the main features of its constitution. Simultaneously, he was aware of the close connection between the meaning of authority and the meaning of equality of conditions in modern times and discovered the signs of the irreversible. Political philosophy was not cut off from social analysis and history.

However accurate his clairvoyance may have been, Tocqueville seems to me to have partially misunderstood what was at stake in the transformation of power (of its character and its image) in democracy. I would like to insist on this last point, that could enlighten the philosophical opposition to modern democracy to which I have already alluded.

Fascinated as he was by the contrast of the new order, founded upon equality of conditions, with the old hierarchic order, Tocqueville has constantly referred to the model of aristocratic society, as though this had not been broken into pieces by monarchy long before the emergence of democratic society. Significantly, Tocqueville was never interested in the symbolic function of the king at the time when his power was supposed to embody the kingdom and to proceed from God, or His substitutes, justice and reason. Consequently, he seems not to have measured how extraordinary was the appearance of a government deprived of any capacity for incorporation or any pretention to absolute legitimacy.

First, power becomes unrepresentable in democracy. Perhaps it was not exactly visible before, but it seemed organically linked to the body of the king. As this mortal body was supposed to be connected with an immortal body, the perennial nature of the state and the substantiality of the body politic were ensured. In contrast, democratic power appears as essentially problematic. In one sense, it continues to maintain the internal cohesion of the community and to guarantee its identity in space and time as though it were coming from without. In another sense, it is said to emerge from within society itself. At once external to society and within it, its nature is tacitly accepted as purely symbolic. Second, because the holders of public authority are institutionally prevented from occupying the place of power, this place appears as empty for the first time. Third, because the exercise of public authority results from a periodic competition between the political parties and this competition itself derives from social conflicts, power turns out to be dependent on political and social antagonisms and finally anchored in the division of society. Fourth, just as power loses its capacity to incorporate the community, it can no longer claim to include in itself the ultimate principles of law and knowledge. The government in place must incessantly demonstrate its legitimacy and its competence, yet the foundations of law and knowledge cannot be fixed or guaranteed by anyone. Last, in consequence of this change, the general standards of social relationship become upset in each field of experience. The status of each entity in confrontation with another, whatever the domain, may be doomed to be called into question. We witness a dissolution of the ultimate landmarks of certainty.

This is not the weakness but the greatness of democratic life, so long as it remains vivid. We know that this experience can result in relativism. However, the questioning about what is right or wrong, just or unjust, real or imaginary, does not imply accepting any opinion with indifference. Questioning is a way of recognizing that there is something to be sought, something to be opposed to the authoritarian answers that one usually draws from the past. I am not sure that Tocqueville should have rejected the analysis I have just sketched out, in the wake of his writings. Indeed, he was one of the rare thinkers who spoke of the disorders of democracy in its praise.

To conclude, I should say that political philosophy today requires in the first place the assumption that legitimacy cannot be detached from the continuous debate about the legitimate and the illegitimate. Consequently, I will ask this last question that relates to the first one I asked: does not the philosopher's ignorance or contempt of modern democracy proceed from the reluctance to recognize the interrogation at the heart of social life, precisely while they claim the right of thought to radical questioning?

20

The Political Origins of Democracy

Dick Howard

POLITICS AFTER "THE" REVOLUTION

The heading under which I introduce these remarks points toward the conclusion at which I will arrive. It also suggests some of the premises from which these reflections begin. First of all, I am bothered by the abuse of the concept of democracy that assimilates it simply to the interests of the so-called free world. This same refusal of simplification for political ends holds for another abuse of the concept of democracy that has taken root recently in France, especially among an intelligentsia seeking to make amends for its former sins of philo-communism. To awaken from the dream of happy tomorrows and to uncover everywhere the seeds of totalitarianism is not a politics. But these twin abuses are not without significance. Claude Lefort, who cannot be accused of either deviation, suggests an orientation for further analysis when, instead of opposing a "critique" of totalitarianism to a praise of democracy, he subtitles *L'invention democratique* "The Limits of Totalitarian Domination."[1] Democracy and totalitarianism are not simply antithetic. The analysis of their relation has to pass through the mediation by the *political* structure of modern societies, which I will define as republican. As a political form, democracy expresses a society's self-understanding, its vision of the good life, which cannot be fixed by a simple formula or procedure. Democracy is not a fact but the expression of the *sense* of social action. Its relation to totalitarianism makes clear that this sense must be constantly reaffirmed if it is not to degenerate.

I was going to begin these remarks under the heading "post-revolutionary politics." Aside from the fact that I dislike the modish application of "posts" that has gained public favor recently and covers over the
need for analysis, the title would have led to confusion because I do not
intend to talk about what should be done once "we" have "taken power."
The implicit assumption made by "revolutionary politics" separates
power from politics; it introduces a premodern image in which the political sphere is conceived as if it were a thing or a place that could be occupied and whose command could bring about social transformations
that would, ultimately, permit the political state to "wither away" because society would be capable of self-government. I speak of politics after "the" revolution to indicate the refusal of the idea of a transparent society that has become, finally, reconciled with itself and in which, as
Engels put it, the government over men has been replaced by the administration of things. That representation of "revolutionary politics" ignores the symbolic role of the political and denies its difference from
other social facts. But to give up on "the" revolution does not imply the
acceptance of the established order. It is necessary to understand the
philosophical *origin* of this attitude whose empirical foundation is, no
doubt, the fact that we are living "after" the totalitarian revolution. But
this totalitarianism itself remains to be explained. Its origin is found in the
political structure of democracy itself.

My introductory title suggests another premise of my argument.
That dichotomy of politics and power that I reject is founded on a representation that imagines political forms as if they were things. "Democracy" is opposed to "totalitarianism" as if each were a fixed essence that
is unchanged by any relation into which it enters. Beyond the obvious
methodological criticism of that representation of politics, I want now to
draw from it a positive implication. At the time of the American Revolution—which, it should be recalled, *was* a revolution—many people spoke
of "the democracy" as a thing, or rather as a threat that weighed on the
newly independent state. "The democracy" was the masses, the popu-
lace, or what philosophical jargon calls "civil society." The threat that it
represented should not be reduced to its simple economic consequences;
the threat was political, symbolic, endangering the meaning of those actions by which the colonists had become a free people. The American
Revolution, it will be recalled, claimed to be republican; it felt itself
threatened by the mercantile spirit for the same reason that "the democracy" was a threat: the *res publica*, the public thing, had to be protected
against all private interests, be they *majoritary* or *minoritary*. This republican argument can be "demystified" by a progressive or a Marxist historian; but the reductionism supposed by that demystification is not a

politics. The politics I propose to consider here will take as its premise the development of the American Revolution that realized, in its way, the republic.

One last premise needs to be mentioned. When "the" revolution is not identified with the Bolshevik Revolution, it is often conceived in terms of the French Revolution. But the French model poses problems of its own. Was it the work of July 14? The night of August 4? Or the more "radical" movements that continue in a linked process up to the fall of Robespierre, if not beyond? If I introduce the French Revolution into these reflections, it is not to return to the famous thesis of Hannah Arendt, which suggests that the American Revolution succeeded because it knew how to remain at the political level whereas the French Revolution was undermined by the contradictions imposed on it by the "social question." That dichotomous formulation is too simple for the historian, too exclusive for the philosopher. Once again, politics is not reducible to a thing, whose essential nature can be opposed to another fixed identity; politics is concerned with the way in which a society makes sense of itself by means of an appeal to what it *is* not and can never fully become. Because politics expresses the symbolic dimension of society, it is always confronted by its own inherent historicity. I introduce the French Revolution into my premises because its analysis by François Furet, in *Penser la Revolution Française,* permits me to treat the question of democracy without falling into political manichaeism, which distorts the nature of the political. The origin of that manichaeism explains why politics is inherently symbolic and historical.

THE MODERNITY OF REVOLUTION

What is one trying to explain when one analyzes a revolution? Attention can be directed to its objective causes, the material necessities that explain why things had to take the course they did. But the existence of these causes does not explain the modality of action, the process by which men and women become conscious of those so-called material necessities. The problem comes from the separation of the subject and the object. Thus, Furet shows how Tocqueville's analysis of the *ancien régime* has to be completed by the study of the new modes of political behavior by new actors described by Cochin. But the problem remains: how is one to conceptualize the unity of that juxtaposition of the two approaches? The concept of "thinking" *(penser)* in the title of Furet's study has philosophical resonances. "The" revolution is neither what existed before nor what came to exist after. The historian wants to reproduce the unity of the material foundation and a mode of action. But that unity no longer exists. "The" revolution is known only from its manifestations; it expresses the symbolic sense of a historical action. The Before and the After can be represented; but "the" revolution has to be thought as its own origin. Conceived in this manner, the revolution inaugurates *modernity*.

This identification of a revolutionary origin and modernity has to be elucidated. When we speak of a science or an art, an institution or a state, as modern, we are affirming that the structure being analyzed is autonomous and self-legitimating. We are saying that its *genesis* and the *norm* that legitimates that institution are *immanent* to it. From this point of view, the two moments unified in "the" revolution can be conceptualized as that of its genesis and that of its normativity. This is why the revolution can be called *modern*. But we know that the path that began on July 14, 1789, was tortuous; we know that Thermidor was followed by a succession of regimes whose conclusion was the Empire and its defeat; indeed, Furet affirms that in a certain sense, the entire history of modern France (which was perhaps concluded in 1981, or in 1986) can be conceived of as the vain pursuit of the promise that I am calling the *entry into modernity,* and that Furet calls the *Republic*.[2] The categories of genesis and normativity can explain what Furet calls the *skids (dérapages)* in the path of the revolution. These skids, in turn, permit me to clarify what I mean by the concept of origin.

Without going into the historical details, one can say that there is a skid in an originary structure when the constitutive tension between genesis and normativity becomes either too loose or unbearable for its actors, who are then driven to break out of it. The result can be a politics in which genesis determines normativity; an example would be the Jacobin moment in which the appeal to *le Peuple* results in the elimination of all constitutional protections for real people. The result can also be a politics in which normativity determines genesis; an example would be the politics of the Directory that was so concerned with assuring its own legitimacy that it made the established institutions inoperable. Other forms of this skid away from the originary revolutionary unity are possible. What served as a genetic principle can invert itself and function as a norm; an example would be the appeal to *la Patrie en danger*. Similarly, what served as a legitimating norm can be inverted to serve as an animating principle of society; an example would be the abandomnent of its role by the Constituant Assembly in favor of the Convention. Because they function within an originary unity, genesis and normativity are related to one another as *reversible*.[3] This reversibility is not an empirical fact; it operates within the domain of meaning; it is political.

These brief allusions, which could be developed if we had the time, describe a structure that reappears, for example, in the art forms called *modern,* but also in a politics that claims to be revolutionary. The debate between reformists and revolutionaries, between Social-Democrats and Bolsheviks, can be replayed in these same terms. Reformists appeal apparently to the genetic pole whereas revolutionaries insist on the normative demand. But Rosa Luxemburg was a "genetic revolutionary" who defended the need for democracy against Lenin and against the Bolshevik seizure of power. Similarly, Karl Kautsky's radical orthodoxy became the basis of a reformist strategy for which acting before the structural logic of capitalism had prepared its downfall was giving in to a provocation. The result of these necessarily fruitless theoretical jousts, condemned by the one-sidedness of their empirical options, returns us to that other revolution, the American, whose republican institutions pose the question of democracy. Let me first insist, once again, on the fact that an orginary structure, defined by the copresence of genesis and normativity is revolutionary and modern to the degree that it is constituted in a manner that avoids the "skid" toward one or the other of its constitutive poles. "The" revolution, which wants to go beyond that constitutive dichotomy by replacing, for example, formal or political democracy by its real or social incarnation is to be rejected just as is "the" revolution that would come into being to realize the Laws of History or Science.

(This is the point at which the analysis of totalitarianism could be introduced, were there time. As opposed to the classical forms of despotism or tyranny, totalitarianism is specifically modern. Like democracy, it is born of the revolution that breaks with the ancien régime that was structured as a *political society.* The destruction of that unity of society with its political representation produces a political state that is both separate from and yet dependent on society. The space opened between the two poles makes possible the practice of democracy; but the same democratic space expresses the tension defined by the originary structure of "the" revolution. Democracy is constantly threatened by the "skids" built into its very structure. The totalitarian temptation is founded on a critique of the inherent instability of democracy and the necessary empirical incompleteness of its supposed realization, which could be only symbolic. The totalitarian move can take the genetic form of a demand for "real democracy," eliminating the difference between state and society; or it can take the form of a normative appeal (to the Science of History, but also to the Nature of the *Volk*) to overcome the artificiality of the public space. In both cases, the constitutive unity-in-difference of modernity is destroyed by the attempt to eliminate difference and efface the threat of the new by realizing it in the here-and-now. Democracy is par excellence historical; totalitarianism seeks the end of what Marx euphemistically called *prehistory*. An unsatisfactory or incomplete democracy can be changed from within; the "limits to totalitarian domination" take the form of a return of the suppressed pole that restores the conditions for democracy by returning to society the possibility of political action that the empirical "realization" of Natural or Historical Law claimed to produce.

THE MODERN STATE AS REPUBLICAN

I insisted on the fact that the authors of the American Constitution of 1787 feared equally "the democracy" and private mercantile interest. Their republic was intended to control what since Hegel has been called *civil society*. In the Remark to Paragraph 258 of his *Philosophy of Right*, Hegel criticizes the politics for which the protection of the individual and his or her interests would determine the activity of the state. The state is not to be confused with civil society; its specific end is not "the security and protection of property and personal freedom." Hegel's state can be interpreted as republican; it determines the "true content and the goal" of the individual. Hegel explains why the "principle of the modern state" has such an "incredible strength and depth" in Paragraph 260. Its secret is that it permits "the principle of subjectivity to realize itself as an *autonomous pole*" and at the same time to *"return it to the substantial unity* in which it is preserved."[4] This Hegelian argument could be interpreted as recognizing and seeking to give form to the originary structure we have described. But even if it is republican, Hegel's state is hardly democratic. Marx's path began from the demystification of the "political illusion" he found in Hegel. In our terms, Marx criticizes Hegel for being simply a normative philosopher. The "substantial unity" engulfs the "autonomous pole," eliminating the tension constitutive of democracy by treating the symbolic nature of the political as a *really realized* or *"objective"* spirit. But Marx's solution is based on the representation of a civil society and a proletariat that would be the genetic foundation of a "true" politics, which would not need to refer at all to a state for its unification. Like Hegel, but by a symmetrical error, Marx breaks the constitutive tension of modernity; he, too, wants to "realize" the political.

Before returning to the Americans through this brief detour into the culmination of German Idealism, it should be noted that Kant provides the philosophical basis from which a modern democratic theory could be derived. His critical theory attempts to maintain the duality of genesis and normativity; it explains the peculiar but necessary "dialectic" that constantly threatens to explode the tension and lead it into skids. Working from his own philosophical form of the constitutive tension furnished by the first two *Critiques*, Kant analyzes the critical activity itself in the *Critique of Judgment*. The theory of reflective judgment formulated there is crucial to any attempt to think modern politics. Kant's last writings, which address questions of politics, confirm this orientation. For example, the essay "On the Common Saying: 'This may be true in Theory, but it does not Apply in Practice' " (1793) criticizes the error committed by the revolutionaries. They have not understood the implication of the form of reflective judgment. They assume that the "social contract" *really* took place; they justify this purported revolutionary goal as the realization anew of a real achievement that supposedly has been perverted by power. Kant rejects this theoretical justification of practice at the same time that he nonetheless insists on the practical relevance of properly understood theory. The key to that theory is the distinction between the subsumptive universalizing judgment, which eliminates particularity, and the reflective judgment, which begins from particularity to propose, in public communication, a universal form adequate to it. The beautiful is affirmed explicitly as the "symbol" of the concrete ethical life (in Paragraph 59) whereas the teleology of nature revealed to the reflective judgment is given an explicit political form by its comparison to the French Revolution (in Paragraph 65).

In his great "post-Jacobian" proposal for "Perpetual Peace" (1795), Kant remains a supporter of the French Revolution, whose foundation he attempts to understand. The reflective judgment affirms the republican solution and rejects the attempt to found a "real democracy" by identifying the executive and the legislative branches. That kind of democracy would leave no public space in which political judgment could be formed. The crucial role of the reflective political judgment is said by Kant to be an "affirmative and transcendental principle of public right," whose formulation is that "All maxims which *require* publicity if they are not to fail in their purpose can be reconciled with both right and politics." Only in the republican form is this publicity guaranteed. The Americans, in effect, anticipated the argument of the philosopher. But the philosopher of modernity offers the critical tools with which to understand the limits, and possibilities, of the American achievement, which cannot be reduced to its material achievements or failings.

If the American Revolution is characterized by its republican spirit and if that spirit is truly anchored in the Constitution of 1787, its *democratic* realization provides a critical standpoint from which to analyze that Revolution. Although the historians still debate when the rupture with the revolutionary phase took place, all admit that the Founding Fathers would not recognize the contemporary manifestation of their new society. The obvious source from which to begin an analysis of the relation

between this political form and its social realization is Tocqueville's attempt to generalize from its lessons. Claude Lefort suggests an approach
to Tocqueville that permits us to develop the implications of the structure
of modernity by applying the concept of "reversibility."[5] In a word,
Tocqueville's first volume seems to define democracy as a "social fact"
whose political, cultural, and moral consequences he analyzes. But
Tocqueville is not an empirical sociologist, he is a political theorist. In
Lefort's formulation, social equality is here the visible, political freedom
is its "invisible" political correlate, which Tocqueville is trying to understand. But things are not so simple; the relation can invert itself. Apparently empirical liberty can become the visible foundation of an invisible
equality that democratic politics attempts to realize. This reversed orientation dominates Tocqueville's second volume, whereas the first approach characterizes his first volume. Tocqueville's equality could be replaced here by "civil society," and his "freedom" by the republican
institutional structure. The two are inseparable, functioning alternatively
as genesis and normative legitimation; equality can engender forms of
freedom but its isolated pursuit threatens them; freedom demands conditions of social equality but when pursued for the sake of private ad-
vancement it comes to threaten that equality. Tocqueville's conclusion
returns us to contemporary politics: I like democracy, he says, not because of what it is, but because of what it makes people do (*fait faire*).

THE POLITICAL ORIGINS OF DEMOCRACY

   Tocqueville sees the heart of American democracy in its rich associational life. The preservation of associational democracy is due to the
fact that the goals of the groups are neither too great nor too insignificant;
association becomes a habit, a mode of behavior that is at once political
and social. This median role incarnates the reversibility stressed by Lefort: democracy maintains itself by straddling the political and the social,
correcting its skids as it attaches itself to the flesh of national history. But
Tocqueville's description should not lead to an idealization of democracy; the movement of self-correction is constantly threatened from
within. The history of the United States can just as well be told in terms
of its "skids," whose amplitude is perhaps increasing! Democracy is not
a thing whose essence is fixed; the constitutive tension that defines it explains also the possibility of its distortion. If the goals of associative life
are too great; the attempt to realize them breaks with the symbolic unity
of the democratic polity from the side of society that seeks to make itself
fully political. If the goals are too small, the symbolic unity is destroyed

from the side of politics that is left to the control of others. Once again, Tocqueville is offering an analysis of democracy as political; his apparently empirical illustration is not simply sociological.

The critique of "really existing democracy" is not the property of the "left." Indeed, the notion of a "left" needs to be rethought once the belief in a Sense of History is jettisoned along with the faith in "the" Revolution. Contemporary neoconservative theory demonstrates unintentionally the need for a revision in our political definitions. It proposes a critique of a democracy whose excesses are said to threaten to make society ungovernable. For the neoconservatives, democracy must be limited to preserve democracy. This solution explains why its proponents are called neo*conservative;* it also helps define a modern "left." When political options are conceived without reference to *the* Sense of History, conservatives and radicals can be distinguished by their attitudes toward popular participation. What bothers the worthy neoconservative protectors of democratic society is the birth of what are called *new social movements*. These movements are new in that they present themselves neither as the representatives of particular social interests, nor as political actors whose goals concern society as a whole. Their novelty can be understood in terms of the originary structure. They are the carriers of a practical critique of "really existing democracy" insofar as that democracy leans either too far toward politics or too far toward particular social interests. That is to say, these movements carry with them a democratic civil society in the making.

This briefly sketched analysis suggests a "post-revolutionary" definition of the distinction left-right in terms of their respective attitudes toward democracy. But that conceptual distinction does not yet found a politics. The new social movements are not born like mushrooms after the rain. The explanation of their *origin* demands a return to the problem of revolution and to the republican politics proposed by Kant. Analyses as different as those of Habermas, Gorz, Ferguson and Cohen, or Laclau and Mouffe,[6] all run into difficulty when confronted with the question of the *origin* of democracy; they treat it as the reaction of a threatened *Lebenswelt,* an existential choice, a rational decision, or a discursive given. None of them is able to think the *political question* posed by the new social movements conceived as a democratic civil society in the making. The result is that, once the movement no longer moves, those who wish to remain active politically find themselves condemned to adopt diverse "revolutionary" formulas from the past; the search for a new political subject occupies some, whereas others debate the demystification of the ill deeds of the interests. This seems to be the point at which the left finds itself today; but it is no more the "last word" than is the state of contemporary American democracy.

The "post-revolutionary" politics that I am proposing can be conceptualized in terms of republican theory. What characterizes that theory throughout the ages[7] is the concern to avoid the centralization of power in the hands of a single person, group, interest, or even a political institution. This republican demand was well understood by the authors of the Constitution of 1787. *If* their republic has become a *social* democracy without at the same time losing its political soul, this is because the domination of one branch of government, one material interest, or one legal codification has been avoided—barely at times! The point is not to complain that politics has done too little, or that it has been kept out of the hands of its rightful possessors. These empirical facts are founded by a *political* structure that remains their "invisible" corollary. A radical politics whose aim is the restoration of the kind of participatory politics that Tocqueville described as American associational democracy has to make visible the political structure that frames the republic. This does not mean addressing "the democracy," any more than it is possible to appeal to the (re)creation of "the" proletariat or "the" revolution. Republican theory and the history of the American republic point to a different orientation.

American history suggests a mode of conceptualizing the new social movements. They are not "the democracy" feared by the Framers of 1787. The Americans had gone through a historical experience between 1763 and 1776, which led them to declare their independence in ringing tones of natural right. They had attempted to give institutional form to their political creed in thirteen states and a Confederation and they had come to see the dangers of a politics that ignores its specific form and limits. The attempt to incarnate materially the popular sovereignty that independence had achieved led to theoretical paradox and practical confusion. The new Constitution, inaugurated by the phrase "We, the people," recognized the plurality of interests among the people; the popular sovereignty it affirmed was to be present in each of its carefully checked and balanced branches of government. Because it is present everywhere, this popular sovereignty is incarnate nowhere; it is symbolic and political, not empirical and social. If the Constitution can be seen as excluding the "social question" from the political sphere,[8] its claim to represent popular sovereignty takes on its full sense in the light of the double lesson drawn from Kant. Kant's reflective judgment prevents us from conceiving of politics as a science or an applied morality; his republican theory insists on the necessary existence and preservation of a public space in which that judgment can be practiced. This republican politics also expresses the goals of the great French liberal who loved democracy for what it *fait faire*.

The ambiguous but really existing democracy in America, whose history has not ended, is founded by its republican political institutions. If we want to see the benefits of democracy extended at the same time that we admit that the civil society represented by the new social movements cannot be created from outside of that society, our politics must aim first of all at the realization of the *republic*. Democracy is its result, not its cause. This does not change, or *make less necessary,* empirical struggles within society, but it does affect their political *sense*. Politics cannot be reduced to the pragmatic question of who gets what from whom. The political is not defined by the social. On the contrary, politics defines those questions around which social action — that "revolutionary" transformation that society exercises on itself—becomes possible. Modern societies, inaugurated by the rupture signified by the American and French Revolutions, are always already political. There is no reason why contemporary politics should exist only in the deformed mode of competition among existing social interests. A radical democratic politics that reactivates the normative republican institutional framework can be generated by the ability of new social movements to realize the implications of their own political existence.

21

Art and Democracy in Habermas

Claude Piché

We should begin by restricting the scope of this inquiry and orienting ourselves to the theme chosen for this round table, The Critique of Society and Problems of Democracy. We will discuss the "critique of society" by examining the critical theory of the Frankfurt School, particularly the work of its best-known heir, Jürgen Habermas. Our investigation of the modern "problem of democracy" will be confined to the phenomenon of art and the social role of art in democracy. At stake, therefore, is the relation between art and democracy in the recent texts of Habermas.

The following preliminary observation will serve as our point of departure. With the publication in 1985 of *Der philosophische Diskurs der Moderne*, Habermas implicitly *abandons* the terrain of philosophical aesthetics in the sense that, for him, art no longer represents a privileged object of philosophical discourse. This observation is drawn from a reading of the appendix to the chapter devoted to Derrida.[1] Philosophy is no longer responsible for the interpretation of the work of art or for the integration of the work of art into society, as Habermas implicitly delegates this task to art criticism. The innovative potential of art is manifested in a way far too unpredictable and sporadic to be amendable to philosophical discourse. Art bears the mark of "contingency";[2] it can be apprehended only empirically, reflected upon only a posteriori. This attitude appears to be a reversal of Habermas's earlier position, particularly if one considers the hope engendered by the well-known lecture delivered in Frankfurt in 1980, "Modernity versus Postmodernity." Gérard Raulet,

265

Martin Jay, and Richard Bernstein[3] perceived this lecture as a promising breakthrough for Habermas's critical theory of society. *The Theory of Communicative Action,* which appeared in 1981, confirmed the importance of aesthetic considerations for the architectonic of this social theory, to the extent that it was reasonable to expect that the problem of art would be central to the argumentation presented in *Der philosophische Discurs der Moderne.*

Moreover, Habermas is forced to acknowledge that the *aesthetics* of modernity constitute a privileged approach for those who wish to define the characteristics of modern times in general. In the short Preface to this book, however, Habermas, sets aside this aspect of the question. "Since the late eighteenth century modernity has been raised to the status of a philosophical topic in this discourse. The philosophical discourse of modernity has much in common with its aesthetic ounterpart; they overlap each other in many ways. I was obliged, however, to limit my topic; these lectures *do not* deal with modernism in art and in literature."[4] Habermas excuses this omission by appeal to limitations of space and refers us to the works of three theoreticians of aesthetics: Rudolph Bürger, Hans-Robert Jauss, and Albrecht Wellmer. Wellmer's important role in the development of Habermas's aesthetic theory will be examined shortly. For the moment, however, we will merely reiterate our initial observation that in his latest book Habermas shows signs of disillusionment with respect to the problem of art. This disillusionment is manifested in the sharp distinction he draws between philosophy and art criticism, the latter having henceforth an exclusive competence in the aesthetic domain.

In what follows, we will attempt to explain why Habermas's efforts in the field of aesthetics ultimately led him to such a negative account of art. We will seek the cause of his disappointment in the heart of his critical theory of society. In short, Habermas's theory of communication prevents him from appreciating the specificity of the aesthetic phenomenon. Our discussion will proceed by way of the following three stages: the paradox of modernity; art as a medium of learning and a medium of communication; and the cognitive potential of art.

THE PARADOX OF MODERNITY

Although the theory of communication was adumbrated in Habermas's earlier works,[5] it is not until the publication, in 1971, of "Vorbereitende Bemerkungen zu einer Theorie der kommunikativen Kompetenz"[6] that it enters forcefully into his writings. Before 1971, Habermas had developed his critical theory from the perspective of a theory of knowledge, whereas since then the theory of communicative action has dominated the development of his theory of society. As is well known, the elaboration of his theory of communicative action remains the central aim of all of Habermas's inquiries. *Knowledge and Human Interests* sets out to be a critique of positivism and, in the 1960s, it was precisely in this sort of critique that Habermas saw the potential for emancipation. A certain number of internal difficulties induced him to reorient his enterprise, however. He has realized that his epistemological critique is still far too dependent on traditional philosophy and its claim to be able to delineate absolute foundations. Recall that *Knowledge and Human Interests* appeals to a certain form of transcendentalism (or quasi-transcendentalism). One of the problems incurred by this approach is its complete dependence on the subject-object relation (here *Gattungssubjekt*). With the assistance of his theory of communication, Habermas intends to eliminate the *aporias* of the philosophy of subjectivity by relying directly on a theory of intersubjectivity secured from all relapses into the monologism of instrumental reason.[7] According to Habermas, the theory would have a much greater chance of realizing its ideal of emancipation if it were founded, from its inception, on communicative rationality. Only the theory of communicative action can provide the normative foundations necessary for a critical theory of society. In fact, the theory of communicative action is intimately related to the Enlightenment ideal of the accession of all to maturity, to democracy. In the Preface to the 1981 edition of *Philosophical-Political Profiles*[8] Habermas insists that the task of the *Auflärung* must not be limited to the establishment, from the perspective of a theory of science or an epistemological critique, of a mediation only between science and the life world. The task of philosophy is to consider and show the fruitfulness, for this life world, of every dimension of modern rationality, including morality and art. Only the theory of communicative action is in a position to integrate, in addition to the perspective of the cognitive-instrumental sphere, the dimensions of the moral-practical and aesthetic-expressive spheres.

The revival of the Weberian scheme of the rationalization processes familiar to Western society is evident in the preceding enumeration of the three cultural spheres. The gradual severing of modern culture from tradition results in the institution of autonomous spheres that develop in relation to the logic internal to each. We also witness the increasing specialization of the three spheres: science and technology; universalistic morality and positive law; and autonomous art and art criticism. In each case, the specialization of tasks is pushed to the point that only an expert can perform them competently. The efficacy of the process of rationalization increases in relation to the automony, yet also to the esoteric nature of each of the spheres, to such an extent that they become inaccessible to the public. Having adopted this Weberian diagnosis, Habermas sees the paradox of rationality as the greatest challenge now facing philosophy. The challenge must be met because the project of modernity still demands completion. In his article "Modernity versus Postmodernity," Habermas poses the question in the following way:

> The differentiation of science, morality, and art, which characterizes, according to Weber, the rationalism of the Western culture, means both that the segments treated by the specialist have become autonomous and, *at the same time,* that these segments have split off from a tradition that continues to develop naturally in the hermeneutics of everyday communication. This splitting off is the problem that results from the development, according to their own sets of laws *(Eigengesetzlichkeit),* of the different domains of values . . . [9]

The problem may be summarized as follows: on the one hand, we witness the increasing and necessary autonomy of each of the cultural spheres; on the other, there is a rupture in the continuity between these cultural spheres and daily life. Modernity is an unfinished project so long as the gap between culture and the lived world remains to be filled. It is actually the Enlightenment ideals of emancipation and democracy that are slow to be realized and that, ultimately, is the source of Habermas's fundamental motivation. It is not that he wishes to renounce the specialization of the expert (on the contrary, for Habermas, specialization is the indispensable condition for the development of modern reason), but that he wishes to show the fruitfulness of specialization for everyday life.

It is from this perspective that we must grasp the intervention of the theory of communication in Habermas's work. Our modern societies are characterized by this sense of rupture; there are breakdowns in the communication among citizens, between society and culture, even among the cultural spheres themselves, and this is due to the specificity of the inner logic of each. The imperative of communication, that is to say the ideal of the Enlightenment, is so determinative for Habermas that the theory of communicative action founded on the formal pragmatics of language dictates the entire architectonic of his cultural system. In this way, science, morality, and art are divided according to the three validity claims that are reunited in every speech act: the claim to truth, the claim to normative rightness, and the claim to authenticity (or truthfulness). For example, in the conclusion of his great work, *The Theory of Communicative*

Action[10] Habermas provides a glimpse of the development of the three philosophical disciplines that correspond to the three validity claims: the theory of science, the theory of law and morality, and aesthetics.

ART AS A MEDIUM OF A LEARNING EXPERIENCE
AND A MEDIUM OF COMMUNICATION

The preceding overview is essential for an understanding of the status that Habermas accords philosophical discourse concerning art. Here aesthetics takes its place within a theory of modernity or, more precisely, within a theory of modern rationality. The inclusion of art in a theory of modern rationality is also explained in the following way: to the extent that an argument (one that brings to light diverse motives and reasons) is possible and even legitimate in this case, art harbors a cognitive potential.[11] Art implies a certain "type of knowledge"[12] and for this reason is of philosophical interest. The corresponding philosophical task is the articulation of the conditions of the possibility of such knowledge. Thus art is correctly viewed as the "medium of a learning experience" to the extent that the "reconstructive sciences," inspired by Piaget and adopted by Habermas, may be applied without difficulty to aesthetics.[13] Thus, in the early 1980s, Habermas's project in the aesthetic domain parallels his agenda in the realms of science and ethics, for he claims, particularly in *The Theory of Communicative Action,* to be able to identify the conditions necessary for the production of aesthetic knowledge by showing that aesthetic experience is intimately related to the "intuitive mastery of a system of rules."[14] Here we can see that Habermas is ready to study the inner logic of the aesthetic phenomenon and, in so doing, to preserve intact its autonomy against all attempts at reduction. Habermas has, moreover, always respected the fundamental autonomy of the movement of art in modernity,[15] and he has clearly indicated his reservations concerning a desublimated art and the "profane illumination" in the art of the masses (Benjamin).

The problem that arises from the heart of Habermas's aesthetics, however, is provoked by a theoretical interference: the arguments put forth in a discussion of a work of art gravitate toward a validity claim presented in terms of *authenticity.* This concept refers back to the notion of expressiveness in which Habermas circumscribes the sphere of art: the aesthetic-expressive. That is to say, the intrinsic quality of a work of art depends on the degree to which the artist's expression in the work of art is authentic. "In this context reasons have the peculiar function of *bring-*

ing us to see a work or performance in such a way that it can be perceived as an *authentic expression* of an exemplary experience, in general as the embodiment of a *claim to authenticity.*"[16] Shortly thereafter Habermas is warned that the categories of truth and authenticity are inadequate for the task of discerning the cognitive specificity of the work of art. Habermas soon became sympathetic to Albrecht Wellmer's view that the claim to authenticity is too restrictive. In *Der philosophische Diskurs der Moderne* Habermas makes the following observation: "A. Wellmer has shown that the inner coherence of a work of art, the so called artistic truth, cannot so easily be said to rely on authenticity or truthfulness."[17] We should not underestimate the consequences of this concession but it would be advisable to pause here to consider the causes of the first error.

The theoretical interference to which we alluded earlier is presented in the following way: *the requirement of authenticity originates in the theory of communication.* The pragmatics of language here determines a priori if not the content of art, at least the standard of measure by which it will be judged. Does not the primacy of communication interfere here with the inner logic of art? Habermas formally maintains his respect for the autonomy of art but, in fact, he subjects art to the logic of communication. Because he wishes to use communicative reason to resolve, at all costs, the paradox of rationality, he is led to introduce into the aesthetic domain a completely extrinsic standard of measure. We have seen that modern reason has the two opposing characteristics of specialization and autonomy, on the one hand, and social emancipation and *Aufklärung,* on the other. The dominance of the latter in Habermas's position leads him to overemphasize the theory of communication and to let it interfere with the specialized cultural spheres, with the culture of experts.

In sum, communication is primary in Habermas's approach to art. This is manifested by, among other things, the occurrence of the theme of "reception"[18] in the article "Modernity versus Postmodernity." Art is truly a "medium of communication,"[19] to borrow an expression Habermas applies to Schiller. Thus for Habermas, the conception of art as a medium of communication takes precedence over its construal as a "medium of a learning experience"[20] in which the cognitive potential of art is acknowledged. Moreover, because the rigid and all-encompassing validity claim of authenticity is no longer at his disposal for the definition of the aesthetic sphere, Habermas relinquishes the hope of being able to highlight in advance the direction taken by diverse artistic experiences. The following sentence constitutes a clear admission: "I do not know whether or not the results of Piaget's genetic psychology are as appropriate for the analysis of this 'level of learning' as they are for the analysis of the stages of postconventional conception of law and morality. I tend to be rather skeptical."[21] In this assertion Habermas implicitly abandons the philosophical aesthetics proposed in *The Theory of Communicative Action*. Just as in the case of the theory of science and the theory of morality, philosophical aesthetics was supposed to be edified with the help of the reconstructive sciences, as is the case with the genetic psychology of Piaget. In *Der philosophische Diskurs der Moderne,* Habermas still retains the hope of isolating the conditions for the possibility of scientific and moral discourse *(Diskurs),* but he no longer believes this can be done for the aesthetic critique *(Kritik).* Such is the meaning of the dichotomy he henceforth establishes between truth and taste.[22] Only science and ethics have univocal access to the truth; the concept of truth cannot be applied to art except in a metaphorical sense (in the passage cited later concerning Wellmer, Habermas introduces the expression *artistic truth* in quotation marks!), unless art reveals itself in a communication process with the life world. Yet, in that case, philosophy no longer plays the role of the mediator between art and the life world, as is the case for science and ethics. This mediation is now the task of art criticism construed as an empirical investigation. Philosophy is prepared to play the role of "interpreter"[23] between the culture of experts and life world only in the realms in which philosophy succeeds in bringing to light the criteria of the relevant procedures (i.e., apophantic truth for science, moral rectitude for ethics); that is to say, only in the realms in which philosophy was originally able to play the role of *"Platzhalter."* In *Der philosophische Diskurs der Moderne,* Habermas only draws out the consequences of this position: in the absence of an all encompassing criterion such as authenticity, philosophy cannot function as a mediator.

THE COGNITIVE POTENTIAL OF ART

Once the communicative criterion of truthfulness proved to be insufficient, the cognitive potential of art was no longer of primary importance for Habermas. Before concluding we should no doubt examine more closely the reasons for which Habermas ultimately adopted this position. In fact, the criterion of truthfulness does not linger over that which is expressed by the aesthetic subject. We have seen that when the artist is viewed as a transmitter in communication with his public, the demand for authenticity qualifies his mode of expression. How then does Habermas characterize the content of the aesthetic experience communicated? It is important to refer to an article, published in 1984, "Questions and Counterquestions," which is very explicit on this subject. At first Habermas applies himself, with good reason, to the task of circumscribing the aesthetic sphere within the exterior world. After delimiting this sphere, Habermas proceeds to define its contents.

Authentic experiences of this type are possible only to the extent that the categories of the patterned expectation of organized daily experiences collapse, that the routines of daily action and conventions of ordinary life are destroyed, and the normality of foreseeable and accountable certainties are suspended. ... At the same time, this decentering indicates an increased sensitivity to what remains unassimilated in the interpretive achievements of pragmatic, epistemic and moral mastery of the demands and challenges of everyday situations; it effects an openness to the expurgated elements of the unconscious, the fantastic, and the mad, the material and the bodily —thus to everything in our speechless contact with reality which is fleeting, so contingent, so immediate, so individualized, simultaneously so far and so near that it escapes our normal categorical grasp.[24]

In a close reading of these lines, one is first struck by the marginal role of art in daily life and in the other cultural spheres. This depiction of art's marginal position is reminiscent of a point Habermas makes in *Legitimation Crisis:* art is interested in "residual needs";[25] that is to say, in all that is left unfulfilled by the economic and political systems, as well as by the cultural system in the form of science and morality. As mentioned in the preceding passage, in all these domains a "mastery" asserts itself, be it pragmatic, epistemological, or moral. Art, therefore, appears to be the domain of nonmastery, perhaps even of the nonmasterable: art concerns itself with the residual, with that which is "unassimilated." From this perspective, the content of art is seen to reside in that which "escapes our usual categorical grasp." In the beginning of the extract, Habermas alludes to the collapse of these "categories" of daily experience. This is surprising because one ends up with the impression that the content of art has to do with that which eludes all categories, with that which is particular, singular, and immediate, to the point that the general concept is excluded. It is as though Habermas considers aesthetics in terms of its etymological sense of *aithésis,* as an object of pure sensibility. But in the domain of art, such an exclusive dualism between concept and intuition borders on the dogmatic. Habermas no doubt considers himself here to be the legitimate heir of his mentor, Adorno.[26] Yet it is important to note that, for the latter, the categories of material life are also present in a work of art. This does not mean that they are denied but that they are often transfigured. Let us turn to Adorno himself, to whom Habermas's lecture, "Modernity versus Postmodernity," is officially dedicated.

The formative categories of art are not simply different in kind from those outside. They actively seek to impart what is particular to themselves to the outside world. In the latter the prevailing forms are those that characterize the domination of nature, whereas in art, forms are being controlled and regimented out of a sense of freedom ... If art had nothing at all to do with logic and causality, it would be an idling motion without any link to its other; if it took them too literally, it would succumb to their spell. What allows art to pull away from the spell, and not by much, is its dual essence which causes permanent conflict.[27]

Habermas also speaks of the "inner logic"[28] of the autonomous work of art, yet he does not indicate how the concept fits into this logic, if in fact it does.

It is possible to trace the difficulties Habermas encounters in grasping aesthetic experience by closely examining his readings of Kant's *Critique of Judgement* as it is summarized in the extended version of the lecture "Modernity versus Postmodernity." At first he acknowledges his complete agreement with Kant concerning the delimitation of art in modernity as a distinct cultural sphere. Habermas enumerates the following four traits: art is concerned strictly with "taste"; it takes refuge in fiction, in "appearance"; it is detached from all "interest"; and it "transcends" daily reality.[29] Later Habermas attempts to provide a "positive determination" by proposing a reinterpretation of the theme of genius centered around "authentic expression." This interpretation is far removed from Kant as well as, if one may trust the criticisms of Wellmer, from the aesthetic phenomenon itself. Even more telling is Habermas's brief account of the principal elements of Kant's aesthetics. Though we need not suspect Habermas of deliberate concealment, in each case he omits all references to conceptuality and, therefore, to the cognitive aspect of art. Thus, whereas elsewhere he claims to be willing to acknowledge the cognitive element of art, all references to it are suppressed in his reading of Kant. As a result, Habermas considers the "free play of imagination" but not the free play of imagination and understanding. He considers the "play of the faculties of representation" *(Vorstellungsvermögen),* but not the play of the faculties of knowledge *(Erkenntnisververmögen).* The expressions cited are indeed present as such in Kant, but they disclose only one dimension of the problem. Moreover, Habermas speaks in general of the "laws proper" *(Eigengsetzlichkeit)*[30] to each of the three cultural spheres, yet he avoids this expression in speaking of art in particular, preferring Weber's more neutral term, *Eigensinn.*[31] Nevertheless, for Kant it was a question of the "legality" *(Gesetzmässigkeit*[32]*)* proper to the faculty of judgment as a superior faculty of knowledge (at which time this faculty recovers its autonomy in the aesthetic domain!). In fact, Habermas emphasizes the dimension of sensibility, not to mention sensuality (*zweckfreier Kunstgenuss*[33]) of the aesthetic experience to such an extent that eventually the connection between art and modern *rationality* is obscured.

Communication is certainly not a category entirely foreign to aesthetic experience. It is well known that, for Kant, communicability *(Mitteilbarkeit)* is constitutive for the judgment of taste. The claim that this judgment will be shared by all is indicative of its universality even though, in this case, universality is connected not to a determinant concept but to an exemplification; that is to say, to something concrete and beautiful — the work of art. Kant did not dismiss the communicative moment, this social moment proper to beauty. On the contrary, in his transcendental critique he devotes himself to an explicit justification of the claim to universal communicability made by the judgment of taste. Habermas, in turn, ventures into the terrain of philosophical aesthetics, but only long enough to understand the defeat of a category derived from his theory of communication after its unfortunate integration into the aesthetic sphere. From that point onward, the only thing Habermas would recognize was a critique that Kant would have characterized as empirical and psychological. But this raises the following question: is *Aufklärung* well served when art is reduced to the role of an exit, when it is nothing more than a safety valve that releases the pressure of the residual and irrational needs of society? What distance then separates autonomous art from the art of the masses, which is subject to economic recuperation through its commercialization and political recuperation through ideology? Occasionally one gets the impression that Habermas acknowledges the cognitive dimension of art only when it filters by osmosis into the two other cultural spheres, science and morality, and this position leads to the heteronomy of art to the extent that it becomes either realistic or "engagé."[34]

We must hope that Habermas will be led to reexamine and reinforce his thesis, so pertinent in other respects, concerning the cognitive character of modern autonomous art. Perhaps it is when one fully acknowledges the inner logic of a work of art that the work best serves democracy.

Translated by Elizabeth Ennen

VIII The Future of Continental Philosophy

22

The Future of Continental Philosophy

Joan Stambaugh

The various branches of continental philosophy, that is, the French and Germans including Wittgenstein, have in common a need to get out of metaphysics and metaphysical thinking. This need is expressed, for example, in the title of Heidegger's work, *The End of Philosophy and the Task of Thinking*. The end of philosophy has been thought and written about a lot, but less has been said about the second half of this title, the task of thinking. However, according to Heidegger, the future of nonmetaphysical philosophy lies in what he calls the *task of thinking*.

When asked in the *Spiegel* interview what philosophy could do to ameliorate the world situation today, Heidegger replied with a laconic "nothing." If philosophy is equivalent to metaphysics for Heidegger, the remaining task seems to be to cultivate and be open to a nonmetaphysical thinking. What is this kind of thinking and how can it come about?

In contrast to metaphysical, representational, calculative thinking, Heidegger has always spoken of a more "authentic" way of thinking that comes to be called both *Besinnung* and *Andenken,* usually translated as meditative thinking and remembrance. I am critical of these translations but must confess that I have no better alternative. However, I should like to discuss this kind of thinking and see just how it concretely differs from metaphysical thinking whose characteristics are objectifying, reifying, substantializing, and conceptualizing. Briefly stated, metaphysical thinking distorts and manipulates what is by perpetrating the activity of "Framing," which orders and interprets everything in the schema of cause and effect. The metaphysics of Judeo-Christianity extends this

275

schema, culminating in the idea of God as cause of the world. Predestination and fate are similarly thought as a kind of "cause." Our entire understanding of the world and ourselves is tainted by this concept of causality. After all, why should the conception of God and destiny be restricted to being an ultimate *cause,* to being a cause at all?

What Heidegger has to say about "the end of philosophy" is much more dramatically striking and moving than what he has to say about the task of thinking. His descriptions of the technologization of the earth and man are powerful and unforgettable. The relation of man and Being at the completion of metaphysics requires a great deal of thought and is, to say the least, intricate. It is perhaps best epitomized by the following statement: "Being's remaining absent is the withdrawal of itself keeping to itself with its unconcealment that it promises in its refusing self-concealment."[1] More simply stated, being presences in remaining absent and *only* as this remaining absent. Man, however, is heedless of the extreme need and danger here; he is oblivious to the fact that thinking thus fails to provide a shelter for the arrival of Being. Much has been written and will continue to be written on this situation at the end of metaphysics.

We, however, shall try to stick with the task of thinking and move within much simpler questions. In nontechnical terms, occasionally even in non-Heideggerian terms, what sort of thinking is at stake here? What does this nonrepresentational, noncalculative, nonsubstantializing, nonobjectifying, nonmanipulating thinking look like? First of all, it does not originate with and procede from an ego.

> With Husserl, the realm of consciousness is not questioned, much less broken through. Heidegger adds: moreover, it cannot be broken through as long as one starts with the Ego cogito; for the fundamental constitution of the Ego cogito (just like that of Leibniz's monads) is to have no windows at all through which something could come in or go out. Thus the Ego cogito is a closed sphere. The idea of "coming out" of this closed space is self-contradictory. Thus the necessity of beginning with something other than the Ego cogito.[2]

Heidegger's consistent critique of Descartes is well known, but the implications of beginning with something other than the ego and the ego cogito bear further consideration. If philosophy does not begin with the "inside," with the ego, where does it begin? In *Being and Time,* Heidegger was still speaking about the self, but that "self" was fundamentally conceived as an outside-of-itself, an *ek-stasis,* ek-sistence. With the rejection of an inside, an ego, has Heidegger also rejected the concept of self? He probably has. We can surmise that the concept of self was too traditional and too close to the concept of ego to be of much use to him philosophically. More important than the concern about the loss of ego, self, or person in Heidegger's thought is his discussion of a nonrepresentational mode of thinking and experiencing. "What is important is to have a fundamental experience of the thing itself. If one starts with consciousness, one cannot have this experience. To do this we need a realm other than that of consciousness. This other realm is called *Da-sein*."[3] In speaking about this kind of experiencing, Heidegger is not speaking about an ego or self to which this experiencing *belongs,* but about the *thing,* the thing itself. *Thing itself,* of course is not meant in the sense of Kant's thing-in-itself, but in the direction of Husserl's call "to the things themselves." Whereas Husserl's things are in consciousness, however, Heidegger's are in the world. According to Heidegger, Husserl remains trapped in the immanence of consciousness. All representational thinking is trapped in the immanence of consciousness because it refers back to itself. It cannot get "outside" itself to the thing: "re- in modern thinkers (Re-presentation) refers back to the Ego cogito. Re- is here: 'back to me.' "[4]

Nonrepresentational thinking does not think "itself"; it is not reflexive. Nor, by definition, does it *represent* the thing or anything else. All representation simply gets in the way of the thing. In contrast, *Da-sein* is ek-static: it is already outside itself. It does not have to go from inside to outside; it *begins* outside. "In contrast to the immanence in consciousness that expressed the 'being' in Bewusstsein (being conscious, consciousness), the 'being' in *Da-sein* names being-outside-of."[5]

Yet, later, after having established the "outside-of-itself" element of *Da-sein,* Heidegger adds the dimension of the "in," not the inside. This is not something new, but rather a new emphasis on being-in-the-world. "Today ... I would no longer simply speak of Ekstase, but of standing within the opening/clearing *(Inständigkeit in der Lichtung).* ... From now on man stands ecstatically face to face with what something itself is and no longer over against it mediated by a representation."[6]

Standing-within *(Inständigkeit)* is far removed from any self-contained reflexivity. What we stand within is not our consciousness or subjectivity, but the world. As always with Heidegger, what is most important in these characterizations are the *prepositions:* out, in, within (between). The opening/clearing was one of Heidegger's favorite words for the transparency of Being as opposed to its opaqueness, its self-concealment. Heidegger tells us that thinking is beginning to prepare the conditions for an entry into a realm that is nothing "human."[7] Let us turn now to the two terms for nonmetaphysical thinking: *Besinnung* and *Andenken.*

BESINNUNG

The translation "meditative thinking" for *Besinnung* is headed in the right direction in that it presents a contrast to representational, calculative thinking but "meditation" will not do for what Heidegger has in mind. First of all, there are many different forms of meditation. Some forms attempt to concentrate on one thing; others on nothing; still others on following the breath. One dictionary, not a very good one, defines meditation as follows: "to plan in the mind, think with a view to planning or acting." This sounds closer to calculative thinking than to *Besinnung*.

Most forms of meditation involve some kind of "turning within." This is true of Eastern forms as well as those of Marcus Aurelius, Descartes, and Husserl, but Heidegger's *Besinnung* does not coincide with a "turning within."

One might think that "contemplation" would do the trick. But in *Wissenschaft und Besinnung* Heidegger discusses the Roman translation of *theorein* as *theoria*, which reads *contemplari* and *contemplatio*. Heidegger states that this translation obliterates the meaning of the Greek words. "*Contemplari* means to put something into one section and fence it in there. *Templum* is the Greek *temenos* that comes from a completely different experience from *theorein*. *Temnein* means to cut, to divide. The indivisible is the *atmeton, a-tomon,* atom."[8] So we see that this will not do either.

"Reflective thinking" might be somewhat better if we could distance the meaning of this word in the German tradition from Kant to Hegel. Heidegger himself, however, is quite firm in stating that he is not talking about *Reflexion*. "We are not talking *about* thinking. We remain outside of mere reflection that makes thinking its object. Great thinkers, first Kant and then Hegel, recognized what is unfruitful about this reflection. Thus they had to attempt to reflect themselves out of this reflection."[9] The difficulty here is not merely a problem of translation; it is a question of meaning.

The term *Besinnung* is not a technical philosophical term, for example, out of German Idealism. It is a common, everyday term with a rich variety of possible meanings. It has its roots in both the mental and physical spheres. The root noun *Sinn* has both significations of "meaning" and of "sense," as in the senses *(die Sinne)*. Thus, *Besinnung* is really a kind of "sensing" that includes the whole being, body and mind.

Pursuing the primordial meaning of the word *noein*, Heidegger states:

Noein implies a perceiving which never was nor is a mere receiving of something. The *noein* perceives beforehand by taking to mind and heart. The heart is the wardship guiding what lies before us, though this wardship itself needs that guarding which is accomplished in the *legein* as gathering. *Noos* and *nous*, therefore, do not originally signify what later develops into reason; *noos* signifies the minding that has something in mind and takes it to heart. Thus *noein* also means what we understand by scenting — though we use the word mostly of animals, in nature.

Man's scenting is divination *(Ahnen)*. But since by now we understand all knowledge and all skill in terms of the thinking of logic, we measure "divination" by the same yardstick. But the word means more. Authentic divination is the mode in which essentials come to us and so come to mind, in order that we may keep them in mind. This kind of divination is not the outer court before the gates of knowledge. It is the great hall where everything that can be known is kept concealed.[10]

The preposition *an* as the root of *Ahnen* establishes the connection with *Andenken*. We shall return to this later.

Human *Wittern* (scenting) is *Ahnen* (divination). It is not introspective. Rather, it is directed toward what comes toward us, toward the "future" in Heidegger's sense of that word. Wild animals *wittern* (scent); they sense something coming, usually possible danger. They do not meditate, contemplate, or reflect. With all senses alert, they "know" something is coming. We humans have almost totally lost our ability to sense. We do not sense that a storm is coming, the weather report has already informed (or misinformed) us of that. As far as our sense organs go, we rely almost entirely on our sense of sight in orienting ourselves to the world. If we live in large cities, we have lost much of our senses of hearing and smell simply out of sheer self-defense. We still may just be able to sense how a person close to us feels. Not only do we not have a "sixth" sense, we do not even use the five that we have.

> To take a direction that a matter has already taken of itself is called in our language *sinnan, sinnen* (to sense). To enter into meaning *(Sinn)* is the essence of *Besinnung*. This means more than simply making oneself conscious of something. We are not yet in *Besinnung* when we are in consciousness, *Besinnung* is more. It is the releasement to what is worthy of question.[11]

Besinnung is not ordinary consciousness. It is the releasement from representational, calculative thinking. What it releases for is less easy to name or even anticipate. When I say that I have anticipated an emergency, this means that I have prepared and planned for it, taking certain measures to ensure safety.

ANDENKEN

Let us go back to what was said in *What Calls for Thinking* about *Ahnen*. Its root is the preposition *an*, to, toward. One might think of the song of Beethoven, "An die Ferne Geliebte ("To the Distant Beloved"). The song expresses a kind of *Andenken*, an intense turning toward the beloved who is far away. *Andenken* for Heidegger is not to be confused with the tourist's use of that word when he buys, for example, a Black Forest cuckoo clock, a souvenir, an *Andenken* that he can look at in his home in New Jersey and thus recall his summer vacation. For Heidegger, *Andenken* is not even primarily related to the past at all, at least not in the ordinary sense of that word.

Appealing to the older, impersonal use of *ahnen* in the construction *"es anet mir,"* *"es anet mich."* Heidegger distances the idea that *I* think toward something by reversing the direction: *it* comes *to* me, comes over me. Any "subjective" element, which, after all, is a feature of representational thinking, is excluded.

Any time I think of a past event and remember it, I am re-presenting it. This is not what Heidegger means by *Andenken*. At the end of the book on Hölderlin with that title, he states:

> What is poetized in the poem *"Andenken"* is the presencing and the essential time-space of a thinking that must remain unknown to all traditional doctrines of thought. Re-collecting *(andenkend)* thinking thinks of the festival that has been by thinking ahead to what is coming. But this re-collection backwards and forwards thinks before both [the festival and what is coming] toward destining *(das Schickliche)*. Thinking toward destining belongs to destiny. Such "thinking" belonging-to *(Angehören)* is the originating coming-to-presence of re-collection *(des Andenkens)*.[12]

This is one of the fullest, most complex (and virtually untranslatable into nonbarbaric English) statements about *Andenken*. But there are other simpler, more perspicuous ones. "The conversation itself is the thinking of destining. And because the conversation is remembrance *(Erinnerung)*, this thinking is an *Andenken*. Because this thinking thinks re-collectively *(andenkend)* and never only represents what is objectively present, it must at the same time think towards what is coming."[13]

Finally, we must briefly examine what Heidegger has to say about a term related to Andenken: "memory" *(Gedächtnis)*. Just as *Andenken* is not at all restricted to the past, neither is memory. The English *memory* comes from the Lain *memor,* to be mindful. Thus, even the English term does not have the exclusive emphasis on the past that it has come to have in common parlance. Heidegger treats the term *Gedächtnis* as the "non-universal" unity of all thinking, similar to the way in which *Gestell* (framing) is the unity of all the various activities of *stellen*. The analogy in everyday language that he appeals to is *das Gebirge*, the mountain chain as the nonuniversal, nonsubsumptive unity of a group of mountains *(die Berge)*. Heidegger brings in the old word for thought *(Gedanc,* an earlier form of *Gedanke)* and relates thinking *(Denken)* to thanking *(Danken)*. "The root or originary word says: the gathered, all-gathering thinking that recalls."[14]

Heidegger has described for us a kind of nonmetaphysical thinking. He has also, to a considerable extent, brought about this kind of thinking himself. Repeatedly he emphasizes that we cannot of our own will forcibly change our way of thinking. The very force employed would ensure and entrench our further imprisonment in metaphysical thinking. His term for our appropriate attitude is *Gelassenheit*, releasement. *Gelassenheit* is not passive. It is a letting go of all conceivable kinds of calculation that include, for example, measuring oneself against, comparing, competing, and "keeping score." The list is endless. What does *Gelassenheit* do? It waits and perdures. It does not interfere and impose.

Any writer or artist knows what it means to wait. Thomas Mann sat at his desk every morning for four hours. Sometimes ideas came; other times they did not. Sometimes he was not able to write anything. But if he had not sat at his desk every morning waiting, the ideas would never have come at all. Perduring in this case might correspond to the actual working out of the ideas.

A final instance of this thinking would be the thinking of the fourfold. Man does not stand *over against* the fourfold; he stands *within* it; he is an integral part of it. "They [things] do not appear *by means of* human making. But neither do they appear without the vigilance of mortals. The first step toward such vigilance is the step back from the thinking that merely represents—that is, explains—to the thinking that responds and recalls."[15]

We could quietly fold our hands, resting them on our laps and say: well, it's all up to the destiny of Being; we have nothing to say about it and we can do nothing. But for Heidegger the destiny of Being is never without man and man is never without the destiny of Being. Strange as it may sound, Being *needs* man. The term *brauchen*, developed in the Anaximander essay and elsewhere, means to need and make use of. Being needs and makes use of man in Heidegger's very special interpretation of the word *use*. " 'To use' accordingly suggests: to let something present come to presence as such; *frui*, to brook, to use, usage, means: to hand something over to its own essence and to keep it in hand, preserving it as something present."[16] Heidegger's late word for Being, *Ereignis*, is a *relational* term. It does not name some transcendent Being out there; it names the belonging-together, the being appropriated to each other of man and Being.

Thus, there is something we can do. Instead of manipulating, calculating, explaining, and looking for causes and reasons why, all of which are activities that right now are threatening the destruction of our existence, we can learn to practice listening and responding, opening ourselves to Being or as Meister Eckhart called it, to *Istigkeit,* to isness. This would be something rather new for philosophers. It is a humble claim. It neither builds a magnificent metaphysical system nor develops a brilliant new logic. It does not even solve all the problems of language, nor does it get so obsessed with language as to give up on it, attempting to demand of language things that language simply cannot do. This thinking simply lets things be what they are, keeping open to and mindful of them, responding to them in Saying or, in non-Heideggerian terms, giving them expression. Our response and giving expression are an absolutely integral part of our experience, not something external to that experience; they are not subjective and are not arbitrary. As Meister Eckhart put it: "Whoever has understood this sermon, let it be his. Had no one been here, I would have had to preach it to this poor-box."[16]

23

The Secularization of Philosophy

Gianni Vattimo

A trend that I propose to call the *secularization of philosophy* has become relevant with the widespread cultural diffusion of hermeneutics in the last two decades. If one wanted to indicate a tendency in current philosophical thought that could be considered the latest *koinē* in philosophy, comparable to Marxism in the 1950s and 1960s, or structuralism in the 1970s, one could probably argue that hermeneutics has assumed this role, even though its methods and areas of diffusion are different. For instance, hermeneutics does not bear the same political implications as Marxism. Hermeneutics indicates a philosophical tendency that was first expressed by Hans-George Gadamer in *Wahrheit und Methode* (1960). In characteristic manner, he elaborates, "urbanizes" (as Habermas said), and perhaps even secularizes the results of Heideggerian ontology. This tendency has gone on to become enriched, complicated, and perhaps also diluted within boundaries that have become vast and vague in recent years. The significant moments in this transformation were above all the elaboration that Gadamer himself gave of "practical philosophy," an elaboration that caused Gadamer's own version of hermeneutics to undergo a secularization, thus presenting itself as the philosophical *koinē* of our society. (I am thinking, for example, of the essays in *Die Vernunft im Zeitalter der Wissenschaft*, 1976). The reception (with Kantian contaminations) that Gadamer's work underwent at the hands of thinkers like Habermas with his "theory of communicative competence" and Apel with his "a priori of the unlimited communication" furthered this tendency along; with the diverse contributions made by philosophers like Ricoeur

283

(in which it is coupled with the ontology of the liberty of existential as-cendency). A significant contribution to the diffusion of the hermeneutic thematic was brought about by the methodological self-consciousness of literary criticism in America and, more generally, by the methodical self-consciousness of the social sciences. A decisive step toward the secular-ization of hermeneutics has been made by Richard Rorty in *Philosophy and the Mirror of Nature,* a work that can be invoked to clarify what is intended by secularization of philosophy in connection with the spread-ing of hermeneutics as the *koiné* of current philosophy.

In his book, Rorty criticizes the ideal of foundation that has domi-nated Western philosophy since its inception. This dominance first oc-curred in the form of a search for primary principles, the *ontos on,* a search for Being as the stable structure that legitimizes and provides a foundation for the world of experience. In modern times, the foundational ideal of philosophy no longer manifests itself as the knowledge of a par-ticular "level" of reality that provides a basis for the others, as do the Ar-istotelian first principles. Instead, grasping the conditions of all valid knowledge through reflection is the way in which, under different forms, the foundational ideal of thought persists in contemporary philosophies from neo-kantianism to phenomenology to neopositivism. The mirror of nature in the title of Rorty's book is the conscious subject. Philosophy, in its various critical-epistemological versions, looks toward this mirror with the intent of making it capable of reflecting, without limits and im-precisions, the real, the world "out there." The importance of Rorty's book, at least from the viewpoint of hermeneutics, consists in pointing out that the deep transformation of philosophy in the twentieth century does not result from those trends that were presented as more radically critical of traditional metaphysics, like neopositivism or even phenome-nology, in that these trends maintain a foundational attitude toward phi-losophy. Phenomenology and neopositivism appear especially tied to the mentality of foundation, for Rorty, insofar as they present philosophy mainly as epistemology.

The departure from the ideal of foundation radically occurs in the thought of Heidegger, Dewey, and the late Wittgenstein: the legacy of these thinkers is seen more clearly in hermeneutics than in any other phil-osophical orientation. Taking Rorty's idea in a direction that he himself did not follow but that without a doubt corresponds to his intentions, we can say that the importance of Heidegger does not consist only in his hav-ing emphasized the connection between Being and language. Rather, above all it lies in thinking of Being as an event and not as a structure. As long as Being is brought back to language (according to the *Brief uber den Humanismus,* language houses Being) that foundational ideal can be maintained, although transferred to the plane of language (as it actually happens in the neopositivistic variety of philosophy of language). We can see something of the sort of the neo-kantian interpretations of the linguistic turn of philosophy: Apel speaks of a "semiotization of kantianism" as characterizing contemporary philosophy. In this sense, the a priori that makes experience possible and guarantees the objectivity of knowledge as well as the rationality of action are language structures, but they conserve the universality and nonhistorical character of the *a priori* in Kant. Only if the connection between Being and language takes place in the perspective of the radical finitude of existence, as happens in Heidegger, does one go beyond the belief in foundation. In Heidegger's ontology, Being not only occurs in language, but it simply occurs—the linguistic a priori are from time to time historically qualified; they are not structures but messages. Between the various linguistic worlds there is not the connection that metaphysics has established between individuals belonging to the same species. They are not tied by the fact of making up one universal type with specific differences. Rather, unity is provided by a sort of "family resemblance" (I believe that Wittgenstein's term can be applied to Heidegger's concept of the historicity of *Wesen,* essence) in the sense of a transmission that does not imply the permanence of an identity, but only the continuity of a "chain." This is what Heidegger expresses with the term *Geschick.* Being is not *Grund,* that is, principle, *arché,* or foundation; it is *Geschick,* a sending or message or transmission. The natural languages that make experience of the world possible are historical-natural languages. They occur from time to time as responses to other languages that in turn are already responses and interpretations.

Only insofar as hermeneutics remains faithful to the inheritance of Heidegger's ontology, which can legitimately be termed *nihilistic,* does it radically accept the implications of the historical finitude of language and Being, thus secularizing philosophy. Heidegger's forerunner along this path was Nietzsche. The implications of the announcement that "God is dead" are not to be found only in the content of this statement (which holds that the epoch of stable structures is over because we do not need them anymore; therefore the epoch of thought as foundation has ended) but also and above all in its form as an announcement that does not describe a structure (the nonexistence of God), but rather reports an event. It is perhaps in this respect above all that Nietzsche represents the inheritance of thought that we have yet to assimilate fully. Indeed, what does thinking in an historical moment mean when thought is no longer conceivable as foundation—neither in the classical-metaphysical sense nor in the modern-epistemological sense? We can understand the centrality of the question *"Was heisst Denken?"* in Heidegger's work only if we place it against this background.

To speculate about the "secularization" of hermeneutics as the latest philosophical *koinē* within our culture is to also ask what it means to think when thinking no longer regards itself as foundational. Those who speak of the end of philosophy, in fact, already give a response to this question: they identify philosophy with foundational thought and point out that now "there is nothing left" of such thinking (as is the case of Being in the process of nihilism). But can we really abandon metaphysics, heir of the philosophy of the past, and thereby abandon "foundation" as a simple opinion we can no longer believe in? The "errors" of the ethics, metaphysics, and art of the past, have colored the world and make it interesting. Should we not, then, keep on celebrating in relation to them, "feats of memory," as Nietzsche said? If we take leave from metaphysics and Platonism, will this really be a simple reversal of the Platonic hierarchy, a reversal that places the world of the appearances in the position of the true world? If, as Nietzsche writes in *Twilight of the Idols,* the true world (Platonic ideas, the stable essences) has finally become a fable, then the apparent world has disappeared along with the true world, for the apparent world has no longer a term with which to compare and refute itself. What remains after the fabulization of the true world is not the apparent world as the only world — thus the only true one — but the history of the fabulization. Thought is a "feast of memory," or as Heidegger says more explicitly, *An-denken,* recollection. Once the ideal of thought as foundation has been consumed, tied as it is to the idea of Being as the foundational structure, all that remains is simply the system of appearance, the world of data ascertained by the sciences and put at our disposal by technology. This world, were it isolated from the story of fabulization, would fatally take the strong characteristics of the "true" Platonic world. Among the terms with which Heidegger more insistently alludes to the nonmetaphysical essence of language, we find the word *Sage:* this word is not only to be understood in terms of the language of the origin, but rather, I believe, as meaning a "fable" in the sense of Nietzsche's notion of fabulization.

Therefore, if we look for the postmetaphysical essence of thought, that is, a type of thought that no longer performs the task of providing a foundation, then we must move to the horizon of *Sage,* the horizon of fable and recollection. These represent the way in which thought responds to Being as an "event" and a "sending," *Ereignis* and *Geschick.* Memory of an event (which is quite different from "verifying," recording, or ascertaining a fact) is precisely what thinking as *Andenken* bases its legitimacy on. To say that the secularization of philosophy is the meaning we have to recognize in the spreading of hermeneutics as the contemporary *koinē* involves also the recommendation that secularization is taken seriously and carried out. But this can be recommended only on the basis of a "story." We have no *Grund* for affirming that philosophy must no longer be foundational thought: there is only a certain reconstruction of events in the development of philosophy as the unfolding and consuming of the ideal of foundation. An example of a story is provided by Nietzsche's reconstruction in the previously mentioned chapter of *Twilight of the Idols,* in which he discusses the real world that becomes fable. Heidegger gives another example in his reconstruction that outlines "metaphysics as the history of Being." On the other hand, there is a certain interpretation (fabulization) of the correspondence between this theoretical consummation of the notion of the fundamental and the transformation of the conditions of individual and social existence induced in our world by science and technology, seen in their relation to metaphysics.

Thus, for Nietzsche, God dies because the conditions of existence have been made less extreme, but this security has happened because of the rationalization of social life that the hypothesis of God as fundamental made possible. For Heidegger the end of metaphysics, which implies the end of foundational thought, happens as a result of its factual realization in the world of *Getstell,* the world of planetary technology and organization. To be legitimate in its form of Andenken, therefore, secularized philosophy narrates a certain history composed of "disciplinary" events (the course of past philosophy, reconstructed and experienced according to certain preconceptions, prejudices, hypotheses) and external historical events (the conditions of modern existence, the transformations tied to the passage, if it can be called such, from modernity to postmodernity). These two aspects of the tale corroborate and clarify each other, without any claim for demonstrative strength. Their persuasiveness is "hermeneutic"; that is, measured in terms of the capacity to gather the appeals addressed to them and above all to respond with discourses that stimulate further responses.

We may also say that the thesis of the recollective, nonfoundational character of thought is offered as an interpretation of the sense of existence in the conditions of the late modern era. Its persuasiveness must be measured not on the basis of proof and foundations, but on the basis that it makes sense; that is, it permits us to connect multiple aspects of experience into an articulated unity and then permits us to speak about it with others.

This outlines the role that is to be attributed to secularized thought and further justifies the use of Heidegger's term *recollection. Andenken* does not resolve and "appropriate" reality, indicating and grasping the *Grund,* but makes the world practicable by reconstructing a continuity. We thus see that the relation of nonfoundational thinking to foundational thinking is not that of getting rid of an old suit. It is not total dissociation but rather that which Heidegger has called *Verwindung:* a secularization that maintains, distorts, and recalls that to which it is connected as its past and then takes leave of it. The metaphysical foundation, in the classical Aristotelian formulation, wanted to take possession of the real in its totality, gathering the causes and the principles on which everything depends. Such an attitude postulates, therefore, a moment of unity, the grasping of the whole in a punctual experience (which is the model of the evidence as the metaphysical experience of the truth). Secularized thinking maintains (and distorts) this need for unity, searching for it as a continuity (like Nietzsche's genealogy) of family resemblances, of historical-destinal linkings and interpretations of messages.

What Nietzsche said is probably true: the comprehensibility and practicability of the world, in terms of recalling a continuity, properly belongs to an epoch of at least relative security. It is late-modern man that no longer expects reassurance from the *archai* that he has learned to consider as temporary, mystifying, and human, all too human. Yet humanity cannot give up bestowing sense upon the world and existence, and for this reason it still needs continuity, which constitutes a form of secularized foundation. The continuity that postmetaphysical philosophy can provide has to fight against at least two main forms of discontinuity that threaten existence in late modernity; the discontinuity of the specialized scientific and technical languages and of the spheres of values (politics, morals, economy, erotics, religion — I am thinking of the work of Max Weber among others); and the discontinuity between past and present. The first kind of discontinuity orientates philosophy toward the necessity of reconstructing again and again a "viable" image of the world out of the transformations produced by the sciences. This task could be described as that of construction of a new "cosmology," which would not claim to summarize and unify the scientific knowledge of the physical or even the human world (psychology, anthropology, and sociology are also involved), but simply to provide a sort of "rhetorically persuasive" synthesis, called *divulgation* (also in the sense of vulgarization, popularization . . .). Habermas has recently spoken of a function of philosophy as *Dolmetscher,* and I think this could be one of the senses of the term. Of course, it is possible (and maybe more adequate to the operational, non-cognitive nature of modern science) that unifying the "results" of the sciences has to be accomplished by philosophy on the moral rather than on the cognitive level. The continuity between the sciences and everyday life, in this sense, should be looked for through a moral critique of the technical applications of science which orientates and limits these applications in terms of values accepted by society and which expresses itself in the language and the shared culture of that society. This is the way Gadamer has designed the task of hermeneutics as "practical" philosophy, in the essays of *Reason in the Age of Science* I mentioned earlier.

The language and the culture of a society, of a historical community, is threatened by the second form of discontinuity that postmetaphysical philosophy is faced with: the discontinuity between present and past.

This specific discontinuity has been from the beginning the main theme of hermeneutics. Thus, it may not be necessary to discuss it here. What does seem important to emphasize is that the continuity between present and past, which hermeneutics strives to reconstruct again and again through the activities of interpretation of the past (such are the *Geisteswissenschaften,* which were the original field of hermeneutics, both as actual research and as epistemological reflection), is not to be separated from the continuity between the different spheres of knowledge and of values. This has to be stressed, because hermeneutics very often tends to be interpreted only as a discipline related to the *Geisteswissenschaften,* thus perpetuating a separation between "science" and "humanities" that reestablishes a deep discontinuity in the very moment in which one recognizes the hermeneutic essence of philosophy.

A philosophy that conceives of its task in these terms of *Dolmetscher* is also secularized in a further sense. It loses all the scientific characteristics that had given it prestige in antiquity and in modern rationalism. It gets closer and closer to the vagueness, impurity, and changeability of everyday language. The *logoi* into which the philosopher has to jump, following the Platonic Socrates, are the actual discourse of an historical community. The jump is nevertheless required, because one has to jump out of the abstractness and separation of the specialized language and the autonomous spheres of value. A conversation is still needed, only it no longer has anything to do with the scientific formalization of the metaphysical ratio. Not only Socarates' jump, but also another classical image of philosophy must be retrieved and "transformed" or secularized: Hegel's image of philosophy as the owl of Minerva, which takes flight in the sunset. Secularized philosophy does not stand as the absolute basis of specialized knowledge (as its foundation or as its critically explicit methodology). It comes after specialized knowledge, as its conclusion; not as a supreme synthesis organizing the various truths of the incomplete bodies of knowledge of each specialty, but as a kind of superficial synthesis that has the characteristics of edification.

These are only some of the various characteristics one can recognize in contemporary philosophy, once one has taken secularization of philosophy into account; that is, once one has attempted to assume toward the philosophical tradition the "hermeneutic attitude" to which we were alluding. Secularization is both a direction that a part of contemporary philosophy is taking and a task for our moral and theoretical self-consciousness. I would like to mention one more point that seems to me crucial, because it concerns the "critical" role of philosophy. Does not a secularized philosophy, which conceives of itself as an organon of the recomposition of the continuity of the natural-historical language of a community, risk reducing itself to a mere defense and apology of the existent status? Will not the continuity that it tries to maintain and reestablish, by means of its synthesizing interpretation and edification in the end be only that of the established tradition, of the consolidated canon and common sense? The fact has to be stressed that secularized thought is not speculative thinking but recollection; this means that it does not look at Being as if from an external viewpoint, but recalls it from within the event of Being, answering the messages of Being through interpretations that, in turn, are opened to new responses. Recollective thinking is not only the turn to the past, but also the projection onto the future in the form of expectation, conjecture, judgment and choice. If that which speaks to us and determines, *bestimmt* or intones, our thinking is the event (though only "narrated" and not demonstrated) of the "death of God" of foundational thought; it is just in such an event, recalled and not speculatively described, that we can find indications for future choices and orientations. Secularized philosophy becomes philosophy of secularization; all we have "at our disposal," as Nietzsche said in *Human, All Too Human,* is what we have received from the historical transmission: forms, values, languages — "errors" handed down to us by the humanity of the past. This is the only "Being" we are to meet, in ourselves and in the world. If this transmission reaches us with the characteristics of secularization, our response cannot help taking secularization into account. To remember our past means to assume it as a possible guide for our expectations and choices. These are always risky because not deductively guaranteed, but they are not unreasonable and arbitrary either. The announcement of the death of God, in the sense of Nietzsche, constitutes the end of the thought of foundation, authority, and *Grund;* thus, the end of every man of violence and of that kind of violence accompanying the "sacred." Nietzsche's announcement, together with Heidegger's announcement of the end of metaphysics, does not only recall an event in the past, but it also and above all recalls (draws attention to) responsibilities that have to be assumed for the future — choices, judgments and critical positions to be taken in respect of the existent. These responsibilities and choices, as far as we can see (on the basis of a "recollection" of what is transmitted to us by the philosophy of the past but also by the new conditions of social existence in the late modernity), seem to point to the direction of secularization as a progressive consummation of all the strong, reassuring, and also violent characteristics of Being, with all the ethical, even political implications this process involves. To let philosophy really unfold in the form of recollection, Being must become memory and "background" rather than an imposing and obliging presence. Secularization is not only a destiny of philosophy; it affects Being itself as well: in the epoch of the end of metaphysics Being finally occurs as what eludes any firm grasp and vanishes.

24

Translating the Differences: The Futures of Continental Philosophy

David Wood

There are philosophers for whom the history of philosophy is the history of the failure of philosophy to either solve its problems or to make substantial progress on them. For them, philosophy simply requires renewed and collective commitment to the development and implementation of research programs. Only then will we have results we would not be ashamed to show to our scientific colleagues. The problem of what philosophy itself might be, what its limits might be, how it might be possible to proceed after a confrontation with the question of limits — these are preliminary difficulties that need resolving if someone raises them, but are then best forgotten.

Such a vision constructs and constitutes the future in conformity with the model of purposive action. On such a model one might submit progress reports to the authorities explaining why one needed just a little more time to finally sort out a hitherto neglected piece of philosophical undergrowth.

Now there is, perhaps, a place for something of this in continental philosophy. When Professor Spiegelberg speaks of the need for more work on the phenomenology of the look — an expansion of the Sartrean problematic — he is giving voice to Husserl's original construal of phenomenology as opening up great new vistas of research, a graduate director's dream. But if such work could once have been carried on with the forgiveable innocence of a project of renewal, it is no longer possible with quite that innocence. My claim is that it is the distinctive commitment of continental philosophy to continually reinscribe the question of the nature and limits of philosophy that makes it worth preserving. In more Heideggerean words, the being of philosophy is to put its being into question. This is not all that continental philosophy should do, but it is a distinct commitment. The continuing practice of philosophy rests on the light or shadow cast by such self-interrogation, and continental philosophy has long played host to this self-consciousness.

We might be reminded here of the opening remarks in Derrida's discussion of Lévinas ("Violence and Metaphysics,") where he suggests that the questions surrounding the death of philosophy are the only ones "today capable of founding the community, within the world, of those who are still called philosophers. . . . A community of the question about the possibility of the question."[1] If we take seriously the project of dialogue with some of those who may currently seem deaf, then there is every hope that this community will be expanded and continental philosophy will live on.

It is indeed hard to see how to begin to think of "The Future of Continental Philosophy" without addressing a whole series of preliminary issues that the very title raises. It has itself given a central place to reflection on time in general and the future in particular. Philosophizing, or if you prefer, thinking, no less than any other human activity, operates within something like a temporal horizon, which involves an active relation to tradition, as well as to "the future." Although Hegel, Nietzsche, Husserl, Heidegger, and Derrida may seem merely to have filled out that horizon differently, they in fact bear witness to a series of transformations of our understanding of and confidence in the very concept of horizon. Heidegger and Derrida in particular inaugurate the breakdown of rectilinear time. (Heidegger, in *On the Way to Language,* writes about not wanting to get anywhere, but, for once, to get to where we are already; Derrida has written about wanting to get to the point at which he does not know where he is going, and, elsewhere, as being able to conceive of the future only in terms of absolute danger.) One is tempted to say that the question of the future of continental philosophy can be satisfactorily addressed only by reabsorbing it within continental philosophy, and that it is precisely in the sophistication with which continental philosophy, would treat such a question that its right to a future is best attested.

I shall not, however, attempt here the working through of this historical trajectory, but rather parade my puzzlement and a few of my doubts about any direct addressing of this question. First some doubts. Given the notorious uncertainty of the future, we are surely not being called on to predict. Is the demand then for "speculation" or perhaps "exhortation?" No doubt some of this will have happened, and I urge you to treat such pronouncements, even my own, with extreme caution. What place do they have in philosophy, you might ask. I am puzzled about the very phrase *continental philosophy*. With an editorial involvement in a new series of excellent books being published by Routledge under this very title, I am committed to it, but it takes little reflection on our topic to realize that it is built on an ambiguity. Is the question about continental philosophy taken as a given (like "the future of dairy farming")? Or is the question whether, and if so how (long), there will continue to be a kind of philosophy distinguishable as "continental"? On this second reading, the question would be precisely: does whatever is distinctive and important about continental philosophy provide a basis for its continuing to be constituted as a unity of some sort? In other words, if Hegel, Nietzsche, Husserl, Heidegger, Sartre, Derrida, Kristeva, and so on are all continental philosophers, as are those who study, develop, and continue their work, is there some intellectually convincing reason that (say) excludes a Wittgenstein or a Frege? At this point it is easier to define continental philosophy via various alternative approaches: phenomenology, existential philosophy, hermeneutics, post-structuralism, and so forth. But in a sense the question arises again: what is it that excludes the positivism of (for instance) the Vienna Circle?

The answer, of course, is tradition. What these approaches share is a reference set, which allows them to be constituted as a largely self-contained, self-referring tradition. We do not have to agree on any specific story of (say) the relation between Derrida and Husserl to acknowledge the intimacy of the bond betrayed by Derrida's reading of Husserl. (We do not, for example, have to suppose that Derrida dismisses phenomenology. I would add here that it is as foolish for phenomenologists to ignore Freud, Foucault, or *La Voix et le phénomène* as it is for those fired up by deconstruction to forget Derrida's own insistence on the need to go through phenomenology, particularly to avoid falling back into vulgar empiricism. Indeed, the full extent of Derrida's involvement in the problematics of transcendental phenomenology has only recently begun to be generally appreciated. I am thinking here of the work of Rodolphe Gasché.)

But such a reference to tradition, though inevitable, is not unproblematic. Its force will depend on what position one takes up within phenomenology. Tradition is a founding operational concept for Husserl, Heidegger, and Gadamer, but hardly so for Derrida or Lyotard. If we need to make use of the concept of tradition to legitimate a certain closure of texts and philosophers, one that would determine the shape of continental philosophy to come, do we not have to ignore the fact that this concept is itself contested within continental philosophy? Perhaps, it should be pointed out that the emphasis on the permanent possibility of dialogue in Gadamer can have something of the same effect as the loosening of the prescriptive grip of tradition suggested by Derrida and Lyotard; in dialogue one opens oneself to the possibility of changing the position from which one is talking, the possibility of one's own tradition transformed.

Clearly, there is a long history of interaction between continental philosophy and its other, the philosophy that lies outside it. But there is an equally long history of verdicts of dissatisfaction with the results. If Gadamer and Derrida hardly seemed "to make contact" in their *Text and Interpretation* discussion, how much less did Derrida and Searle? Impasse easily leads to insult and back to isolation. This does no one any credit, and I want to suggest important theoretical reasons for renewing our efforts at dialogue across the always already fractured frontiers separating continental philosophy from what it is not.

The unity and integrity of continental philosophy, with all its carefully managed internal debates, is emminently deconstructable. Was not continental philosophy born in the United States in the late 1930s as the name of the enterprise of protecting and preserving the heritage of European, especially German, philosophy, in the face of a very different, largely hostile native tradition? Was it not born in a defensive gesture, a traumatic reaction to apparently overwhelming external pressures, not wholly unrelated to the general problem of integrating various emigré traditions into the United States? Continental philosophy, I am suggesting, is a kind of American (and to a lesser extent British) philosophy, an artefact of history. Heidegger is not in himself a continental philosopher. He is a German philosopher appropriated by "continental philosophy" in America.

This is not a bad thing. But we can ask whether the defensiveness that gave rise to continental philosophy is still necessary, or whether there might not come a time when we would have the confidence to put away our continental philosophy badges and become more simply . . . philosophers.

There are two sorts of objection to this proposal. The first is that it rests on a philosophical error, and the second is that it is politically dangerous, even suicidal. First the philosophical error. Does it not assume that all philosophers are "really talking about the same problems," which is naive, historical, totalizing, and so on. Of course, no such thing is assumed. What is claimed—and here I perhaps venture half a step beyond Gadamer—is that something like dialogue is always possible. For even where straightforward dialogue breaks down, dialogue about the possibility of dialogue or dialogue soaked in the difficulty of dialogue remains an option. Moreover, to put it more positively, the experience of the difficulties of translation-dialogue in which idiomatic and conceptual problems "interfere" with the purity of natural communication is one of the paradigmatic philosophical experiences. (Derrida has gone so far as to identify philosophy with the problem of translation, and Heidegger's "Dialogue between a Japanese and an Inquirer" attests to his own sense of the philosophical intensity and fruitfulness of such meetings or translations.) These experiences of course are in some sense dangerous, but in that danger lies exhilaration, for it is precisely between discourses that one's everyday assurances are shaken. Of course, if philosophy is about the construction of an edifice of established truths, this would be most frustrating.

The second objection is political. I am too sanguine, it will be said, about the inherent virtue and attractiveness of continental philosophy, about the maturity of its current development, and about the intellectual robustness of its devotees. Translation of course can just be the name for appropriation and domination. Even Rorty must feel the shudder of history when institutions seek his lesser clones to handle their continental philosophy. We have all read unrecognizable travesties of Heidegger and Derrida, written in the belief that whatever can be said can be said in plain English. But dispiriting as these can be, they actually offer the opportunity for posing the very philosophical questions about tradition and translation that the plain English advocates are repressing. I would add here that the insistence on plain English is not just an expression of linguistic imperalism directed outward at those who swim in other waters. It is also a sign of a poverty of dwelling in English, indeed in language. I would not wish to question in any way the importance of the German philosophical tradition from Kant and Hegel through German Idealism to Nietzsche and Heidegger, but is not the accompanying celebration of the German language at least in part the celebration of the language that happens to be its medium? Heidegger attempts to transform our relationship to the language in which we dwell, to fulfill that dwelling. It is not fundamentally an invitation to learn to live in German, however valuable that may also be.

Continental philosophy offers exemplary models of meditating on, dwelling in, and performatively relating to language and could encourage a renaissance in the philosophical use of English (or indeed any language). Professor Spiegelberg's list of synonyms for look (peer, peep, gape, stare, glance) — a list that celebrates differences — seems to point in just this direction. My hope, then is that a greater dialogical confidence on the part of continental philosophy will open the way to the recovery of the philosophical power of the English language, which in both its literature and lexical wealth is arguably the richest the world has ever known.

The ultimately political importance of this is incalculable. English is already the world language, the language into which all other languages will eventually be translated and in which they will yield up their truth. The fate of the planet may be bound up with the state of this language here.

I do not say that continental philosophy should begin an international crusade to save English, but that the response to those who would translate Heidegger into plainspeak should first be to encourage an enrichment in our 'dwelling' in the English language so as to begin to meet this challenge.

And perhaps because it has so long had to resist appropriative translation continental philosophy is in the best position to promulgate an ethics of translation which, put simply, consists in an undying respect for what is other, for what resists translation, for the gap, the remainder, the space in-between.

Notes

1. SUBVERSION OF SYSTEM/SYSTEMS OF SUBVERSION

1. E.g. Richard Bernstein, *Praxis and Action*, (Philadelphia, 1971), pp. 85 ff.

2. Jacques Derrida, *Dissemination*, trans. Barbara Johnson (Chicago, 1981), p. 5.

3. Martin Heidegger, "Letter on Humanism," in *Basic Writings*, trans. David Farrell Krell (New York, 1977), p. 208.

4. Martin Heidegger, *Schelling's Treatise on the Essence of Human Freedom*, trans. Joan Stambaugh (Athens, Ohio, 1985), pp. 22–61.

5. Martin Heidegger, "The End of Philosophy and the Task of Thinking," in *Basic Writings of Martin Heidegger* edited by David Farrell Krell (New York, 1977), p. 383.

6. On metanarrative see J.-F. Lyotard, *The Postmodern Condition*, trans. Geoff Bennington (Minneapolis, 1984), pp. 31–37. The Plato to NATO metanarrative has become considerably less plausible (has opened itself to deconstruction) since the writing of the essay in 1986.

7. Jacques Derrida, *Speech and Phenomena*, trans. David B. Allison (Evanston, 1973), p. 102.

8. Jacques Derrida, *Positions*, trans. Alan Bass (Chicago, 1981), p. 44.

9. Hegel, *The Difference Between Fichte's and Schelling's System of Philosophy*, trans. H. S. Harris and Walter Cerf (Albany, 1977), p. 122.

10. References are to Hegel. *The Phenomenology of Spirit*, trans. A. V. Miller (New York, 1977).

11. Hegel, *Samtliche Werke* (Leipzig, 1925), vol. 18, p. 202.

12. Cf. my article "Notes on the Animal Kingdom of the Spirit," *Clio* (Spring 1979):323–338.

13. Derrida, *Dissemination*, p. 13.

14. Derrida, *Of Grammatology*, trans. Gayatri Chakrovorty Spivak (Baltimore, 1976), p. 26.

15. In his paper "Hegel and the Subversion of System: *Der Fall Adornos*," Martin Donougho follows Adorno in suggesting such a reading between the lines of Hegel.

2. ESSENCE AND SUBVERSION IN HEGEL AND HEIDEGGER

Preliminary versions of this essay were read at the Heidegger conference, at SPEP, and at the New School for Social Research. Each time, it received very valuable criticism, from people too numerous to list. I would like to thank them all, especially Annemarie Gethmann-Siefert and Martin Donougho.

1. "Ich weiss selber noch nicht hinreichend deutlich, wie meine 'Position' gegenüber Hegel zu bestimmen ist—als 'Gegenposition' wäre zu wenig; die 'Positions'—Bestimmung hängt mit der Frage nach dem Geheimnis des 'Anfangs' zusammen. . . . Immer wieder habe ich mich gegen die Rede vom 'Zusammenbruchs' des Hegelschen Systems gewendet. Zusammengebrochen, das heisst herabgesunken ist, was folgte—Nietzsche mit einbezogen." Quoted by Gadamer in *Das Erbe Hegels,* ed. Hans-Georg Gadamer and Jürgen Habermas (Frankfurt: Suhrkamp, 1979), p. 89, note 3; when originals are cited, all translations are my own unless otherwise noted.

2. In addition to the cited work by Gadamer, we can call attention to the five studies published in English as *Hegel's Dialect,* trans. P. Christopher Smith (New Haven and London: Yale University Press, 1976); for Sartre's use of Hegel and Heidegger in the formulation of his concept of Nothingness, cf. Jean Paul Sartre, *L'être et le néant* (Paris: Gallimard, 1943), pp. 47–57.

3. Georg Wilhelm Friedrich Hegel, *Wissenschaft der Logik,* ed. Georg Lasson, 2 vols. (Hamburg: Felix Meiner, 1932), vol. 2, pp. 3–6, 202 ff; English translation by A. V. Miller, *Hegel's Science of Logic* (London: Allen and Unwin, 1969), pp. 389 ff, 569 ff, hereinafter cited as WDL.

4. Martin Heidegger, *Vorträge und Aufsätze,* 3rd ed., 3 vols (Pfullingen: Neske, 1967), vol. 1, p. 29 f; the translation is from Robert Bernasconi, *The Question of Language in Heidegger's History of Being* (Atlantic Highlands, N.J.: Humanities Press, 1985), p. 75; also cf. pp. 65–70, 73–75, 77f for discussions of essence in Heidegger.

5. Martin Heidegger, "Vom Wesen des Grundes" in Martin Heidegger, *Wegmarken* (Frankfurt: Klostermann, 1967) p. 58; Martin Heidegger, "Vom Wesen der Wahrheit" in *Wegmarken*, pp. 81 f, hereinafter cited as WW.

6. WW, p. 89.

7. Martin Heidegger, "Das Wesen der Sprache" in Martin Heidegger, *Unterwegs zur Sprache*, 4th ed. (Pfullingen: Neske, 1971), pp. 174 f, hereinafter cited as UZS; Martin Heidegger, *Was Heisst Denken?* (Tübingen: Niemeyer, 1971), p. 85; WW, p. 97.

8. Cf. my "Language and Appropriation: The Way of Heideggerean Dialogue" in *The Personalist* 60 (1979):384–396.

9. Heidegger, *Was Heisst Denken?* pp. 114 f; WW, p. 93.

10. Martin Heidegger, *Grundprobleme der Phänomenologie*, ed. Fr. W. von Hermann (Frankfurt: Klostermann, 1975), pp. 105, 176, 178 f, 216, 218; "Hegel's Begriff der Erfahrung" in Martin Heidegger, *Holzwege*, 4th ed. (Frankfurt: Klostermann, 1963), pp. 191 f; "Hegel und die Griechen" in *Die Gegenwart der Griechen, Festschrift für H. G. Gadamer* (Tübingen: Niemeyer, 1966), p. 45; Martin Heidegger, *Zur Sache des Denkens* (Tübingen: Niemeyer, 1969), pp. 68–73.

11. Jacques Taminiaux, "Finitude and the Absolute: Remarks on Hegel and Heidegger" in *Heidegger: the Man and the Thinker*, ed. Thomas Sheehan (Chicago: Precedent, 1981), p. 205.

12. Alexandre Kojève, *Introduction à la lecture de Hegel* (Paris: Gallimard, 1947).

13. Martin Heidegger, *Hegels Phänomenologie des Geistes*, ed. Ingtraud Görland (Frankfurt: Klostermann, 1980), pp. 1–46.

14. Ausser der Rechtsphilosophie (1821) und einigen Rezensionen hat Hegel in der Berliner Zeit nichts mehr veröffentlicht, was von grundsätzlicher Bedeutung für seine Philosophie war. Seine Vorlesungstätigkeit arbeitet das System aus, das bereits 1817 in der Heidelberger Enzyklopädie die entscheidende und endgültige Gestalt bekam." Heidegger, ibid., p. 7.

15. I have attempted to give that strategy in my "Hegel's Philosophical Languages," *Hegel-Studien* 14 (1979):183–196. The text from which that strategy can be clarified is given in the *Encyclopedia der Philosophischen Wissenschaften* and is to be found at Georg Friedrich Wilhelm Hegel, *Werke*, eds. Karl Markus Michel and Eva Modenhauer, 20 vols. (Frankfurt: Suhrkamp, 1970–71), hereinafter cited as *Werke*, vol. 10, pp. 463 f. But that text is changed radically between the 1827 and 1831 editions. It follows that Hegel did not have a clear grasp on how his system functioned until the last five years of his life.

16. Heidegger, *Hegels Phänomenologie des Geistes*, pp. 23, 38 f.

17. Martin Heidegger, "Die onto-theologische Verfassung der Metaphysik" in Martin Heidegger, *Identität und Differenz* (Pfullingen: Neske, 1957), pp. 36 f.

18. This broad usage of *truth* dates, at least from the standard Platonic sense, throughout the dialogues, of τα 'αληθη, true entities, not as judgments or propositions but as "the Forms," attainment of which is the goal of Platonic dialogue. For the relation of absolute knowing and truth in Hegel, cf. Werner Marx, *Heidegger and the Tradition*, trans. Theodore Kisiel (Evanston: Northwestern University Press, 1971), pp. 43–59.

19. "for whatever a thing 'truly' has in it that is not part of the 'notion' cannot be spoken of:" WDL, vol. 2, p. 409; cf. Georg Wilhelm Friedrich Hegel, *Philosophie des Rechts*, in *Werke*, vol. 7, #21 Zus, hereinafter cited as RPH; paragraph numbers also hold for the English translation: *Hegel's Philosophy of Right*, trans. T. M. Knox (Oxford: Clarendon Press, 1952); Georg Wilhelm Friedrich Hegel, *Enzyklopädie der philosophischen Wissenschaften*, in *Werke*, vols. 8–10, vol. 8, #24, Zus. 2; paragraph numbers also hold for Georg Wilhelm Friedrich Hegel, *Hegel's Science of Logic*, trans. William Wallace, 3rd ed. (Oxford: Clarendon Press, 1975); Georg Wilhelm Friedrich Hegel, *Vorlesungen über die Ästhetik*, in *Werke*, vols. 13–15, hereinafter cited as Aesth., vol. 13, pp. 137 f, 150 f; English translation *Hegel's Lectures on Aesthetics*, trans. T. M. Knox, 2 vols. with consecutive pagination (Oxford: Clarendon Press, 1975), pp. 100 f, 110.

20. Graeme Nicholson, "Heidegger on Thinking," *Journal of the History of Philosophy* 13 (1975):491–503.

21. Cf. Jan van der Meulen, *Hegel und Heidegger: Order Widerstreit und Widerspruch* (Meisenheim/Glan: Westkulturverlag, 1953), pp. 43 ff.

22. Hegel, *Enzyklopädie*, in *Werke*, vol. 8, #24, Zus, #2; cf also #12, #172, Zus, #213 Zus, #246 Zus; Aesth., vol. 13, p. 105/74.

23. Heidegger, WW, pp. 77–80; Martin Heidegger, *Sein und Zeit*, 11th ed. unchanged (Tübingen: Niemeyer, 1967), pp. 214–226; German pagination given marginally in Martin Heidegger, *Being and Time*, trans. John Macquarrie and Edward Robinson (New York: Harper and Row, 1962). Also cf. "die Sprache," UZS, p. 15; "Das Wesen der Sprache," UZS, p. 160; *Zur Sache des Denkens*, p. 77; this passage also recognizes what I am calling the localism of Hegel's definition of truth: "Die Rede von der 'Wahrheit des Seins' hat in Hegels 'Wissenschaft der Logik' ihren berechtigten Sinn, weil Wahrheit hier die Gewissheit des absoluten Wissens bedeutet."

24. I borrow the term *local* from Arthur Fine, *The Shaky Game: Einstein Realism and the Quantum Theory* (Chicago: University of Chicago Press, 1986), pp. 136–150.

25. Cf. ibid.; Richard Rorty, *Philosophy and the Mirror of Nature* (Princeton: Princeton University Press, 1979), pp. 373 ff.

26. First, in the *Differenzschrift* (1801), in *Werke*, vol. 2, pp. 46; English translation, *The Difference between Fichte's and Schelling's Conception of Philosophy*, ed. H. S. Harris and Walter Cerf (Albany: SUNY Press, 1977), pp. 113 f; last, in the Preface to the Second Edition of WDL (1831), WDL, vol. 1, pp. 9–

31. My understanding of these relies on E. L. Fackenheim, *The Religious Dimension in Hegel's Thought* (Bloomington: Indiana University Press, 1967), pp. 15 ff.

27. WDL, vol. 1, 9–31.

28. *Poetics*, 1450b36; *Politics*, 1326a 33 seq; cf. *Metaphysics*, 1078b1.

29. Aesth., vol. 13, pp. 127, 151 f/91, 111 f.

30. Martin Heidegger, "Der Ursprung des Kunstwerkes" in Heidegger, *Holzwege*, 4th ed. (Frankfurt: Klostermann, 1963), pp. 31–36, hereinafter cited as OWA; English translation in Martin Heidegger, *Poetry Language Thought*, trans. Albert Hofstadter (New York: Harper and Row, 1971), pp. 42–47.

31. For Heidegger's concept of "hint," see my "Language and Appropriation," pp. 388 f.

32. This is the only kind of presence, according to the Logic of Judgment, that really counts for philosophy; WDL, vol. 2, pp. 265 ff/624 ff.

33. "die gesamte Welt der phantasiereich ausgebildeten Vorstellungen," Aesth., vol. 15, pp. 228, 240 f, 243, 254 f, 272–963, 976, 984 f, 997. Also cf. Georg Wilhelm Friedrich Hegel, *Hegel's Idea of Philosophy*, ed. and trans. Quentin Lauer (New York: Fordham University Press, 1974), pp. 111 f, 115, 122 f. It will be recognized that I am not using *content* in Hegel's sense. In that sense, the re-organizing force itself, the "infinitude" of Spirit, becomes the *content*, and this is one content that art cannot convey. But that does not affect my point here, for which *content* means, more or less, "what is empirically presented."

34. E.g., in the "reconciliation with reality" presented in the *Philosophy of Right*, RPh, pp. 26 f/12.

35. Aesth., vol. 13, pp. 272, 275/208, 210 f.

36. RPH 421 n/168 n; Emil Fackenheim has referred to this footnote as "cryptic," and the present paper may be understood as an effort to understand that crypticity: Emil Fackenheim, *Encounters Between Judaism and Modern Philosophy* (New York: Basic Books, 1973), p. 126. The *Philosophy of History* contains a passing reference to the anti-Jewish activities of the Inquisition, which as they were not carried out in a modern state are rather different from the type of oppression discussed here: *Werke*, vol. 12, p. 510; English translation *The Philosophy of History*, trans. J. Sibree (New York: Dover Books, 1956), p. 429.

37. WDL, vol. 1, pp. 160–164/170–173.

38. WDL, vol. 1, pp. 154/163; the inner meaning here lost is that gained in the section of the Logic just previous to "Being-for-Self," that of "Infinity": WDL, vol. 1, pp. 125–146/137–156.

39. diese Eitelkeit, welche sich jede Wahrheit zu vereiteln, daraus in sich zurückzukehren versteht und an diesem eignen Verstande sich weidet, der alle

Gedanken immer aufzulösen und statt alles Inhalts nur das trockne Ich zu finden weiss, ist eine Befriedigung, *welche sich selbst überlassen werden muss;* denn sie fleiht das Allgemeine und sucht nur das Fürsichsein. Georg Wilhelm Friedrich Hegel, *Phänomenologie des Geistes,* ed. Johannes Hoffmeister (Hamburg: Meiner, 1952), pp. 69 f (hereinafter cited as PHG); English translation, *Hegel's Phenomenology of Spirit,* trans. A. V. Miller (Oxford: Oxford University Press, 1977), p. 52; emphasis added.

40. Shlomo Avineri, "A Note on Hegel's Views on Jewish Emancipation," *Jewish Social Studies* 25 (1963):145–151.

41. RPH, pp. 18 f/5 f.

42. Georg Wilhelm Friedrich Hegel, *Vorlesungen über die Geschichte der Philosophie,* in *Werke,* vols. 18/20, vol. 20, pp. 402 f; this passage is missing from the English translation, *Hegel's Lectures on the History of Philosophy,* trans. E. S. Haldane and Frances H. Simson, 3 vols. (London: 'Routledge and Kegan Paul, 1896); also cf. Georg Friedrich Wilhelm Hegel, *Philosophie des Geistes,* in *Werke,* vol. 10, #456 Zus.; paragraph numbers also hold for Georg Friedrich Wilhelm Hegel, *Hegel's Philosophy of Mind,* trans. William Wallace and A. V. Miller (Oxford: Clarendon Press, 1971).

43. Hegel, *Werke,* vol. 20, pp. 387/vol. 3, 479.

44. Hegel, *Werke,* vol. 20, pp. 418 f; omitted from English translation.

45. Hegel wrote to the Prussian ministry of education about the dangers of too much freedom of the press; what enraged him was the *Literaturzeitung's* accusation that he had earlier attacked Fries personally. As Rosenkranz reports, Hegel "versicherte, an Fries als Privatmann nicht im mindesten, nur an seine verderblichen Grundsätze gedacht zu haben." The incident is excerpted in Hegel, *Werke,* vol. 8, pp. 519 ff.

46. "Indem ihr Negieren nichts effektuiert . . . so kehren sie nicht in sich zurück, erhalten sich nicht, und sind nicht." WDL, vol. 1, pp. 162/171.

47. For the impotence of nature, cf. the discussion in Fackenheim, *The Religious Dimension in Hegel's Thought,* pp. 112 ff; for the prose of modernity, cf. my "Contradiction and Resolution in the State: Hegel's Covert View," *Clio* 15 (1986):379–390.

48. As Hegel notes in the pages adduced.

49. See my "Hegel's Anarchistic Utopia," *Southern Journal of Philosophy* 22 (1982):203–210.

50. Heidegger, *Sein und Zeit,* p. 164.

51. Hans-Georg Gadamer, "Being, Spirit, God," in *Heidegger Memorial Lectures,* ed. Werner Marx, trans. Steven W. Davis (Pittsburgh: Duquesne University Press, 1982), p. 67.

52. Cf. my "Authenticity and Interaction: the Account of Communication in *Being and Time*," *Tulane Studies in Philosophy* 32 (1984):45–52.

53. For this, cf. Martin Heidegger, "Bauen Wohnen Denken" and "Das Ding," in Martin Heidegger, *Vorträge und Aufsätze*, 3 vols., 3rd ed. (Pfullingen: Neske 1967), vol. 2, pp. 19–60; and "Hölderlins Erde und Himmel" in Martin Heidegger, *Erläuterungen zu Hölderlins Dichtung*, 4th ed., expanded (Frankfurt: Klostermann, 1971), pp. 152–181. I have been guided by the discussion in Joseph Kockelmans, *On the Truth of Being* (Bloomington: Indiana University Press, 1984), pp. 102–121; in contrast to earlier commentators, who see an actual identity between the Two-fold and its later filling-in as the Fourfold, Kockelmans posits something more akin to my notion of "prevailing."

54. Heidegger, "Bauen Wohnen Denken," pp. 23 f.

55. Even then it would have to identify the essential vagueness of world with the Hegelian "impotence of nature," out of which come the forms of finite thought worked up by science: cf. Fackenenheim, *Encounters between Judaism and Modern Philosophy*, and Heidegger, *Sein und Zeit*, pp. 83–88.

56. Even here, the system functions constitutively as well; for once we judge Fries in terms of his response to the idea of the infinite essence of man, we can recognize him for a concretion of the "excluding One," which feature can then be viewed as "constitutive" of him the way extension, for example, is constitutive of intuitions for Kant. As usual, what for Kant is a rigid distinction for Hegel turns into a dialectical interplay.

57. Joan Stambaugh, "Time and Dialectic in Hegel and Heidegger," *Research in Phenomenology* 4 (1974):87–97.

58. Aristotle, *Poetics*, chapter 7 f; cf. Hegel, PhG, p. 558/487.

59. PhG, pp. 489 f/424.

60. Hegel, Aesth., vol. 14, pp. 267, 270, 302–329/631, 633, 660–680.

61. Heidegger, OWA, pp. 46/58.

62. OWA, pp. 32/42.

63. Hegel, *Werke*, vol. 12, pp. 36, 311/18, 254 f.

64. Cf. RPH, #57 Anmerkung, 66 Anmerkung.

65. For the "Gestell," see Kockelmans, *On the Truth of Being*, pp. 245–248.

3. HEGEL AND THE SUBVERSION OF SYSTEM:
DER FALL ADORNO

1. T. W. Adorno, *Minima Moralia: Reflections from a Damaged Life* [1951] (London: New Left Books, 1974), p. 50; cf. G. W. F. Hegel, *Phänomenologie des Geistes* (Frankfurt: Suhrkamp, 1970), p. 24. See also "Aspekte [der Hegelschen Philosophie]" in *Gesammelte Schriften*, vol. 5 (Frankfurt: Suhrkamp, 1973), especially the editors' note p. 386.

2. "Selected Aphorisms from the Atheneum" [1798] #53, in F. Schlegel, *Dialogues on Poetry and Literary Aphorisms* (University Park: Pennsylvania State Press, 1968); translation amended. On the importance of the early romantics for Adorno see Jochen Hörisch, "Herrscherwort, Geld und geltende Sätze. Adornos Aktualisierung der Frühromantik und ihre Affinität zur post-strukturalistischen Kritik des Subjekts" in *Materielen zür ästhetischen Theorie. Th. W. Adornos Konstruktion der Moderne*, ed. B. Lindner and W. Martin Lüdke (Frankfurt: Suhrkamp, 1979) pp. 369–398. Adorno had planned to use another Schlegel aphorism as motto for his *Asthetischen Theorie:* "In dem, was man Philosophie der Kunst nennt, fehlt gewöhnlich eins von beiden; entweder die Philosophie oder die Kunst." See the editors' Afterword, *Asthetische Theorie* (Frankfurt: Suhrkamp, 1970), p. 544. Even the title has a Schlegelian ring to it.

3. Adorno, *Negative Dialectics* [1966] (New York: Seabury Press, 1973); in *Gesammelte Schriften*, B. 6 (Frankfurt: Suhrkamp, 1973), hereinafter cited in the text as ND, followed by German then English pagination.

4. "Skoteinos" in "Drei Studien zu Hegel," *Gesammelte Schriften*, vol. 5, pp. 326–375; citations in text are to this edition.

5. G. W. F. Hegel, *Wissenschaft der Logik*, vol. 1 [1812], 2nd ed. [1831] (Hamburg: Meiner, 1934), p. 66; the second edition leaves the wording unchanged.

6. On the notion of "constellation" see *Negative Dialectics*, pp. 165 f, 163 f. History is both outside and inside the object, stored up, sedimented. It is something already known but repressed, demanding a recognition by the thinking subject. This liability (of both cognition and object known) cannot be tied down to determinate concepts, however.

7. Adorno's attempted defense of Hegel against the abstraction to which his thought is constantly liable would answer Jean-Francois Lyotard's complaint (in *Discours, figure* [Paris: Klincksieck, 1971]) that Hegel privileges language over the image, the significant over the figurative. Adorno urges us to attend to the ways in which the dialectic puts language to work, rather than to the speculative "profit" that results.

8. See Hegel, *Phenomenologie*, Chapter 6 b, esp. 465–466.

9. The reference is to the end of Chapter 6 and the transition to Chapter 7, on religion. In the *Encyclopaedia* the crucial passage is from objective and thus

finite spirit—in the shape of Schleiermacher's subjective, private model of civic conscience *(Gewissen)*—to absolute spirit, a form of religious, cultic activity.

10. Albrecht Wellmer, "On the Dialectic of Modernism and Postmodernism," *Praxis* 4, no. 4 (1985):337–362, quote on 350.

11. *Phenomenologie,* pp. 580–582.

12. See "Différance" [1968], in *Margins of Philosophie* (Brighton: Harvester Press, 1982), pp. 1–27, specifically pp. 13–14.

13. *Wissenschaft der Logik,* vol. 1, p. 102.

14. Ibid., p. 106.

15. Michael Theunissen, *Sein und Schein. Die kritische Funktion der Hegelschen Logik* (Frankfurt: Suhrkamp, 1980).

16. *Asthetische Theorie* (Frankfurt: Suhrkamp, 1970), p. 398; *Aesthetic Theory* (London: Routledge, 1984), p. 376. Hereinafter cited in the text as AT.

17. Roland Barthes, "From Work to Text" [1971], in *Image-Music-Text* (London: Fontana, 1977) pp. 155–164.

18. *Vorlesungen über die Asthetik Werke,* vol. 14 (Frankfurt: Suhrkamp, 1970), pp. 140–141; *Hegel's Aesthetics. Lectures on Fine Art* (Oxford: Clarendon Press, 1975), p. 527.

19. See my "The Semiotics of Hegel" *Clio* 11, no. 4 (1982).

20. Adorno: "Disintegration is the truth of integral art" (AT, p. 455, 425); Mozart or the late Beethoven undermine the very classical style they were instrumental in forging.

4. KIERKEGAARD'S STAGES ON LIFE'S WAY: HOW MANY ARE THERE?

1. It has to be pointed out, as far as this paragraph and the next are concerned, that Kierkegaard's concern in *The Point of View* is not strictly speaking with the *stages.* What is referred to as *the aesthetic* is the entire pseudonymous authorship, which of course contains a presentation of all three stages. These works are contrasted with the purely religious works that were published under Kierkegaard's own name and parallel to the aesthetic or pseudonymous ones. That there is a close connection between the issue raised explicitly in *The Point of View* and the issue of the relationship between the three stages is to a considerable extent demonstrated later, even though it seems to be simply assumed at this point.

2. Søren Kierkegaard, *Purity of Heart Is to Will One Thing,* trans. Douglas V. Steere (New York: Harper and Row, 1938), p. 206.

3. Søren Kierkegaard, *The Present Age*, trans. Alexander Dru (New York: Harper and Row, 1962), p. 33.

4. Ibid., p. 53.

5. Ibid., p. 56.

6. Ibid., p. 81.

7. Ibid., p. 79.

8. Søren Kierkegaard, *Concluding Unscientific Postscript to the Philosophical Fragments*, trans. David F. Swenson; completed and edited by Walter Lowrie (Princeton: Princeton University Press, 1941). Hereinafter cited as *Postscript*.

9. In attributing to Kierkegaard the views expressed in the *Postscript*, I am for the sake of simplicity ignoring the considerably important scholarly question of the relationship between Kierkegaard's own thought and that of his pseudonyms.

10. *Postscript*, p. 188.

11. Ibid., p. 182.

12. Ibid., p. 188.

13. "Equilibrium between the Aesthetical and the Ethical in the Composition of Personality," Søren Kierkegaard, *Either/Or: a Fragment of Life*, vol. 2, trans. Walter Lowrie (New York: Anchor Books, 1959) pp. 159–338.

14. I attribute things indifferently to Kierkegaard and Judge William; see note 9.

15. Kierkegaard, *Either/Or II*, p. 184.

16. Ibid., p. 215.

17. Ibid., p. 227.

18. Ibid., p. 173.

19. Ibid., p. 258.

20. Ibid., p. 231.

21. Ibid., p. 256.

22. Ibid., p. 267.

23. Ibid., p. 164.

24. Ibid., p. 194.

25. Ibid., p. 164.

Notes   307

26. Søren Kierkegaard, *Fear and Trembling* and *The Sickness Unto Death*, trans. Walter Lowrie (New York: Doubleday Anchor Books, 1954), p. 147.

27. Kierkegaard, *Purity of Heart*, pp. 205–206.

5. KIERKEGAARD'S PHENOMENOLOGY OF FAITH AS SUFFERING

1. Søren Kierkegaard, *Concluding Unscientific Postscript*, trans. David F. Swenson and Walter Lowrie (Princeton: Princeton University Press, 1941). Hereinafter cited in the text as CUP.

2. Kierkegaard is careful never simply to repudiate the finite for the infinite, the relative for the absolute. His formula is that we are "simultaneously to sustain an absolute relationship to the absolute end, and a relative relationship to relative ends" (CUP, p. 371; cf. pp. 347, 377). Thus he praises Abraham for still wishing to be a father in his old age and for believing that "God is concerned about the smallest things." He is awed that "the finite tastes just as good to him as to one who never knew anything higher . . . " And he ends up describing the knight of faith as "the heir to the finite." Kierkegaard, *Fear and Trembling/Repetition*, trans. Howard V. Hong and Edna H. Hong, vol. 4 of *Kierkegaard's Writings* (Princeton: Princeton University Press, 1983), pp. 18, 34, 40, 50. Hereinafter cited in the text as FT.

3. *Hegel's Science of Logic*, trans. A. V. Miller (London: George Allen and Unwin, 1969), hereinafter cited in the text as SL.

4. The German text reads, "In seiner unbestimmten Unmittelbarkeit ist es nur sich selbst gleich and auch nicht ungleich gegen Anderes, hat keine Verschiedenheit innerhalb seiner, noch nach aussen." Hegel, *Wissenschaft der Logik*, ed. Georg Lasson (Hamburg: Felix Meiner, 1934).

5. *The Logic of Hegel*, trans. William Wallace (Oxford: Oxford University Press, 1892), p. 158.

6. Like T. S. Eliot, Kieregaard wants to affirm the identity of action and suffering. His ears would perk up when Eliot's Thomas Becket says, with reference to the chorus of women:

> They know and do not know, what it is to act or suffer.
> They know and do not know, that action is suffering
> And suffering action. Neither does the agent suffer
> Nor the patient act. But both are fixed
> In an eternal action, an eternal patience
> To which all must consent that it may be willed
> And which all must suffer that they may will it,

That the pattern may subsist, for the pattern is the action
And the suffering, that the wheel may turn and still
Be forever still.

(T. S. Eliot, *Murder in the Cathedral,* [New York: Harcourt, Brace and World, 1935], pp. 21–22). But Kierkegaard would not appreciate the "Eastern" and "pantheistic" overtones of this formulation. He would want to formulate the identity of action and suffering more positively than the "Neither/nor" of Eliot, claiming that a certain kind of suffering simply is a certain kind of action and that faith practices this identity.

7. Describing the similar dialectic at work in Hegel's *Philosophy of Right,* Klaus Hartmann suggests that each stage is incomplete (and thus immediate) until it reaches the fullness of inclusion that is "a non-indebtedness to any further stage. . . . At the final stage, there is no unintegrated opposite left over; the whole is presented as the result of imperfect antecedents, as *their* perfection and completion." Klaus Hartmann, "Towards a new systematic reading of Hegel's Philosophy of Right," in *The State and Civil Society: Studies in Hegel's Political Philosophy,* ed. Z. A. Pelczynski (Cambridge: Cambridge University Press, 1984), p. 118, his italics. Hegel's own words are equally helpful. As abstract, incomplete parts find their proper place in more inclusive wholes, the former "have their independent self-subsistence superseded." They are seen to have "no independent validity." Hegel, *Philosophy of Right,* trans. T. M. Knox (Oxford: Oxford University Press, 1942), paragraphs 129–130.

8. The claim by Aristotle that true happiness is to be found in virtue rather than in pleasure, wealth, or honor (status) marks the same move from the Aesthetic to the Ethical.

9. *Søren Kierkegaard's Journals and Papers,* ed. and trans. Howard V. Hong and Edna H. Hong (Bloomington: Indiana University Press, 1967–78), vol. 4, 4603. Hereinafter cited in the text as JP. N. B.: References are to entry numbers, not page numbers in any given volume.

10. Another immediacy of the Ethical is developed even more strongly in FT but not picked up as explicitly in CUP. It is the immediacy of society's rules and values with reference to a transcendent divine will. See Merold Westphal, *Kierkegaard's Critique of Reason and Society* (Macon, Ga.: Mercer University Press, 1987), Chapter 5.

11. C. Stephen Evans puts it this way. "The religious life arises as a possibility when the ethical project of actualizing oneself through choice suffers shipwreck. Whereas the ethical life is essentially self-sufficient, the religious life has an essentially dependent element. No longer convinced of individual self-sufficiency, the religious exister strives to allow himself to be transformed by God. . . . Achieving this sort of God-relationship, in which a person becomes the recipient of God's action, is nonetheless an activity — in fact the most strenuous activity imaginable." C. Stephen Evans, *Kierkegaard's Fragments and the Postscript:*

The Religious Philosophy of Johannes Climacus (Atlantic Highlands, N. J.: Humanities Press, 1983), p. 13. Here again, one can see the difference between Kierkegaard's identification of action and suffering and Eliot's. See note 6.

12. See Westphal, *Kierkegaard's Critique*, Chapter 6.

13. See ibid., Chapter 7.

14. *Philosophical Fragments/Johannes Climacus*, trans. Howard V. Hong and Edna H. Hong, vol. 2 of *Kierkegaard's Writings* (Princeton: Princeton University Press, 1985), Chapter 2. Hereinafter cited in the text as PF.

15. Kierkegaard, *Training in Christianity*, trans. Walter Lowrie (Princeton: Princeton University Press, 1944), pp. 108, 195, 232, 238. Hereinafter cited in the text as TC.

16. Kierkegaard, *The Gospel of Suffering and The Lilies of the Field*, trans. David F. Swenson and Lillian Marvin Swenson (Minneapolis: Augsburg Publishing House, 1948), p. 50. Hereinafter cited in the text as GS.

17. John William Elrod, "Climacus, Anti-Climacus and the Problem of Suffering." *Thought* 55 (1980):306–319.

18. Evans puts much the same point in socio-political terms. "When all is said and done, however, it cannot be denied that Climacus is not a social activist. . . . This may be grounded in the thesis that the ethical task is something that can be carried on under any political or economic conditions. Climacus consistently maintains a sharp separation of 'the inner and the outward,' with a tendency to depreciate the significance of the latter." *Kierkegaard's Fragments*, p. 89. It is as hard to disagree with this point as it is with Elrod's about Climacus's "idealistic ontology."

19. Kierkegaard, *The Point of View for My Work as an Author*, trans. Walter Lowrie (New York: Harper and Row, 1962), p. 91. Hereinafter cited in the text as PV.

20. Elrod, "Climacus," p. 313.

21. Ibid., p. 312.

22. This dialectic is evidently Hegelian. For example, the liberal theory of property rights presented under Abstract Right in PR is not to be attributed to Hegel. It is presented to reveal its abstract—that is, incomplete—character and to show the need for a richer context in which it can find its rightful—that is, qualified and relativized—place.

23. Mark C. Taylor, *Kierkegaard's Pseudonymous Authorship: A Study of Time and the Self* (Princeton: Princeton University Press, 1975), pp. 21–24.

24. Ibid., pp. 20, 24.

25. Stephen N. Dunning, *Kierkegaard's Dialectic of Inwardness: A Structural Analysis of the Theory of Stages* (Princeton: Princeton University Press, 1985). See especially the summary on page 251.

26. Kierkegaard, *The Sickness unto Death*, trans. Howard V. Hong and Edna H. Hong, vol. 19 of *Kierkegaard's Writings* (Princeton: Princeton University Press, 1982), hereinafter cited in the text as SUD.

27. Dunning, *Kierkegaard's Dialectic*, p. 241.

28. Ibid., p. 240.

29. Plato, *Phaedo*, 66a–e.

30. John D. Caputo, "Kierkegaard, Heidegger and the Foundering of Metaphysics," in *International Kierkegaard Commentary: Repetition* (Macon, Ga.: Mercer Press, forthcoming); and *Radical Hermeneutics* (Bloomington: Indiana University Press, 1987). Caputo's argument is found in both works cited, especially the essay in the *Repetition* volume. The reference to the *Phaedo* is my attempt to illustrate his point as I have understood it. Irene Harvey helps us see the link between Kierkegaard's concern for becoming and Derrida's project when she writes, "It might have been possible to think of *differance* as temporality itself, had this term not so thoroughly been usurped by the 'metaphysics of presence' and the sense of Being as an eternal Now, which therein contains the sense of both past and future." Irene E. Harvey, *Derrida and the Economy of Differance* (Bloomington: Indiana University Press, 1986), p. 127. Derrida himself highlights the difference between *différance* and the immediacy demanded in the *Phaedo*. "The play of differences supposes, in effect, syntheses and referrals which forbid at any moment, or in any sense, that a simple element be *present* in and of itself, referring only to itself. Whether in the order of spoken or written discourse, no element can function as a sign without referring to another element which itself is not simply present. . . . Nothing, neither among the elements nor within the systems, is anywhere ever simply present or absent. There are only, everywhere, differences and traces of traces." Jacques Derrida, *Positions*, trans. Alan Bass (Chicago: University of Chicago Press, 1981), p. 26. Saussurean linguistics is essentially theological because "it refers to an absolute logos to which it is immediately united." *Of Grammatology*, trans. Gayatri Chakravorty Spivak (Baltimore: Johns Hopkins University Press, 1976), p. 13.

31. Derrida, *Positions*, p. 32.

32. The mirror image and the older King James image, "through a glass darkly," are wonderfully Derridean, suggesting that neither God nor the world is ever "simply present" (see note 30) and that the unmediated access to the real to which the *Phaedo* aspires through recollection is not a possibility for existence as we know it.

33. Derrida, *Grammatology*, pp. 7–8.

34. Ibid., p. 49.

35. Ibid., p. xiii.

36. Ibid., p. 6, his italics.

37. Jacques Derrida, *Margins of Philosophy,* trans. Alan Bass (Chicago: University of Chicago Press, 1982), pp. 130–131.

6. WHERE THERE'S A WILL THERE'S A WAY: KIERKEGAARD'S THEORY OF ACTION

1. Albert Camus, *The Myth of Sisyphus and Other Essays* (New York: Random House, 1955), pp. 3–48.

2. Alasdair MacIntyre, *After Virtue* (Notre Dame, Ind.: University of Notre Dame Press, 1984), p. 47.

3. Ibid., p. 40.

4. One writer who has perceived this clearly is George Stack, who has written two articles on Aristotle and Kierkegaard's understanding of choice. See "Kierkegaard's Analysis of Choice: The Aristotelian Model," *The Personalist* 52: 643–661; and "Aristotle and Kierkegaard's Concept of Choice," *The Modern Schoolman* 46:11–23.

5. Davidson's views are found in his famous "Actions, Reasons, and Causes," and other papers can be found in *Essays on Actions and Events* (Oxford: Oxford University Press, 1980). Donagan's theory of action can be found in his *Choice: The Essential Element in Human Action* (London: Routledge, 1987). The following account of what I call the Aristotelian tradition in action theory is heavily indebted to Donagan's account.

6. *Søren Kierkegaard's Journals and Papers,* vol. 2 (Bloomington: Indiana University Press, 1970), entry 1241, p. 59.

7. Søren Kierkegaard, *Concluding Unscientific Postscript,* trans. David F. Swenson and Walter Lowrie (Princeton: Princeton University Press, 1941), p. 143. I have modified the translation slightly, following the Danish first edition of the *Samlede Vaerker,* Gyldendals (Copenhagen, 1902), p. 133. In the following references from the *Postscript* the first page number will be to the Swenson-Lowrie translation; the second will be from the above Danish edition. Translations in some cases are my own.

8. Kierkegaard, *Postscript,* p. 302/293.

9. Ibid., p. 306/296.

10. Ibid., p. 299/290.

11. Ibid., p. 299 n/290 n.

12. See, Kierkegaard, *Journals and Papers*, entry 1268, p. 73 in vol. 3.

13. Kierkegaard, *Postscript*, p. 279/270.

14. Ibid., p. 144 n/133 n.

15. At this point a natural objection to the notion of will suggests itself. If we say actions are events that are caused by acts of will, then what is the status of acts of will themselves? Are they also caused by acts of will? If so, a vicious regress appears to be in the offing. On the other hand, if acts of will are simply directly originated, why cannot the same be true of other actions? To respond to this objection, we must, I think, distinguish acts of will from full-blooded actions in the normal sense of the word *action*. An act of will is an actualization of a human capacity and in that sense is an act, but one can quite consistently hold that there are acts in that sense that are the causes of human actions in the fuller sense. Because, in Kierkegaard's view as we shall see, there is a sense in which the act of will is the crucial element in the whole action, to the extent that it can be considered to be what the action really is, strictly speaking, it is understandable that there should be some confusion here. Perhaps the clearest way to view the matter is to distinguish an "ordinary language" sense of action, where actions frequently involve bodily movements (such as carrying out the garbage, closing the door), from those basic acts that are acts in a stricter philosophical sense. The former are caused by acts of will. The latter are originative in character and, in Kierkegaard's view, are in a sense the "true" actions (see the next section). These basic acts of willing are the locus of "agent causality" if I am right in interpreting Kierkegaard as a libertarian. (Again, see the discussion of this later in the text.) Hence, the infinite regress does not occur, because acts of will are originative. However, it is not arbitrary to say that oridinary actions are not originative in the same primitive way, because there is a basic difference in character between acts of will and actions in the full, ordinary sense.

16. Kierkegaard, *Postscript*, p. 302/293.

17. See the following passage, for example: "If and when it [significance] comes, it is Providence that superimposes it upon his ethical striving within himself, and so it is not the fruit of his labor." Ibid., p. 123/112.

18. Ibid., p. 121/110.

19. Ibid.

20. Ibid., pp. 303–304/294.

21. Harry Frankfurt, "The Principle of Alternate Possibilities," *Journal of Philosophy* 64, no. 23 (1969):829–839.

22. Donald Davidson, "How is Weakness of the Will Possible?" *Essays on Actions and Events*, pp. 21–42.

23. Ibid., p. 41.

24. Davidson, "Intending," in ibid., p. 98.

25. Ibid., p. 99.

26. Davidson, "How is Weakness of the Will Possible?" p. 42.

27. "The laws whose existence is required if reasons are causes of actions do not, we may be sure, deal in the concepts in which rationalizations must deal." Davidson, "Actions, Reasons, and Causes," in ibid., p. 17.

28. Kierkegaard, *Philosophical Fragments,* ed. and trans. Howard V. Hong and Edna H. Hong (Princeton: Princeton University Press, 1985), p. 76 *Samlede Vaerker,* vol. 4, p. 240.

30. MacIntyre, *After Virtue,* p. 103.

7. LOVE AND PERFECT COINCIDENCE IN A SARTRIAN ETHICS

1. Jean-Paul Sartre, "Merleau-Ponty," *Situations,* trans. Benita Eisler (Greenwich, Conn.: Fawcett Publications, 1965), p. 161 n.

2. My most comprehensive treatment of these and other issues pertaining to ethics is to be found in *Sartre's Ethics of Authenticity* (University: University of Alabama Press, 1989).

3. Sartre, "Materialism and Revolution," *Literary and Philosophical Essays,* trans. Annette Michelson (New York: Collier Books, 1962), p. 237.

4. Maurice Merleau-Ponty, "Sartre and Ultrabolshevism," *Adventures of the Dialectic,* trans. Joseph Bien (Evanston: Northwestern University Press, 1973), pp. 147, 98.

5. Herbert Marcuse, "Sartre's Existentialism," *Studies in Critical Philosophy,* trans. Joris de Bres (Boston: Beacon Press, 1972), p. 189.

6. The following section is a condensation and reworking of Chapter 6 of my book *Sartre's Ethics of Authenticity,* and is included here with permission.

7. Sartre, *Being and Nothingness,* trans. Hazel E. Barnes (New York: Philosophical Library, 1956), p. 627.

8. Mary Warnock, *The Philosophy of Sartre* (New York: Barnes and Noble, 1967), p. 131.

9. Sartre, *Cahiers pour une morale* (Paris: Gallimard, 1983), p. 26.

10. Sartre, *Critique of Dialectical Reason,* trans. Alan Sheridan-Smith (Atlantic Highlands, N.J.: Humanities Press, 1976), p. 439.

11. Sartre, *The Devil and the Good Lord,* trans. Kitty Black (New York: Vintage Books, 1960), p. 145.

12. See Joseph H. McMahon's discussion of this, *Humans Being: The World of Jean-Paul Sartre* (Chicago: University of Chicago Press, 1971), p. 117.

13. Sartre, *Men without Shadows,* trans. Kitty Black (London: Hamish Hamilton, 1949), pp. 119, 145, 146.

14. Michel Contat and Michel Rybalka, *The Writings of Jean-Paul Sartre,* vol. 1, trans. Richard C. McCleary (Evanston: Northwestern University Press, 1974), p. 92.

15. Sartre, *The Chips Are Down,* trans. Louise Varese (New York: Lear, 1948), p. 92.

16. Ibid., p. 186.

17. Contat and Rybalka, *The Writings of Jean-Paul Sartre,* pp. 163–164.

18. Sartre, *Dirty Hands,* trans. Lionel Abel, in *No Exit and Three Other Plays by Jean-Paul Sartre* (New York: Vintage Books, 1955), p. 233.

19. Sartre, *The Devil and the Good Lord,* pp. 97, 99, 111, 128.

20. Ibid., p. 133.

21. Ibid., p. 147.

22. McMahon, *Humans Being,* p. 187. I fear seeing her as "a feminine force" may lead McMahon in an unprofitable direction. Anna's love is "feminine" in the sense that she offers Kean a love that is sexual and that she envisions as involving marriage. Otherwise her love has much in common with that of Hoederer, as the following analysis makes clear. The dangers of importing objectionable societal notions of the feminine into analysis of Sartre's work have been adequately shown by Margery L. Collins' and Christine Pierce's analysis ("Holes and Slime: Sexism in Sartre's Psychoanalysis," *Women and Philosophy,* ed. Carol C. Gould and Marx W. Wartofsky [New York: G. P. Putmans's Sons, 1980], pp. 113–116) of Wiliam Barrett's presentation of Sartre. At the same time, I should add that Collins' and Pierce's disparagement of female characters in Sartre's literary works is challenged seriously by characters like Hilda and Anna.

23. Sartre, *Kean,* trans. Kitty Black, in *The Devil and the Good Lord and Two Other Plays* (New York: Vintage Books, 1960), pp. 194, 195.

24. Ibid., pp. 213, 220, 276.

25. Sartre, *What Is Literature?* trans. Bernard Frechtman (New York: Harper and Row, 1965), p. 269.

26. Sartre, *The Devil and the Good Lord,* p. 145.

27. Ibid., p. 111.

28. Ibid., p. 146.

29. Sartre, *Kean*, p. 279.

30. Ibid., p. 256.

31. Sartre, *Cahiers*, p. 430.

32. Ibid., p. 523.

33. Sartre, *Being and Nothingness*, p. 371.

34. Sartre, *What Is Literature?* p. 52.

35. Ibid., p. 53.

36. Ibid., p. 49.

37. Sartre, *Cahiers*, p. 95.

38. Ibid., pp. 288, 290, 292, 293.

39. Ibid., p. 299.

40. Ibid., p. 296.

41. Ibid., p. 295.

42. Ibid., p. 296.

43. Ibid., pp. 295–296.

44. Ibid., pp. 54, 296–297.

45. De Beauvoir, *Adieux: A Farewell to Sartre*, trans. Patrick O'Brian (N.Y.: Pantheon, 1984), p. 119, expresses her outrage over statements Levy "extorted" from Sartre, including the weakening of the notion of fraternity, a notion that, she says, had been "so strong and firm in the *Critique of Dialectical Reason*." Levy does try to get Sartre to agree that talk of fraternity is "mythology."

46. "The Last Words of Jean-Paul Sartre, An Interview with Benny Levy," trans. Adrienne Foulke, *Dissent* (Fall 1980):414.

8. AUTHENTICITY, CONVERSION, AND THE CITY OF ENDS IN SARTRE'S *NOTEBOOKS FOR AN ETHICS*

1. *Being and Nothingness*, trans. Hazel Barnes (New York: Philosophical Library, 1956), p. 70.

2. *Cahiers pour une morale* (Paris: Gallimard, 1983). I take full responsibility for all translations, but I must acknowledge the invaluable assistance of Patricia Radzin. See also "Self-Portrait at Seventy," in *Life/Situations*, trans. P. Auster and L. Davis (New York: Pantheon, 1977), pp. 60, 74.

3. As far as philosophical works are concerned, *Cahiers* was written after *Existentialism Is a Humanism* (1946), *Materialism and Revolution* (1946), and *Anti-Semite and Jew* (1946) and at the same time as *What Is Literature?* (1947). De Beauvoir's *Pyrrhus et Cineas* (1944) and *The Ethics of Ambiguity* (1946) both predate the *Cahiers*.

4. *The Foundation and Structure of Sartrean Ethics* (Lawrence: University of Kanasa Press, 1979).

5. Unless otherwise indicated my discussion of pure reflection is based on *Cahiers* pp. 12, 13, 18, 425, 488–490, 495–497, 577–578.

6. *Being and Nothingness*, p. 627.

7. Like *Being and Nothingness*, *Cahiers* insists that all persons no matter how oppressed or mystified are always prereflectively conscious of their freedom, see pp. 373, 401, 488.

8. *Cahiers*, pp. 433, 486.

9. Ibid., pp. 495, 578.

10. *Being and Nothingness*, pp. 159 ff, 581.

11. *Cahiers*, p. 490. See the whole discussion pp. 488 – 492, 497, and 577–578.

12. Ibid., p. 495.

13. Ibid., pp. 162, 549.

14. Ibid., p. 501.

15. Ibid., p. 498. See also pp. 502, 507–508, 514, 543. Basically the same point is made in *Existentialism and Humanism*, trans. P. Mairet (London: Eyre Methuen Ltd., 1973), pp. 54–56.

16. *Cahiers*, pp. 499–502, 508–514, 543–546. *Being and Nothingness*, Introduction, Section 4; Part 1, Chapter 1.

17. *Cahiers*, pp. 464, 530.

18. Ibid., pp. 135–137, 455, 464, 499–504, 512–513, 549–552.

19. Ibid., pp. 137, 464, 500–501.

20. *Existentialism and Humanism*, p. 51. For a more detailed discussion of this argument see *The Foundation and Structure of Sartrean Ethics*, Chapter 3.

21. Places where he indicates that man should create the "maximum" of being are *Cahiers*, pp. 500, 501, 503–505, 507, 513, 522.

22. Ibid., pp. 16–18, 22–23, 63–64, 396–398, 429–430, 444, 484–485. For his remarks on childhood see ibid., pp. 199 ff, 352.

23. Ibid., p. 380. But elsewhere he states that this alienation is *not* oppression (pp. 396, 429), apparently reserving the latter term for more overt domination.

24. Ibid., pp. 338, 341, 380, 398, 484. Places where Sartre states that oppression is the result of human choice are pp. 13, 353, 395–396.

25. Ibid., p. 394. See also pp. 16 and 502. Yet Sartre also states (429) that man *cannot* escape from "primitive alienation," viz. primacy of the other. This has to be incorrect as the following analysis shows.

26. Ibid., pp. 26 and 433–434 respectively. See also pp. 91, 113–114, 128, 293.

27. Ibid., pp. 26 and 380. The conflict between human beings described in *Being and Nothingness* also has its roots in man's desire to be God, a desire that conversion refuses to indulge. See *Being and Nothingness*, pp. 361–363, 412, 526.

28. *Cahiers*, pp. 17–18, 54–55, 95, 421, 430, 434, 487, 515, 521–524.

29. Ibid., pp. 95, 109, 148–149, 174–176, 421, 487, 522.

30. Ibid., pp. 55, 109, 487.

31. Ibid., p. 177. See also pp. 148–149. *Being and Nothingness*, pp. 408–410.

32. *Cahiers*, pp. 148–149, 177, 346, 487.

33. Ibid., pp. 287–299. Some places where comprehension is mentioned in *Being and Nothingness* are pp. lxiii, 251, 289, 291, 439. It is not used there primarily to refer to awareness of others.

34. *Cahiers*, p. 299.

35. Ibid., pp. 16–17, 22, 52–54, 119–120, 300, 302, 416–417, 430, 516, 522–524. Sameness becomes a central notion in the *Critique of Dialectical Reason*. Obviously, much of what Sartre discusses here will find its fruition in the group of the *Critique*. But even there the exact ontological status of this "synthetic totality" will remain unclear.

36. *Cahiers*, p. 515. See also pp. 17–18, 295.

37. *Being and Nothingness*, p. 412. See also note 27 above.

38. *Cahiers*, pp. 285–297.

39. Ibid., pp. 150–151, 294–295, 443–444, 515.

40. "L'Ecriture et la Publication," interview with M. Sicard, *Obliques* nos. 18–19 (1979):14. Other places where he evaluates this early ethics are *Sartre by Himself*, filmscript trans. R. Seaver (New York: Urizen Books, 1978), pp. 76–

81; "The Last Words of Jean-Paul Sartre," trans. A. Foulke, *Dissent* (Fall 1980):405; "Self-Portrait at Seventy," pp. 60, 74–75; *On a raison de se revolter* (Paris: Gallimard, 1974), pp. 78–79. See also M. Contat and M. Rybalka, *The Writings of Jean-Paul Sartre, A Bibliographical Life,* vol. 1, trans. R. McCleary (Evanston: Northwestern University Press, 1974), pp. 228, 249–250, 295. For a good discussion of Sartre's three moralities, consult R. Stone's introduction to his translation of F. Jeanson's *Sartre and the Problem of Morality* (Bloomington: Indiana University Press, 1980).

41. "L'Ecriture et la Publication," p. 15; "The Last Words," pp. 411–413; *Sartre by Himself,* p. 80.

9. "MAKING THE HUMAN" IN SARTRE'S UNPUBLISHED DIALECTICAL ETHICS

1. The phrase *making the human* is our translation of Sartre's expression "faire l'homme."

2. Jean-Paul Sartre, *Being and Nothingness: An Essay on Phenomenological Ontology,* trans. Hazel E. Barnes (New York: Philosophical Library, 1956).

3. Jean-Paul Sartre, *Cahiers pour une morale* (Paris: Gallimard, 1983).

4. Jean-Paul Sartre, *Sartre by Himself,* a film directed by Alexandre Astruc and Michel Contat, trans. Richard Seaver (New York: Urizen Books, 1978), pp. 78–80; and Jean-Paul Sartre, interview by Michel Sicard, in *Obliques,* nos. 18–19 (1979):14.

5. Jean-Paul Sartre, *Critique of Dialectical Reason,* vol. 1, trans. Alan Sheridan-Smith, ed. Jonathan Rée (London: NLB/Verso, 1976); *Critique de la raison dialectique,* vol. 2 (Paris: Gallimard, 1985). Hereinafter cited as CDR.

6. Michel Contat and Michel Rybalka, *The Writings of Jean-Paul Sartre,* vols. 1 and 2, trans. Richard C. McLeary (Evanston: Northwestern University Press, 1974), vol. 1, p. 449.

7. Jean-Paul Sartre, *L'Idiot de la famille,* vols. 1 and 2 (Paris: Gallimard, 1970) and vol. 3 (Paris: Gallimard, 1972).

8. So far this effort, which Sartre and Lévy called "Pouvoir et liberté," has resulted in a set of interviews and a book by Benny Lévy: "L'Espoir, maintenant . . . ," *Le Nouvel Observateur,* nos. 800, 801, and 802 (March 10, 17, and 24, 1980); *Le nom de l'homme: dialogue avec Sartre* (Lagrasse: Verdier, 1984). Unfortunately, Lévy's book contains only small fragments of the tapings. Simone de Beauvoir expressed "consternation" at the "vague, yielding philosophy that Victor [Lévy's pseudonym] attributed to [Sartre]" and at Lévy's "influence" over a diminished Sartre in these interviews: *Adieu: A Farewell to Sartre,* trans.

Patrick O'Brian (New York: Pantheon, 1984), pp. 119–120. For a discussion of the status of these interviews in Sartre's own mind, see Sonia Kruks, "Sartre's *Cahiers pour une morale:* Failed Attempt or New Trajectory in Ethics?" *Social Text,* nos. 13–14 (Winter–Spring 1986):186–187. For Lévy's more recent views on morality, see: Stuart L. Charmé, "From Maoism to the Talmud (With Sartre Along the Way): An Interview with Benny Lévy," *Commentary* 78, no. 6, December 1984):48–53.

    9. Contat and Rybalka, *Writings,* vol. 1, p. 449; Sartre, *Sartre by Himself,* pp. 78–81.

    10. Sartre, interview by Michel Sicard, *Obliques,* nos. 18–19 (1979):14. *New York Times,* March 18, 1965. Cf. also Contat and Rybalka's bibliographical entry in *Obliques,* p. 347, and our "Sartre's *Morality and History:* A First Look at the Notes for the 1965 Cornell Lectures," in *Sartre Today,* ed. Ronald Aronson and Adrien Van Den Hoven (Detroit: Wayne State University Press, forthcoming).

    11. For an overview of these texts, and a summary of the *Notes for the 1964 Rome Lecture,* see our "Dialectical Ethics: A First Look at Sartre's Unpublished *1964 Rome Lecture Notes" Social Text,* nos. 13–14 (Winter–Spring 1986): 195–215.

    12. Only one-seventh of the notes for the lecture were published. They appeared as "Determinism and Freedom" in Contat and Rybalka, vol. 2, pp. 241–252. Other extracts from the *1964 Rome Notes* have appeared in Francis Jeanson, *Sartre* (Paris: Desclée de Brouwer, 1966), pp. 137–138, and in Benny Lévy, *Le nom de l'homme.*

    13. Letter to R. V. Stone postmarked February 21, 1986. Her words were: *"le point culminant."* Given that the *1964 Rome Notes* are more finished and easily published than the *Cahiers pour une morale,* far more valid in Sartre's mind than that renounced work and more pertinent to Sartre's central and life-long concern with ethics than any *inedita* so far published, it is puzzling that those charged with publishing Sartre's *inedita* so far have not seen fit to make this key work public. We hope publication of this "culmination" of Sartre's ethical thought will not be delayed further.

    14. We take Sartre's play *The Condemned of Altona* to be a meditation on mass suicide as one possible reponse of the bourgeoisie to its own "subhumanity."

    15. As usual, Sartre's humanism here is unlike most secular and religious humanisms in that it rests neither on an atemporal human essence preceding action nor on a valorization of our present condition. "Existentialism Is a Humanism," *Existentialism from Dostoevesky to Sartre,* ed. Walter Kaufmann (New York: Meridian Press, 1956), pp. 289–291. Cf. hints at "a true and positive humanism" in CDR, vol. 1, pp. 800–805.

    16. Sartre, "Existentialism Is a Humanism," pp. 296–297, 308.

17. Lévi-Strauss's *The Savage Mind* appeared just two years before Sartre spoke; Altusser's work was taking shape. For this background, see Mark Poster, *Existential Marxism in Postwar France: From Sartre to Althusser* (Princeton: Princeton University Press, 1975), pp. 306–361.

18. Cf. "Imperatives" in CDR, vol. 1, pp. 187–192.

19. Ibid., pp. 67, 191.

20. Jeanson, *Sartre,* p. 137.

21. In CDR, vol. 1, the distinction between *group* and *series* is not between singular (individual) and plural, but rather between practical agents acting either in a series or in a group. Cf. pp. 255–258, 370–373, 384, 396–400.

22. Ibid., pp. 161–162, 193, 225.

23. Jeanson, *Sartre,* p. 137.

24. "Contribution to the Critique of Hegel's Philosophy of Right," in *Marx-Engels Reader,* 2d ed, ed. Robert C. Tucker (New York: W. W. Norton and Co., 1978), p. 17. This distinction is present both in the early Marx (ibid., pp. 78–79, 85) and in *Capital,* vol. 1, trans. S. Moore and E. Aveling (New York: International Publishers, 1967), pp. 310, 571.

25. *Marx-Engels Reader,* p. 162.

26. Jeanson, *Sartre,* p. 138.

27. Jean-Paul Sartre, *Saint Genet, Actor and Martyr,* trans. Bernard Frechtman (New York: George Braziller, 1963).

28. Jean-Paul Sartre, *The Devil and the Good Lord,* trans. Kitty Black (New York: Alfred A. Knopf, 1960).

29. "Nevertheless, spirit, as Hegel says, is anxiety. But this anxiety horrifies us. We must eliminate it and arrest spirit by ejecting its springwork of negativity. Unable to get rid of this malignant postulation completely, the right-thinking man castrates himself; he cuts the negative moment away from his freedom and casts out the bloody mess. Fredom is thus cut in two; each of its halves wilts away separately. One of them remains within us. It identifies forever Good with Being, hence with what already is." *Saint Genet,* p. 24. Compare *Saint Genet* on Manicheism (pp. 24–31) with CDR, vol. 1, pp. 132–134, 736.

30. Sartre, *Saint Genet,* p. 186 n.

31. Cf. Linda A. Bell, "Loser Wins: The Importance of Play in a Sartrean Ethics of Authenticity," in *Phenomenology in a Pluralistic Context,* ed. William L. McBride and Calvin O. Schrag, Selected Studies in Phenomenology and Existential Philosophy, no. 9 (Albany State University of New York Press, 1983), pp. 5–13. Bell argues that " 'loser wins' constitutes an authentic deliverance from the problem of futility" (p. 6) and "Whatever Sartre's ethics, it must confront the

recognition that in terms of consequences, all human actions are on a par—they all fail" (p. 9). We suggest this failure is *ontological;* the actual human praxis can be an existential success. The "loser wins" game is not meant to resolve this alleged futility; but rather it is a way that inauthentic consciousness (i.e., before a "radical conversion") accepts losing, accepts oppression within a practico-inert ideology. Yet, as Goetz shows, playing out "loser wins" can lead to radical rejection of oppressive ideologies, opening a novel future *beyond* this game.

32. Sartre, *The Devil and the Good Lord,* p. 140.

33. Ibid., p. 149. Our translation.

34. CDR, vol. 1, pp. 771–772.

35. See, for example, Allen W. Wood, "Marx's Immoralism," in *Marx en perspective,* ed. Bernard Chavance (Paris: Editions de l'Ecole des Hautes Etudes en Sciences Sociales, 1985), pp. 681–698.

36. See, for example, Kai Nielsen, "Marxism and Morality," unpublished paper delivered to the Radical Philosophy Association at the Socialist Scholars' Conference, New York, New York, April 11, 1986. Two useful review essays on this literature are A. P. Simons "Marxism and Morals," *Ethics* vol. 93, no. 4 (July 1982):792–800; Kai Nielsen, "Morality and Ideology: Some Radical Critiques," *Graduate Faculty Philosophy Journal* 8, nos. 1–2 (Spring 1982).

37. Sartre, *The Psychology of the Imagination,* trans. anonymous (New York: Philosophical Library, 1948), pp. 268–269.

38. *Being and Nothingness,* p. 626. Cf. CDR, vol. 1, pp. 80–88.

39. At the level of fundamental needs that Sartre is dealing with here, the issue of so-called false needs does not arise. In his talk with Fidel Castro, Sartre seems to indicate a rejection of the notion of false needs. *Sartre on Cuba,* trans. anonymous (New York: Ballentine Books, 1961), pp. 134–135. Sartre later agreed that late capitalism engenders false needs. See Sartre, "France: Masses, Spontaneity, Party," in *Between Existentialism and Marxism,* trans. John Mathews (New York: Pantheon Books, 1974), pp. 124–125. In his unpublished notes toward *Investigations for a Morality,* he sketched a distinction between need and desire that might allow for a true-false need distinction.

40. To be sure, Marx says "the realm of necessity" is the *"basis"* for "the realm of freedom" — and Sartre's description of "making the human" could serve as a description of this latter realm. (*Capital,* vol. 3, trans. Ernest Untermann [Chicago: Charles H. Kerr, 1909], pp. 954–955.) However, Marx also clearly indicates freedom can penetrate the realm of necessity itself, so long as "the associated producers [are] rationally regulating their interchange with Nature." Ibid., p. 820.

41. Sartre, with Philippe Gavi and Pierre Victor, *On a raison de se révolter* (Paris: Gallimard, 1974), p. 118.

10. WOMAN'S EXPERIENCE: RENAMING THE DIALECTIC
OF DESIRE AND RECOGNITION

1. Paul Ricoeur, *Freud and Philosophy: An Essay on Interpretation*, trans. Denis Savage (New Haven: Yale University Press, 1977).

2. Paul Ricoeur, "Fatherhood: From Phantasm to Symbol," trans. Robert Sweeney, in *The Conflict of Interpretations: Essays in Hermeneutics*, ed. Don Ihde (Evanston: Northwestern University Press, 1974).

3. It is important to note that the shift from the focus on sisterhood to a focus on motherhood has entailed a shift away from the politics of *non*motherhood, the politics of abortion. But the liberatory attempt to reclaim and reconstruct motherhood *began* with women who found themselves suffering from the alienation of enforced motherhood — women who found themselves pregnant when they did not want to be and were forced either to have an unwanted child or to risk death with an illegal abortion. The contemporary concern with motherhood, as a politics of reproduction, cannot forget its origin: it must remain first and foremost woman's right to choose *not* to reproduce, the right to *not* mother. Within contemporary progressive social movements an abstract understanding of the domination of nature has led to support for the antiabortion movement. For a critique of this position, see my review essay, "Man-Made Motherhood and Other Sleights of Hand," *Phenomenology + Pedagogy* 3, no. 3 (1986).

4. Here I include the theories of Lacan and Irigaray as giving no new account of heterosexual desire as a female-male relation.

5. This concept of sisterhood was clarified in a conversation with Frieda Forman.

6. Woman as Other became the starting point for an understanding of what all women share, the starting point for a universal understanding of the experience of male domination and a new political practice. However, this has led to an exploration of differences among women and to the present allegiances of women to smaller and more "particular" or exclusive groups. From thinking and acting on the belief that all women are sisters, women have regrouped into specific forms of separatism based on race, sexual preference, religion, and ethnic identity. This multiplicity of Otherness challenges the solidarity that once made the women's movement powerful even as it discloses the importances of understanding the nonidentity of women. The question of the shared ground of sisterhood raised by this multiplicity is intensified by the fact that, as the politics of the women's liberation movement is institutionalized as feminism, sisterhood is sometimes invoked by women only to do intimate violence to other women.

7. The reclaiming of motherhood is a contentious issue within feminist theory. Dinnerstein and Chodorow see only negative features in human development due to the absence of the father from early child care: male domination of woman and the domination of nature are seen as reactions to the overwhelming and unbearable power of the mother experienced by the preverbal, prerational infant. In

contrast, feminists like Rich, Ruddick, Ryan, and Whitbeck see positive features in mother-raised children; mothering is said to provide the basis for the transformation of society through a model of the nondominating relation between the self and the Other. See Adrienne Rich, *Of Woman Born: Motherhood as Experience and Institution* (New York: W. W. Norton and Co., 1976); Sara Ruddick, "Maternal Thinking," in *Mothering: Essays in Feminist Theory*, ed. Joyce Trebilcot (Totowa, N.J.: Rowman and Allanheld, 1984); Joanna Ryan, "Psychoanalysis and Women Loving Women," in *Sex and Love: New Thoughts on Old Contradictions*, ed. Sue Cartledge and Joanna Ryan (London: Women's Press, 1984); Caroline Whitbeck, "Maternal Instinct" and "Afterword," in Trebilcot, *Mothering;* Iris Young, "Is Male Gender Identity the Cause of Male Domination?" in Trebilcot, *Mothering*. My account of the relation between motherhood and sisterhood within feminism is not meant to be exhaustive but to allow for a reconsideration of the relation. For an interesting discussion of sisterhood as friendship, as a relationship of recognition between two women, see Janice G. Raymond, *A Passion for Friends: Toward a Philosophy of Female Affection* (Boston: Beacon Press, 1986); and Carroll Smith-Rosenberg, "The Female World of Love and Ritual: Relations between Women in Nineteenth-Century America," in *The Signs Reader: Women, Gender and Scholarship*, ed. Elizabeth Abel and Emily K. Abel (Chicago: University of Chicago Press, 1983), pp. 27–55.

8. Herbert Marcuse, *Counterrevolution and Revolt* (Boston: Beacon Press, 1972), p. 78. Marcuse keeps searching for the revolutionary subject all through the 1960s and 1970s but then writes against this search and returns to an expanded working class as the revolutionary subject within a focus on the concept of "surplus-consciousness." See Marcuse, "The Reification of the Proletariat," *Canadian Journal of Political and Social Theory* 3 (Winter 1979):20–23.

9. Judith Butler, response to "Women: The One and the Many" by Elizabeth Spelman, paper presented to the American Philosophical Association, Washington, D.C., December 29, 1985.

10. Theodor W. Adorno, *Negative Dialectics*, trans. E. B. Ashton (New York: Seabury Press, 1973), p. 191.

11. Ibid., p. 309.

12. Ibid., p. 12.

13. Theodor W. Adorno, *Minima Moralia: Reflections from Damaged Life*, trans. E. F. N. Jephcott (London: New Left Books, 1974), p. 87. A wonderful poem in *Ceremony* by Leslie Marmon Silko (Harmondsworth: Penguin Books, 1986) echoes this relation between naming and the creative activity of the spider:

> ts'its'tsi'nako, Thought-Woman,
> is sitting in her room
> and whatever she thinks about
> appears.

She thought of her sisters,
Naut'ts'ity'i and I'tcts'ity'i,
and together they created the Universe
this world
and the four worlds below.

Thought-woman, the spider,
named things and
as she named them
they appeared.

14. Theodor W. Adorno, "Commitment," *New Left Review* (September–December 1974) 85.

15. Max Horkheimer, *Eclipse of Reason* (New York: Seabury Press, 1974), p. 179.

16. Betty Friedan, *The Feminine Mystique* (New York: Dell Publishing Co., 1963).

17. This essay is excerpted from Chapter 5 of my book *Woman, Nature, and Psyche* (New Haven: Yale Unviersity Press, 1987) and is reprinted here with permission of the press.

11. LITERATURE AND PHILOSOPHY AT THE CROSSROADS: PROUSTIAN SUBJECTS

1. Marcel Proust, *Remembrance of Things Past* (New York: Random House, 1982), vol. 2, p. 121. All quotations in English will refer to this edition and follow in the text. "Et puis ces sentiments particuliers, toujours quelque chose en nous s'efforce des les amener à plus de vérité, c'est-à-dire des les faire se rejoindre à un sentiment plus général, commu à toute l'humaniteé, avec lequel les individus et les peines qu'ils nous causent nous sont seulement une occasion de communier: ce qui mêlait quelque plaisir à ma peine, c'est que je la savais une petite partie de l'universel amour." *A la recherche du temps perdu* (Paris: Bibliothèque de la Pléiade), vol. 2, p. 120. All quotations in French refer to this edition, vol. 1–3.

2. My translation. "Au fond, toute ma philosophie revient comme toute philosophie vraie à justifier, à recontruire ce qui est." Cited in Anne Henry, *Théories pour une ésthétique* (Paris: Klincksieck, 1981), p. 260.

3. "Le redressement de l'oblique discours intérieur," vol. 3, p. 890.

4. "Une oeuvre où il y a des théories est comme un objet sur lequel on laisse la marque du prix," vol. 3, p. 882.

5. "L'impression est pour l'écrivain ce qu'est l'expérimentation pour le savant, avec cette différence que chez le savant le travail de l'intelligence précède et chez l'écrivain vient après," vol. 3, p. 880.

6. "Elle n'était plus animée que de la vie inconsciente des végétaux ... Son moi ne s'échappait pas à tous moments, ... par les issues de la pensé inavouée et du regard. Elle avait rappelé à soi tout ce qui d'elle était au dehors; elle s'était réfugiée, enclose, résumé, dans son corps. En le tenant sous mon regard, dans mes mains, j'avais cette impression de la posséder tout entière que je n'avais pas quand elle était réveillée," vol. 3, p. 70.

7. "Quelquefois, comme Eve naquit d'une côte d'Adam, une femme naissait pendant mon sommeil d'une fausse position de ma cuisse. ... Si, comme il arrivait quelquefois, elle avait les traits d'une femme que j'avais connue dans la vie, j'allais me donner tout entier à ce but: la retrouver, comme ceux qui partent en voyage pour voir de leurs yeux une cité désirée et s'imaginent qu'on peut goûter dans une réalité le charme du songe. Peu à peu son souvenir s'évanouissait, j'avais oublié la fille de mon rêve," vol. 1, pp. 4–5.

8. "La brume, dès le réveil, avait fait de moi, au lieu de l'être centrifuge qu'on est par les beaux jours, un homme replié, désireux du coin de feu et du lit partagé, Adam frileux en quête d'une Eve sédentaire, dans ce monde différent," vol. 2, p. 346.

9. "O grandes attitudes de l'Homme et de la Femme où cherchent à se joindre, dans l'innocence des premiers jours ... ce que la Création a séparé, où Eve est étonnée et soumise devant l'Homme au côte de qui elle s'éveille, comme lui-même, encore seul, devant Dieu qui l'a formé," vol. 3, p. 79.

10. "Elle est une soif de savoir grâce à laquelle, sur des points isolés les uns des autres, nous finissons par avoir successivement toutes les notions possibles, sauf celle que nois voudrions," vol. 3, p. 86.

11. Vol. 3, p. 384.

12. "Une théorie désire d'être exprimée entièrement," vol. 1, p. 563.

13. Vol. 3, p. 106.

14. Vol. 3, p. 899.

15. Vol. 2, p. 63.

16. Vol. 3, p. 897.

17. "La jalousie est bon recruteur qui, quand il y a un creux dans notre tableau, va nous chercher la belle fille qu'il fallait," vol. 3, p. 916.

18. "Et tout se compose bien, grâce à la présence suscitée par la jalousie de la belle fille dont déjà nous ne sommes plus jaloux et que nous n'aimons plus," vol. 3, p. 917.

19. Vol. 1, p. 858.

20. ''Elles sont, ces femmes, un produit de notre tempérament, une image, une projection renversées, un 'négatif' de notre sensibilité. De sorte qu'un romancier pourrait, au cours de la vie de son héros, peindre presque exactement semblables ses successives amours et donner par là l'impression non de s'imiter lui-même mais de créer, puisq'il y a moins de force dans une innovation artificielle que dans une répétition destinée à suggérer une vérité neuve,'' vol. 1, p. 894.

21. Beneath the social veneer of the Baron de Charlus, one can glimpse a woman: ''Ce à quoi me faisait penser cet homme, qui était si épris, qui se piquait si fort de virilité, à qui tout le monde semblait odieusement efféminé, ce à quoi il me faisait penser tout d'un coup, tant il en avait passagèrement les traits, l'expression, le sourire, c'était à une femme,'' vol. 2, p. 604.

22. Gilles Deleuze, *Proust and Signs,* (New York: Georges Braziller, 1972), p. 99.

23. ''Les invertis, qui se rattachent volontiers à l'antique Orient ou à l'Age d'or de la Grèce, remonteraient plus haut encore, à ces époques d'essai où n'existaient ni les fleurs dioïques, ni les animaux unisexués, à cet hermaphroditisme initial dont quelques rudiments d'organes mâles dans l'anatomie de la femme et d'organes femelles dans l'anatomie de l'homme semblent conserver la trace,'' vol. 2, p. 629.

24. Roland Barthes, *Recherche de Proust* (Paris: Seuil, 1980), pp. 37–39.

25. ''Comme il n'est de connaissance, on peut presque dire qu'il n'est de jalousie que de soi-même,'' vol. 3, p. 386.

12. PHILOSOPHY BECOMES AUTOBIOGRAPHY: THE DEVELOPMENT OF THE SELF IN THE WRITINGS OF SIMONE DE BEAUVOIR

1. Simone de Beauvoir, *Force of Circumstance,* trans. Richard Howard (New York: Harper Colophon Books, 1964), p. 23.

2. Simone de Beauvoir, *The Ethics of Ambiguity,* trans. Bernard Frechtman (New York: Citadel Press, 1970), p. 78.

3. Simone de Beauvoir, *The Second Sex,* trans. and ed. by H. M. Parshley (New York: Vintage Books, 1974), p. xxxiv.

4. Michèle Le Doeuff, ''Simone de Beauvoir and Existentialism,'' *Feminist Studies* 6 (1980):277–289.

5. Jean-Paul Sartre, ''Existentialism Is a Humanism,'' in *Existentialism,* ed. Robert Solomon (New York: Modern Library, 1974), p. 202.

6. Le Doeuff, p. 286. Beauvoir and Sartre read, critiqued, and edited nearly everything that each other wrote. Was Beauvoir's shift toward "determinism" in *The Second Sex* an influence upon Sartre and a cause of his own shift, represented in works like *Baudelaire* (1950), *Saint Genet* (1952), and *Critique of Dialectical Reason* (1960), toward the concrete, the material, and toward Marx and Freud? Sartre had tackled psychoanalysis in *Being and Nothingness*, but he did so to strongly disagree with it and deny the existence of an unconscious. In *The Second Sex*, Beauvoir goes much further with Freud than Sartre did in *Being and Nothingness*.

7. Beauvoir, *The Second Sex*, pp. xx–xxi.

8. Beauvoir, "Merleau-Ponty et le pseudo-sartrisme," in *Privilèges* (Paris: Gallimard, 1955), pp. 203–272. Originally published in *Les Temps modernes* 10, nos. 114–115 (June–July 1955):2072–2122.

9. Carol Ascher's excellent book on Beauvoir, *Simone de Beauvoir: A Life of Freedom* (Boston: Beacon Press, 1981), never mentions the article on Merleau-Ponty nor the book, *Privilèges*. Terry Keefe's book, *Simone de Beauvoir: A Study of Her Writings* (Totowa, N.J.: Barnes and Noble Books, 1983), devotes less than one page to the essay, for he claims it is insignificant "outside of the context of the heated political disputes in France in the nineteen-fifties" (p. 123). Anne Whitmarsh's book, *Simone de Beauvoir and the Limits of Commitment* (Cambridge: Cambridge University Press, 1981), which focuses on "the ethical, social and above all political implications" of Beauvoir's commitment to leftist politics (quote from p. 1), mentions the article in a parenthesis that gives only its title (p. 101). Neither of two recently published studies of Beauvoir, both of which focus on *The Second Sex*, mention the article nor the book, *Privilèges:* Mary Evans, *Simone de Beauvoir: A Feminist Mandarin* (London: Tavistock, 1985), and Judith Okely, *Simone de Beauvoir* (New York and London: Virago/Pantheon, 1986).

10. Merleau-Ponty had been friends with Beauvoir longer; Terry Keefe's index lists Merleau-Ponty as "Jean Pradelle" also. Pradelle was Beauvoir's name for the friend of hers of whom Zaza, her best friend, became enamored, a romance that ended in Zaza's death, whether of emotional or physical reasons remains unclear. See Beauvoir, *Memoirs of a Dutiful Daughter*, trans. James Kirkup (New York: Harper Colophon Books, 1974), pp. 245–360, especially 245–251 and 260 et passim to the end of the book.

In their recently published biography of Beauvoir, *Simone de Beauvoir: A Life*, trans. Lisa Nesselson (New York: St. Martin's Press, 1987), Claude Francis and Fernande Contier provide the story behind these events, a story that Beauvoir revealed to them. See pp. 83–88 and 376–377.

11. This originally appeared as articles in *Les Temps modernes* in 1952 and was later published in book form in *Situations VI: Problèmes du Marxisme*, vol. 1. For full citation, see note 2, p. 96 of the English translation of Merleau-Ponty's *Adventures of the Dialectic*, trans. Joseph Bien (Evanston, Ill.: Northwestern University Press, 1973).

12. Beauvoir, *Force of Circumstance*, p. 318.

13. Jean-Paul Sartre, *Being and Nothingness*, trans. Hazel Barnes (New York: Washington Square Press, 1966), p. 125.

14. Beauvoir, *Privilèges*, p. 207.

15. Ibid., p. 207, quote of Jean-Paul Sartre.

16. Ibid., p. 206. To defend Sartre against Merleau-Ponty, Beauvoir overlooked her own earlier remarks on the contrast between Sartre and Merleau-Ponty in her review of *The Phenomenology of Perception*, published in *Les Temps modernes*, in 1945. There she stated: "Whereas Sartre in *Being and Nothingness* first emphasizes the opposition of the for-itself and the in-itself . . . Merleau-Ponty, on the contrary, adheres to describing the concrete character of the subject which is never, according to him, a pure for-itself . . . " (*Les Temps modernes* 1, no. 2 (1945):366–367), my translation.

17. Keefe, p. 44.

18. A nicely turned phrase of J. Schneewind, in conversation.

19. Others have remarked on this also. Cf. Keefe, pp. 32–33.

20. Beauvoir, *The Ethics of Ambiguity*, pp. 35–36.

21. Simone de Beauvoir, *Memoirs of a Dutiful Daughter*, pp. 11–12. This was published first in 1958 in France.

22. Ibid., pp. 30–31.

23. Beauvoir, *The Ethics of Ambiguity*, p. 40.

24. Beauvoir states this both in *Memoirs*, p. 360, and in *The Prime of Life*, p. 285. She later, in *Force of Circumstance*, p. 649, criticized those women who had read *Memoirs* because they liked her description of an upbringing they shared, yet were disinterested in her later explanations of how she had escaped it; that is, specifically, the story of her writing career.

25. Beauvoir, *Memoirs*, p. 360.

26. Simone de Beauvoir, *The Prime of Life*, trans. Peter Green (Cleveland: World Publishing Co., Meridian Books, 1962), p. 9. *Memoirs* and *The Prime of Life* were published in France, respectively, in 1958 and 1960. The fourth of Beauvoir's autobiographies is *Tout Compte Fait* (Paris: Editions Gallimard, 1972); the English translation is *All Said and Done*, trans. Patrick O'Brian (New York: G. P. Putnam's, 1974).

27. Beauvoir, *The Prime of Life*, p. 9.

28. Beauvoir, *The Ethics of Ambiguity*, p. 119.

29. Beauvoir, *Force of Circumstance*, pp. 66–68. She says here that she was most irritated by this book, of all the books she had written, particularly by

its idealism: "I was in error when I thought I could define a morality independent of a social context. I could write an historical novel without having a philosophy of history, but not construct a theory of action. . . . Why did I write *concrete liberty* instead of *bread . . . ?*"

30. Beauvoir, *The Ethics of Ambiguity,* p. 25.

31. Ibid., p. 156.

32. Beauvoir, *Memoirs,* p. 360.

33. Ibid., p. 282.

34. Beauvoir, *The Ethics of Ambiguity,* p. 73.

35. Beauvoir, *Memoirs,* p. 55.

36. Ibid., p. 61.

37. Ibid., p. 56.

38. Ibid., p. 87 and *The Prime of Life,* p. 34.

39. *Memoirs,* pp. 166–167.

40. Ibid., p. 295.

41. Beauvoir, *The Prime of Life,* p. 54.

42. Ibid., p. 38.

43. Ibid., p. 171.

44. Ibid., p. 54.

45. Simone de Beauvoir, *La Force de l'âge* (Paris: Editions Gallimard, 1960), p. 66. "Castor" was Sartre's nickname for Beauvoir.

46. Beauvoir, *The Prime of Life,* p. 54.

47. Ibid., p. 178.

48. Ibid., p. 452.

49. Ibid., pp. 21, 22, 26–27, et passim.

50. Ibid., p. 26.

51. Ibid., p. 23.

52. Ibid., p. 208.

53. Cf. "Epilogue," *Force of Circumstance,* pp. 643–658.

54. Beauvoir, *The Prime of Life,* p. 289.

55. Ibid., p. 285.

56. Beauvoir, *The Ethics of Ambiguity*, pp. 72–73.

57. Beauvoir, *The Prime of Life*, p. 295.

58. Ibid., p. 433.

59. Beauvoir, *The Prime of Life*, p. 474.

60. Ibid., p. 479.

61. Ibid., p. 385.

62. Beauvoir, *Memoirs*, p. 169.

63. Beauvoir, *The Prime of Life*, p. 292. Though this remark, as it stands, is contradictory to Sartre's claim in *The Transcendence of the Ego*, I believe it simply amounts to a case of careless terminology. The French reads: "je crois encore aujourd'hui à la théorie de 'l'ego transcendantal'; le moi n'est qu'un objet probable, et celui qui dit *je* n'en saisit que des profils; autrui peut en avoir une vision plus nette ou plus juste." From *La Force d l'âge*, p. 377.

64. Ibid. The English misses a great deal. Translator Peter Green phrased it: " . . . self-knowledge is impossible, and the best one can hope for is self-revelation."

65. Beauvoir, *Force of Circumstance*, p. 276.

13. DIALOGUE AND DISCOURSES

I thank John O'Neill for looking through the manuscript and giving a more flexible body to my thoughts. A German version of this essay has been published in Bernhard Waldenfels, *Der Stachel des Fremden* (Frankfurt: Suhrkamp, 1990).

1. The link between dialogue and dialectic is demonstrated by Heidegger in his interpretation of Hegel's concept of experience. Martin Heidegger, *Holzwege* (Frankfurt: V. Klostermann, 1950), pp. 169, 177. In Gadamer's well-known study on Hegel und die antike Dialektik" these ideas are put into an historical context. Hans-Georg Gadamer, *Hegels Dialektik* (Tübingen: Niemeyer, 1971).

2. I shall not answer the question of how far the dialogue as *staged and practiced* by Plato is covered by Plato's own idea of dialogue and its dialectical sublimation.

3. In what follows I shall take up some issues largely treated in my earlier studies *Das sokratische Fragen* and *Das Zwischenreich des Dialogs* (Den Haag: M. Nijhoff, 1961 and 1971). In doing so, I try to revise my former attempts, which are still too much directed to an all-encompassing "order without twilight." In this sense, see my book *Ordnung im Zwielicht* (Frankfurt: Suhrkamp, 1987).

4. Trying to deepen this problem we should have to take notice of recent form of a logic of questioning whose beginnings point back to Aristotle's *Analytica Posteriora* (II, 1–2).

5. This kind of "discourse" does not have much to do with the concept used in my own paper. Habermas's "discourse" can be regarded as a new variant of the old form of dialogue, tempered only by a certain separation of power and reduced to a formal rationality. See my critique in *In den Netzen der Lebenswelt* (Frankfurt: Suhrkamp, 1985), Chapters 5 and 6.

6. G. Calogero, *Philosophie du dialogue* (Brussels: Editions de l'Université de Bruxelles, 1973).

7. Michel Foucault, *L'ordre du discours* (Paris: Gallimard, 1971).

8. J.-F. Lyotard, *Le différend* (Paris: Minuit, 1984).

9. M. Theunissen, *Der Andere* (Berlin: De Gruyter, 1977), p. 490.

10. See, e.g., Foucault, *L'archéologie du savoir* (Paris: Gallimard, 1969), p. 125; and my critical remarks on Foucault's theory of discourse in *In den Netzen der Lebenswelt*, Chapter 6, and in my *Phänomenologie in Frankreich* (Frankfurt: Suhrkamp, 1983).

11. Maurice Merleau-Ponty, *Signes* (Paris: Gallimard, 1960), p. 150.

12. On the reciprocity of perspectives see recently R. de Folter in Grathoff and Waldenfels, *Sozialität und Intersubjektivität. Phänomenologische Perspektiven der Sozialwissenschaften im Umkreis von Aron Gurwitsch und Alfred Schütz*, (Übergänge 1) (München: W. Fink, 1983), and on Piaget's logic of reversibility, criticized from a phenomenological point of view, see K. Meyer-Drawe, *Leiblichkeit und Sozialität* (Übergange 7), (München: W. Fink, 1984).

13. Maurice Merleau-Ponty, *La prose du monde* (Paris: Gallimard, 1969).

14. Here I refer to Levinas's early essay, *Le temps et l'autre*, published in 1947, where many of the later thoughts are already anticipated. Levinas, *Le temps et l'autre* (Montpellier: Fata Morgana, 1979).

15. Ibid., p. 196.

16. Merleau-Ponty, *La prose du monde*, p. 29.

17. E. Husserl, *Ideen zu einer reinen Phänomenologie und phänomenologischen Philosophie*, vol. II (Husserlinana IV), (Den Haag: M. Nijhoff, 1952), p. 111.

18. Merleau-Ponty, *Le visible et l'invisible* (Paris: Gallimard, 1964), pp. 254, 299.

19. Husserl, *Ideen zu einer reinen Phänomenologie und phänomenologischen Philosophie*, pp. vol. II, 98. 259.

20. See Julia Kristeva's *Polylogue* where Bakhtin's ideas are taken up within a semiotic framework. In what follows, I shall refer especially to Bakhtins articles "Das Wort in Roman" and "Zur Methodologie der Literaturwissenschaft," in *Die Ästhetik des Wortes* ed. and trans. by R. Grubel (Frankfurt: Suhrkamp, 1979). See also R. Lachmann's volume on *Dialogizität* (München: W. Fink, 1982).

21. Bakhtin, *Die Ästhetik des Wortes*, p. 185.

22. Ibid., p. 204.

23. Ibid., p. 351.

24. Ibid., p. 354.

14. BEYOND SIGNIFIERS

1. "L'interrogation philosophique sur le monde ne consiste donc pas à se reporter du monde même à ce que nous en disons, puisqu'elle se réitère à l'intérieur du language," in Maurice Merleau-Ponty, *The Visible and the Invisible*, ed. Lefort, trans. Lingis (Evanston, Ill.: Northwestern University Press, 1968), pp. 96–97. *Le Visible et l'Invisible*, ed. Lefort (Paris: Gallimard, 1964), p. 132.

2. M. Merleau-Ponty, "The Primacy of Perception and Its Philosophical Consequences," in *The Primacy of Perception*, ed. and trans. Edie (Evanston, Ill.: Northwestern University Press), p. 13.

3. Merleau-Ponty speaks to this issue, but his speaking was silenced a quarter-century ago, hence he did not—could not—respond to such key texts as Derrida's *De la Grammatologie*, which was published in 1967, six years after Merleau-Ponty's untimely death. (Jacques Derrida, *De la Grammatologie* [Paris: Les Editions de Minuit, 1967]; *Of Grammatology* trans. Spivak [Baltimore: Johns Hopkins University Press, 1976].) It might be worthwhile to note here that Merleau-Ponty does address himself to Derrida—whose prominence in France was growing long before the publication of *Grammatology*—but he does not name Derrida in his reference to contemporary linguistics.

4. Although post-hermeneutic skepticism and semiological reductionism emerge from the works of Heidegger and Saussure, neither of these figures, as I interpret the primary texts, espoused the standpoint derived from his thought.

5. M. Heidegger, *Being and Time*, trans. Macquarrie and Robinson (New York: Harper and Row, 1962), Section 32, pp. 188–195.

6. M. Heidegger, "The Origin of the Work of Art," in *Poetry, Language, Thought*, trans. Hofstadter (New York: Harper and Row, 1971), p. 78.

7. Ibid., p. 72.

8. Ibid., p. 73.

9. M. Heidegger, *An Introduction to Metaphysics*, trans. Manheim (New York: Doubleday, 1961), p. 11.

10. Heidegger, "What Are Poets For?" in *Poetry, Language, Thought*, p. 132.

11. Heidegger, *An Introduction to Metaphysics*, p. 42.

12. Ibid., p. 37.

13. M. Heidegger, "Hölderlin and the Essence of Poetry," in *Existence and Being*, ed. Brock, trans. Scott (Chicago: Henry R. Regnery, 1949), p. 287. The original German language version of this essay was published in 1936.

14. Heidegger, *An Introduction to Metaphysics*, p. 41.

15. Ibid., p. 11.

16. M. Heidegger, " . . . Poetically Man Dwells . . . ," in *Poetry, Language, Thought*, p. 215.

17. "Language is the house of Being because language, as saying, is the mode of Appropriation." M. Heidegger, "The Way to Language" in *On the Way to Language*, trans. Hertz (New York: Harper and Row, 1971), p. 135. German language version published in 1959.

18. To the extent that semiological laws are grounded in sociological laws, at least one science seems to defy the reduction.

19. Ferdinand de Saussure, *Course in General Linguistics*, ed. Bally and Sechehaye in collaboration with Reidlinger, trans. Baskin (New York: Philosophical Library, 1959).

20. I say "for the most part compatible" because the scientific realism implicit in Saussure's appeal to sociology, history, physiology, and so on would be regarded as naive by contemporary proponents of semiological reductionism.

21. De Saussure, *Course*, p. 16.

22. That is, the sign unites a signified (concept) and a signifier (sound-image). Ibid., p. 66.

23. Ibid., p. 113.

24. Ibid., p. 91.

25. Ibid., p. 71.

26. "Without the help of signs we would be unable to make a clear-cut, consistent distinction between two ideas. Without language, thought is a vague, uncharted nebula. There are no pre-existing ideas, and *nothing is distinct before the appearance of language*." Ibid., pp. 111–112, emphasis added.

27. "The linguistic entity exists only through the associating of the signifier with the signified. Whenever only one element is retained, the entity vanishes; instead of a concrete object we are faced with a mere abstraction." Ibid., pp. 102–103. Also see pp. 65 ff.

28. Ibid., p. 104.

29. "Each linguistic term is a member, an articulus [joint, knuckle, turning point] in which an idea is fixed in a sound and a sound becomes the sign of an idea." Ibid., p. 113.

30. Ibid., p. 113.

31. "The arbitrary nature of the sign explains . . . why the social fact alone can create a linguistic system. The community is necessary if values that owe their existence solely to usage and general acceptance are to be set up; by himself the individual is incapable of fixing a single value." Ibid., p. 113. It is interesting to note the conflict with Heidegger here. The latter grants this power of linguistic institution to the poet—who stands *apart from the community* and listens to the gods.

32. Here I exchange Saussure's convention for the one I am employing, but, I trust, without altering his intent. See *Course*, pp. 66–67.

33. Ibid., p. 213.

34. See Heidegger, *Being and Time*, Section 6.

35. It is clear from the French text that the antecedent of "it"—in all four instances in this sentence—is "language."

36. M. Merleau-Ponty, *La prose du monde*, ed. Lefort (Paris: Gallimard, 1969). *The Prose of the World*, ed. Lefort, trans. O'Neill (Evanston, Ill.: Northwestern University Press, 1973).

37. Ludwig Wittgenstein, *Tractatus Logico-Philosophicus*, trans. D. F. Pears and B. F. McGuinness (London: Routledge and Kegan Paul, 1961), prop. 6.54, p. 151.

38. Ibid., prop. 5.6, p. 115.

39. Ibid., props. 2.223, 2.224, 4.002.

40. Ibid., prop. 6.522, p. 151.

41. Ibid., prop. 7, p. 151.

42. M. Heidegger, "The Way to Language," in *On the Way to Language*, trans. Peter D. Hertz (New York: Harper and Row, 1971), p. 134. "Weil wir Menschen, um die zu sein, die wir sind, in das Sprachwesen eingelassen bleiben und daher niemals aus ihm heraustreten können, um es noch von anderswoher zu

umblicken, erblicken wir das Sprachwesen stets nur insoweit, als wir von ihm selbst angeblickt, in es vereignet sind." "Der Weg zur Sprache," in *Unterwegs zur Sprache* (Pfullingen: Neske, 1959), p. 266.

43. The profound misreading of this essay by an otherwise astute critic prompts me to enter two disclaimers here. First, my endorsement of Merleau-Ponty's assertion that the perceptual world is epistemologically foundational does not commit me to anything resembling the sense data or protocol experiences that play a foundational role in positivist theorizing. The sense of foundation that informs the standpoint taken here is that of *Fundierung*, a term Merleau-Ponty appropriates from Husserl and modifies to reflect his own nonidealistic understanding of the transcendental functions of constitution and sedimentation. To acknowledge the sedimentation of culture in experience (the intertwining of the founding and founded, or what Merleau-Ponty later called the reversibility of the flesh of the world) is to deny the possibility of separating the two but, at the same time, to preserve the truth that positivism sought in vain to capture in its own theorizing. That is the truth of the transcendence of the perceptual world. Second, my use of the terms *immanence* and *transcendence* is specifically intended to undercut rather than reaffirm the dualism of traditional Cartesian ontology. As I use the terms, they name correlative rather than mutually exclusive aspects of human experience. The transcendence of the perceived world is a revealed transcendence, and that which is immanent within human experience ultimately refers beyond itself to a source within the phenomenal world. The primary flaw I find in the thesis of linguistic immanence is that it presupposes a discontinuity between language and experience such that the autonomy attributed to the former denies its gounding and contextualization in the latter. That is, in its fascination with the narcissistic and infrareferential aspects of language, it denies the fact that language is intrinsically allusive, extrareferential, and parasitic as well. Both of these issues are treated at length in *Merleau-Ponty's Ontology* (Bloomington: Indiana University Press, 1988). See Chapters 1 ("The Cartesian Origins of Empiricism and Intellectualism"), 2 ("The Paradox of Immanence and Transcendence"), and 10 ("Language: Foundation and Truth").

44. M. Merleau-Ponty, *Phenomenology of Perception,* trans. Colin Smith (London: Routledge and Kegan Paul, 1962), p. xiv. "Le plus grand enseignement de la réduction est l'impossibilité d'une réduction complète." *Phénoménologie de la perception* (Paris: Gallimard, 1945), p. viii.

45. J. Derrida, *Of Gammatology* p. 7. "Il n'est pas de signifié qui échappe . . . au jeu des renvois signifiants qui constitue le langage." *De la Grammatologie,* p. 16.

46. J. Derrida, 'Différance," in *Margins of Philosophy,* trans. Alan Bass (Chicago: University of Chicago Press, 1982), p. 12. *"Il n'y a pas de présence avant la différance sémiologique et hors d'elle"* "La Différance," in *Marges de la philosophie* (Paris: Les Éditions de Minuit, 1972), p. 12.

47. Ibid., p. 11. "La Différance," pp. 11–12.

48. Derrida, "Deconstruction and the Other" in "Dialogue with Jacques Derrida" in Richard Kearney, *Dialogues with Contemporary Continental Thinkers* (Dover, N.H.: Manchester University Press, 1984), pp. 123–124. I am indebted to John D. Caputo for drawing my attention to this text.

49. Derrida, "Différance," p. 23. "La trace n'est jamais comme telle en présentation de soi." "La Différance," p. 24.

50. Derrida, "Différance," p. 24. "La Différance," p. 25.

15. MERLEAU-PONTY AND *L'ÉCRITURE*

1. Jacques Derrida, *Of Grammatology,* trans. G.C. Spivak (Baltimore: Johns Hopkins University Press, 1974), p. 8.

2. Maurice Merleau-Ponty, *Phenomenology of Perception,* trans. C. Smith (London: Routledge and Kegan Paul, 1962), p. 196.

3. Ibid., pp. 196–197.

4. Jacques Derrida, *Writing and Difference,* trans. A. Bass (Chicago: University of Chicago Press, 1978), p. 27.

5. Ibid.

6. Ibid., p. 28.

7. What I do *not* say here: in working through this difficulty after *Phenomenology of Perception,* Merleau-Ponty maintained the perspective of perceiver perceiving content of perception. In fact, Merleau-Ponty found a way of interrogating perception beginning at the point, so to speak, where the perceiver-perceived structure originates. But this is not to say that Merleau-Ponty abandoned his earlier work as wrong because it is carried out from the perspective of perceiver perceiving content of perception. In fact, in the work after *Phenomenology of Perception,* Merleau-Ponty does not deny a perceiver-perceived structure. He finds a way of beginning where it originates. This is made possible by the disclosure of "reversibility." And this holds open the possibility of finding that "function that creates meanings and communicates them." For an extended discussion of this issue see my *Merleau-Ponty: Language and the Act of Speech* (Lewisburg, Pa.: Bucknell University Press, 1982).

8. Maurice Merleau-Ponty, *The Visible and the Invisible; Followed by Working Notes,* ed. C. Lefort, trans. A. Lingis (Evanston, Ill.: Northwestern University Press, 1968), pp. 147–148.

9. Ibid., p. 148.

10. Ibid., p. 129.

11. Ibid.

12. *Of Grammatology*, p. 6.

13. The issue is not whether one can establish "*l'écriture*" as the unspoken, or unwritten, of Merleau-Ponty's work, nor whether one can in some way appropriate Merleau-Ponty's writings for the work of Jacques Derrida, but rather how Merleau-Ponty's writings displace speech from a "purely intelligible" that would not rely at all on the sensible—indeed, how they point to "the trace" that is neither strictly of the visible nor strictly of the invisible, and in so doing undo what represses "*l'écriture*" by excluding it, as fallen away from a "purely intelligible," from the set margins of philosophy as metaphysics. That displacement permits an appearance of "*l'écriture*."

14. *The Visible and the Invisible*, p. 268.

15. See p. 198.

16. *Writing and Difference*, p. 77.

17. *The Visible and the Invisible*, p. 125.

18. Ibid.

19. The issue is not whether one can in some way recapture or reappropriate "*l'écriture*" for the work undertaken by Merleau-Ponty, but rather that if in seeking to unfix or liberate writing, Derrida would simply erase the interrogation of "the trace" that is begun in *The Visible and the Invisible*, *l'écriture* is ruled out, or to use Derrida's phrase, this means the death of writing.

20. *Writing and Difference*, p. 300.

16. DOCILE BODIES, REBELLIOUS BODIES: FOUCAULDIAN PERSPECTIVES ON FEMALE PSYCHOPATHOLOGY

An expanded version of this essay appears in *Gender/Body/Knowledge: Feminist Reconstructions of Being and Knowing*, eds. Alison Jaggar and Susan Bordo (New Jersey: Rutgers University Press, 1989) and is part of a larger cultural study, *The Body and the Reproduction of Gender* (Berkeley: University of California Press, forthcoming). Other pieces of my analysis of eating disorders have been developed in "Anorexia Nervosa: Psychopathology as the Crystallization of Culture" (*The Philosophical Forum* 17, no. 2 [Winter 1985]: 73–103), "Reading the Slender Body," in *Body/Politics: Women and the Discourses of Science*, eds. Mary Jacobus, Evelyn Fox Keller and Sally Shuttleworth (New York: Routledge, 1990: 83–112), and "The Feminist Challenge to the Concept of Pathology," in *The Body in Medical Thought and Practice*, ed. Drew Leder, (Kluwer, forthcoming).

I wish to thank Douglass College for the time and resources made available to me as the result of my visiting scholarship for the Laurie Chair in Women's Studies, Spring 1985. My time there, and my participation in the Women's Studies Seminar, greatly facilitated much of the initial research for this piece. Earlier versions of this paper were delivered at the philosophy department of State University of New York at Stony Brook and the University of Massachusetts conference on Histories of Sexuality. To all those who commented on those versions I express my appreciation for stimulating suggestions and helpful criticisms.

1. Pierre Bourdieu, *Outline of a Theory of Practice*, (Cambridge: Cambridge University Press, 1977), p. 94.

2. On our cultural obsession with slenderness, see Kim Chernin, *The Obsession* (New York: Harper and Row, 1981); Susie Ohrbach, *Hunger Strike* (New York: W. P. Norton, 1985) and Susan Bordo, "Anorexia Nervosa: Psychopathology as the Crystallization of Culture."

3. On "docility," see Michel Foucault, *Discipline and Punish* (New York: Vintage Books, 1979), pp. 135–169. For a Foucauldian analysis of feminine practice, see Sandra Bartky, "Foucault, Feminity and the Modernization of Patriarchal Power," in *Feminism and Foucault*, ed. Diamond and Quinby.

4. Over the last decade, there has been an undeniable increase in male concern over appearance. Study after study confirms, however, that there is still a large "gender gap" in this area. Research conducted at the University of Pennsylvania in 1985 found men to be generally satisfied with their appearance, often, in fact, "distorting their perceptions [of themselves] in a positive, self-aggrandizing way." ("Dislike of Own Bodies Found Common among Women," *New York Times*, March 19, 1985) Women, on the other hand, were found to exhibit extreme negative assessments and distortions of body perception. Other studies have suggested that women are judged more harshly than men when they deviate from dominant social standards of attractiveness. The April 1986 *Psychology Today* reports that, alhthough the situation for men has changed recently, the situation for women has more than proportionately worsened, too. Citing results from 30,000 responses to a 1985 survey of perceptions of body image, and comparing similar responses to a 1972 questionnaire, the magazine reports that the 1985 respondants were considerably more dissatisfied with their bodies than the 1972 respondants, and notes a marked intensification of concern among men. Among the 1985 group, the group most dissatisfied of all with their appearance, however, were teen-age women. Women today are by far the largest consumers of diet products, attenders of spas and diet centers, and subjects of intestinal by-pass and other fat reduction operations.

5. Michel Foucault, *Discipline and Punish*, p. 136.

6. On the "gendered" and historical nature of these disorders: the number of female to male hysterics has been estimated as anywhere from 2:1 to 4:1, whereas as many as 80 percent of all agoraphobics are female (Annette Brodsky

and Rachel Hare-Mustin, *Women and Psychotherapy* [New York: Guildford Press, 1980], pp. 116, 122). Although more cases of male eating disorders are being reported recently, it is estimated that close to 90 percent of all anorexics are female (Paul Garfinkel and David Garner, *Anorexia Nervosa: A Multidimensional Perspective* [New York: Brunner/Mazel, 1982], pp. 112–113). For a sociohistorical account of female psychopathology, with particular attention to nineteenth-century disorders (but having, unfortunately, little mention of agoraphobia or eating disorders), see Elaine Showalter, *The Female Malady* (New York: Pantheon Books, 1985.) For a discussion of social and gender issues in agoraphobia, see Robert Seidenberg and Karen DeCrow, *Women Who Marry Houses* (New York: McGraw-Hill, 1983.) On the clinical history of anorexia nervosa, see Garfinkel and Garner, *Anorexia Nervosa: A Multidimensional Perspective*.

7. There is evidence that in the case of eating disorders this is rapidly changing. Anorexia and bulimia, originally almost exclusively limited to upper- and upper-middle-class white families, are now touching ethnic populations (blacks, East Indians) previously unaffected, and all socioeconomic levels (Garfinkel and Garner, *Anorexia Nervosa*, pp. 102–103). In contemporary North America, no groups are exempt from the power of popular imaginery; it merely takes some time for fashions, for example, that appear in *Vogue* to make their way into J.C. Penney's catalogue.

8. See Garfinkel and Garner, *Anorexia Nervosa*, p. 100, for a list of studies suggestive of a striking increase in the frequency of eating disorders over the last twenty years. On the "epidemic" of hysteria and neurasthenia, see Showalter, *The Female Malady* and Carroll Smith-Rosenberg, *Disorderly Conduct* (Oxford: Oxford University Press, 1985).

9. On the "delicate lady," see Martha Vicinus, ed., *Suffer and Be Still* (Bloomington: Indiana University Press, 1972), esp. pp. x–xi. On medical and scientific conceptions of feminity, see Carol Nadelson and Malkah Notman, *The Female Patient* (New York: Plenum Press, 1982), p. 5; Vicinus, *Suffer and Be Still, p. 82; Peter Gay, The Bourgeois Experience, vol. 1 (New York: Oxford University Press, 1984); Showalter, The Female Malady.*
The delicate lady, an ideal that had very strong class connotations (as does slenderness today), is not the only conception of feminity to be found in Victorian cultures. But is was arguably the single most powerful ideological representation of feminity in that era, affecting women of all classes (including those without the material means to fully realize the ideal).

10. Smith-Rosenberg, *Disorderly Conduct*, p. 203.

11. Showalter, *The Female Malady*, p. 129.

12. Betty Friedan, *The Feminine Mystique,* (New York: Dell, 1962), p. 36.

13. I. G. Fodor, "The Phobic Syndrome in Women," in *Women in Therapy,* ed. V. Franks and V. Burtle (New York: Brunner/Mazel, 1975), p. 119. See also Kathleen Brehony, "Woman and Agoraphobia: A Case for the Etiological Signif-

icance of the Feminine Sex-Role Stereotype," in *The Steretyping of Women*, ed. Violet Frank and Esther Rothblum (New York: Springer, 1983).

14. The exploration of these multidetermined "axes" of the slenderness ideal is the full project within which this chapter is located; see Bordo, "Anorexia Nervosa: Psychopathology as the Crystallization of Culture," and "Reading the Slender Body." For other interpretive perspectives on the slenderness ideal, see Chernin, *The Obsession;* and Ohrbach, *Hunger Strike*.

15. The connection between traditional constructions of feminity and the control of female appetite is discussed in Helena Michie, *The Flesh Made Word* (New York: Oxford University Press, 1987).

16. Aimee Liu, *Solitaire* (New York: Harper and Row, 1979), p. 123.

17. Striking, in connection with this, is Catherine Steiner-Adair's 1984 study of high school women, which reveals a dramatic association between problems with food and body-image and emulation of the cool, professionally "together" *and* gorgeous "Superwoman." On the basis of a series of interviews, the high-schoolers were classified into two groups — one that expressed scepticism over the Superwoman ideal, the other that thoroughly aspired to it. Later administration of diagnostic tests revealed that 94 percent of the "superwomen" group fell into the eating disordered range of the scale; 100 percent of the other group fell into the non-eating disorder range. Media images notwithstanding, young women today appear to sense — either consciously or through their bodies — the impossibility of simultaneously meeting the demands of two spheres whose values have been historically defined in utter opposition to each other.

18. Bordo, "Anorexia Nervosa: Psychopathology as the Crystallization of Culture," pp. 86–87.

19. Dianne Hunter, "Hysteria, Psychoanalysis and Feminism," in *The [M]Other Tongue*, ed. Shirley Nelson Garner, Claire Kahane and Madelon Sprenger (New York: Cornell University Press, 1985), p. 114.

20. Catherine Clément and Hélène Cixous, *The Newly Born Woman*, trans. Betsy Wing (Minneapolis: University of Minnesota Press, 1986), p. 42.

21. Ibid., p. 95.

22. Charles Bernheimer and Claire Kahane, eds. *In Dora's Case: Freud-Hysteria-Feminism* (New York: Columbia University Press, 1985), p. 1.

23. Seidenberg and DeCrow, *Women Who Marry Houses*, p. 31.

24. Smith-Rosenberg, *Disorderly Conduct*, p. 208.

25. Ohrbach, *Hunger Strike*, p. 102. When one looks into the many autobiographies and case studies of hysterics, anorexics, and agoraphobics, one is struck by the fact that these are, indeed, the sorts of women one might expect to be frustrated by the constraints of a specified female role. Freud and Breuer, in

Studies on Hysteria (and Freud, in the later *Dora*) constantly remark on the ambition, independence, intellectual ability, and creative strivings of their patients. We know, moreover, that many of the women who would later go on to become the leading social activists and feminists of the nineteenth century were among those who fell ill with hysteria or neurasthenia. It has become a virtual cliche that the typical anorexic is a perfectionist, driven to excel in all areas of her life. Though less prominently, a similar theme runs throughout the literature on agoraphobia.

One must keep in mind that, in drawing on case studies, one is relying on the perceptions of other, acculturated individuals. One suspects, for example, that the popular portrait of the anorexic as a relentless "overachiever" may be colored by the lingering (or perhaps resurgent) Victorianism of our culture's attitudes toward ambitious women. One does not escape this hermeneutic problem by turning to autobiography; but in autobiography one is at least dealing with social constructions and attitudes that animate the subject's own psychic reality. In this regard the autobiographical literature on anorexia in particular is strikingly full of anxiety about the domestic world and other themes that suggest deep rebellion against traditional notions of feminity. See Bordo, "Anorexia Nervosa," pp. 87–90.

26. Kim Chernin, *The Hungry Self: Women, Eating and Identity* (New York: Harper and Row, 1985).

27. Liu, *Solitaire*, p. 36.

28. Bordo, "Anorexia Nervosa," p. 87. Liu's body symbolism is thoroughly continuous with dominant cultural associations. Brett Silverstein's studies testify empirically to what is obvious from every comedy routine involving a dramatically shapely woman: namely, our cultural association of curvaceousness and incompetence. ("Correlates of the Thin Standard of Bodily Attractiveness for Women," *International Journal of Eating Disorders,* forthcoming.) The anorexic is also quite aware of the social and sexual vulnerability involved in having a female body. Many, in fact, were sexually abused as children.

29. Showalter, *The Female Malady,* p. 48.

30. Smith-Rosenberg, *Disorderly Conduct,* p. 207.

31. Ohrbach, *Hunger Strike,* p. 000.

32. Susan Brownmiller, *Feminity* (New York: Fawcett Columbine, 1984).

33. Toril Moi, "Representations of Patriarchy: Sex and Epistemology in Freud's *Dora,*" in *In Dora's Case,* ed. Bernheimer and Kahane, p. 192.

34. "The Waist Land: Eating Disorders In America," 1985, Gannett Corporation, MTI Teleprograms.

35. "Fat or Not, Fourth-Grade Girls Diet Lest They Be Teased or Unloved," *Wall Street Journal* (February 11, 1986).

17. SEX, GENDER, AND THE POLITICS OF DIFFERENCE

1. Annie Leclerc, *Patrole de femme* (Paris: Grasset, 1974).

2. Christine Delphy, "Protofeminism and Antifeminism," in *Close to Home: A Materialist Analysis of Women's Oppression*, trans. and ed. Diana Leonard (Amherst: Unviersity of Massachusetts Press, 1984).

3. Annie Leclerc, *Hommes et femmes* (Paris: Grasset, 1985), pp. 73–74: "On admet sans doute un peu trop vite que ce sont des femmes qui luttent contre ou avec des hommes. Est-ce bien aux hommes qu'elles ont affaire? A ceux qui n'ont aucun pouvoir, ni scientifique, ni technique, ni économique, ni meme sexuel? Sont-ce des hommes ou pas? Dès qu'on sort de la réference strictement biologique de l'identité sexuelle physiquement repérable, il est bien difficile de savoir de quoi on parle."

4. Luce Irigaray, *Parler n'est jamais neutre* (Paris: Les Editions de Minuit, 1985), pp. 226–230.

5. Ibid., pp. 105–106; cf. Luce Irigaray, *Le langage des déments*, (the Hague: Mouton, 1973).

6. Julia Kristeva, "The Ethics of Linguistics," in *Desire in Language*, trans. Thomas Gora, Alice Jardine, and Léon S. Roudiez, ed. Léon S. Roudiez (New York: Columbia University Press, 1980). For a reply see Eleanor H. Kuykendall, "Questions for Julia Kristeva's Ethics of Linguistics," in *The Thinking Muse*, ed. Iris Young and Jeffner Allen (Bloomington: Indiana University Press, 1989).

7. Shoshana Felman, *The Literary Speech Act: Don Juan with J. L. Austin, or Seduction in Two Languages*, trans. Catherine Porter (Ithaca, N.Y.: Cornell University Press, 1983).

8. Luce Irigaray, *Ce sexe qui n'en est pas un* (Paris: Les Editions de Minuit, 1977).

9. Luce Irigaray, *This Sex Which Is Not One*, trans. Catherine Porter with Carolyn Burke (Ithaca, N.Y.: Cornell University Press, 1985).

10. Anne Healey and G. J. Judge, *A Reference Grammar of Modern French* (London: Edward Arnold, 1983), p. 57.

11. Monique Wittig, "The Mark of Gender," in *The Poetics of Gender*, ed. Nancy K. Miller (New York: Columbia University Press, 1987), pp. 68–69. Cf. an earlier version of the article published in *Feminist Issues* 5 (1985):5–6.

12. Healey and Judge, *A Reference Grammar*, pp. 70–71.

13. Luce Irigaray, *Ethique de la différence sexuelle* (Paris: Les Editions de Minuit, 1984), p. 130: "Les énoncés masculins sont généralement déjà transformés à la *troisième personne*. Le sujet s'y trouve masqué dans le monde, la vér-

ité. Mais cet univers est sa construction. Le *il* est une transformation, une transposition du *je*. Sorte d'effacement de l'énonciation dans un édifice de langage. Dénégation aussi de qui a produit cette grammaire, ce sens, et leurs règles."

14. Ibid., p. 128.

15. Ibid., pp. 100–108.

16. Irigaray, *Parler n'est jamais neutre*, p. 9.

17. Ibid., p. 10.

18. RATIONALITY, RELATIVISM, FEMINISM

1. I have written elsewhere about the project of grounding a unitary feminist standpoint. My essay, "The Feminist Standpoint: A Matter of Language," belongs to a growing body of theoretical work on this problem, mostly within the socialist-feminist tradition. See the work of Nancy Hartsock, Alison Jaggar, Iris Young, and, for an overview and analysis of the state of the art, Sandra Harding, "The Instability of the Analytical Categories of Feminist Theory," *Signs: Journal of Women in Culture and Society* 11 (1986):645–664.

2. Geneviève Lloyd, *The Man of Reason* (Minneapolis: University of Minnesota Press, 1984).

3. Ian Hacking, "Language, Truth, and Reason," in *Rationality and Relativism,* ed. Martin Hollis and Steven Lukes, (Cambridge, Mass.: MIT Press, 1982), pp. 48–66.

4. Barry Barnes and David Bloor, "Relativism, Rationalism, and the Sociology of Knowledge," in *Rationality and Relativism,* ed. Martin Hollis and Steven Lukes (Cambridge, Mass.: MIT Press, 1982), p. 27.

5. In my view, political, epistemological, and philosophical commitments are three discriminable, though overlapping, facets of the commitments we make — explicitly or implicitly — as feminists. Any commitment to relativism is thus multifaceted, and distinctions among relativisms can occur as philosophical distinctions, as more specifically epistemological distinctions, or as political distinctions. Moreover, these distinctions cut across those due to subject matter, such as that between relativism about rationality and relativism in ethics. They also cut across distinctions due to domain of contrast, such as the distinction between cultural relativism and gender relativism. For more discussion of these distinctions between philosophical stance, political standpoint, and epistemological perspective, see my "The Feminist Standpoint: A Matter of Language," *Hypatia: A Journal of Feminist Philosophy* 2, no. 1 (1987):123–148; and "When and How to Be Intelligible and Unintelligible," unpublished manuscript of a talk to the American Philosophical Association, April 1985.

6. Evelyn Fox Keller, *A Feeling for the Organism* (San Francisco: W. H. Freeman, 1983). Keller's account of this marginalization is that McClintock did not pursue the methods of the new molecular biology, continuing to consider organisms as whole individuals rather than as collections of chemicals. This is a resistance, on McClintock's part, of the tendencies toward reductionism in the life sciences. But this reductionism is itself imbued with the notion that the closer a theory is to the physical sciences, the more objective the theory can be. Thus I do not think that I am diverging very much from Keller's own interpretation.

7. In my way of thinking about the turn from traditional epistemology, it is important to acknowledge the influence not only of Strawson, but also of Stanley Cavell and of Richard Rorty. Through the influence of Naomi Scheman, I have come to formulate issues facing feminist philosophy in terms of a feminist turn. See her "Othello's Doubt/Desdemona's Death: The Engendering of Scepticism," in *Power, Gender, Values,* ed. Judith Genova (Edmonton, Alberta: Academic Printing and Publishing, 1987). The question for feminist philosophy is whether the feminist turn can be more effective than the linguistic turn in overturning traditional epistemology.

8. P. F. Strawson, *Skepticism and Naturalism: Some Varieties* (New York: Columbia University Press, 1985).

9. It seems that Aristotle himself offered an argument of this sort to show that philosophizing is inescapable. It occurs, as a fragment of the *Protrepticus,* in Alexander's commentary on the *Topics:* "for instance, if someone should say that it is not necessary to philosophize, since searching for this very thing, whether one ought to philosophize or indeed not philosophize, is called philosophizing (as [Aristotle] says in the Protrepticus), as well as pursuing philosophical contemplation" ("Protrepticus fragment 2." in Ross, *Aristotelis fragmenta selecta;* see Barnes's revised Oxford translation, vol. 2, p. 2404). I am indebted to Robin Smith for remarking on this similarity and pointing me to the text.

10. These questions, considered rhetorically, suggest a way to characterize the Lacan-influenced French feminists: they offer a philosophical stance committed to the centrality of theory of gendered knowledge.

11. Iris Young has pointed out that, on my account, gender theory cannot consist in the speaking of specifically female experience. Our disagreement is not so pointed as it might appear. I do not deny the significance for gender theory of women's taking the floor and speaking specifically female experience. I take it to be a political project to empower women to speak in this way. But the successes of this political project, in my account, are data for gender theory and not to be identified with gender theory itself. Perhaps, if we women spoke with one voice it would be fine to conflate our speaking with the theoretical product of our making sense of what we say. But we do not have a single voice, and this is just the problem that gives rise to a specifically philosophical enterprise in coming to terms with gender.

12. Barbara Smith, *Home Girls: A Black Feminist Anthology* (New York: Kitchen Table, Women of Color Press, 1983).

13. Barbara Smith, "Home," in ibid., pp. 67–68. See also Barbara Smith and Beverly Smith, "Across the Kitchen Table: A Sister-to-Sister Dialogue," in *This Bridge Called My Back,* ed. Cherrie Moraga and Gloria Anzaldua (Watertown, Mass.: Persephone Press, 1981).

14. For many kinds of help with this essay, I am grateful to the Philosophy Department and the Women's Studies Program of the University of Colorado at Boulder, to the students in my Fall 1986 seminar on naturalism, to students in the 1987 feminism and philosophy tutorial at Wesleyan University, and to Harriette Andreadis, Dorothy Leland, Joe Rouse, Michael Stocker, Ken Westphal, and Iris Young.

20. THE POLITICAL ORIGINS OF DEMOCRACY

This is my English translation of a paper originally presented in French at the Toronto SPEP meeting, whose revised version was published in *La Lettre International* (Paris), no. 15 (January 1988).

1. Claude Lefort, *L'invention démocratique. Les limites de la domination totalitaire* (Paris: Fayard, 1981). Lefort's analysis of the relation of totalitarianism and democracy can only be alluded to in the present context. For a fuller discussion, cf., *The Marxian Legacy* (Minneapolis: University of Minnesota Press, 1988), and especially the Afterword to the second edition.

2. The parenthetical suggestion that the Socialist victory of 1981 may have ended this secular history of the Revolution is due to Jacques Julliard. See *Defining the Political* (London: Macmillan; and Minneapolis: University of Minnesota Press, 1988).
Furet writes that "The history of the French nineteenth century in its entirety can be considered as the history of a struggle between the Revolution and the Restoration across episodes dated 1815, 1830, 1848, 1851, 1870, the Commune, the 16th of May 1877. Only the victory of the republicans over the monarchists at the beginning of the Third Republic marks the definitive victory of the Revolution in the depths of the country: the lay teacher of Jules Ferry, the missionary of the values of '89, is the symbol more than the instrument of that long victorious battle. The integration of the villages and peasantry of France into the republican nation through the principles of '89 would have taken at least a century." *Penser la Révolution Francaise* (Paris: Gallimard, 1978), pp. 16–17. But this is only the victory of the principles of 1789; for the more radical, "the" revolution could be identified with the Rousseauian-Jacobin dream which remained, or remains, alive in the dream of a socialist or communist revolution. On the implications of Furet's argument, see my essay on "The Origins of Revolution," *Journal of the British Society for Phenomenology,* vol. 14, no. 1, January, 1983, reprinted in *The Politics of Critique,* and Claude Lefort's "Penser la Révolution dans la Révolution Française," in *Essais sur le politique* (Paris: Seuil, 1986).

3. The concept is elaborated by Claude Lefort's essay on Tocqueville, to which I shall refer in a moment. Its philosophical basis is formulated by Merleau-Ponty's phenomenological ontology. My claim is that this relation is specific to modernity, and that its elaboration depends on the presence of the political as the horizon which gives sense to this unity-in-difference.

4. *Rechtsphilosophie,* Paragraphs 258, 260, translation mine.

5. "Réversibilité: Liberté politique et liberté de l'individu," in *Essais sur le politique;* English translation in *Telos,* no. 63 (Fall 1985).

6. Habermas's position is articulated systematically in his *Theorie des kommunikativen Handeln* and numerous articles; Gorz's in *Adieu au proletariat* and numerous more recent articles; Ferguson and Cohen's in *On Democracy;* and Laclau and Mouffe's in *Hegemony and Socialist Strategy.* Habermas and Gorz's theories are analyzed in the Afterword to the second edition of *The Marxian Legacy;* Laclau and Mouffe's in "Another Resurrection of Marxism" in *Defining the Political.* Ferguson and Cohen's is muckraking for the most part; theoretically its application of "Rawlsianism" adds nothing to the political debate because its "Kantian constructivism" operates still within the world defined by the first two *Critiques.*

7. Cf., William R. Everdell, *The End of Kings. A History of Republics and Republicans* (New York: Free Press, 1983). Everdell begins his analysis with Samuel and Solon and carries it through the Watergate affair. The popular, biographical, and narrative form of his account does not invalidate its main theoretical argument. The abuses Everdell sees in the Nixon administration have recurred in the recent debacle of the Reagan administration; cf. *Defining the Political,* ch. 17.

8. This is of course the accusation of the "progressive historians," expressed classically in 1913 by Charles Beard's *An Economic Interpretation of the Constitution.* Beard tries to show how the Framers wrote a document whose defense of the interests of the minority was intended to protect private property from the hands of the citizenry who might revolt against *social* domination.

21. ART AND DEMOCRACY IN HABERMAS

1. J. Habermas, *Der philosophische Diskurs der Moderne* (Frankfurt: Suhrkamp, 1985); hereinafter cited as PDM. Cf. the Appendix, "Exkurs zur Einebnung des Gattungsunterschiedes zwischen Philosphie und Literatur," particularly pp. 243–247.

2. PDM, p. 373.

3. See Gérard Raulet's note to his translation, "La modernité: un projet inachevé," *Critique* 413 (October 1981):968–969. Martin Jay, "Habermas and

Modernism'' in *Habermas and Modernity*, ed. R. J. Bernstein (Cambridge Mass.: MIT Press 1985), pp. 125–139. Finally, Richard J. Bernstein "Introduction," *Habermas and Modernity*, p. 28.

4. PDM, p. 7 (translation and italics ours).

5. See among others *Erkenntnis und Interesse*. (Frankfurt: Suhrkamp, 1973), p. 311.

6. J. Habermas, "Vorbereitende Bemerkungen zu einer Theorie der kommunikativen Kompetenz," *Theorie der Gesellschaft oder Sozialtechnologie*, with N. Luhmann. (Frankfurt: Suhrkamp, 1971), pp. 101–141.

7. For this change in "paradigm" and its consequences for the concept of classical critical theory, see our "Entre la philosophie et la science: Le reconstructionnisme herméneutique de J. Habermas," *Dialogue* 25 (Spring 1986):119–142.

8. J. Habermas, *Philosophisch-politische Profile* (Frankfurt: Suhrkamp, 1981, enlarged edition), p. 12; hereinafter cited as PPP.

9. J. Habermas, "Die Moderne — ein unvollendetes Projekt" in *Kleine politische Schriften I–IV* (Frankfurt: Suhrkamp, 1981), p. 454. Our translation was inspired by the shorter English version of this lecture by S. Ben-Habib under the title "Modernity versus Postmodernity," *New German Critique* 22 (Winter 1981):9.

10. J. Habermas, *Theorie des kommunikativen Handelns* (Frankfurt: Suhrkamp, 1981), vol. 2, p. 585.

11. J. Habermas "Die Moderne," p. 453.

12. J. Habermas, "Questions and Counterquestions," in *Habermas and Modernity*, p. 200.

13. Ibid., p. 201.

14. J. Habermas, "Rekonstruktive vs. verstehende Sozialwissenschaften," *Moralbewusstsein und kommunikatives Handeln* (Frankfurt: Suhrkamp, 1983), p. 40.

15. J. Habermas, *Strukturwandel der Öffentlichkeit* (Neuwied and Berlin: Luchterhand, 1976), pp. 52–53. By the same author see "Über Kunst und Revolution," in *PPP*, pp. 261, 264. Cf. also by the same author "Ein Interview mit der New Left Review," in *Die neue Unübersichtlichkeit* (Frankfurt: Suhrkamp, 1985), p. 240.

16. J. Habermas, *Theorie des kommunikativen Handelns*, vol. 1, p. 41 (cited from Thomas McCarthy's translation, *The Theory of Communicative Action: Volume 1*, p. 20). On the following page, Habermas speaks of an "authentic work," which is something entirely different!

17. PDM, p. 366 (translation ours). Cf. A. Wellmer, "Wahrheit, Schein und Versöhnung," now in *Zur Dialektik von Moderne und Postmoderne* (Frankfurt: Suhrkamp, 1985), among others pp. 31, 36.

18. J. Habermas, "Die Moderne," p. 460. For an analysis of certain difficulties arising from H.-R. Jauss's aesthetics of reception, see our "Expérience esthétique et herméneutique philosophique," in *Texte* 3 (Toronto, 1984), pp. 179–191. See also H.-R. Jauss, "Réponse à Claude Piché" in ibid., pp. 193–201.

19. PDM, p. 64. Cf. A. Wellmer, "Reason, Utopia, and Enlightenment," in *Habermas and Modernity*, p. 63.

20. J. Habermas, "Questions and Counterquestions," p. 201.

21. Ibid.

22. PDM, p. 245.

23. J. Habermas, "Die Philosophie als Platzhalter und Interpret" [1981], in *Moralbewusstsein und kommunikatives Handeln*, pp. 25–26. See also the Preface to the 1981 edition of PPP, p. 12.

24. J. Habermas, "Questions and Counterquestions," pp. 200, 201.

25. J. Habermas, *Legitimationsprobleme im Spätkapitalismus* (Frankfurt: Suhrkamp, 1975), p. 110. On this subject also see Peter Bürger's *Theorie der Avantgarde* (Frankfurt: Suhrkamp, 1974), p. 33.

26. J. Habermas, "Einleitung zum Band 1000 der edition suhrkamp" [1979], in *Kleine politische Schriften I–IV*, p. 435. For an opposing viewpoint, see T. W. Adorno, *Ästhetische Theorie* (Frankfurt: Suhrkamp, 1977), p. 489.

27. T. W. Adorno, *Ästhetische Theorie* (cited from the translation by C. Lenhardt [London: Routledge and Kegan Paul, 1984], pp. 199–200).

28. J. Habermas, "Questions and Counterquestions," p. 200.

29. J. Habermas, "Die Moderne," p. 456.

30. Ibid., pp. 453, 454.

31. Ibid., pp. 455, 456, 458.

32. E. Kant, *Kritik der Urteilskraft* (Hamburg: Meiner, 1968), p. 118.

33. J. Habermas, "Die Moderne," p. 456.

34. J. Habermas, "Die Philosophie als Platzhalter und Interpret," p. 25. (See now J. Habermas "Heinrich Heine und die Rolle des Intellektuellen in Deutschland" [1986] in *Eine Art Schadensabwicklung* [Frankfurt: Suhrkamp, 1987], pp. 41–42.)

22. THE FUTURE OF CONTINENTAL PHILOSOPHY

1. Martin Heidegger, *Nietzsche* (Pfullingen: Neske, 1961), vol. 2, p. 390.

2. Martin Heidegger, *Vier Seminare* (Frankfurt: Klostermann, 1977), p. 121.

3. Ibid.

4. Ibid., p. 58.

5. Ibid., p. 121.

6. Ibid., p. 122.

7. Ibid., p. 128.

8. *Vorträge und Aufsätze* (Pfullingen: Neske, 1954), p. 54.

9. *Was Heisst Denken* (Tübingen: Niemeyer 1954), p. 9.

10. *What Calls for Thinking?* trans. Fred D. Wieck and J. Glenn Gray (New York: Harper and Row, 1968), p. 207.

11. *Vier Seminare*, p. 68.

12. *Hölderlins Hymne "Andenken,"* (Frankfurt: Klostermann, 1982), p. 194.

13. Ibid., p. 165.

14. *What Calls for Thinking?* p. 139: "Das anfängliche Wort der 'Gedanc' sagt das gesammelte, alles versammelnde Gedenken. 'Der Gedanc' sagt soviel wie das Gemüt, der muot, das Herz."

15. *Poetry, Language, Thought,* trans. A. Hofstadter (New York: Harper and Row, 1971), p. 181.

16. *Early Greek Thinking,* trans. David Farrell Krell and Frank Capuzzi (New York: Harper and Row, 1975), p. 53.

17. *Deutsche Predigten und Traktate* (München: Carl Hanser Verlag, 1955), p. 273. *Nolite timere eos.*

24. TRANSLATING THE DIFFERENCES: THE FUTURES OF CONTINENTAL PHILOSOPHY

1. Jacques Derrida, "Violence and Metaphysics: An Essay on the Thought of Emmanuel Levinas," *Writing and Difference* (Chicago: University of Chicago Press, 1978), p. 79.

Bibliography

Adorno, Theodor. *Aesthetic Theory,* trans. C. Lenhardt, ed. Gretel Adorno and Rolf Tiedemann. London: Routledge and Kegan Paul, 1984.

Adorno, Theodor. *Minima Moralia: Reflections from Damaged Life,* trans. E. F. N. Jephcott. London: New Left Books, 1974.

Adorno, Theodor. *Negative Dialectics,* trans. E. B. Ashton. New York: Seabury Press, 1973.

Anderson, Thomas C. *The Foundation and Structure of Sartrean Ethics.* Lawrence: University of Kansas Press, 1979.

Ascher, Carol. *Simone de Beauvoir: A Life of Freedom.* Boston: Beacon Press, 1981.

Avineri, Shlomo. "A Note on Hegel's Views on Jewish Emancipation." *Jewish Social Studies* 25 (1963):141-151.

Barthes, Roland. "From Work to Text." In *Image-Music-Text,* trans. Stephen Heath, pp. 155-164. New York: Hill and Wang, 1977.

Barthes, Roland. *Recherche de Proust.* Paris: Seuil, 1980.

Bell, Linda. "Loser Wins: The Importance of Play in a Sartrean Ethics of Authenticity." In *Phenomenology in a Pluralistic Context,* ed. William McBride and Calvin O. Schrag. Albany: SUNY Press, 1983.

Bell, Linda. *Sartre's Ethics of Authenticity.* University: University of Alabama Press, 1989.

Ben-Habib, Seyla. "Modernity versus Postmodernity." *New German Critique,* 22 (Winter 1981).

Bernheimer, Charles, and Claire Kahane, eds. *In Dora's Case: Freud-Hysteria-Feminism.* New York: Columbia University Press, 1985.

Bernstein, Richard. *Praxis and Action.* Philadelphia: University of Pennsylvania Press, 1971.

Bernstein, Richard, ed. *Habermas and Modernity.* Cambridge: MIT Press, 1985.

Bordo, Susan. "Anorexia Nervosa: Psychopathology as the Crystallization of Culture." *The Philosophical Forum* 17, no. 2 (Winter 1985):73-103.

Bordo, Susan. *The Flight to Objectivity: Essays on Cartesianism and Culture.* Albany: SUNY Press, 1987.

Bordo, Susan, and Alison Jaggar, eds. *Gender/Body/Knowledge: Feminist Reconstructions of Being and Knowing.* New Brunswick: Rutgers University Press, 1989.

Bourdieu, Pierre. *Outline of a Theory of Practice*. Cambridge: Cambridge University Press, 1977.

Bowman, Elizabeth, and Robert Stone. "Dialectical Ethics: A First Look at Sartre's Unpublished *1964 Rome Lecture Notes.*" *Social Text*, 13–14 (Winter–Spring 1986):195–215.

Bowman, Elizabeth, and Robert Stone. "Sartre's *Investigations for a Morality:* A First Look at the Notes for the 1965 Cornell Lectures." In: *Sartre Today*, ed. Ronald Aronson and Adrien Van Den Hoven. Detroit: Wayne State University Press, 1988.

Brehony, Kathleen. "Women and Agoraphobia: A Case for the Etiological Significance of the Feminine Sex-Role Stereotype." In *The Stereotyping of Women*, ed. Violet Frank and Esther Rothblum. New York: Springer, 1983.

Brodsky, Annette, and Rachel Hare-Mustin. *Women and Psychotherapy*. New York: Guildford Press, 1980.

Brownmiller, Susan. *Femininity*. New York: Fawcett Columbine, 1984.

Camus, Albert. *The Myth of Sysiphus and Other Essays*. New York: Random House, 1984.

Charmé, Stuart. "From Maoism to the Talmud (With Sartre Along the Way): An Interview with Benny Lévy." *Commentary* 78, no. 6 (December 1984):48–53.

Chernin, Kim. *The Hungry Self: Women, Eating and Identity*. New York: Harper and Row, 1985.

Chernin, Kim. *The Obsession*. New York: Harper and Row, 1981.

Clément, Catherine and Hélène Cixous. *The Newly Born Woman*, trans. Betsy Wing. Minneapolis: University of Minnesota Press, 1986.

Contat, Michel, and Michel Rybalka. *The Writings of Jean Paul Sartre*, trans. Richard C. McCleary. Evanston: Northwestern University Press, 1974.

Contier, Fernande, and Claude Francis. *Simone de Beauvoir: A Life*, trans. Lisa Nesselson. New York: St. Martin's Press, 1987.

Davidson, Donald. *Essays on Actions and Events*. Oxford: Oxford University Press, 1980.

de Beauvoir, Simone. *Adieu: A Farewell to Sartre*, trans. Patrick O'Brian. New York: Pantheon Books, 1984.

de Beauvoir, Simone. *All Said and Done*, trans. Patrick O'Brian. New York: J. P. Putnam, 1974.

de Beauvoir, Simone. *The Ethics of Ambiguity*, trans. Bernard Frechtman. New York: Citadel Press, 1970.

de Beauvoir, Simone. *Force of Circumstance*, trans. Richard Howard. New York: Harper Colophon Books, 1964.

de Beauvoir, Simone. *Memoirs of a Dutiful Daughter*, trans. James Kirkup. New York: Harper Colophon Books, 1974.

de Beauvoir, Simone. *The Prime of Life*, trans. Peter Green. Cleveland: Meridian Books, 1962.

de Beauvoir, Simone. *The Second Sex*, trans. H. M. Parshley. New York: Vintage Books, 1974.

de Saussure, Ferdinand. *Course in General Linguistics*, ed. Charles Bally and Albert Sechehaye, trans. Wade Baskin. New York: Philosophical Library, 1959.

Deleuze, Gilles. *Proust and Signs*. New York: Georges Braziller, 1972.

Delphy, Christine. "Protofeminism and Antifeminism." In *Close to Home: A Materialist Analysis of Women's Oppression*, trans. Diana Leonard. Amherst: University of Massachusetts Press, 1984.

Derrida, Jacques. "Deconstruction and the Other: Dialogue with Jacques Derrida." In *Dialogues with Contemporary Continental Thinkers*, ed. Richard Kearney. Manchester: Manchester University Press, 1984.

Derrida, Jacques. *Dissemination*, trans. Barbara Johnson. Chicago: University of Chicago Press, 1981.

Derrida, Jacques. *Margins of Philosophy*, trans. Alan Bass. Chicago: University of Chicago Press, 1982.

Derrida, Jacques. *Of Grammatology*, trans. Gayatri Chakrovorty Spivak. Baltimore: John Hopkins University Press, 1976.

Derrida, Jacques. *Positions*, trans. Alan Bass. Chicago: University of Chicago Press, 1981.

Derrida, Jacques. *Speech and Phenomena*, trans. David B. Allison. Evanston: Northwestern University Press, 1973.

Derrida, Jacques. *Writing and Difference*, trans. Alan Bass. Chicago: University of Chicago, 1978.

Diamond, Irene, and Lee Quinby, eds. *Feminism and Foucault: Reflections on Resistance*. Boston: Northeastern University Press, 1988.

Dillon, M. C. *Merleau-Ponty's Ontology*. Bloomington: Indiana University Press, 1988.

Donougho, Martin. "The Semiotics of Hegel." *Clio* 11, no. 4 (1982).

Dunning, Stephen. *Kierkegaard's Dialectic of Inwardness: A Structural Analysis of the Theory of Stages*. Princeton: Princeton University Press, 1985.

Elrod, John William. "Climacus, Anti-Climacus and the Problem of Suffering." *Thought*, 60 (1980):303–319.

Evans, Mary. *Simone de Beauvoir: A Feminist Mandarin*. London: Tavistock, 1985.

Evans, Stephen. *Kierkegaard's Fragments and the Postscript: The Religious Philosophy of Johannes Climacus*. Atlantic Highlands, N.J.: Humanities Press, 1983.

Everdell, William. *The End of Kings. A History of Republics and Republicans*. New York: Free Press, 1983.

Fackenheim, Emil. *Encounters between Judaism and Modern Philosophy*. New York: Basic Books, 1973.

Fackenheim, Emil. *The Religious Dimension in Hegel's Thought*. Bloomington: Indiana University Press, 1967.

Felman, Shoshana. *The Literary Speech Act: Dan Juan with J. L. Austin, or Seduction in Two Languages*, trans. Catherine Porter. Ithaca: Cornell University Press, 1983.

Fine, Richard. *The Shaky Game: Einstein Realism and the Quantum Theory*. Chicago: University of Chicago Press, 1986.

Fodor, I. G. "The Phobic Syndrome in Women." In *Women in Therapy*, ed. V. Franks and V. Burtle. New York: Brunner/Mazel, 1974.

Foucault, Michel. *Discipline and Punish*, trans. Alan Sheridan. New York: Vintage Books, 1979.

Frankfurt, Henry. "The Principle of Alternate Possibilities." *The Journal of Philosophy* 66, no. 23 (1969):829–839.

Friedan, Betty. *The Feminine Mystique*. New York: Dell Publishing, 1963.

Froman, Wayne. *Merleau-Ponty: Language and the Act of Speech*. Lewisburg, PA.: Bucknell University Press, 1982.

Gadamer, Hans Georg. *Hegel's Dialectic*, trans. P. Christopher Smith. New Haven: Yale University Press, 1976.

Gadamer, Hans-Georg. "Being, Spirit, God." In *Heidegger Memorial Lectures*, ed. Werner Marx, trans. Steven W. Davis. Pittsburgh: Duquesne University Press, 1982.

Garfinkel, Paul, and David Garner. *Anorexia Nervosa: A Multidimensional Perspective*. New York: Bruner/Mazel, 1982.

Gay, Peter. *The Bourgeois Experience*. New York: Oxford University Press, 1984.

Habermas, Jürgen. *Communication and the Evolution of Society*, trans. Thomas McCarthy. Boston: Beacon Press, 1979.

Habermas, Jürgen. *Legitimation Crisis*, trans. Thomas McCarthy. Boston: Beacon Press, 1976.

Habermas, Jürgen. *The Theory of Communicative Action*, trans. Thomas McCarthy. Boston: Beacon Press, 1984.

Hacking, Ian. "Language, Truth and Reason." In *Rationality and Relativism*, ed. Martin Hollis and Steven Lukes. Cambridge: MIT Press, 1982.

Harding, Sandra. "The Instability of the Analytical Categories of Feminist Theory." *Signs: Journal of Women in Culture and Society* 2 (1986):645–664.

Hartmann, Klaus. "Towards a New Systematic Reading of Hegel's *Philosophy of Right*." In *The State and Civil Society: Studies in Hegel's Political Philosophy*, ed. Z. A. Pelczynski. Cambridge: Cambridge University Press.

Harvey, Irene. *Derrida and the Economy of Differance*. Bloomington: Indiana University Press, 1986.

Hegel, G. W. F. *The Difference Between Fichte's and Schelling's Conception of Philosophy*, ed. H. S. Harris and Walter Cerf. Albany: SUNY Press, 1977.

Hegel, G. W. F. *Hegel's Lectures on the History of Philosophy*, trans. E. S. Haldane and Frances H. Simson. London: Routledge and Kegan Paul, 1896.

Hegel, G. W. F. *Hegel's Philosophy of Mind*, trans. William Wallace and A. V. Miller. Oxford: Clarendon, 1971.

Hegel, G. W. F. *Hegel's Science of Logic*, trans. A. V. Miller. London: George Allen and Unwin, 1969.

Hegel, G. W. F. *The Phenomenology of Spirit*, trans. A. V. Miller. New York: Oxford University Press, 1977.

Hegel, G. W. F. *The Philosophy of History*, trans. J. Sibree. New York: Dover Books, 1956.

Heidegger, Martin. *Being and Time*, trans. John Macquarrie and Edward Robinson. New York: Harper and Row, 1962.

Heidegger, Martin. *An Introduction to Metaphysics*, trans. Ralph Manheim. New York: Doubleday Books, 1961.

Heidegger, Martin. "Letter on Humanism." In *Basic Writings*, ed. and trans. David Farrell Krell. New York: Harper and Row, 1977.

Heidegger, Martin. *On the Way to Language*, trans. Peter Hertz. New York: Harper and Row, 1971.

Heidegger, Martin. *Poetry Language Thought*, trans. Albert Hofstadter. New York: Harper and Row, 1971.

Heidegger, Martin. *Schelling's Treatise on the Essence of Human Freedom*, trans. Joan Stambaugh. Athens: University of Ohio Press, 1985.

Horkheimer, Max. *Eclipse of Reason*. New York: Seabury Press, 1974.

Howard, Dick. *Defining the Political*. London: Macmillan and Minneapolis: University of Minnesota Press, 1988.

Howard, Dick. *The Marxian Legacy*, 2d ed. Minneapolis: University of Minnesota Press, 1988.

Howard, Dick. *The Politics of Critique*. Minneapolis: University of Minnesota Press, 1988.

Howard, Richard. "Reversibility: Political Liberty and the Liberty of the Individual." *Telos*, 63 (Fall 1985).

Hunter, Dianne. "Hysteria, Psychoanalysis and Feminism." In *The [M]Other Tongue*. New York: Cornell University Press, 1985.

Irigaray, Luce. *This Sex Which Is Not One*, trans. Catherine Porter with Carolyn Burke. Ithaca: Cornell University Press, 1985.

Jacobus, Mary, Evelyn Fox Keller, and Sally Shuttleworth, eds. *Women, Science and the Body Politic: Discourses and Representations*. New York: Routledge, 1990.

Jeanson, Francis. *Sartre and the Problem of Morality*, trans. Robert C. Stone. Bloomington: Indiana University Press, 1980.

Keefe, Terry. *Simone de Beauvoir: A Study of Her Writings*. Totowa, N.J.: Barnes and Noble Books, 1983.

Keller, Evelyn Fox. *A Feeling for the Organism*. San Francisco: W. H. Freeman, 1983.

Kierkegaard, Søren. *The Concept of Anxiety*, trans. Reidar Thomte. Princeton: Princeton University Press, 1980.

Kierkegaard, Søren. *Concluding Unscientific Postscript to the Philosophical Fragments*, trans. David F. Swenson. Princeton: Princeton University Press, 1941.

Kierkegaard, Søren. *Either/Or: A Fragment of Life*, trans. Walter Lowrie. New York: Anchor Books, 1959.

Kierkegaard, Søren. *Fear and Trembling/Repetition*, trans. Edna and Howard V. Hong. Princeton: Princeton University Press, 1983.

Kierkegaard, Søren. *Fear and Trembling and the Sickness unto Death*, trans. Walter Lowrie. New York: Doubleday Anchor Books, 1954.

Kierkegaard, Søren. *The Gospel of Suffering and The Lilies of the Field*, trans. David and Lillian Swenson. Minneapolis: Augsburg Publishing House, 1948.

Kierkegaard, Søren. *The Present Age*, trans. Alexander Dru. New York: Harper and Row, 1962.

Kierkegaard, Søren. *Philosophical Fragments/Johannes Climacus*, trans. Edna and Howard Hong. Princeton: Princeton University Press, 1985.

Kierkegaard, Søren. *The Point of View for My Work as an Author,* trans. Walter Lowrie. New York: Harper and Row, 1962.

Kierkegaard, Søren. *Purity of Heart Is to Will One Thing,* trans. Douglas v. Steere. New York: Harper and Row, 1938.

Kierkegaard, Søren. *Søren Kierkegaard's Journals and Papers,* ed. and trans. Edna and Howard Hong. Bloomington: Indiana University Press, 1967–78.

Kierkegaard, Søren. *Training in Christianity,* trans. Walter Lowrie. Princeton: Princeton University Press, 1944.

Kockelmans, Joseph. *On the Truth of Being.* Bloomington: Indiana University Press, 1984.

Kristeva, Julia. *Desire in Language,* trans. Thomas Gora, Alice Jardine, and Leon Roudiez. New York: Columbia University Press, 1980.

Kruks, Sonia. "Sartre's *Cahiers pour une morale:* Failed Attempt or New Trajectory in Ethics?" *Social Text,* nos. 13–14 (Winter–Spring 1986):186–187.

Kuykendall, Eleanor. "Questions for Julia Kristeva's Ethics of Linguistics." In *The Thinking Muse,* eds. Iris Young and Jeffner Allen. Bloomington: Indiana University Press, 1989.

Le Doeuff, Michèle. "Simone de Beauvoir and Existentialism." *Feminist Studies* 6 (1980):277–289.

Liu, Aimée. *Solitaire.* New York: Harper and Row, 1979.

Lloyd, Geneviève. *The Man of Reason.* Minneapolis: University of Minnesota Press, 1984.

Lyotard, Jean François. *The Postmodern Condition,* trans. Geoff Bennington. Minneapolis: University of Minnesota Press, 1984.

MacIntyre, Alasdair. *After Virtue.* Notre Dame: University of Notre Dame Press, 1984.

Marcuse, Herbert. *Counterrevolution and Revolt.* Boston: Beacon Press, 1983.

Marcuse, Herbert. "Sartre's Existentialism." In *Studies in Critical Philosophy,* trans. Joris de Bres. Boston: Beacon Press, 1972.

Marcuse, Herbert. "The Reification of the Proletariat." *Canadian Journal of Political and Social Theory* 3 (Winter 1979):20–23.

Marx, Werner. *Heidegger and the Tradition,* trans. Theodore Kisiel. Evanston: Northwestern University Press, 1971.

McCumber, John. "Authenticity and Interaction: the Account of Communication in *Being and Time.*" *Tulane Studies in Philosophy,* 32 (1984):45–52.

McCumber, John. "Hegel's Anarchistic Utopia." *Southern Journal of Philosophy* 22 (1982):203–210.

McCumber, John. "Hegel's Philosophical Languages." *Hegel Studien* 14 (1979):183–196.

McCumber, John. "Language and Appropriation: The Way of Heideggerian Dialogue." *The Personalist* 60 (1979):344–396.

McMahon, Joseph. *Human Being: The World of Jean Paul Sartre.* Chicago: University of Chicago Press, 1971.

Merleau-Ponty, Maurice. *Phenomenology of Perception,* trans. Colin Smith. London: Routledge and Kegan Paul, 1962.

Merleau-Ponty, Maurice. *The Prose of the World,* ed. Claude Lefort, trans. John O'Neill. Evanston: Northwestern University Press, 1973.

Merleau-Ponty, Maurice. "Sartre and Ultrabolshevism." In *Adventures of the Dialectic,* trans. Joseph Bien. Evanston: Northwestern University Press, 1973.

Merleau-Ponty, Maurice. *The Visible and the Invisible,* ed. Claude Lefort, trans. Alphonso Lingis. Evanston: Northwestern University Press, 1968.

Michie, Helena. *The Flesh Made Word.* New York: Oxford University Press, 1987.

Mills, Patricia. "Man-Made Motherhood and Other Sleights of Hand." *Phenomenology + Pedagogy* 3, no. 3 (1986).

Mills, Patricia. *Woman, Nature and Psyche.* New Haven: Yale University Press, 1987.

Nadelson, Carol, and Malkah Notman. *The Female Patient.* New York: Plenum Press, 1982.

Nicholson, Graeme. "Heidegger on Thinking." *Journal of the History of Philosophy* 13 (1975):491–503.

Ohrbach, Susie. *Hunger Strike.* New York: Norton, 1985.

Okely, Judith. *Simone de Beauvoir.* New York and London: Virago/Pantheon, 1986.

Poster, Mark. *Existential Marxism in Postwar France: From Sartre to Althusser.* Princeton: Princeton University Press, 1975.

Rich, Adrienne. *Of Woman Born: Motherhood as Experience and Institution.* New York: W. W. Norton, 1976.

Ricoeur, Paul. "Fatherhood: From Phantasm to Symbol," trans. Robert Sweeney. In *The Conflict of Interpretations: Essays in Hermeneutics,* ed. Don Ihde. Evanston: Northwestern University Press, 1974.

Ricoeur, Paul. *Freud and Philosophy: An Essay On Interpretation,* trans. Denis Savage. New Haven: Yale University Press, 1977.

Rorty, Richard. *Philosophy and the Mirror of Nature.* Princeton: Princeton University Press, 1979.

Ryan, Joanna. "Psychoanalysis and Women Loving Women." In *Sex and Love: New Thoughts on Old Contradictions,* ed. Sue Cartledge and Joanna Ryan. London: Women's Press, 1984.

Raymond, Janice. *A Passion for Friends: Toward Philosophy of Female Affection.* Boston: Beacon Press, 1986.

Sartre, Jean-Paul. *Being and Nothingness,* trans. Hazel Barnes. New York: Philosophical Library, 1956.

Sartre, Jean-Paul. *The Chips Are Down,* trans. Louise Varese. New York: Lear, 1948.

Sartre, Jean-Paul. *Critique of Dialectical Reason,* trans. Alan Sheridan-Smith. Atlantic Highlands, N.J.: Humanities Press, 1976.

Sartre, Jean-Paul. *The Devil and the Good Lord,* trans. Kitty Black. New York: Vintage Books, 1960.

Sartre, Jean-Paul. "Existentialism is a Humanism." In *Existentialism from Dostoevsky to Sartre,* ed. Walter Kaufmann. New York: Meridian, 1956.

Sartre, Jean-Paul. "France: Masses, Spontaneity, Party." In *Between Existentialism and Marxism,* trans. John Mathews. New York: Pantheon Books, 1974.

Sartre, Jean-Paul. Interview by Michel Sicard. *Obliques,* nos. 18–19 (1979).

Sartre, Jean-Paul. "The Last Words of Jean-Paul Sartre: An Interview with Benny Lévy," trans. Adrienne Foulke. *Dissent* (Fall 1980).

Sartre, Jean-Paul. *Men without Shadows,* trans. Kitty Black. London: Hamish Hamilton, 1949.

Sartre, Jean-Paul. "Materialism and Revolution." In *Literary and Philosophical Essays,* trans. Annette Michelson. New York: Collier Books, 1962.

Sartre, Jean-Paul. "Merleau-Ponty." In *Situations,* trans. Benita Eisler. Greenwich, CT.: Fawcett Publications, 1965.

Sartre, Jean-Paul. *The Psychology of the Imagination,* trans. anonymous. New York: Philosophical Library, 1948.

Sartre, Jean-Paul. *Saint Genet: Actor and Martyr,* trans. Bernard Frechtman. New York: Georges Braziller, 1963.

Sartre, Jean-Paul. *Sartre on Cuba,* trans. anonymous. New York: Ballantine Books, 1961.

Sartre, Jean-Paul. "Self-Portrait at Seventy." In *Life/Situations,* trans. P. Auster and L. Davis. New York: Pantheon Books, 1977.

Sartre, Jean-Paul. *What Is Literature?* trans. Bernard Frechtman. New York: Harper and Row, 1965.

Scheman, Naomi. "Othello's Doubt/Desdemona's Death: The Engendering of Skepticism." In *Power, Gender, Values,* ed. Judith Genova. Edmonton, Alberta: Academic Printing and Publishing, 1987.

Seidenberg, Robert, and Karen DeCrow. *Women Who Marry Houses.* New York: McGraw-Hill, 1983.

Shapiro, Gary. "Notes on the Animal Kingdom of the Spirit." *Clio* (Spring 1979):323–338.

Showalter, Elaine. *The Female Malady.* New York: Pantheon Books, 1985.

Silverman, Hugh J. *Inscriptions: Between Phenomenology and Structuralism.* London and New York: Routledge, 1987.

Simons, A. P. "Marxism and Morals." *Ethics* 93, no. 4 (July 1982):792–800.

Smith-Rosenberg, Carroll. "The Female World of Love and Ritual: Relations between Women in Nineteenth-Century America." In *The Signs Reader: Women, Gender and Scholarship,* ed. Elizabeth and Emily Abel. Chicago: University of Chicago Press, 1983.

Smith, Barbara, and Beverly Smith. "Across the Kitchen Table: A Sister-to-Sister Dialogue." In *This Bridge Called Me Back,* eds. Cherrie Maraga and Gloria Anzaldua. Watertown, MA: Persephone Press, 1981.

Smith, Barbara, ed. *Home Girls: A Black Feminist Anthology.* New York: Kitchen Table–Women of Color Press, 1983.

Stack, George. "Aristotle and Kierkegaard's Concept of Choice." *The Modern Schoolman* 46:11–23.

Stack, George. "Kierkegaard's Analysis of Choice: The Aristotelian Model." *The Personalist* 52:643–661.

Stambaugh, Joan. "Time and Dialectic in Hegel and Heidegger." *Research in Phenomenology* 4 (1974):87–97.

Strawson, P. F. *Skepticism and Naturalism: Some Varieties.* New York: Columbia University Press, 1985.

Taminiaux, Jacques. "Finitude and the Absolute: Remarks on Hegel and Hei-degger." In *Heidegger: the Man and the Thinker,* ed. Thomas Sheehan. Chicago: Precedent, 1981.

Taylor, Mark. *Kierkegaard's Pseudonymous Authorship: A Study of Time and the Self.* Princeton: Princeton University Press, 1975.

Treblicot, Joyce, ed. *Mothering: Essays in Feminist Theory.* Totowa, NJ: Rowman and Allanheld, 1984.

Vicinus, Martha, ed. *Suffer and Be Still.* Bloomington: Indiana University Press, 1972.

Warnock, Mary. *The Philosophy of Sartre.* New York: Barnes and Noble, 1967.

Wellmer, Albrecht. "On the Dialectic of Modernism and Postmodernism." *Praxis* 4, no. 4 (1985):337–662.

Westphal, Merold. *Kierkegaard's Critique of Reason and Society.* Macon, Ga.: Mercer University Press, 1987.

Whitmarsh, Anne. *Simone de Beauvoir and the Limits of Commitment.* Cambridge: Cambridge University Press, 1981.

Winant, Terry. "The Feminist Standpoint: A Matter of Language." *Hypatia: A Journal of Feminist Philosophy* 2, no. 1 (1987):123–148.

Wittgenstein, Ludwig. *Tractatus Logico-Philosophicus,* trans. D. F. Pears and B. F. McGuinness. London: Routledge and Kegan Paul, 1961.

Wittig, Monique. "The Mark of Gender." In *The Poetics of Gender,* ed. Nancy Miller. New York: Columbia University Press, 1987.

Wood, Allen. "Marx's Immoralism." In *Marx en perspective,* ed. Bernard Chavance. Paris: Editions de l'Ecole des Hautes Etudes en Sciences Sociales, 1985.

Wood, David, and Robert Bernasconi, eds. *Derrida and Differance.* Evanston: Northwestern University Press, 1988.

Contributors

Thomas C. Anderson is professor and chair of the Philosophy Department at Marquette University. He is author of *The Foundation and Structure of Sartrean Ethics* (University of Kansas Press, 1979) and numerous articles on Marcel, Sartre, de Beauvoir, and questions of ethics and religion.

Linda Bell is professor of philosophy at Georgia State University. She is author of *A Sartrean Ethics of Authenticity* (University of Alabama Press, 1989). She contributed to the 1983 SPEP/SUNY volume *Phenomenology in a Pluralistic Context*, edited by William McBride and Calvin Schrag.

Susan Bordo is assistant professor of philosophy at Le Moyne College. She is author of *The Flight to Objectivity: Essays on Cartesianism and Culture* (SUNY Press, 1987) and coeditor (with Alison Jaggar) of *Gender/Body/Knowledge: Feminist Reconstructions of Being and Knowing* (Rutgers University Press, 1988). She has also contributed to *Soundings, Signs,* and *The Philosophical Forum.*

Elizabeth A. Bowman is visiting assistant professor of French at Middlebury College. She taught previously at Memphis State University after completing her doctorate at Columbia University on "The Moral Impasse and the Possibility of the Human: A Study of Jean-Paul Sartre's Ethics and his Political Theater" (1987). She has also coauthored a paper on Sartre's dialectical ethics with Robert V. Stone for *Social Text.*

Martin Dillon is professor of philosophy at the State University of New York at Binghamton. He is author of *Merleau-Ponty's Ontology* (Indiana University Press, 1987) and has written numerous articles on Merleau-Ponty, Nietzsche, Sartre, Kant, and topics in phenomenological psychology, philosophy and literature, and existential thought.

Martin Donougho is assistant professor of philosophy at the University of South Carolina. He has written a variety of articles for such journals as *Philosophy and Social Criticism, Hegel-Studien, Clio, Post Script, The Journal of Aesthetic Education,* and the *Alaska Quarterly Review.*

C. Stephen Evans is professor of philosophy and curator of the Howard and Edna Hong Kierkegaard Library at St. Olaf College in Northfield, Minnesota. He has written a number of books, including *The Quest for Faith: Reason and Mystery as Pointers to God* (1986), *Philosophy of Religion: Thinking About Faith* (1985), *Kierkegaard's 'Fragments' and 'Postscript': The Philosophy of Johannes Climacus* (Humanities Press, 1983), and *Preserving the Person: A Look at the Human Sciences* (1977).

Wayne Froman is associate professor of philosophy at George Mason University. He is author of *Merleau-Ponty: Language and the Act of Speech* (Bucknell University Press, 1982) and of a variety of articles in continental philosophy.

Dick Howard is professor of philosophy at the State University of New York at Stony Brook and senior fellow at the Research Institute on International Change at Columbia University. He has written a number of books including a second edition of his 1977 *The Marxian Legacy* (University of Minnesota Press, 1988), *From Marx to Kant* (1985), *La naissance de la pensée politique américaine* (1987), and *Defining the Political* (University of Minnesota Press, 1988), and *The Politics of Critique* (University of Minnesota Press, 1988).

Eleanor H. Kuykendall is associate professor and chair of philosophy at the State University of New York College at New Paltz. She is also coordinator of the Linguistics Program there. Editor of *Philosophy in the Age of Crisis* (1970), she is author of articles on Sartre, Irigaray, and feminist linguistics.

Claude Lefort is director of Studies at the Ecole des Hautes Etudes en Sciences Sociales in Paris. He is author of many books including a series of essays on Merleau-Ponty entitled *Sur une colonne absente, Le Travail de l'oeuvre Machiavel, The Forms of History*. He is one of the most important political philosophers writing in France today.

John McCumber is associate professor of philosophy at Northwestern University. Author of numerous articles in continental philosophy, especially concerning Hegel, Heidegger, and Habermas, his book *Poetic Interaction* appeared with University of Chicago Press in 1989.

Christie McDonald is professor in the Department of French at the University of Montreal. She has written *The Extravagant Shepherd, The Dialogue of Writing*, and *Dispositions*.

John M. Michelsen is associate professor of philosophy at the University of Victoria. He has written articles on Santayana, Plato, and Kierkegaard in *Transactons of the Charles S. Peirce Society, Diotima*, and *Analecta Husserliana*.

Patricia J. Mills is associate professor of political theory in the department of political science at the University of Massachusetts at Amherst. Author of *Woman, Nature, and Psyche* (Yale University Press, 1988), she has also written on marginality and otherness, the "woman question," motherhood, and Hegel.

Claude Piché is professor agrégé in the Department of Philosophy at the University of Montreal. Author of *Das Ideal, ein Problem der Kantischen Ideenlehre* (Bouvier, 1984), he has also published articles on Husserl, Heidegger, Kant, Habermas, aesthetic experience, and hermeneutics.

Jo-Ann Pilardi is assistant professor of philosophy and women's studies at Towson State University. She has written on Simone de Beauvoir in *Feminist Studies* and in *History of Women Philosophers*, and on Hegel, Freud, and feminist studies in *Hypatia*.

Gary Shapiro is professor of philosophy at the University of Kansas and a member of the Executive Committee of the International Association for Philosophy and Literature and program committee member of the American Society for Aesthetics. He edited the volume *Hermeneutics: Question and Prospects* with Alan Sica (University of Massachusetts Press) and his book on Nietzsche is forthcoming Indiana University Press.

Joan Stambaugh is professor of philosophy at Hunter College of the City University of New York. She is translator of various texts by Heidegger (including *The End of Philosophy, Identity and Difference*, and *Schelling*), and author of *Untersuchungen zum Problem der Zeit bei Nietzsche* (Nijhoff, 1959) and *Nietzsche's Thought of Eternal Return* (Johns Hopkins University Press, 1972).

Robert V. Stone is associate professor of philosophy at the C. W. Post Center of Long Island University. He is author of various papers on Sartre's ethics including *Social Text* and the *Revue Internationale de Philosophie* and is translator of Francis Jeanson's *Sartre and the Problem of Morality* (Indiana University Press, 1980). He has also contributed to *The Philosophy of Jean-Paul Sartre* (Schilpp Library of Living Philosophers) and *Explorations in Phenomenology* (Nijhoff).

Gianni Vattimo is professor of theoretical philosophy at the University of Torino, where he has also held the position of chair of the Faculty of Letters and Philosophy. He has been visiting professor at SUNY/Albany, Yale, and NYU. Editor of *Rivista di Estetica*, he has written over a dozen books, including *The End of Modernity* (Johns Hopkins University Press, 1989). His other books focus on Aristotle, Heidegger, Nietzsche, Schleiermacher, and his own notion of weak thought.

Bernhard Waldenfels is professor of philosophy at the Ruhr-University Bochum, West Germany. His books include *Das sokratische Fragen. Aporie, Elenchos, Anamnesis* (Hain, 1961), *Das zwischenreich des Dialogs. Sozialphilosophische Untersuchungen in Anschluss an E. Husserl* (Nijhoff, 1971), *Der Spielraum des Verhaltens* (Suhrkamp, 1980), *Phänomenologie in Frankreich* (Suhrkamp, 1985), and *Ordnung im Zwielicht* (Suhrkamp, 1987).

Merold Westphal is professor of philosophy at Fordham University. He is author of *History and Truth in Hegel's Phenomenology* (Humanities, 1979), *God, Guilt, and Death: An Existential Phenomenology of Religion* (Indiana University Press, 1984), and *Kierkegaard's Critique of Reason and Society* (Mercer, 1987).

Terry Winant is assistant professor of philosophy at the California State University at Fresno. She taught previously at the University of Wisconsin—Madison. She has written "How Ordinary (Sexist) Discourse Resists Radical (Feminist) Critique" and "The Feminist Standpoint: A Matter of Language" in *Hypatia: A Journal of Feminist Philosophy*, and an article on Sartre in the *Southern Journal of Philosophy*.

David Wood is senior lecturer in philosophy and programme director of the Centre for Research in Philosophy and Literature at the University of Warwick. He is author of *The Deconstruction of Time* (Humanities, 1989) and *Philosophy at the Limit* (Unwin Hyman, 1990). He is also coeditor of various books including *Heidegger and Language* (1981), *Time and Metaphysics* (1982), *Derrida and Differance* (1988), *Exceedingly Nietzsche* (1988), and *The Provocation of Lévinas* (1988).

About the Editor

HUGH J. SILVERMAN is Professor of Philosophy and Comparative Literature at the State University of New York at Stony Brook. He has taught at Stanford University and has been Visiting Professor at Duquesne University, New York University, the University of Warwick (England), the University of Nice (France) the University of Leeds (England), and the University of Torino (Italy). Author of *Inscriptions: Between Phenomenology and Structuralism* (Routledge, 1987), editor of *Piaget, Philosophy and the Human Sciences* (Humanities, 1980), coeditor of *Jean-Paul Sartre: Contemporary Approaches to his Philosophy* (Duquesne, 1980), *Continental Philosophy in America* (Duquesne, 1983), *Descriptions* (SUNY, 1985), *Hermeneutics and Deconstruction* (SUNY, 1985), *Critical and Dialectical Phenomenology* (SUNY, 1987), *The Horizons of Continental Philosophy: Essays on Husserl, Heidegger, and Merleau-Ponty* (Kluwer, 1988), *Postmodernism and Continental Philosophy* (SUNY, 1988), *The Textual Sublime: Deconstruction and its Differences* (SUNY, 1990), and translator of various works by Merleau-Ponty, he is also editor of the Routledge *Continental Philosophy* series, including *Philosophy and Non-Philosophy since Merleau-Ponty* (1988), *Derrida and Deconstruction* (1989), *Postmodernism—Philosophy and the Arts* (1990), and *Gadamer and Hermeneutics* (1991). He served as Executive Co-Director of the Society for Phenomenology and Existential Philosophy for six years (1980–86) and is currently Executive Director of the International Association for Philosophy and Literature.

INDEX

Absolute, the, 55, 91
  absolute knowing, 17–18, 28, 61
  as foundation of language, 178
Absurd, 46, 52, 60, 73
Abyss (*Ab-grund*), 180, 184
Action
  Aristotle's theory of, 73–77
  causality of, 80–81
  external, 81
  intellectualizing of, 51–53
  Kierkegaard's theory of, 77
Adolescence, 152
Adorno, 11, 130, 272
  Aesthetic Theory, 38
  *Aspekte der Hegelschen
    Philosophie,* 31, 32
  Dialectic of Enlightenment, 35, 38,
    123–124
  Minima Moralia, 31
  Negative Dialectics, 32
Aesthetic, stage, 43–45, 47, 57, 79
Agency, 81, 84–85
  autonomous, 115, 120
Agoraphobia, 207
Alienation, 104
  of morals, 114–115
American Revolution, 254–255, 259
Andenken (remembrance,
    recollection), 275, 280–282, 286
Anorexia Nervosa, 207–209
Appearance, 14
  of language, 194
Appropriation (*Ereignis*), 281–282,
  286
Arendt, Hannah, 246

Art
  Adorno, 38–39
  and Critical Theory, 265–274
    passim
  Hegel (poetry), 21–23, 28, 32, 38–
    39
  as learning experience, 269
  as truth, 138–139, 144, 179–181
Authenticity
  Habermas, 269–271
  Kierkegaard, 45, 49
  Sartre, 90–91, 95, 100–101
Autobiography, 150–162
Autonomy, 115, 120, 158
  of epistemology, 234–236

Bakhtin, Mikhail, 175
Beautiful Soul, 35–36
Beauty (Proust), 141
de Beauvoir, Simone
  Ethics of Ambiguity, 145, 147
  Force of Circumstance, 146, 161
  Memoirs d'une jeune fille rangee,
    152, 155–156
  "Merleau-Ponty and Psuedo-
    Sartrism," 148–150
  The Prime of Life, 154, 158
  The Second Sex, 147
Beginnings (*archai*) 10, 288
Begriff, 8
Binary oppositions
  good/evil, 113
  inside/outside, 4–11
  man/woman, 140
  perception/reflection, 136–137

367